WILLIAMSTON ANTHOLOGY

Volume I

This is a work of fiction. All of the characters, events, and organizations portrayed in this novel are either products of the authors' imaginations or used fictitiously.

Williamston Anthology - Volume 1

Copyright © Williamston Theatre 2016

Each play is the copyright of the playwright or adaptor.

All rights reserved. No part of this book may be reproduced in any form by any electronic or mechanical means including photocopying, recording, or information storage and retrieval without permission in writing from the authors.

ISBN-13: 978-1944540135
ISBN-10: 194454013X

Published by Sordelet Ink
www.sordeletink.com

WILLIAMSTON ANTHOLOGY

Volume I

An Anthology of Plays
from 10 Years
of Great Theatre

Published by
Sordelet Ink

The Williamston Theatre's mission is to produce professional theatre that excites and engages our audiences while challenging us all to explore our lives. This mission statement is supported by the following objectives: to be an integral part of the cultural fabric of Michigan; to pursue innovative collaboration in every aspect of our work; to establish a home for Midwest artists; to engage audiences of diverse ages, cultures and economic backgrounds.

We believe that theatre can enrich our lives and make a positive difference in our community, both culturally and economically. We believe that theatre should be accessible and affordable to everyone, whether they live in a large coastal city or a small Midwestern town. We believe that there are voices in the Midwest worth hearing, and our goal is to create moving, entertaining, professional theatre for, by, and about this part of the world.

In 2014, the American Theatre Wing recognized the Williamston Theatre as one of the most promising small theatre companies across the country with its National Theatre Company Award. With support from a strong donor base, the theatre was able to purchase its building in 2014, securing both its financial stability and its future in the Williamston downtown for seasons to come.

As the only professional, resident theatre in the central Michigan area, the Williamston Theatre fills an important role in providing high-quality theatre experiences for its community, and in keeping the voice of the Midwest alive and vibrant. Since opening in 2006, the Williamston Theatre has mounted six full productions each season including, by the conclusion of our 10th season in August 2016, fourteen World Premieres. We're honored to present those new plays to you, here, in this anthology.

CONTENTS

FOREWORD

FLAP
by Annie Martin
1

VOICES OF THE MIDWEST: MAIDENS, MOTHERS, & CRONES
by Annie Martin and Suzi Regan
55

VOICES OF THE MIDWEST: FLYOVER U.S.A.
by Dennis E. North and Joseph Zettelmaier
105

IT CAME FROM MARS
by Joseph Zettelmaier
161

VOICES OF THE MIDWEST: HOME
by Annie Martin and Suzi Regan
223

OEDIPUS by Sophocles
adapted by Annie Martin and Tony Caselli
283

NORTHERN AGGRESSION
by Joseph Zettelmaier
326

WILLIAMSTON THEATRE

THE WILLIAMSTON THEATRE FOUNDERS

John Lepard, Executive Director

Tony Caselli, Artistic Director

Chris Purchis, Managing Director

Emily Sutton-Smith, Development Director

Foreword

The way in which the Williamston Theatre started would probably make a pretty good script. I will pitch it to you:

"A ragtag team of misfits decides to start a professional theatre in a Mid-Michigan town with a population the size of a Carnival Cruise Ship. While enduring a national recession and a leaky roof, our heroes rally the town around their cause, and find that even the craziest of dreams can come true."

Pretty romantic, huh? And over the course of the last ten years, a lot of wonderful things have happened for the ragtag cofounders: Tony Caselli, Chris Purchis, Emily Sutton-Smith and me, but the thing that I am most proud of is the family of patrons and artists we have gathered. It is part of our mission to employ Michigan talent in all areas of our theatre, including actors, directors, stage managers, set, lighting, costume, and sound designers prop masters, and technical directors. Our aim is to keep our home-grown talent here in our state.

Another of our missions is to tell stories for, by, and about people in this part of the world, and that is where this anthology comes in.

Michigan has a voice, and that voice is conveyed through our playwrights. In an atmosphere of nurturing and trust, these talented wordsmiths have allowed us to take their ideas, add the artistry of our designers, actors, and directors, and bring to life the stories of the Midwest.

I hope you enjoy these, our earliest world-premiere plays.

John Lepard
Executive Director
Williamston Theatre

Flap

A PLAY BY
ANNIE MARTIN

Cast of Characters

GAIL: late 40s–early 50s, soon-to-be divorced woman
NAOMI: late 40s–early 50s; Gail's new neighbor
BILL: Gail's soon-to-be ex-husband
SAM: early 20s, bat catcher

Time and Place:
Present day, the outside of a house in a Detroit suburb

FLAP received its world premiere on July 5, 2007 at Williamston Theatre (Williamston, MI). It was directed by Lynn Lammers. Set design by Bartley H. Bauer, Lighting Design by Laura Munson, Costume Design by Melanie Schuessler, Sound Design by Emily Sutton-Smith, Stage Managed by Erica N. Koski.

The cast was as follows:

GAIL: Teri Clark Linden
NAOMI: Dana Brazil
BILL: Brian Harcourt
SAM: Jesse Miller

For production rights, contact Annie Martin at annielmartin@gmail.com.

FLAP

ACT I

(A front porch. Behind it is a large door and large glass windows. Outside on the porch are boxes and moving materials. Inside more boxes are slightly visible. GAIL is walking around the inside of the house. She is looking out the window impatiently. She finally takes out her phone and dials)

GAIL
Hi Lizzy. *(pause)* Well I was just wondering if you were gonna come over and... *(sniffling)* I'm fine. Everything looks like it's here. *(pause)* I'm trying to get settled. *(opening a box)* So, I kind of need your help. I can't move half of this stuff by...

(Something whips by her)

GAIL
(to the air) What? *(into the phone)* No. Sorry. My back can't take... *(walking further offstage)* ...any more lifting. I've got to move the furni—

(Offstage, GAIL lets out a blood-curdling scream. GAIL comes running and flapping into view)

GAIL
YEOW!!

(She throws the phone down and runs out the door, slamming it behind her)

GAIL
(screaming) Oh my god! Oh my god! *(jumping up and down)* Oh! My! God! *(She checks herself, tries taking deep breaths. She looks around and picks up a rock. She tosses it in her hand a few times as if she's trying out the weight and feel. She goes to the door and looks in. She starts to cry and then immediately stops. GAIL goes in, shutting the door behind her. All is quiet for a moment until we hear another scream and the sound of glass breaking as the rock flies through a window. GAIL comes running and rams directly into the door)*

GAIL
Aaagghh!

(She opens the door and slams it. Her nose is bleeding)

GAIL
No. *(looks at the house)* No. *(then yells)* NO!

NAOMI
Hey there neighbor.

(NAOMI has appeared in the yard)

NAOMI
I heard your hollering.

GAIL
Yes.

NAOMI
I'm Naomi Campbell. Obviously not the supermodel.

GAIL
Obviously.

NAOMI
I'm in the brick house right there. *(points)* Your screams pierced right through.

GAIL
I've got a…

NAOMI
I didn't catch your name.

GAIL
Name?

NAOMI
What people call you?

GAIL
Gail.

NAOMI
Well, Gail, welcome.

GAIL
Uh, thanks. Listen, I'm a little busy here so…

NAOMI
I saw those movers. Seemed slightly…

GAIL
Unprofessional?

NAOMI
Stoned. But I suppose I would be too if I had to lug furniture around all day. Probably helps relax the muscles.

GAIL
Well, they scratched my antique cobbler's table.

NAOMI
Maybe it'll just add character. I'd love to see it. *(heads for the door)* I mean it's a cobbler's table. There's gotta be some scratches on it already, right? *(opens the door)*

GAIL
BAT! Bat, bat, bat, bat. Bat in the house!

(NAOMI jumps back)

NAOMI
Gail, you probably shouldn't have bats in your house.

GAIL
I know.

NAOMI
They're like mice with wings.

GAIL
I hate mice.

NAOMI
Disease carriers—Plague.

GAIL
Maybe you could help me?

NAOMI
Oh yeah, well I don't think so. Bats and me… We don't mesh well.

GAIL
I got it.

(pause)

NAOMI
Gail, you do know you've been bleeding since I got here?

GAIL
Yes.

NAOMI
Just checking. *(takes off her t-shirt, leaving her only in a sports bra. Tries to hand it to GAIL)* Here you go.

GAIL
What?

NAOMI
For your nose.

GAIL
No.

NAOMI
Well, you're not going back in there. What else you gonna use?

GAIL
It would ruin it.

NAOMI
Naw. I've been sweating in the yard all day, it's already ruined. *(sniffs)* And it's a little ripe.

GAIL
Perfect.

NAOMI
Here. Take it.

GAIL
Um…

NAOMI
Take it.

GAIL
Fine, okay.

(NAOMI tosses the t-shirt to Gail)

NAOMI
You need to tip your head back.

GAIL
(smells the shirt) I know. *(reluctantly holds the shirt to her nose)*

NAOMI
There you go. *(pause)* You're welcome.

Put pressure on.

GAIL
I don't think I can take anymore.

NAOMI
(pauses) Well, if you're talking about the nose, then you're pressing too hard.

GAIL
This can't be a good sign.

NAOMI
The bleeding will…

GAIL
The bat. Bats can't be lucky.

NAOMI
Well…

GAIL
And then running into the door with my nose.

NAOMI
It's really not unlucky. It's more unfortunate.

GAIL
And I think I knocked my front tooth loose. Great. Hopefully it'll fall out and I'll be toothless.

NAOMI
Might be a good look for you.

GAIL
I can't afford to fix them. Can't go in there. *(points to the house)* Can't go out without teeth.

NAOMI
Gail. Gail.

GAIL
I'll probably get a blood clot in my brain—it'll start hemorrhaging and I'll die out here because I can't get into my house. And you know what? Nobody'll care. It won't even make the papers.

I'll be eaten out here by birds, shrivel up like a prune. No dignity, nothing like that and you know what... when some people find out what a horrible and lonely death I've had, they'll be happy. They'll laugh and say I got what I deserved. But I don't want to die. Die alone and afraid of... of the bat and I'll still be toothless.

NAOMI
Wow!

GAIL
Toothless and dead.

NAOMI
Listen, I'll come. I'll be here.

GAIL
Yeah?

NAOMI
You think I want to smell a rotting corpse in this heat? *(looks at GAIL)* You watch - that bat will probably just fly out through that hole the rock... it was a rock I saw coming through that window, right?

(GAIL nods)

NAOMI
We'll just wait, OK?

(GAIL nods again)

NAOMI
We'll just wait.

(GAIL takes the shirt away from her nose)

GAIL
I feel like it might have stopped.

NAOMI
Yeah. *(looking at it)* Yeah. It looks like it.

GAIL
(holding up the shirt) I'll wash this.

NAOMI
Whenever. No worries.

(NAOMI sits. They look at the house)

NAOMI
Moving can certainly suck.

GAIL
Yes it can.

NAOMI
But this house, well, I've always liked it.

GAIL
Really?

NAOMI
Oh yeah. If not for my house, which I love, I'd definitely buy this one.

GAIL
I just got a vibe walking through it. And that fireplace—that's what really sold me.

NAOMI
How could it not?

GAIL
The carved wood mantel. The Pewabic tile—you can't buy craftsmanship like that today.

NAOMI
I've always loved the fact that Christopher designed it and then she threw him in it. Cracks me up.

GAIL
Who threw what?

NAOMI
Maggie Fritzer. The Fritzers.

GAIL
Who?

NAOMI
You know.

GAIL
No. I don't.

NAOMI
Mad Maggie Fritzer? Back in 1956?

GAIL
The name is sort of familiar.

NAOMI
Are you from the area at all?

GAIL
I was born in Detroit and then we moved out to the suburbs.

NAOMI
And you don't remember Mad Maggie? This was her house. Mad Maggie lived here with her husband, Christopher, and their two kids. I don't remember their names... they're not important to the story. Maggie was this terrific wife and mother—a real stand out in the neighborhood.

GAIL
She died here, didn't she?

NAOMI
One evening, Christopher comes home. You know I don't think anyone ever called him Chris, at least not in anything I've heard. Don't you think that's funny?

GAIL
No.

NAOMI
Well, he comes home and the kids are out—someplace else—again it doesn't matter. All that matters is they weren't home. Maggie was making his dinner. Typical 1950s thing. Anyway, story is they had some sort of argument. Christopher wanted to leave, take the kids, start a new life away from her.

GAIL
Why? Why would he want that?

NAOMI
I don't know. It doesn't matter.

GAIL
He just comes home and says this without any warning?

NAOMI
Men are bastards. Anyway Maggie loses it—something snaps. She takes the pot roast out of the oven and clobbers him to death with it.

GAIL
This happened here?

NAOMI
Right in your kitchen.

GAIL
My realtor never mentioned this.

NAOMI
But that's not it. Then Mad Maggie chops him up using his prized tools out in the garage, buries his head out back here, and used his limbs as kindling in the fireplace.

GAIL
Oh my god.

NAOMI
I know. In fact—now I should tell you that this part is just a myth, but when the police arrived, Mad Maggie was supposedly with her children standing around that exact fireplace making s'mores.

GAIL
The head was buried out here?

NAOMI
Don't worry. They found it and buried it someplace else.

GAIL
How could nobody tell me?

NAOMI
It was the trial of the century—that's how they billed it.

GAIL
Somebody was murdered here.

NAOMI
People have lived in it since. Life went on. Except for the tour buses.

GAIL
Tour buses?

NAOMI
Because of the house's history, there's a local bus tour that takes people around to see where famous murders and deaths happened. You know, they go past the Red Fox where Jimmy Hoffa was. It's actually pretty cool. I took it with my—

(GAIL explodes into tears)

NAOMI
Oh. Oh. *(starts to rub Gail's back)* It's hard. I know.

GAIL
(sobbing)
You... this... I...

NAOMI
You've looked on the verge since I got here.

GAIL
I've been on the verge for months.

NAOMI
It's okay. I sensed something was a little off. But you know what? Everything will work out. It will.

GAIL
You don't know that.

NAOMI
Yes I do. I mean, it's not like you're gonna murder someone in there, right?

GAIL
Who knows?

NAOMI
(GAIL just stares at NAOMI) I do feel real bad. I figured you knew.

GAIL
Well, I didn't

NAOMI
I mean, if I were you and I didn't know, I'd be raising hell about now.

GAIL
I don't have the energy to move again ... or the money.

NAOMI
Listen, there's been a few families in there since.

GAIL
Were they happy?

NAOMI
(pause) Well, everyone has their issues, Gail. But I think they were, yeah. I think the Adams were the first to move in after the... and then the next were the... oh... the... Polish people... the something-ski... Kelwinskis. Mrs. Kelwinski passed away—not in the house though. She was older.

GAIL
So it was natural causes?

NAOMI
I wasn't there, Gail. And then Mr. Kelwinski went to live in Arizona. And then the last folks were Jim and Sharon. You met them. Been great neighbors.

GAIL
They seemed nice.

NAOMI
Oh they are. Really. Just good people. Raised all three kids here, but when they finally all left Jim and Sharon decided to head up North to their place near Grayling.

GAIL
I think they mentioned that.

NAOMI
Those three kids though. What a bunch of assholes. You have to wonder what turns kids into numbnuts because I can't believe Jim and Sharon were bad parents.

GAIL
Sometimes you never really know what happens in a family unless you are part of it.

NAOMI
They had a good childhood. Lots of love and laughing. So see it's not all bad here.

GAIL
I don't know.

NAOMI
You know what? It's a beautiful evening out. We should have ourselves a little housewarming party or something.

GAIL
I just want the bat out.

NAOMI
(interrupting) A bat party! Perfect. I'll be right back. Okay? Don't go anywhere.

GAIL
Don't worry…

(NAOMI runs offstage)

GAIL
My keys are inside.

(GAIL sits out with her head in her hands. A few seconds later, a long rumbling is heard offstage and it gets closer. GAIL perks up a bit. Around the corner comes NAOMI with a wheelbarrow full of stuff)

GAIL
That was quick.

NAOMI
Good, you're still here.

GAIL
Where else would I go?

NAOMI
Brought out the welcome wagon—I prepacked it before I came over…just in case.

GAIL
Uh-huh.

NAOMI
Any movement in there?

GAIL
No.

NAOMI
Well, he'll come out sooner or later. (Begins to unfold lawn chairs) Four bucks at CVS. Can't beat it. (grabs something from the wheelbarrow and tosses it to GAIL) Heads up.

(The package hits GAIL right in the face—the nose)

GAIL
Ah!

NAOMI
Sorry. You've got some bad hand-eye coordination.

GAIL
(picks up the package) Frozen peas?

NAOMI
For the nose. To keep swelling down. Frozen peas fix anything.

(GAIL puts it on her nose)

NAOMI
You're welcome. *(pause)* You're gonna have a hell of a face tomorrow. Two black eyes and all. What do you want - Cuervo or Jack?

GAIL
Excuse me?

(NAOMI holds up a Jose Cuervo and Jack Daniels bottle)

GAIL
Do you have any water?

NAOMI
Gail.

GAIL
Yes.

NAOMI
You really want water at a time like this?

(Pause)

GAIL
Cuervo.

NAOMI
There we go.
(hands her the bottle)

GAIL
Should I just... drink...
(indicating drinking from the bottle)

NAOMI
A toast.
(unscrewing her cap)
To new neighbors.

GAIL
Fine.

NAOMI
You have to say it.

GAIL
To new—

NAOMI AND GAIL
—neighbors.

NAOMI
Cheers. *(they clink and swig)* I brought crackers too. Just in case we need some absorption.

(NAOMI gets up and goes to the window, looks in)

NAOMI
I don't see much... nope... wait... you don't have a bird, do you?

GAIL
No.

NAOMI
Then the bat's still there. And a phone is ringing.

GAIL
That'll be my daughter.

NAOMI
Ahh. A daughter, huh?

GAIL
Two actually.

NAOMI
Two... Wow. They don't live here?

GAIL
They will - they do. Sometimes.

NAOMI
Oh.

GAIL
Well I mean Sarah, she's 16 and never home - always with friends and Lizzy, she's a freshman at MSU.

NAOMI
They should be helping you.

GAIL
You'd think, but they...well...You know teenagers.

NAOMI
No I don't.

GAIL
Well they have some issues, but well, I'm very lucky

NAOMI
Well then... *(holding up her bottle)* ...to your daughters.

GAIL
To Sarah and Liz.

(They clink and swig)

GAIL
You have any kids?

NAOMI
Depends on who you ask. *(looking at the sky)* It's gonna be a full moon tonight.

GAIL
Figures.

NAOMI
Doesn't it? *(pause)* I swear every time something goes wrong, there's always something like that, isn't there?

GAIL
Something like what?

NAOMI
Full moon... a typo... Santa... an angry god... the weather... it's always something.

GAIL
Well, here's to it always being something.

NAOMI
There you go!

(They clink and swig)

NAOMI
We gotta figure this thing out.

GAIL
Screw it.

NAOMI
You don't want the bat ...

GAIL
He can have the house.

NAOMI
Well, he's got it.

GAIL
(getting up to go to the window) Of course, you do realize that it's a male.

NAOMI
It has to be.

GAIL
Flying in, taking what he wants.

NAOMI
Bastard.

GAIL
You're right. He is a bastard. *(looks in the window)* BASTARD!

NAOMI
He looked like a fat bastard too.

GAIL
He'll probably drop dead of a heart attack.

NAOMI
Yeah. *(knocking on the window)* We're waiting for you to die, fatty.

GAIL
(knocking again) One way or another, you're gonna get it.

NAOMI
(knocking) Die! You hear that, you're gonna die!

GAIL
(knocking) Yeah. You hear us. You're gonna...

(*A loud thud against the glass—the bat flies into it. The ladies go flying backwards, scared shitless and screaming. They stumble back, the Cuervo bottle hits NAOMI in the face—the nose—and she falls to the ground. Her Jack bottle spills on the ground. She's bleeding*)

NAOMI
Good god.

GAIL
You okay?

NAOMI
Save the bottle. J.D.!

GAIL
(*picks up the bottle*) I got it.

NAOMI
Oh my god.

GAIL
Let me see.

NAOMI
You've got a damn kamikaze bat in there.

GAIL
That's what I tried to tell...

NAOMI
(*interrupting*) He attacked me.

GAIL
It was actually the Cuervo bottle.

NAOMI
It was that bat.

GAIL
We should try to stop the bleeding.

NAOMI
(*looking at her J.D bottle*) How much did I lose?

(*GAIL grabs NAOMIs sweaty, bloody t-shirt off the ground*)

GAIL
There wasn't a lot left. (*hands it to NAOMI*) Here.

NAOMI
It's got blood on it.

GAIL
It mine.

NAOMI
Gail, I don't know you well enough to...

GAIL
It's got your sweat too.

NAOMI
Give me your shirt. (*touches her nose*)

GAIL
My shirt?

NAOMI
I'm gushing here.

GAIL
I can't. I've only got a bra underneath.

NAOMI
Crimey, Gail. What do you call this? (*pointing to her bra*)

GAIL
Technically, that's a sports bra.

NAOMI
What kind of neighbor are you? We're girls. I've seen what you're selling.

GAIL
Fine. Fine. (*takes off her shirt*)

NAOMI
Everything is like pulling teeth with you.

GAIL
(*handing over the shirt*) What's that mean?

NAOMI
(*Plugging up her nose*) Exactly what you think.

GAIL
I just gave you my shirt.

NAOMI
After I pleaded.

GAIL
Please.

NAOMI
You're gonna argue with an injured woman?

GAIL
Let me help you.

NAOMI
No. I'm fine.

GAIL
Fine.

(Silence. GAIL walks around, grabs the frozen peas, and brings them to NAOMI, dropping them in front of her)

GAIL
I am sorry.

NAOMI
Why? I'm sorry for being such a crab ass with you.

GAIL
Well, your nose.

NAOMI
Yours too. *(pause)* Hey, this is our first official squabble.

GAIL
I guess.

NAOMI
You know what this means?

GAIL
No.

NAOMI
(holding up her Jack bottle) To feuds.

GAIL
Feuds.

(They both swig)

NAOMI
To broken women.

GAIL
Yes!

(Swig)

GAIL
We're gonna look like twins.

NAOMI
It's just good fodder for the neighbors.

GAIL
I wonder what they'll say.

NAOMI
That we got in a fight.

GAIL
No.

NAOMI
Well, that's what I'm gonna tell them.

GAIL
Naomi.

NAOMI
Come on. It'll be funny.

GAIL
Their first impression of me would be that I got into a fight.

NAOMI
It'll be great.

GAIL
Who's gonna actually believe that?

NAOMI
Doesn't matter. It's a neighborhood - nothing is actually as it seems.

GAIL
But—

NAOMI
Trust me, the fact that I will have two black eyes will play greatly to your favor.

GAIL
Are you that hated?

NAOMI
Of course not. I'm just a little feared.

GAIL
Really?

NAOMI
I think, yeah.

GAIL
Why?

NAOMI
Well it probably started when I called Peter a fatty.

GAIL
Peter?

NAOMI
He's this 5 year old, totally self destructive... Listen it's too long of a story

(Car lights. Sound of a car pulling into the driveway)

NAOMI
(holds up her bottle) To long stories. *(waits for GAIL)* Gail. Come on.

GAIL
To long stories.

NAOMI
To being feared.

GAIL
To being feared.

(They clink and swig)

NAOMI
To fatty Peter.

GAIL
I'm not drinking to that.

NAOMI
You just wait. You will.

(NAOMI swigs)

BILL
(off-stage) Gail!

NAOMI
Oh, a knight to save us from the bat?

GAIL
Great.

(BILL enters)

BILL
Gail, what the hell?

NAOMI
Hello to you too.

GAIL
What the hell what?

BILL
Lizzy called me frantic. She said she heard a horrible scream and glass breaking.

GAIL
She called you instead of the police?

NAOMI
We're fine.

BILL
What are you wearing? And what happened to your face?

NAOMI
The latest from Paris.

(BILL looks at NAOMI)

NAOMI
(points to herself) Naomi Campbell.

BILL
(ignoring her) Gail, can you please explain

to me why—

GAIL
No.

BILL
Our daughter is in tears.

GAIL
And called you and not the police.

BILL
She thought you were dead.

GAIL
Again, she called you and not the—

BILL
I'm her father. Of course she called me, now what—

GAIL
Stop yelling at me.

BILL
Jesus, here you go again. I'm not yelling, I'm...

GAIL
If you're so concerned, why didn't you call the police?

BILL
I thought it'd be easier to come over and see...

GAIL
This isn't your problem.

BILL
Of course it is.

GAIL
I'm not your wife anymore.

BILL
I wish that were true.

NAOMI
Oh, so you're getting divorced?

BILL
I'm trying.

GAIL
Don't worry, it's coming.

BILL
Did you sign them?

GAIL
I haven't had a lot of time, Bill. Look around. I've been a little busy, but it's on my list of things to do.

BILL
All you have to do is sign it. A signature. That's it.

GAIL
Bill, I don't have any idea where they are. In a box someplace I imagine. You'll just have to be patient and wait for me to unpack.

BILL
(pulls out papers from his coat) You always did manage to misplace everything. Here. *(tries to hand her the papers)* An extra copy.

GAIL
So that's why you decided to play hero and come over.

BILL
No. I came because Lizzy was ...

GAIL
Well, I'm not going to be pressured into signing.

BILL
Well, at least take them.

GAIL
No. I have my own.

BILL
Why are you trying to prolong the inevitable?

GAIL
What's your big hurry? Huh?

BILL
I want to move on.

GAIL
Well, I need to look them over and make sure...What is that? *(points at him)* What the hell is that?

BILL
What?

GAIL
Oh my god, an earring?

BILL
Let it go.

GAIL
(to NAOMI) Do you see this?

NAOMI
He's expressing his freedom.

BILL
It's not a big deal.

GAIL
It looks ridiculous.

BILL
Whatever, Gail. I'm trying to move...

GAIL
Move on...I heard you. What's next? You gonna buy a Porsche?

BILL
Come on. Your lawyer's already been over the papers. Everything is... fair.

GAIL
Is it fair to hide money and empty the savings? Naomi, does that sound fair?

NAOMI
No.

BILL
How many times... Gail, for Christ's sake, you know that was my mother's money. She left that for me.

GAIL
You didn't have a problem spending my inheritance. Did it buy you that thing there? *(pointing again to his ear)*

BILL
It was $10, you know...I don't understand why you're doing this? You don't make sense.

GAIL
I don't have to explain myself. Not now, not ever.

BILL
I actually came by to see if everything was okay. That was my reason for coming.

GAIL
Right, and you just happened to have the papers on you. You can't control the situation and you certainly can't control me.

BILL
Gail, I don't want to. I don't even want to be part of your life anymore. Don't you get it?

GAIL
(pause) I don't love you either, Bill. Okay. So get back in your car and get off my property.

BILL
Obviously you're under stress.

GAIL
You think? You think you're helping?

BILL
That's why I came.

NAOMI
Should I leave?

BILL
Yes.

GAIL
(to NAOMI) Don't move.

NAOMI
No problemo! I got your back. *(holds up her bottle. GAIL and NAOMI clink and swig)*

BILL
Are you drunk?

NAOMI
Bill, it is the cocktail hour.

BILL
Cocktails are typically served in a glass.

NAOMI
Well, obviously we aren't your typical gals. Now I think Gail— *(turns to GAIL)* —and you let me know if I'm wrong— *(back to BILL)* —but I think Gail wants you to take your business elsewhere.

BILL
I didn't come to fight.

NAOMI
Of course not.

GAIL
Naomi, you see him. You see what he's doing.

BILL
I was concerned. Worried.

GAIL
Look around, everything is fine.

(Long pause)

GAIL
Well we aren't bleeding anymore.

NAOMI
Nope. I've stopped.

GAIL
So we're fine.

NAOMI
Except for the bat.

BILL
Bat?

NAOMI
He hit that glass pretty hard.

BILL
You have a bat?

GAIL
You think he might be dead?

NAOMI
At least severely injured.

BILL
It's in the house?

NAOMI
Keep up Bill. Of course it's in the house.

BILL
A little bat is …

GAIL
It's not little.

NAOMI
It's a huge sucker.

BILL
They're harmless. And easy to get rid of. *(starts toward the door)*

GAIL
Hey!

BILL
All you have to do… *(hands on the door)*

GAIL
You're not going in there.

BILL
It will take me—

GAIL
(stands in front of the door) This is my

house. Not yours.

BILL
You're scared of ants. This is a little more than that, dontcha think?

NAOMI
(taps his shoulder) We don't need your help.

BILL
Naomi, just let me…

NAOMI
We can handle it.

BILL
(to GAIL) You're gonna sit out here all night. I know you, Gail.

GAIL
You don't know me. You've never known me. You didn't know when I was unhappy. You didn't care then and you don't care now.

BILL
You're drunk. You don't know what you're saying. I'm going in. *(pushes GAIL aside)*

NAOMI
(grabs his shirt) Whoa tiger.

BILL
Get your hands off me.

NAOMI
We've been out here strategizing in regards to that bat and we now know what we have to do.

GAIL
Huh?

NAOMI
Yeah. So, thanks for your offer, Billy, but the ex and I got this.

GAIL
Yeah. We do. We do?

NAOMI
Oh we do.

GAIL
So, you can leave. *(to NAOMI)* Right?

NAOMI
Yep. *(to BILL)* And I'll make sure she calls Liz.

BILL
I think I'll stay.

GAIL
I can handle this.

BILL
So why get upset if I stick around?

GAIL
This isn't your business. Listen to me. You never listen.

BILL
I listen. All the time. You don't want to sign the papers. I heard you. But that means we're still married. Meaning I own half of this place. I can do what I want and I think I'll wait, unless… *(waves the papers)*

GAIL
You think that's gonna get me to sign 'em even quicker? Boy, you're even stupider than I gave you credit for.

NAOMI
Whoa, Whoa, Whoa. Bill, you're welcome to stay. It'll be good to have you on call just in case we need your assistance.

GAIL
(to NAOMI) No.

NAOMI
Yes. But Bill, you've got to stand back… in fact, stand over there. *(points out into the yard)* We need to concentrate.

BILL
Oh you need room for your plan? Sure, I'll stand right there.

NAOMI
No. There. Way over.

BILL
(smiling) Fine.

GAIL
Good.

(BILL grabs a lawn chair)

NAOMI
Uh, no. Sorry. Those are mine and we're using them.

BILL
What do you need with...

NAOMI
You can't possibly understand the plan.

BILL
Fine. I'll be over there. Call me when you want it done.

(BILL walks away as NAOMI and GAIL watch)

NAOMI
(yelling out to him) Keep going. *(pause)* Keep going.

GAIL
(to NAOMI) Naomi.

NAOMI
Do you think he'll just keep going?

BILL
(yelling back) This is it. I'm not going any further.

NAOMI
Ten-four, buddy.

(NAOMI and GAIL look at each other)

GAIL
So?

NAOMI
Oh, we're fucked.

GAIL
Naomi.

NAOMI
Remember me and bats... We don't mix.

GAIL
I thought you had a plan.

NAOMI
I did. I got him way out there

GAIL
I can't let him in there. I can't. It's my place. Not his.

NAOMI
I know.

GAIL
No, you don't.

NAOMI
He's not going in. I promise.

GAIL
I'm not signing that thing. He can't force me. He can't come in here trying to control me, blame me. This is exactly the opportunity he's been looking for. Make me look like an idiot. He's so happy. Look at him out there. Smirking. Patronizing you. Waiting for my failure.

NAOMI
Okay. But first, doll, look at him out there. He's getting eaten by mosquitoes. Second, at least he came out here to check on you. Obviously, people were worried.

GAIL
She didn't even call...

NAOMI
...the police, I know. Get over it. So your daughter handles crisis poorly. Good to know. Make a note of it, file it, and move on.

GAIL
She's just so damn mad at me. She's punishing me. It's not fair. And Sarah, she wants to live with him. Him! He didn't even want another child and now she thinks he's awesome. They both hate me.

NAOMI
Of course they hate you.

GAIL
Excuse me?

NAOMI
If they liked you, you'd probably be a crappy mother.

GAIL
Oh well.

NAOMI
Come on, you're the parent. Be the parent. Move past this. We've got a bigger issue at hand.

BILL
(yelling) Is this going to happen today?

NAOMI
Nobody's making you stay, Billy. So cork it. *(to GAIL)* So I think you need to go in.

GAIL
Where?

NAOMI
(motions to the house) There.

GAIL
You're coming.

NAOMI
Well...

GAIL
This is your plan.

NAOMI
Well, sure, but it doesn't include me.

GAIL
Of course it does.

NAOMI
No, it doesn't.

GAIL
Yes.

NAOMI
No.

GAIL
Yes.

NAOMI
No.

GAIL
Naomi.

NAOMI
Gail.

GAIL
You said you had my back.

(Pause)

NAOMI
Then you better share the Cuervo.

(GAIL drinks and hands over the bottle)

NAOMI
Well, the good news is the sucker may possibly be dead already.

GAIL
Yes.

NAOMI
So you'll need to go in and assess the situation.

GAIL
You mean "we".

NAOMI
Just look through the window.

(*They walk to the window. GAIL looks in*)

GAIL
Uh… hmmmm.

NAOMI
You see it?

GAIL
It's hard to tell. Boxes everywhere.

NAOMI
Well?

(*NAOMI passes her the bottle. GAIL swigs it and passes it back. She looks in*)

GAIL
Wait… There he is.

NAOMI
And?

GAIL
He's on the floor.

NAOMI
Dead?

GAIL
No idea.

NAOMI
Open the door.

GAIL
No.

NAOMI
Just to poke it.

GAIL
No.

NAOMI
A little nudge.

GAIL
You.

NAOMI
Your house, your bat.

GAIL
I'm not touching it.

NAOMI
Wait. (*walks out into the yard*)

BILL
(*yells*) Why is this house familiar?

GAIL
(*to NAOMI*) What are you doing?

BILL
Ever since I drove up.

(*NAOMI walks back to GAIL and hands her a large stick*)

NAOMI
Here.

GAIL
So?

NAOMI
Now you don't have to touch it.

GAIL
To see if he moves?

NAOMI
Exactly.

BILL
Did you buy this house from someone we know?

GAIL
(*yells*) Shut up!

(*GAIL opens the door again*)

NAOMI
(*whispering*) Slowly now.

GAIL
Okay. Okay. (*whispering*) Here I go. (*goes to poke the bat. She jerks the stick and the bat is suddenly very much alive*)

GAIL
Ahhh!

NAOMI
It's—

GAIL
Alive.

NAOMI
Shut the—

(GAIL slams the door)

BILL
Is this the Fritzer house?

NAOMI
You should have smashed him.

GAIL
Me?

BILL
(walking over) Please tell me you did not buy Mad Maggie's house?

(Silence and heavy breathing)

BILL
(laughing) Of course you did. Jesus, do you know that the resale of this place will be… Doesn't matter. Jesus.

NAOMI
She didn't know.

BILL
How do you not know? This is why you can't do things alone—you don't think it through.

GAIL
(begins to charge him with the stick) Get out, Bill.

BILL
(laughing further) Gail. I would have helped. I could have told you. . .

(GAIL starts swinging it)

BILL
Don't get mad at me. Put that thing down.

GAIL
Out. Get out.

(BILL continues to laugh and egg her on)

NAOMI
(walking to Gail) Give me that. (grabs stick) It's not worth losing your dignity.

BILL
What dignity?

(NAOMI hits BILL with the stick)

NAOMI
We are trying to work, Bill. (hits him again) Now, stop being a jackass.

BILL
Cut it out. (grabs the stick and they stare at each other)

NAOMI
No. You cut it out. We've been nice… well, I've been fairly nice, but you're acting like a little boy. (pulls the stick from his grip)

BILL
If you'd only let me—

NAOMI
You're not understanding, we don't want you to help.

BILL
I'm trying to be a good guy here.

NAOMI
Good for you. But it's not working. Dontcha see that?

BILL
Naomi, let me be honest. (takes her by the arm and into his confidence) Gail's been a little off lately. Not signing the papers, buying this house, really odd…

NAOMI
So? That's not my business. Here's what I know: We don't, do not, want your help. So you have a choice: stay and stand back or go.

BILL
Naomi...

NAOMI
Scoot. *(hits his butt with the stick)*

BILL
(turns around and walks back out mumbling) Mad Maggie. Figures.

NAOMI
Stop grumbling.

GAIL
I hate him.

NAOMI
Well you married him.

GAIL
Not a proud moment.

NAOMI
Then end the thing, will ya?

GAIL
Well, it's ... it's not a great settlement. I could get more, but I refuse to be rushed.

NAOMI
Well get ready because we're going in there. *(points to the house)*

GAIL
What?

NAOMI
Yes.

GAIL
We?

NAOMI
We.

GAIL
To kill it.

NAOMI
Kill it, catch it, whatever it takes.

GAIL
What are we gonna use?

NAOMI
This. *(holds up the stick)*

GAIL
And me?

NAOMI
Ah... *(both look around)* You got a broom?

GAIL
Kitchen.

NAOMI
Well...

GAIL
I got it. *(picks up the J.D. bottle)*

NAOMI
Eh.

GAIL
Too breakable?

NAOMI
Maybe.

GAIL
(throws it down) Then what?

NAOMI
Bill might have an umbrella or tire iron in his car.

GAIL
No Bill.

NAOMI
Okay.

GAIL
(looks out) Wait, I think I—

(GAIL walks offstage and pulls out the

largest branch you can imagine)

NAOMI
Wow.

GAIL
Perfect.

NAOMI
Can you even lift—

GAIL
Of course. *(the branch sits very awkwardly in her arms)*

NAOMI
Okay then.

(GAIL and NAOMI march to the door and stand. NAOMI grabs the Cuervo and drinks)

GAIL
Hey.

(NAOMI lifts the bottle to GAIL's lips and lets her drink, some dribbles down)

GAIL
Thanks.

BILL
(yells) Good lord, you aren't taking that branch into the house.

NAOMI AND GAIL
Shut up!

GAIL
On the count of three. One.

NAOMI
Remember, leave no compadre behind.

GAIL
Yep. Two.

NAOMI
Talk out. Let me know your position at all times.

GAIL
Three.

NAOMI
Go. Go. Go.

(NAOMI leads the charge. GAIL shuts the door behind them. You can see them inside)

NAOMI
Where is he?

GAIL
I don't know.

NAOMI
I can't see him.

GAIL
Jesus, I'm scared.

NAOMI
Stay with me, Gail

GAIL
I think he's gone.

NAOMI
Really.

GAIL
Yeah, I think…

NAOMI
Oh my God!

GAIL
Naomi!

(BILL is now walking toward the house)

NAOMI
There!

GAIL
Where?

NAOMI
There.

GAIL
Where?

NAOMI
Behind.

(Crashes heard)

NAOMI
Don't hit me.

GAIL
Jesus.

NAOMI
Here he comes again.

GAIL
Get him. Get him

(BILL starts to laugh)

NAOMI
Jesus, he's diving.

GAIL
Divebombing.

NAOMI
He's trying to eat… ARGH!

GAIL
GET AWAY! GET AWAY!

NAOMI
ABORT! ABORT!

(BILL goes to the door and is about to open it)

NAOMI
In my hair!

GAIL
Move. Move.

(Screams. BILL opens the door)

BILL
If you just leave the door…

(NAOMI and GAIL come out flailing and screaming. BILL is struck by GAIL's branch and goes down. They run further into the yard, not noticing the unconscious BILL)

NAOMI
Is he on me?

GAIL
No. No. Me?

NAOMI
No.

GAIL
That thing.

NAOMI
Tormented. Sick.

GAIL
Tried to eat us.

NAOMI
Kill us.

GAIL
Mean.

NAOMI
He was too fast.

GAIL
On speed.

NAOMI
His teeth.

GAIL
I saw.

NAOMI
I can't go back in.

GAIL
No way. Nope. I gotta sell this place.

NAOMI
Yes. Sell it.

GAIL
This house is evil. It's a sign.

NAOMI
We're too wound up. Let's have a drink.

GAIL
I feel sick.

(NAOMI walks back up to the porch area and picks up the bottle by BILL. She opens

it and drinks)

NAOMI
Here.

GAIL
Thanks. *(drinks)*

NAOMI
Gail, we did it. We conquered our fears. Looked death in the eye.

GAIL
We didn't win.

NAOMI
Women against Beast—it's the age-old story.

GAIL
I can't live here. I'm not sharing my house with a bat.

NAOMI
What about Bill? The time has come to let him go in and get the thing. Let him get eaten. *(yelling back out into the yard)* Bill! Bill! It's all yours. Have at it! *(silence)* BILL! *(pause. To GAIL)* I think we pissed him off. Maybe he left.

GAIL
His car's still here. *(pause)* Bill! Bill!

NAOMI
(sees BILL on the ground) What the—

GAIL
It's because I won't do what he wants. Great. He likes to make me suffer.

(NAOMI looks down, discovering the unconscious BILL)

NAOMI
Gail.

GAIL
This is so him.

(NAOMI just points at BILL)

GAIL
What? *(sees BILL)* Oh my...

NAOMI
Yeah.

GAIL
Oh my.

NAOMI
Yeah.

GAIL
Oh my.

NAOMI
Yeah. I know.

GAIL
Is he alive?

NAOMI
I don't know.

GAIL
We should check.

NAOMI
I guess.

GAIL
Naomi.

NAOMI
What?

GAIL
I think I'm drunk.

NAOMI
Yeah.

GAIL
Okay.

NAOMI
We should... what?

GAIL
Flip him over.

NAOMI
But...

GAIL
But what?

NAOMI
I don't think you're supposed to move the body.

GAIL
It's Bill, though.

NAOMI
Okay. On three.

GAIL
One.

NAOMI
Two.

GAIL
Three.

(They flip him over)

NAOMI
He's breathing.

GAIL
There's a strong pulse.

NAOMI
That's good.

GAIL
Yeah. Any marks?

NAOMI
Where?

GAIL
Anywhere?

NAOMI
From what?

GAIL
The bat.

NAOMI
Can bats kill?

GAIL
Probably - if they wanted to. Plus he's allergic to bees.

NAOMI
Oh. Gotcha

GAIL
Just check for marks.

(They search his body)

NAOMI
(looking up his shirt) Pretty hairy guy.

GAIL
Yeah. He's also got a third nipple over there.

NAOMI
Where?

GAIL
To the left of his belly button.

NAOMI
That mole thing?

GAIL
That's no mole.

NAOMI
Eww.

GAIL
What if he has rabies?

NAOMI
Bill has rabies?

GAIL
He does?

NAOMI
Does he?

GAIL
I don't know. I was talking about the bat.

NAOMI
Oh. *(looking at his head)* No. I don't

think it was the bat that did this.

GAIL
You think it was a heart attack? Oh my god, why aren't I calling... I need to call...

NAOMI
His heart's beating.

GAIL
Then a stroke. Jeez, a stroke. I gotta get to a phone.

(GAIL hops up)

NAOMI
You don't want to...

GAIL
He's dying, Naomi. I'm not just going to sit here—

NAOMI
Gail.

GAIL
—while he goes into cardiac arrest.

NAOMI
But...

GAIL
Not enough blood to the brain. Oh god, what if he's a vegetable?

NAOMI
He's going to be—

GAIL
I'm gonna be stuck taking care of him forever. I'm going to your house. I've got to use a phone.

NAOMI
Okay, but I don't have one.

GAIL
You don't have a phone?

NAOMI
Don't believe in them.

GAIL
What's there to believe in? It's a phone.

NAOMI
I prefer letters as a form of communication, plus...

GAIL
Plus what?

NAOMI
Gail, you clobbered him with the branch.

(Silence)

GAIL
So what are you saying?

NAOMI
I'm saying you knocked him out.

GAIL
Me? What about you?

NAOMI
You couldn't even carry your branch? Remember?

(Silence)

GAIL
We should still call for an ambulance.

NAOMI
If you want to. Don't you think it'll look a little funny?

GAIL
No.

NAOMI
Okay then.

GAIL
I accidentally hit him.

NAOMI
I know that. But we're at Mad Maggie's house. *(silence)* You're going through a nasty divorce. *(silence)* The neighbors have probably heard you and Bill

fighting today.

(Pause)

GAIL
Oh.

NAOMI
Yeah.

GAIL
That could look bad.

NAOMI
Especially if he dies.

GAIL
But you said he wouldn't.

NAOMI
He's fine for now. Let's just wait and see if he comes to.

GAIL
Naomi.

NAOMI
He'll be fine… probably.

GAIL
We really can't call them.

NAOMI
Right.

GAIL
What will I tell my girls?

NAOMI
Accidents happen.

GAIL
If he dies, they're gonna give me a name.

NAOMI
Who? Your girls?

GAIL
Everyone. The papers, the news, everyone. I'll be the new Mad Maggie. Mad Gail.

NAOMI
No.

GAIL
Yes.

NAOMI
Well, maybe, but you'll definitely get a new name. Something with alliteration.

GAIL
I didn't mean to.

NAOMI
I'm your witness.

GAIL
Sarah and Liz, they'll never forgive me. Never ever.

NAOMI
You could gut him and you'd be Gutter Gail.

GAIL
They'll think I did this on purpose. They will.

NAOMI
Maybe Guilty Gail.

GAIL
Lizzy just started talking to me again. That only took two months

NAOMI
Gailer the Impaler.

GAIL
But what if he doesn't die?

NAOMI
Oh that's kind of nice.

GAIL
If he wakes up, he's going to be so… he'll take everything. He'll take my house.

NAOMI
That wouldn't be so bad, right?

GAIL
My kids will take his side. Forever. He'll leave me with nothing and a judge will give him whatever he wants after this. I can't go back to having nothing.

NAOMI
So, you want us to what... off him?

(Silence)

GAIL
That's wrong?

NAOMI
I haven't done that in a while.

GAIL
OH MY GOD. OH MY GOD. WHAT ARE WE DOING? WHAT AM I THINKING. WHAT ARE YOU SAYING? OH MY GOD, OH MY GOD. *(runs to a tree or shrubs and vomits)*

NAOMI
Gailer the Impaler—you okay? *(walks over and rubs her back. GAIL moans)*

NAOMI
Gail. Gail. *(shakes her)* Get that Cuervo up and out, girl. *(shakes her again)* Look at me. Look at me. We can solve this. Come on.

GAIL
No, you come on. We're screwed.

NAOMI
Here's what we do. I have a plan.

GAIL
No more of your plans.

NAOMI
Just listen. We—

GAIL
No. *(she puts her hand over NAOMI's mouth)* No more.

(NAOMI pushes her hand away)

NAOMI
I'd prefer you didn't. Let's calm...

GAIL
(again with her hand) Shhh. No more.

(NAOMI slaps GAIL across the face. Both are stunned. GAIL slaps her back. NAOMI and GAIL then both slap each other at the same time. They both look at each other, then proceed to vomit)

NAOMI
You hit like a girl.

GAIL
You didn't even leave a mark.

NAOMI
You didn't even get my nose to bleed again.

(Pause)

GAIL
Are you okay?

NAOMI
Uh-huh. You?

GAIL
Fine.

NAOMI
So what's your plan?

GAIL
Drag him to the car and put him in the back.

NAOMI
Ok. To the trunk.

GAIL
Seat. Back seat. We'll wait ten minutes and see if he comes to.

NAOMI
So, no police?

GAIL
Not yet. We've got to at least get him away from the scene here. Make it look like we care.

NAOMI
Got it. Good plan. I've also got a few gallons of gasoline if we need to burn the car.

GAIL
You scare me.

NAOMI
I think you've got a good plan.

(GAIL points to the Cuervo bottle)

NAOMI
(grabs the bottle) To felonies. *(drinks)*

GAIL
(takes it) To moving. *(drinks)* I hate tequila.

(They both stand over BILL)

NAOMI
Okay. You get the arms. I got the legs. That's always worked best.

GAIL
Alright.

(They grab a hold of BILL)

GAIL
Got him.

NAOMI
Yep.

GAIL
Let's go.

(They pick him up, sort of)

NAOMI
Oh my god.

GAIL
He's put on weight.

NAOMI
He didn't look this heavy.

(They're huffing and puffing when the sound of a bus is heard. Suddenly, NAOMI and GAIL are caught in the glare of two huge headlights)

GAIL
The police. Run!

(GAIL drops BILL's arms and runs off stage)

SPEAKER
(off-stage) And here's Mad Maggie Fritzer's house. Men never looked at pot roast the same way. The house was recently sold again, but... what's going on?

NAOMI
Gail! Wait, it's the tour bus.

SPEAKER
(off-stage) Well, folks, we've got a treat for you today. It looks like they're doing a reenactment.

BLACKOUT

END OF ACT ONE

ACT II

(Fifteen minutes after the end of Act I. NAOMI alone onstage)

NAOMI
Gail? *(pause)* Gail? *(pause)* They're gone. *(pause)* All right, it's time to come out. I'm not foolin' around.

(GAIL comes out from hiding. Leaves and dirt all over her. She carries an arm full of sticks and twigs)

NAOMI
Well, look at you, Miss Piggy. Listen, don't worry. I explained the situation. They aren't calling the police.

GAIL
(places the sticks around the house) Okay.

NAOMI
I mean, I didn't tell them the actual situation. I made one up.

GAIL
Okay.

(GAIL goes back off-stage)

NAOMI
Jake … The tour guide… could not have been sweeter and helped with Bill. I told him Bill has narcolepsy.

(GAIL carries another arm full of sticks and twigs and heads for the house to set them down)

GAIL
Okay.

NAOMI
I know. I was gonna go the alcoholic route, but then well I decided to work the other direction and guess what… Jake's granddaddy used to have it, so it worked out well. *(picks up the tequila bottle)*

GAIL
Okay.

NAOMI
Plus they took some pictures.

GAIL
Okay.

(GAIL heads back off stage)

NAOMI
The sightseers took'em of everything. The whole event. Even one of me in my bra.

(NAOMI heads over to where GAIL disappeared)

GAIL
Okay.

(GAIL reappears again with an arm full of sticks and twigs, but is stopped by NAOMI)

NAOMI
What's going on with you?

GAIL
Nothing. *(moves around NAOMI to the house)*

NAOMI
You seem funny.

GAIL
Okay.

NAOMI
Stop saying okay.

GAIL
Fine.

NAOMI
And none of that "fine" crap either.

GAIL
Sure.

(GAIL heads back out)

NAOMI
Did you hit your head?

GAIL
No.

NAOMI
Then what is going on? What are you doing?

GAIL
(reappears with more sticks) Well...

NAOMI
What is this?

GAIL
I was hiding out there, scared that everything was about to be over - my life was about to be over.

NAOMI
Makes sense.

GAIL
But then, it hit me.

NAOMI
Somebody hit you?

GAIL
No, I just started thinking so clearly. Saw what I needed to do to move on.

NAOMI
You had an epiphany?

GAIL
Exactly.

(GAIL moves back to the house with her sticks and arranges them)

NAOMI
Hm.

GAIL
It's amazing.

NAOMI
You're calm?

GAIL
Total inner peace.

NAOMI
Hm. So where did this inner peace come from?

GAIL
I don't know. But I know now that I've got to purge myself.

NAOMI
Purge yourself?

GAIL
Purge. *(GAIL gets up and looks at her work)* Purge.

NAOMI
Okay.

GAIL
May I? *(pointing to the bottle)*

NAOMI
Yeah. *(hands it over)*

(GAIL takes a sip and continues to hold the bottle)

NAOMI
So this purging...

GAIL
I need to rid myself of everything holding me back. Holding me to the past.

NAOMI
I didn't know you could get rid of that.

GAIL
The past is not the present and cannot be part of my future.

(There is silence as NAOMI thinks about this)

NAOMI
Wait. That's your epiphany? I'm pretty sure you could have got that from Dr. Phil. It sounds a little... kooky.

GAIL
Kooky? Kooky? Is it kooky to want to start anew? Fresh? Again? Is it kooky to want to move away from the dark cloud that's been following you forever? Is it kooky to finally want to be the real you because you've been trapped for years?

NAOMI
Um, it's kooky to be talking about it in your bra with mud all over your face, with an unconscious ex-husband and a terrorist bat. At least I think it is.

GAIL
No. No. You're wrong

NAOMI
I think this is Jose Cuervo talking?

(NAOMI plays with a pack of cigarettes and lights one)

GAIL
It's not the alcohol. Or maybe it is— something has allowed me to be free... you smoke?

NAOMI
I'm thinking about it.

GAIL
What?

NAOMI
Normally I don't, but I found them in Bill's pocket.

GAIL
No. He quit ten years ago.

NAOMI
Well, then maybe he's holding them for—

GAIL
Can I have one?

NAOMI
You smoke?

GAIL
I did.

NAOMI
Then isn't this something you should purge?

(GAIL stares at her)

NAOMI
I'm just saying. *(hands her the pack and the lighter)*

GAIL
No. You're right. Absolutely right.

NAOMI
I am. So give me those back.

GAIL
Bill likes his secrets. Always has. That's why everything needs to be new... fresh

NAOMI
The house is new.

GAIL
No. It's tainted. Things inside it are tainted. The bat is a sign - Get rid of everything.

NAOMI
So, garage sale?

(GAIL drinks cuervo and walks to the house. She gets on all four and starts trying to get the lighter to work)

GAIL
(Keeps trying to get the lighter to work) Let's burn this bitch to the ground.

NAOMI
You can't.

GAIL
Wanna bet? I got insurance. Accidents happen. *(angrier with the lighter)*

NAOMI
(runs over) Gail. No.

GAIL
Good-bye house.

NAOMI
(grabs GAIL) You can't do this.

(They start to wrestle)

GAIL
I thought you'd be with me.

NAOMI
But Bill's in the house

GAIL
Screw Bill.

NAOMI
No, Bill is actually in the house

GAIL
Get off me!

NAOMI
Bill.

GAIL
Naomi.

NAOMI
House.

GAIL
Burn it.

NAOMI
Listen, Bill is in the house.

(BILL gets up from the floor at some point here and looks around)

GAIL
Bill?

NAOMI
He's in the house.

BILL
(wakes up and looks around) What the hell?

GAIL
What happened to the car?

NAOMI
It looked funny to put him in it.

GAIL
But…

(The bat begins to attack BILL)

NAOMI
Jake said we could just slip him in the house.

BILL
AH…Yaaa…

GAIL
With the bat?

NAOMI
I didn't know what else to do.

GAIL
Oh my god.

BILL
(to the bat) Oh it's on. You are dead. Dead!

(BILL goes offstage and returns intermittently with a broom. The battle ensues)

NAOMI
I didn't know he'd wake up.

GAIL
I coulda burned him alive.

NAOMI
I know. *(looking in)* Man, that bat is all over him.

GAIL
He's tearing apart the house!

BILL
Come back here!!

NAOMI
Good news: he's alive.

GAIL
Get him out. Get him out. Look at

what he's doing!

NAOMI
Let him figure this out.

GAIL
He's destroying everything! *(going to the door)*

NAOMI
Hey. Hey. *(stopping GAIL)* He's gonna try and get that thing out.

GAIL
No. No. This isn't …

NAOMI
A half hour ago you were gonna let him in.

GAIL
(to BILL) Bill. Get out. Get out.

(BILL screaming and battling not paying attention to them at all. Losing the fight, BILL runs for the door and his life)

GAIL
Bill, get out of my damn— *(opens the door and clobbers BILL with it)* Oops.

(BILL comes stumbling/running out)

NAOMI
(to BILL) I thought you said you could kill him, Bill.

BILL
(to GAIL once he recovers) WHAT THE HELL ARE YOU DOING?

GAIL
Trying to help?

BILL
(holding his head) Help? HELP?

NAOMI
She was. I was rooting for the bat.

(The ladies both laugh)

BILL
You think this is funny? Funny?

GAIL
No.

NAOMI
A little.

BILL
You're both lunatics! I can't wait to call Harry about this, Gail. Can't wait.

NAOMI
Harry?

BILL
My lawyer.

GAIL
Good. Great.

NAOMI
Bill, I've faced that monster too and you should just be grateful to be alive.

BILL
(rubbing his head) My head.

NAOMI
You got hit pretty good with the door.

GAIL
Plus the branch.

(NAOMI smacks GAIL)

BILL
What branch? *(pause)* Wait a second.

NAOMI
You got in the way.

BILL
You could have killed me.

NAOMI
Could have? Yes. Did we? No.

BILL
Then you put me in with the bat?

GAIL
What was I supposed to do?

BILL
With an angry bat.

GAIL
That was Naomi.

NAOMI
It's true.

BILL
(to Gail) Then what the hell were you doing?

NAOMI
Having a mud facial and a come-to-Jesus meeting in the bushes.

BILL
You just let this woman—

GAIL
I didn't let—

NAOMI
Naomi. It's Naomi.

BILL
—drag me into the den of hell there.

GAIL
I didn't know.

BILL
I don't believe you. You are sick. Sick! Crazy! You will never ever see...

NAOMI
Bill, look at me. I'm being straight with you. She wouldn't have tried to burn down the house had she known you were in there.

(Pause)

BILL
What? What were you doing? *(looks around)*

NAOMI
I was speaking figuratively.

GAIL
It was the alcohol.

NAOMI
It was said in jest.

BILL
(gestures) It looks like a campfire.

GAIL
Just a joke.

BILL
You were going to burn down your house too. Jesus. Jesus. You're worse off then I thought.

NAOMI
It's her house.

BILL
My money bought it.

GAIL
It's my money.

BILL
You're trying to kill me, Gail. I see it. It's come to this, huh?

GAIL
Of course not. I'm just trying to kill the bat and the house and my past.

BILL
You're just like your mother.

GAIL
At least she would have finished the job.

BILL
Yep! I'm right. You are trying to kill me.

GAIL
Oh. Oh. Oh. Yeah. You are right again. Boy you are always right. How's it feel

to be so right. I want to kill you and leave the girls alone. Yep, that's sure right, right, right, right, right.

BILL
Okay. Okay. Let's just...

GAIL
I am not trying to intentionally hurt you. Honestly. You just keep putting yourself in harm's way.

BILL
Listen, Gail. I'm worried. I originally came over worried. You know I don't do anything if I don't have to.

GAIL
Right with the papers.

BILL
Oh right now, I don't even care about those. Honestly. Hear me out. I think you need help. The girls... they can't - I won't let them - see you like this... They know something's been off. It's not just me, it's everyone. *(takes out his cell phone)*

GAIL
I just need a moment. Let's take a moment here.

BILL
You need more than that.

GAIL
I've had a really hard day. A really hard week and month. This isn't me.

BILL
I'm calling 911. And then I'm calling your therapist. I'm sure she'll meet you at the hospital. You need to calm way down and they can help.

NAOMI
Gail, you are okay.

GAIL
I was calm. Before. You should have seen me then. After the bus and the bushes.

BILL
Well obviously something has come loose.

GAIL
No. No.

BILL
I'm going to put a stop to this now. You're obviously a danger to yourself, my things, and myself. You could hurt the girls.

(Pause)

GAIL
Never. Now, you're talking crazy.

BILL
Well they want to stay with me. Why would that be the case, huh?

NAOMI
Because they can get away with anything with you. Because someone is acting like a victim in this situation.

GAIL
That sums it up.

BILL
Let's not get off the point. You're lost, honey. You need psychological help.

GAIL
Don't get that tone. I'm not a two year-old.

BILL
(dials) Yes, hello, I need an...

(NAOMI clobbers BILL over the head with the large branch. He goes down fast and hard)

GAIL
Naomi!

NAOMI
(hangs up the phone) Yeah?

GAIL
Naomi! *(kneels beside BILL)*

NAOMI
Did I draw blood?

GAIL
Maybe...

NAOMI
Well...

GAIL
No.

NAOMI
Then that's pretty good. I couldn't go too hard, but if I went too soft nothing would have happened and he would've been mad. It's a delicate balance to get just the right pressure.

GAIL
What are you thinking?

NAOMI
I'm thinking I'm saving your ass from being arrested or locked up in the looney ward. He was calling 911. Hello? Police?

GAIL
The looney ward?

NAOMI
That's what they do with phone calls like this. Trust me. That place is horrible, especially the food. *(hands bottle to GAIL. They continue to drink throughout the scene)*

GAIL
(drinks) Look at that bump.

NAOMI
Well he's breathing. *(picks up BILL's phone)*

GAIL
He's unconscious.

NAOMI
We bought ourselves some time.

GAIL
Time?

NAOMI
To think about what to do.

GAIL
There was no other way to accomplish that?

NAOMI
I think on my feet.

GAIL
What are we doing?

NAOMI
You tell me.

GAIL
I don't know.

NAOMI
So you aren't having any other epiphanies?

GAIL
No.

NAOMI
You want to try to go sit in the mud again?

GAIL
God. God.

NAOMI
What do you want? I'll help you out Gail, but you've gotta tell me.

GAIL
Don't hit Bill again.

NAOMI
Okay. I won't. It would have helped to have had that piece of information

before. But hey, now I know.

GAIL
(to BILL) Bill. Wake up.

NAOMI
What are you gonna do when he wakes up?

GAIL
I don't know.

NAOMI
Jesus, know something, will you?

GAIL
We are going to jail.

NAOMI
Well technically I hit him. But I guess that probably won't matter to him.

GAIL
No. It won't.

NAOMI
What do you want to do, Gail?

GAIL
(screams) I don't know! Stop asking me!

NAOMI
You have to have a plan. You seem smart, kind of. What do you want—

GAIL
(interrupting and screaming) I want to be happy. Is that too much to ask?

NAOMI
(pause) Okay, well I was talking about down-and-out Bill here, but let's go with you on this.

GAIL
I deserve to be happy.

NAOMI
Well sure. Of course. Everyone does. Except probably Hitler, and Pol Pot…

GAIL
I haven't been happy.

NAOMI
What's happy? Gail, who's really happy?

GAIL
Tons of people.

NAOMI
All the time?

GAIL
It looks that way.

NAOMI
Then they're retarded, Gail. Big old retards. Because look out there, how can you be happy all the damn time?

GAIL
People aren't going through this.

NAOMI
Don't be dense. Of course they are. Okay, maybe not this exact scenario, but trust me, people go through worse.

GAIL
I know that.

NAOMI
Do you? Starvation, earthquakes, tsunamis, floods, poverty, disease. Nobody has a right to be happy all the time. Unless they are too ignorant or stupid to know better.

GAIL
So you're miserable?

NAOMI
I'm content with my life. At this very moment.

GAIL
You're content with this situation?

NAOMI
Well, yeah. I'm looking forward to seeing what's coming next. It's kind

of exciting. But in five minutes, who knows how I'll feel?

GAIL
You happy at the thought of being arrested?

NAOMI
(holds up the bottle) Drinking Cuervo makes me happy, and it's not guaranteed that I'll be arrested, so I'm not gonna worry about it. Jail can actually be fun—depending on where, when, and who you're with. Plus it depends on what you get charged with.

GAIL
I thought I was happy at the idea of divorce. I thought that would make me happy. I was miserable with him.

NAOMI
Wait, you left him?

GAIL
It just wasn't good.

NAOMI
You left him? I don't understand.

GAIL
I had no identity. I was only Bill's wife, Lizzy and Sarah's mom. That's it. I thought the divorce or my breaking the news to him would break him a little, bring him back into the fold.

NAOMI
I'm sure that didn't make him happy.

GAIL
Actually that's exactly what it did. He didn't get upset, he got happy. He had been just as miserable as me. Maybe even more so.

NAOMI
That's a bad thing?

GAIL
Yes.

NAOMI
So you don't want a divorce?

GAIL
No. I do. I think. I just thought he'd be different. Act different.

NAOMI
You can't threaten to divorce someone and then not like their reaction.

GAIL
I know. But with him happy, it makes it my fault too. It wasn't just him.

NAOMI
Good point.

GAIL
Well, that sucks.

NAOMI
Did you want him to beg and plead for you to stay?

GAIL
Yes! After almost 25 years, I deserve that.

NAOMI
Would it have changed things?

GAIL
Maybe. Maybe it would have let me know he still cared. Still desired me.

NAOMI
That plan really blew up in your face.

GAIL
Yeah.

NAOMI
I mean you must think that if he doesn't want you, then who the hell else will? Yikes.

GAIL
Thanks.

NAOMI
Yeah, that's bad.

GAIL
I know.

NAOMI
That's sad. I guess I can see why you might not be in a huge hurry to sign the papers.

GAIL
I thought I knew my life. Knew who I was. Knew who I was married to. But I don't have a clue. How can I be this new person when I'm not sure I knew the old one?

NAOMI
Gail bought this house. Gail has the bat. Everything and every choice you've made today is yours.

GAIL
Oh my god. What does that say about me? *(indicating to the disaster that surrounds them)*

NAOMI
It says you've got some stuff to work on. But focusing on you isn't bad. Maybe you need this opportunity to work just on you.

GAIL
But all I am is lonely. I am going to be alone.

NAOMI
You didn't think about that before?

GAIL
In my head, it turned out much differently than this. I never got to be alone. I thought it would be... better.

NAOMI
It's hard, Gail. Life is hard whether you have a man or whether you go at it alone.

GAIL
Where the hell were you six months ago?

NAOMI
You and Bill... everything still would have dissolved eventually. You just played your cards first. That was smart. Don't be the last one to leave a party, you know what I'm saying. Embrace this change, Gail. Something in the universe is telling you to do this.

GAIL
With angry girls, a bat, a murderer's house and an unconscious ex and...

NAOMI
We can't question the powers.

GAIL
You don't think all this was to tell me I was wrong?

NAOMI
I guess, maybe, sure. But let's spin this into something positive.

GAIL
I wish I had burned the house down.

NAOMI
Who says we can't? We still can. I told you I have gasoline...

GAIL
Maybe I am crazy.

NAOMI
Absolutely.

GAIL
Hey.

NAOMI
What?

GAIL
You're supposed to be cheering me up.

NAOMI
I'm not gonna lie to you.

GAIL
You think I'm crazy?

NAOMI
That's a possibility.

GAIL
So you think Bill's right?

NAOMI
I think he had a few good points.

GAIL
God, Naomi.

NAOMI
What?

GAIL
You must not have a lot of women friends because, normally, in a situation like this, you should just console me and agree with everything I say.

NAOMI
Why?

GAIL
Because that's what girlfriends do.

NAOMI
But we're neighbors.

GAIL
It's what any woman would do.

NAOMI
Well not me.

GAIL
Great. *(yells)* Great!

NAOMI
What do you want me to say?

GAIL
Tell me you understand.

NAOMI
I do. Most of the time. I just met you.

GAIL
Forget it. *(to BILL)* Bill. Bill. I need you to wake up. *(No response. GAIL drops his head)*

NAOMI
See Bill doesn't look happy.

GAIL
He's happy, trust me. A 55 year old with a huge 401K. He's a single woman's dream.

NAOMI
Maybe he deserves some happiness too after years of misery.

GAIL
It wasn't all miserable.

NAOMI
How do you really know that? You just said you didn't know he was so unhappy.

GAIL
I know.

NAOMI
Okay. Okay. I'm just saying that maybe you and he deserve the same thing. You aren't so different.

GAIL
Of course we're different. He has more available to him and his new lifestyle. Me? I'm not in high demand. Women like you and me aren't necessarily commodities in this community.

(BILL begins waking up, unbeknownst to GAIL and NAOMI)

NAOMI
Speak for yourself.

GAIL
You know what I'm saying.

NAOMI
I do. And I'm offended. I'm hotter now than when I was twenty.

GAIL
Really? Well, I guess some of us aren't so lucky.

NAOMI
You know what I did when everything crashed down around me? When my husband went off with another woman? I took a trip to Italy. Yep. One of those group tours. I was all alone, but guess what I did? I bought an old house in the country and fixed it up.

GAIL
In Italy? YOU have a house in Italy?

NAOMI
I hired all these immigrants to work on it. Sure, I was lonely, but after a horribly torrid affair with some hot Italian dude who was just a transitional man, I learned that I had a house full of love - my lesbian friend had her baby...

GAIL
Wait...

NAOMI
Then a young couple from opposite backgrounds got married in my back yard.

GAIL
Naomi. That's a movie.

NAOMI
And then a travelling stranger... a writer found me in my Tuscan villa and we fell in love...

GAIL
That's 'Under the Tuscan Sun'.

NAOMI
What?

GAIL
I saw it in the theatre.

NAOMI
Hmm... Really?

GAIL
With Diane Lane. Yeah.

NAOMI
Well, you get my point.

GAIL
No. Why would you tell me that?

NAOMI
You're getting caught up in the details. My point is you're never too old. The middle ages - the forties, fifties, sixties - are great. Less bullshit and more awesomeness. It's not the end. It's the middle toward the end. But not the end. Didn't you watch the Golden Girls? Hell, they were 100 and got a lot of dates. Granted that was in Florida, but...

GAIL
I'm not a golden girl.

NAOMI
You're close. Point is. . .

GAIL
Point is I'm here, in hell, and bleeding, bruised, and battered. I've almost killed Bill, almost been arrested, almost been eaten by a bat.

NAOMI
Right. Almost. There was no follow through. Hooray for that. And you know what? You'll date if you want to. You'll be alone if that's what you want. You just have to start thinking about what you really want. And being alone, well you've got kids and friends. I'm assuming you have friends, right?

(BILL's car is heard starting)

GAIL
Of course. Some. I guess, but it's not the same. It's...

NAOMI
(sees BILL) One of your problems has been solved.

GAIL
What?

NAOMI
Bill.

GAIL
(looks around for BILL) He's dead?

NAOMI
No. *(points)* There.

GAIL
What?

NAOMI
Bill...

(Tires squealing)

GAIL
(sees it) Bill? What's he doing?

NAOMI
Leaving.

GAIL
Leaving?

NAOMI
This is good.

GAIL
You don't think he'll call the police?

NAOMI
Oh yeah, well maybe. He could.

GAIL
Shit. Why didn't you stop...

NAOMI
I tried. You were flapping your gums.

(A truck pulls into the driveway)

GAIL
You could have... who's this?

NAOMI
You tell me, this is your house.

(A car door opens and shuts)

GAIL
You're the one with the damn plans.

NAOMI
I gave up my plans. I told you to make some of your own.

(SAM enters with a knapsack)

SAM
Um... hi. I'm here for the animals.

NAOMI
Bat guy!

GAIL
Bat guy?

(SAM's eyes look anywhere but at the ladies, who are still in their bras)

NAOMI
Didn't I tell you?

GAIL
Tell me what?

NAOMI
Jake, the tour dude, called the bat guy. To help us out.

GAIL
He did?

NAOMI
He did.

GAIL
(to SAM) You're here!

NAOMI
He's here!

SAM
Yep.

NAOMI AND GAIL
(jumping around him) Yay! Yay!

GAIL
I'm so glad you're here.

NAOMI
You have no idea.

GAIL
What about Bill …

NAOMI
He was fine. Shhh.

SAM
Yea, okay. Um, so…

NAOMI
You're a god-send.

SAM
Sure.

GAIL
Seriously, you are.

SAM
This will just take a few seconds.

GAIL
But you don't understand.

NAOMI
You're exactly what we wanted.

GAIL
You are a dream.

NAOMI
You look like a man who can handle what we got.

GAIL
(to NAOMI) Of course he can.

SAM
(clearly uncomfortable) I just came because of the bat.

GAIL
We know.

NAOMI
That's why I called.

SAM
Just so we're clear.

GAIL
Of course.

SAM
Obviously you guys have been having some fun this evening.

GAIL
Fun?

NAOMI
Fun?

GAIL
What the hell are you talking about?

NAOMI
We've been in the battle for our lives.

GAIL
Look at my nose.

NAOMI
Or mine.

SAM
Okay. Okay.

NAOMI
That's why we needed your help.

GAIL
Before the police come to arrest us.

NAOMI
(glaring at GAIL) She means the bat.

SAM
They won't come to get a bat out. They'll refer you to us.

NAOMI
(to GAIL) See.

SAM
Actually, we were all fighting over

your call. This is Mad Maggie's house, right?

NAOMI AND GAIL
Yes!

SAM
I took the bus tour when I was little, but...

NAOMI
You know, Gail here, had no idea whose house it was when she bought it.

SAM
Are you new in town?

NAOMI
Divorced. Mucky's up the mind.

SAM
Well, you're pretty lucky. A piece of property like this with the history... you'll get a good return on your investment.

NAOMI
Yeah?

GAIL
Really?

NAOMI
What about the house next door? I mean, it's close to Mad Maggie's.

SAM
I can't say for sure. You know what? Let me just get started. So, it's a bat. Just one?

NAOMI
Yes.

GAIL
I have no idea how it got in.

NAOMI
It's big... huge.

GAIL
It was attacking us.

NAOMI
Swooping.

GAIL
Very angry.

NAOMI
She opened the window with a rock and he wouldn't even fly out.

GAIL
It could have rabies.

NAOMI
Or mange.

SAM
Rabies are pretty rare in Michigan.

GAIL
You're gonna kill it, right?

NAOMI
Humanely, of course.

GAIL
Whatever way you can.

SAM
Actually we don't—

GAIL
I want it dead.

SAM
I know they can seem scary.

NAOMI
Do we look scared?

SAM
You are outside.

NAOMI
True.

SAM
You know, bats are actually very important to our ecological systems.

GAIL
He's not doing them any good in there.

NAOMI
Again, it could have rabies. Kill us all.

SAM
But rabies are pretty rare in...

NAOMI
(interrupting) Yeah, yeah. What's your name?

SAM
Sam.

NAOMI
I'm Naomi. *(points to GAIL)* Gail.

SAM
Great. Nice to meet you. I'm gonna get on in.

NAOMI
Good luck.

GAIL
Destroy him.

SAM
(turning back) You know, technically, we do live trappings. We take the animal, in this case, the bat, off the property and dispense it elsewhere.

GAIL
You don't kill it?

SAM
We're not exterminators, no.

NAOMI
So, what's it gonna take, Sam?

SAM
Take?

NAOMI
To get you to off him?

SAM
Ladies, I understand you don't like bats, but they eat thousands of mosquitoes and insects. Do either of you garden?

GAIL
Do I look like Martha Stewart?

NAOMI
I love her show. Even more since the jail thing.

GAIL
I've seen it a couple of...

SAM
(interrupting) I'm just saying these little guys do more good than harm.

GAIL
Are you part of PETA or something?

SAM
No.

NAOMI
A tree hugger?

SAM
I enjoy nature. Yes but I wouldn't consider myself a... listen, I'm just trying to say that bats are misunderstood.

NAOMI
Sam, what's your normal charge?

SAM
For removal?

NAOMI
Yeah. We'll double it.

GAIL
We will?

NAOMI
(to GAIL) You want him dead?

GAIL
Yeah.

SAM
Well it's $150.

GAIL
What?

SAM
Plus it's after seven, so it's another fifty.

NAOMI
Why aren't you driving a better car? With that money...

GAIL
I can't afford to double that.

SAM
Let me just go in there and get him, okay?

GAIL
But I really want it dead.

SAM
Fine.

GAIL
Really.

SAM
I won't charge you extra.

GAIL
I'm really not a bad person, I just don't want him coming back.

SAM
The bat?

NAOMI
Sure, that thing might seek revenge.

SAM
Bats don't seek...

GAIL
I just want him out of my life.

SAM
Okay. Okay. Let me do my job. *(walks toward the door then reaches into his knapsack)*

NAOMI
You should see the equipment he'll use. This new soundwave crap. It's amazing.

GAIL
Two hundred dollars?

NAOMI
I'd pay a thousand for some peace of mind.

(SAM puts on a pair of oven gloves and takes out kitchen tongs and a large Folgers coffee can. He opens the door)

GAIL
Wait a sec!

SAM
(turns) Yeah?

GAIL
Where's your equipment?

SAM
Here. *(holds up the stuff)*

GAIL
Are those kitchen tongs?

SAM
This works best.

GAIL
What am I paying you two hundred for?

SAM
My time and effort. Do you want the bat out?

GAIL
Yes.

SAM
Then, I'll be right back.

(SAM heads into the house)

GAIL
He's gotta know what he's doing, right?

NAOMI
Sure. He's a professional.

(NAOMI *begins picking up her folding chairs*)

GAIL
You think he'll break anything?

NAOMI
Please, all your crap is in boxes.

(NAOMI *puts the chairs in her wheelbarrow*)

GAIL
Yeah, but that bat is … is…

NAOMI
Squirrelly?

GAIL
Yes.

NAOMI
It'll be okay.

GAIL
Yeah. You're right. What are you doing?

NAOMI
I'm going to mosey on home.

GAIL
What?

NAOMI
My work is done.

GAIL
You're leaving at the climax.

NAOMI
Naw. We know what's gonna happen. I'll catch you around.

GAIL
What about Bill … the police? Setting the house on fire?

NAOMI
They would have been here by now. You're fine. And the house? You heard the man, you own history. You're not gonna burn it down cuz of one bad day.

GAIL
But what if—

NAOMI
Gail, I'm right next door.

GAIL
I know.

(NAOMI *heads off*)

GAIL
I'll let you know how it turns out.

(NAOMI *just waves and pushes the wheelbarrow away. GAIL is left alone. She turns to the house and is bitten by a mosquito. As she itches, SAM walks out*)

SAM
Man, I love that fireplace.

GAIL
You got him?

SAM.
Yep.

GAIL
Already?

SAM
(*holds up the coffee can, which is squeaking loudly*) I also got this. (*hands GAIL her purse*)

GAIL
Thanks.

SAM
Yep.

GAIL
So you'll take him and …

SAM
Yep. And you know, it's not a male.

GAIL
Really?

SAM
Definitely female.

GAIL
You're sure?

SAM
Yeah. She's what we call a big brown bat, typical for the area, but much smaller than the name indicates. She's bigger than your normal female, but I think that's because she may be nursing.

GAIL
Nursing?

SAM
She has babies.

GAIL
Babies? She just seemed so angry.

SAM
The swooping. That's a sign of anxiety and fear. She's just trying to protect herself. Picture yourself in some strange place. You'd be freaking out too.

GAIL
Yeah.

SAM
She got lost somehow. Couldn't find her way out. I'm sure it wasn't her ideal situation either.

GAIL
I tried to help. She wouldn't leave.

SAM
Not your problem anymore.

GAIL
It just really wasn't the day for her to fly in here.

SAM
When is a good time, right?

GAIL
(pause) If you let her go, it's far away from here, right?

SAM
Yeah. About thirty miles.

GAIL
Just do that then.

SAM
Oh good. Good.

GAIL
I guess there's no need to kill her, right?

SAM
Yeah.

GAIL
And she'll make a new home.

SAM
Sure. That's two hundred dollars.

GAIL
Of course. *(takes out her purse)* Check okay?

SAM
Fine.

GAIL
Make it out to whom?

SAM
Live Trapping Inc.

GAIL
Great. *(writing)* I mean, she'll do fine out there, right?

SAM
Yeah. She'll adapt.

GAIL
Good.

SAM
Of course, the babies will die.

GAIL
Oh. Really? Oh.

SAM
Can you make sure to include your phone number on there in case there's an issue?

GAIL
Yeah. *(pause)* I know what you're thinking.

SAM
Ma'am, I'm not thinking anything. I mean, I don't think you understand what it's like to be a harmless bat—

GAIL
Oh I understand. I Un-der-stand. *(hands him the check)*

SAM
Thanks. *(starts off)*

GAIL
It's a sanctuary, right?

SAM
Excuse me?

GAIL
For the bat?

(SAM walks over to her)

SAM
Where's your friend?

GAIL
Naomi? She went home.

SAM
Can I be honest with you?

GAIL
About Naomi?

SAM
About this.

GAIL
The bat?

SAM
Meeting men—this isn't the best way. There's the internet, dating services, but this type of half-naked damsel in distress thing just isn't...

GAIL
I'm sorry, I'm confused.

SAM
Your friend mentioned you're going through a divorce. That sucks. Really. My mom went through one last year and she was about your age.

GAIL
Your mom is my age?

SAM
You seem like a real nice woman, Gail. Really. But meeting men in this outfit won't get you anything but trouble.

GAIL
My outfit. Oh, wait, no, you don't understand. I hit my nose then Naomi did. We were bleeding and couldn't go inside and...

SAM
I mean, you're attractive for someone your age, but I have a girlfriend.

GAIL
You really don't understand, Sam.

SAM
Of course I do, the prospect of being your age and having your husband leave you. Probably for a younger woman, right? That's what a lot of men do.

GAIL
Who said he left me?

SAM
You're just giving me that vibe.

GAIL
Oh my god.

SAM
It's gotta be hard.

GAIL
I'm pathetic.

SAM
No. No. I mean, maybe you should see a counselor or something? My mom went to some doctor and she got drugs. She might have been going through some female stuff too. Menopause and such.

GAIL
This is the bottom

SAM
I can get you his name.

GAIL
Yep. Rock bottom.

SAM
She's a lot better now. Joined some society of women with red hats. I bet they'd totally let you in if—

GAIL
Oh my god, Sam, shut up.

SAM
What?

GAIL
I do not want to sleep with you.

SAM
Really?

GAIL
I do not want drugs or red hats. You need to leave. Now.

SAM
I don't want to leave if you're gonna do something crazy.

GAIL
I'm fine.

SAM
You know, my mom saw this Oprah episode…

GAIL
Sam, how old are you?

SAM
Twenty-three.

GAIL
Right. I don't know if you can understand this, but you dispensing this talk is like a dagger in my fucking heart.

SAM
I'm just trying to sympathize.

GAIL
Stop. You're twenty-three. You cannot sympathize.

SAM
But my mom—

GAIL
I don't want to know about your mom. Thank you, Sam. Thank you for everything.

SAM
But you really need something to help with this sadness.

GAIL
You need to go. Now. Go now.

SAM
Are you mad because I rejected you?

GAIL
No. Or yes. Which will make you leave? Two seconds ago you couldn't wait to leave.

SAM
It's just so sad to see you like this.

GAIL
Bye-bye.

SAM
Well, if you want those numbers…

GAIL
I'll call.

SAM
Ask for Sam. G'Night. *(starts to leave)*

GAIL
Wait. Just take her to the end of the street and let her go.

SAM
Really?

GAIL
Let her go back to her babies.

SAM
Gail. Gail. Everything is going to be okay.

GAIL
Hearing you say that makes me want to hurt myself.

(SAM walks to his truck. GAIL watches him leave and then turns to the house)

GAIL
Okay. Okay

(Picking up the papers from BILL, she signs)

GAIL
Okay.

(She goes inside and starts to unpack. NAOMI comes back onstage with beers but starts to look through GAIL's boxes again. GAIL comes outside to get her purse or maybe carry a box and sees NAOMI snooping)

GAIL
Naomi.

NAOMI
Hey there! I figured you could use this. *(hands GAIL a beer)*

GAIL
Thanks. I'm assuming you heard.

NAOMI
Oh, every word. Red hats, huh?

(They laugh or something suggesting that they are amused)

GAIL
By the way, I signed them. *(indicates the divorce papers. NAOMI smiles and toasts)*

NAOMI
You looking for some help with those boxes?

GAIL
Yeah. Come on.

NAOMI
You want me to help?

GAIL
You just offered.

NAOMI
No, I just asked.

GAIL
Well that's offering.

NAOMI
Bull. But since you asked, yeah, I'll help.

GAIL
Is this what you're like?

NAOMI
Is this what you're like? *(pause)* See?

(As they move the boxes, suddenly, we hear a siren and police lights approaching the house)

END OF PLAY

VOICES OF THE MIDWEST

MAIDENS, MOTHERS, & CRONES

A PLAY BY
ANNIE MARTIN & SUZI REGAN

Cast of Characters

All women. This play was originally cast with 4 women and a female troubadour, but it can be performed with as many as 48 women.

TROUBADOUR, female, plays guitar and sings
SANDY: a middle aged (40-50) female, actor; can change name to the actor playing the role
SARAH: an older female (60 or above), actor; can change name to the actor playing the role
TIFFANY: a young female (18-25), actor; can change name to the actor playing the role
EMILY: a female (25-40) female, actor; can change name to the actor playing the role
STAGE MANAGER: the actual play's Stage Manager

WOMAN #1
WOMAN #2
WOMAN #3
WOMAN #4

ROSALIE: an elderly woman

CARRIE: a young female
GIRL #1
GIRL #2
GIRL #3
GIRL #4

WOMAN
JENNY: young girl, 11 or 12; then becomes a woman in her 20s or 30s
MOM
ALEX: Jenny's friend in her 20s or 30; then shifts to a 52 year old
DOCTOR: middle aged OBGYN
KATHY: a young girl, 11-12; can be played by the actor who played MOM earlier in the scene

BONNIE: a young girl, middle school aged
KALI: between 18-50 years old

KRISTI: A middle aged woman; best friends with JULIE
JULIE: A middle aged woman; best friends with KRISTI

FRANNY: Can be any age.

MAYA: Middle aged to older woman

SIAN: A mother; between 25-40 years old

LILLY: cheerleader
JUDY: cheerleader
EILEEN: cheerleader
SAMANTHA: cheerleader
AUDREY: cheerleader

JESSICA: Older woman

BETH: 27 year old veterinarian

JOAN

MOM #1
MOM #2
MOM #3
MOM #4
LITTLE GIRL: played by the troubadour

SHANA: a yoga instructor, young.
THERESA: woman taking SHANA's yoga class

TAMARA
MARIA
ERIN
SUE

THE VOICES FROM THE MIDWEST series of plays was created by the Williamston Theatre to explore and embrace what life is like in our part of the world. Directors and playwrights on the project developed questionnaires, and sent them all over the Midwest, inviting submissions from people of all walks of life. Those submissions were then taken and adapted into three evenings of theatre exploring the life of women, men, and families in the American Midwest.

MAIDENS, MOTHERS, AND CRONES was written, in part, thanks to submissions from the following people: Norma Baker, Juanita Baldwin, Margaret Beard, Sandra Birch, Laurie Binns, Dana Brazil, Judith Bridger, Megan Buckley, Quetta Carpenter, Mariah Cherem, Connie Cowper, Sherry Deatrick, Mary Eckert, Kathy Ellis, Sarah Fruitig, Linda Rabin Hammell, Rachelle Harper, Sandy A. Hopkins, Ameena K. Jier, Kali Jones, Terry Junger, Deborah Kellogg-Lewis, Lynn Lammers, Teri Clark Linden, Cynthia Malow, Annie Martin, Patricia P. Miller, Tiffany Mitchenor, Shirley Munson, Amanda Northrup, Bridgette Redman, Suzi Regan, Kari Ringer, Mary Rux, Barbara Sharpe, Deborah Solo, Emily Sutton-Smith, Clarice Thompson, Jennifer C. Weil, Shey Zenker, and many women who wish to remain anonymous.

MAIDENS, MOTHERS, AND CRONES: VOICES FROM WOMEN OF THE MIDWEST received its world premiere on May 8, 2008 at Williamston Theatre (Williamston, MI). It was directed by Suzi Regan. Set & Lighting Design by Daniel C. Walker, Costume Design by Lori Sands, Music by Suzi Regan. Stage Managed by Megan Buckley. VOICES OF THE MIDWEST series concept by Tony Caselli.

The cast was as follows:

>Sarah Benoit
>Sandra Birch
>Tiffany Denise Mitchenor
>Deborah Solo
>Emily Sutton-Smith

For production rights, contact Williamston Theatre.

MAIDENS, MOTHERS, AND CRONES

ACT I
SCENE ONE

(Lights up and reveal a clearing in the middle of an ancient grove)

TROUBADOUR
Ready?
(starts to sing)
WE ARE THE DAUGHTERS OF OUR GRANDMOTHER'S DAUGHTERS
WE HAVE THE SAME STRONG HANDS, SAME KNOWING EYE
WE THREE WADE
THRU THE MYSTIC WATERS
SEEDED WITH BLOOD, SWEAT AND TEARS
OF ALL THAT IS LIFE

STAGE MANAGER
(calls out)
Cue dancers. Go.

(Out come the actors dancing—auditioning for a play)

TROUBADOUR
WE ARE THE MOON
FULL CIRCLE
HER PHASES
OH, LUNA
WE ARE THE MOON
SILVER SILVER
FULL BODIED
OH, DIANA
WE ARE THE MOON
THE TIME KEEPERS
THE SHAPE SHIFTERS
WE ARE THE MOON
THE RIVER
THE OCEAN
THE TIDE

ACTORS & TROUBADOUR
(sing the chorus together)
WE ARE THE DAUGHTERS OF OUR GRANDMOTHER'S DAUGHTERS
WE HAVE THE SAME STRONG HANDS, SAME KNOWING EYE
WE THREE WADE
THRU THE MYSTIC WATERS
SEEDED WITH BLOOD, SWEAT AND TEARS
OF ALL THAT IS LIFE

TROUBADOUR
WE ARE CREATOR
DESTROYER
THE HUNTER
THE WARRIOR
WE FEED
WE CARRY
WE ROCK
FROM CRADLE
TO GRAVE

WE ARE THE WHALE
THE OTTER
THE TURTLE
THE SPIDER
WE WEAVE LION AND LAMB
IN SACRED MELODY

ACTORS & TROUBADOUR
(singing the chorus together)
WE ARE THE DAUGHTERS OF OUR
GRANDMOTHER'S DAUGHTERS
WE HAVE THE SAME STRONG HANDS,
SAME KNOWING EYE
WE THREE WADE
THRU THE MYSTIC WATERS
SEEDED WITH BLOOD, SWEAT AND TEARS
OF ALL THAT IS LIFE

STAGE MANAGER
Hold please. *(they freeze)* You can have a seat. *(they break)*

SANDY
What is this?

EMILY
I love this song.

SANDY
I didn't know I was auditioning for a musical.

SARAH
Seems to be a little bit of everything.

SANDY
I'm an actor Sarah, not a monkey.

TIFFANY
The audition notice says it's an "exploration of life from the point of view of the modern Midwestern woman."

SARAH
Sandy's right. Doesn't say musical.

SANDY
What? I'm sorry. I'm fallin' asleep here.

STAGE MANAGER
Sandra Birch.

SANDY
I've got a few problems with the script already.

STAGE MANAGER
Sandra Birch?

SANDY
What? Yes?

(pause)

STAGE MANAGER
Read Act I, scene 1, "Home," please.

SANDY
(auditioning with a monologue)
Growing up in a small Michigan town, I would stomp my feet and swear to anyone who would listen to my supposed teenage wisdom that there was nothing worth anything in that town. No life. No culture. And all I wanted to do was move away from what felt like a prison and start my real life. But in the end, I married a factory rat, had kids, and stayed near my hometown and created an actual fulfilling life. My Midwestern life has given me stability and roots. And still has allowed me to grow and succeed. It is my home. And I...

STAGE MANAGER
Stop please.

SANDY
Thank you.

TIFFANY
(to SARAH) What exactly constitutes the Midwest?

SARAH
Well... Michigan.

EMILY
It's Michigan, Ohio, Indiana, Illinois, Missouri, Wisconsin, and Minnesota

TROUBADOUR
And Kansas.

EMILY
No, that's a plain state.

SARAH
The plains are part of the Midwest.

TROUBADOUR
North Dakota?

TIFFANY
Pennsylvania is one.

EMILY and SARAH
No.

SANDY
Iowa?

TUBADOR
If Kansas isn't than Iowa can't be either.

EMILY
This should be in the audition breakdown, don't you think?

TIFFANY
Someone should know.

SANDY
(to the STAGE MANAGER) Megan?

STAGE MANAGER
Sarah. You're next. Can you read Clarissa?

SARAH
Sure.

TIFFANY
How can we keep going if nobody even knows what the Midwest is?

STAGE MANAGER
Can you act like it?

(pause)

TIFFANY
Ok. Yeah.

STAGE MANAGER
Begin when you're ready, Sarah. Can we have a little guitar?

(TROUBADOUR begins to play the guitar)

SARAH
(auditioning as "Clarissa") I technically moved away from the Midwest with my parents at 16 and haven't been back in 47 years. But my core still holds dear the soil and farming of the region... at least in my childhood.

STAGE MANAGER
Sarah, can you pull back your hair, please?

(SARAH puts her hair back)

TIFFANY
Why does the Midwest only mean small towns and farms? I'm a Detroiter. I didn't ever milk a cow.

SANDY
I know.

TIFFANY
There are big cities, urban areas.

SARAH
(to the actors) Can I finish? *(silence)* Thank you. *(becomes Clarissa)* I live in California now. As I drove along a gravel road the other day, I saw a sign nailed on a fence: "organic fruits, vegetables and fresh eggs." Funny...I grew up on organic...it was just food from our yard, garden, and shingled hen house. We knew no other way. I turned off the main road, followed the small lane, and stopped my car beside a weathered building with screened

windows. Inside, I was alone. The note on the front entrance said: "We are on the honor system. Take what you want, weigh it, put the money in the green coffee tin with the blue lid." California dimmed and I took in everything around me: the sights, sound, and taste. I closed my eyes. I had come home.

STAGE MANAGER
Great. Thank you.

TIFFANY
(to SANDY) So Sarah's the crone?

SANDY
Yep.

SARAH
I am not the crone

TIFFANY
Oh, then it's you Sandy?

SANDY
Tiffany, I'm the mother. Megan, I'm the mother, right?

STAGE MANAGER
Probably not. We'll let you know.

SANDY
Oh. Ok. *(to the actors)* This is so insulting. Maiden, Mothers, and Crones… who names a play that?

EMILY
It's not so bad.

SANDY
Call me when you're fifty, Emily.

EMILY
It's beautiful. It's the cycle of life.

SARAH
Um, Crone is a withered old woman. A hag.

SANDY
The playwright probably doesn't even know what it means.

SARAH
It's a woman director – she'll spin it into something, to empower us, right?

TIFFANY
I'd just like it brought to their attention that there needs to be more diversity. Where are the Muslims, the Asians, the Jews…

TROUBADOUR
(interrupting) I'm a Jew.

EMILY
They've only got an hour and a half.

SANDY
And I'm not a mother or a crone. So where does that leave me?

STAGE MANAGER
Tiffany, we'd like you to read the welfare mother.

TIFFANY
(to SANDY) Better off then me.

STAGE MANAGER
Wait. Wait. I'm sorry. The director would like to see the dance again, but this time, we need more energy and would like it in slow motion including the music. Also does anybody object to nudity?

SANDY
(aside) I object to everything.

(Lights change)

SCENE TWO

(Actors chant and march in time)

ALL
WAKE UP
MEDITATE
EAT BREAKFAST
PRAY

LEAVE HOME
GO TO WORK
GO HOME
STAY

OR GO
TO THE GYM
TO A MEETING
TO MY SECOND JOB

OR TALK
OR VISIT
OR WALK
THE DOG

FIX DINNER
CHILL
GET READY FOR BED

READ
REFLECT
CLEAR MY HEAD
AND SLEEP

(This is repeated through the lines below)

WOMAN #1
Wait I forgot to mention finishing the laundry. . . never ending laundry.

WOMAN #2
I don't do cooking. I had the good fortune to finally marry a man who bakes his own bread and stirs up sauces and makes a steak to die for. So, he figures this entitles him to slack on any other household work.

WOMAN #4
There is no relaxation. I can do that in twenty years when I have more time. Until then, I work at home, at the office... I need to make it.

(Chanting stops)

WOMAN #3
I am retired and do as I please.

(Chanting resumes)

WAKE UP
MEDITATE
EAT BREAKFAST
PRAY

LEAVE HOME
GO TO WORK
GO HOME
STAY

OR GO
TO THE GYM
TO A MEETING
TO MY SECOND JOB

OR TALK
OR VISIT
OR WALK
THE DOG

FIX DINNER
CHILL
GET READY FOR BED

READ
REFLECT
CLEAR MY HEAD
AND SLEEP

(Lights change)

SCENE THREE

TROUBADOUR
(with women harmonizing)
MAIDENS, MOTHERS, AND CRONES
MAIDENS, MOTHERS, AND CRONES
MAIDENS, MOTHERS, AND CRONES
MAIDENS, MOTHERS, AND CRONES

ROSALIE
Sit on the edge of the bed
    listen
        to the house settle
        to the memories dance
        to my heart beat in time
            beating to demand attention
Attention all: The clock keeps ticking

Sit on the edge of the bed
        where I used to sleep
            even when he stumbled in
              from a house call
            even when he snored loudly
              enough to chip the paint
            even when he chose to end
              with a hospital bed
                it was in the room
                at the foot of the bed
so we knew we were each here and near

Sit on the edge of the bed
        Night used to be peaceful
        Night used to be quiet
        but night is now too long
            too painful
            too full of the ifs and
            the ands and the buts
I remain unable to lie down
        and take my place in this new bed
            in this new life.

Sit on the edge of the bed
        Until the sun rises
        Until the paper comes
        Until the coffee needs to be made
        Until my distractions arrive

Sit on the edge of the bed
    Tracy is first
    she the young help of 50
    comes through the door
    calling my name.
"yes, yes. I'm still here.
I'm still breathing."
    That gets a laugh every time
Hired help since I have officially retired
    from cleaning
    from cooking
    from the work that
        used to be mine
Tracy will run a bath
    fix breakfast
    and give me a break from night

Sit on the edge of the bed
    The visits begin with my sons, daughters, and the holy ghost
        almost daily
        to do my bills
        to answer my mail
and then come my friends
        who dwindled at first,
        year by year
        and then month by month
        and now week by week
but the last of them still come
        to discuss the weather
            our families
            the obituaries
I get the occasional visits from my grandchildren, the Reverend Miller, and the sweet girls from church

Sit on the edge of the bed
    Move to the family room
        to work on my great-grand-daughter's booties
        or read my large print novel
            which is easier to read but
            almost too heavy to lift
        or watch my Tigers—win or lose
    Tracy makes popcorn and we cheer in silence

while the chair by the window
remains empty
and will continue to be

Sit on the edge of the bed
    and watch nightfall begin
        to creep up again
Tracy makes her way home
and for the first time in 93 years
        I am alone.

So I take my place on the edge of the bed
remember my life
    pray for my family
        and wait for him to come.

(Lights change)

SCENE FOUR

(TROUBADOUR starts to play "When I was a Girl" and CARRIE sings)

CARRIE
(sings)
WHEN I WAS A GIRL
I WANTED TO BE
SOMEONE RICH, FAMOUS, AND FREE.
I'D ACT ON THE SCREEN,
I'D WRITE THE BESTSELLER
AND THEN I'D FIND ME
A MIGHTY NICE FELLER
I'D LEAVE THIS PLACE
WITHOUT A TRACE
NEVER AGAIN TO SHOW MY FACE
WHEN I WAS A LITTLE GIRL

WHEN I WAS A GIRL
I WANTED TO TRAVEL
THE WORLD PAST MY DRIVEWAY
OF SAND AND GRAVEL.
THE LAST SUPPER, DAVID, THE MONA LISA;
SEE THE ARCH, THE SINE,
THE TOWER OF PISA
INVITED TO SEE ART

IN EVERY COURT
LOVE MEN NOT BOYS
IN EVERY PORT
WHEN I WAS A LITTLE GIRL

(Harmonica break)

WHEN I WAS A GIRL
I WANTED TO PLAY
WITH THE BOYS IN MUD
THE DIRT AND THE CLAY
MOMMA SAID NO, NO
GIRLS DON'T GET MESSY
NOW I AM DIRTY
AND A LITTLE TESTY
SURE MAMA I SAID
BUT BROKE MY WORD
OH JOY SWEARIN', SMOKIN'
AND FLIPPIN' THE BIRD
WHEN I WAS A LITTLE GIRL

GIRL #1
Dear Diary,
Oh my gosh, I so want to be a waitress at Friendly's. I'd get to meet so many cool people and eat all the fries I want.

GIRL #2
Dear Diary,
I want to be famous

GIRL #3
Dear Diary,
I am going to be a ballerina. My bun is already perfect... I pin it and use just the right amount of gunk. I don my tights and toe shoes and stand, staring in the mirror. Now, if I just get skinny enough, it would all be perfect.

GIRL #4
I just want to play in the dirt all the time.

GIRL #1
I want to be with my dad. He's so cool

GIRL #2
I believe I can have the American Dream…a great career, a husband and children and a house with a yard. That's why I work real hard because I want it all.

GIRL #3
Dear Diary,
I want to be a cowboy. Not a cowgirl, a cowboy. When my brothers and I play cowboys and Indians, they never let me be anyone but the horse stable manager, but I would be a better cowboy then any of them. I read all the Western Horsemen and love Roy Rogers and will til the day I die.

GIRL #4
Dear Diary,
I need to get as far away from Ohio as I can.

GIRL #1
I've got to figure out how to get to be the elevator operator at Hudson's.

GIRL #2
I just need a pair of glasses

GIRL #3
I am going to have 12 children, all beautiful and generous and they will make a difference in the world.

GIRL #1
Dear Diary,
I want to ride in my pink Barbie Corvette and show off to Carrie, my best friend, because she thinks she's Miss America with her new silver Barbie car.

GIRL #4
My cousin and I are going to get married one day. I just know it.

(lights change)

SCENE FIVE

TROUBADOUR
(sings)
EVER SINCE I WAS A YOUNG GIRL
OLD ENOUGH TO CROSS MY LEGS
THEY TOLD ME TO SIT QUIET
STAND UP STRAIGHT
ACT MY AGE
AND SMILE WHEN MY HEART IS BREAKING
DON'T LOOK DOWN
SMILE WHEN MY WORLD IS FALLING
ALL AROUND ME

NOW THAT I'M A YOUNG WOMAN
TRYING LIKE HELL TO MAKE MY WAY
I FIND IT HARD TO SAY THE THINGS,
YOU KNOW, SAY THE THINGS
I WANT TO SAY
BUT I SMILE WHEN MY HEART IS BREAKING
DON'T LOOK DOWN
SMILE WHEN MY WORLD IS FALLING
ALL AROUND ME

DON'T ASK ME HOW I'M FEELING
I DO NOT KNOW
GOOD GIRLS ALL DIE YOUNG
THEY NEVER LEARN TO GROW UP

SOMEDAY I WANT A BABY
SUGAR AND SPICE
AND EVERYTHING NICE
AND I'LL GIVE TO HER
WHAT WAS GIVEN TO ME
AGE OLD MOTHER KNOWS BEST ADVICE

SMILE WHEN YOUR HEART IS BREAKING
DON'T LOOK DOWN
SMILE WHEN YOUR WORLD IS FALLING
ALL AROUND
SMILE
WHEN YOUR HEART IS BREAKING
DON'T LET THEM KNOW
SMILE WHEN YOUR WORLD IS FALLING
DON'T LET IT SHOW

(lights change)

SCENE SIX

(This scene should have a circular feel to it. Characters morph into others as they grow)

WOMAN
My mother taught me that cold water and soap can take a blood stain out of most everything. What she failed to understand is that nothing removes the humiliation of having your maxipad fall out of your back pack in front of Jimmy Savas the cutest boy in school and him picking it up and laughing. Bastard.

JENNY
(walks in) Hi Mom.

MOM
(kisses her) Hi. What's up?

JENNY
Nothing.

MOM
School ok?

JENNY
Yeah.

MOM
Good. We're having fish.

JENNY
Ugh. I'm not hungry.

MOM
Then you can eat the rice and the veggies.

JENNY
(shrugs) Mom?

MOM
Mh-hmm.

JENNY
Can I ask you a question?

MOM
Mh-hmm.

JENNY
Is it true that water stops blood?

MOM
What?

JENNY
Does water stop blood?

MOM
I don't understand.

JENNY
God. Ok, if you take a shower and you cut yourself, will the bleeding stop?

MOM
I don't think so. I'm not sure. Why?

JENNY
Just wondering.

MOM
That's an odd question.

JENNY
Don't make a big deal out of it.

MOM
Ok. Ok.

JENNY
So, how do you shower when you have your friend?

MOM
Your friend?

JENNY
Yeah. *Your Friend.*

(Pause)

MOM
Did you start your—

JENNY
Yes. Can you just answer my question?

MOM
You started to menstruate?

JENNY
Don't embarrass me.

MOM
Honey, Honey. *(hugs her)*

JENNY
It's not a big deal.

MOM
Of course it is. You're becoming a woman, this is a pretty big day

JENNY
Do not tell dad.

MOM
He's gonna realize it at some point, honey. Oh boy, we need to get you some pads or do you want tampons?

JENNY
I already got stuff.

MOM
You do.

JENNY
At first I used your stuff and then Stacey at school gave me some other stuff.

MOM
Wait, is this your first cycle?

JENNY
No.

MOM
No!

JENNY
I got it a few months ago.

MOM
You didn't tell me.

JENNY
I knew you'd make a big deal out of nothing.

MOM
But… I mean I hope you know you can talk to me about this sort of…

JENNY
Let's just drop it.

MOM
It is a big deal though. Everything is, I mean you can have babies now and it's the beginning of your—

JENNY
I learned that in 4th grade, Mom.

MOM
Ok. Ok.

JENNY
I don't mean to upset you, you know.

MOM
No. No. That's your business. I get it.

JENNY
Ok. I'm gonna go do my homework.

MOM
Ok. *(pause)* Wait. It'll stop in the shower.

JENNY
What?

MOM
Water. It stops the bleeding.

JENNY
Well then what happens when I turn it off? How do I get dried off and stuff?

MOM
You move quickly.

JENNY
I hate this. This sucks.

MOM
It gets better. I promise.

(Time and Lights change. JENNY turns to her friend, ALEX)

JENNY
It's gonna get better right? Can you just tell me to stay calm?

ALEX
Stay calm.

JENNY
Because I'm worrying for nothing.

ALEX
Right. *(pause)* How long has it been?

JENNY
Three weeks.

ALEX
Ok.

JENNY
What's that look for?

ALEX
There's no look.

JENNY
That was a look.

ALEX
Do you think it's just time to invest in a couple of tests to find out for sure?

JENNY
Yeah, I guess. I just keep hoping it comes.

ALEX
For three weeks?

JENNY
Why won't it just come? Please God, please let me get my period. Please. Please. Please.

ALEX
Hon, it's not like you're sixteen and unmarried. You and Joe have been married for five years.

JENNY
But uh, I don't like children. Please come. Please come.

(Time passes, lights change. ALEX turns to the DOCTOR)

ALEX
Maybe it'll still come.

DOCTOR
Alex, I'm pretty sure it won't. That's why we call it menopause. The end of all menstruation.

ALEX
Well, Doc aren't I a little young?

(She looks at her chart)

DOCTOR
No.

ALEX
You don't have to say it like that.

DOCTOR
Alex, you're 52. That's the typical age.

ALEX
So I'm all dried up? I don't have any symptoms.

DOCTOR
You haven't menstruated in 10 months.

ALEX
I know, but...

DOCTOR
That's a pretty big sign. Have you had any irritability or fatigue?

ALEX
I'm an irritable person.

DOCTOR
Hot flashes?

ALEX
I'm warm blooded.

DOCTOR
Change in sex drive?

ALEX
I'm married. I don't have one.

DOCTOR
Alex, this is a change in your body chemistry. Every woman goes through this. The end of—

ALEX
It's just... I didn't even get to say good-bye. I don't feel... ready.

DOCTOR
Well, your body doesn't care. Look at this as just the end of your reproduction cycle. That's it. You don't want to have more children at this point, do you?

ALEX
I like to keep all my options open.

DOCTOR
This might be a sign of some depression. You know, with the chemistry in your body changing, this can affect your hormonal levels which in turn causes depression and anxiety.

ALEX
Or I'm just trying to wrap my brain around this.

DOCTOR
You know a hundred years ago women didn't deal with menopause because they didn't live to experience it.

ALEX
That's your speech? Enjoy it because you could be dead instead?

DOCTOR
Alex. Let me give you a prescription for—

ALEX
Don't give me some pill. Just listen to me.

DOCTOR
Listen to me...

(Time passes and lights change. DOCTOR turns to a bathroom door with her daughter behind it)

DOCTOR
Kathy. *(knocks)* Just listen to me.

KATHY
(crying and yelling) GO AWAY!

DOCTOR
Mrs. Coenfeld called me.

KATHY
MOM!

DOCTOR
Do you want to tell me—

KATHY
NO!

DOCTOR
Honey, just take a deep breath and come out and talk to me.

KATHY
You don't understand!

DOCTOR
I want to help.

KATHY
You can't.

DOCTOR
Let me decide. Now open up.

KATHY
(screams and cries) I GOT MY PERIOD IN 6TH HOUR IN MR. MILLER'S CLASS AND WHEN I GOT UP TO GO TO THE BOARD... THEY... THEY ALL SAW... MY PANTS... ALL OVER MY PANTS.

DOCTOR
Oh.

KATHY
THEY KEPT CALLING ME SPOTTY. SPOTTY. THEY'LL NEVER FORGET.

NEVER. EVER. I CAN'T EVER GO BACK. NEVER. NEVER.

DOCTOR
It happens to everyone.

KATHY
NO IT DOESN'T. NO, NO, NO. NOT TO SCOTT, JIM, TOMMY, NOT TO BOYS.

DOCTOR
They are going to forget. They are going to—

KATHY
EVERYONE STILL CALLS JILL HUGHES POOPY CUZ SHE POOPED HER PANTS.

DOCTOR
Well she's old enough to know better.

KATHY
That happened in first grade.

DOCTOR
Well then you just need to tell them that this is a natural occurrence that happens with every girl and that if they laugh at you they mock their mothers and—

KATHY
You don't get it! You don't know!

DOCTOR
I know.

TROUBADOUR
I know.

ALEX
I know.

JENNY
I know.

KATHY/MOM
I know.

(Lights change)

SCENE SEVEN

ALL
(singing)
SISTERS
SISTERS
THERE WERE NEVER SUCH DEVOTED SISTERS

BONNIE
Dear Diary,
At school today, Jenny, Mary, Joanne, and I all became blood sisters. It was definitely time and we got the idea from that Judy Blume book. So at recess we went to the library with a pin and poked our thumbs. Oh my god, did it hurt. Like so bad. But we are now tied. We are sisters. We are really blood sisters. I hope I don't get sick from this.

KALI
I'm never quite sure what the proper response is when someone asks me if I'm close with my sister. Am I close? We're sisters. Even if I didn't want to be close to her, I'm not sure that's my choice ... we are blood, we are bonded. We are sisters. So close doesn't seem to be the right question. Do I love her? Yes. Hate her? I've had my moments. I mean, we've been friends, enemies, partners, and competitors—sometimes at the same time. She's told me I'm selfish and I've told her she's fat. "I'm an idiot? You're the one who looks like a baboon." We've loved the same boy, despised the same girls, and gotten into a physical altercation that ended with a hair pulling event of a lifetime. We've lip synched into our hair brushes while dancing around the house, wrestle over who would get the bottom bunk, and bickered

over who could take the car out on Saturday. We watched our parents both succeed and fail, clung to each other in times of fear and laughed so hard we peed our pants at some inside joke that only we understood. There have been years when we have barely spoken and years when we talk daily. We are sisters.

(Pause)

When we were little, we always played in the park down the street from our house. Our favorite was the teeter-totter. The back and forth movement trying to be the heavier, the stronger one. Trying to hold down my side leaving her stranded high in the air, helpless and vulnerable until I decide to push up and let her try to take some control, try to hold me up in the air which she of course did. But what really made this our favorite wasn't the tipping the scale from one side to another, it was about finding the balance. Staying in mid-air perfectly straight, but on different sides with our legs dangling from the edges. and laughing. Always laughing and trying to stay balanced forever.

We are sisters.

(Lights change)

SCENE EIGHT

ALL
(sing) LA LA LA LA LA LA LA LA LA LA

(KRISTI is lying in a recliner with IVs into her veins. JULIE is next to her, reading a magazine)

KRISTI
I think I'm just going to shave the rest of it off.

JULIE
(startled) What?

KRISTI
My hair.

JULIE
Oh. Ok.

KRISTI
I look like I'm a squirrel with mange right now. Might as well just shave it off so I don't have to deal with the rest of the clumps.

JULIE
Makes sense.

KRISTI
Yeah.

JULIE
It'll grow back before you know it.

KRISTI
I know.

(Awkward pause)

JULIE
You need some water?

KRISTI
Yes.

(JULIE hands her a water bottle)

KRISTI
Ugh. No. It'll make me puke.

JULIE
Ok.

(Silence. JULIE goes back to reading)

KRISTI
I wish I didn't have to.

JULIE
Didn't have to what?

KRISTI
Shave my own hair off.

JULIE
You don't have to.

KRISTI
I just can't do it myself.

JULIE
Then we'll go to a salon.

KRISTI
Ok.

(Pause)

KRISTI
I don't want to go to a salon. This isn't something I want people to watch me do.

JULIE
Then Jim will do it.

KRISTI
Jim with a razor?

JULIE
He shaves his face everyday.

KRISTI
I know and he comes out with toilet paper splotches covering half his face.

JULIE
He wants to help. Let him.

KRISTI
He'll be too nervous to do it.

JULIE
He'd be happy to.

KRISTI
He's nervous around me now. Like I'm a fragile china doll.

JULIE
He's just worried.

KRISTI
He's nervous, Julie. I should know.

JULIE
Well then we'll figure it out.

(Silence. KRISTI closes her eyes, deep breath)

KRISTI
What's going on with Sam?

JULIE
Oh, nothing much.

KRISTI
Isn't his company going under?

JULIE
It's not a big deal.

KRISTI
Is he losing his job?

JULIE
Yeah.

KRISTI
And that isn't a big deal?

JULIE
Not in the scheme of life. It's just a job. Have you seen this one?

KRISTI
(looks at the magazine) How many times do I have to see a picture of her vagina before she puts on some damn underwear?

JULIE
(looking around) Ssshhhh. Shut up.

(KRISTI smiles)

JULIE
I'm sorry.

KRISTI
Since when did you start apologizing for telling me to shut up?

JULIE
I... nevermind. Forget it.

KRISTI
(pause) Can I see that magazine?

JULIE
(hands it to her) Of course.

(KRISTI looks through it quickly and then begins to tear it apart. Very calmly. JULIE turns to see and is flabbergasted)

JULIE
What are you doing?

(KRISTI just keeps tearing it up)

JULIE
(tries to grab it back from her) What the hell are you doing?

(KRISTI keeps ripping and a small little physical confrontation begins—a little slap fest)

JULIE
Give me that.

KRISTI
No.

JULIE
Kristi, what the hell has... *(KRISTI rips half the magazine and holds on to it)* What are you doing?

KRISTI
What are you doing?

JULIE
What do you mean what am I doing? I... you're... you're acting so... off.

KRISTI
I'm acting off? No you're acting bizarre!

JULIE
Me? What, cuz I brought a goddamn magazine to read. I brought a few... they were for you.

KRISTI
I don't want those magazines.

JULIE
Fine, that's all you have to say. I won't bring them anymore.

KRISTI
Be normal. *(hits her)* Please be normal.

JULIE
I am normal.

KRISTI
No. You're not. You're playing a part. The only honest thing you've said to me today is "shut up." You're not seeing me. See me.

JULIE
I see you. I see you, Kristi.

KRISTI
And?

JULIE
And what?

KRISTI
Tell me what's going on in your life. Tell me the truth. Complain. Bitch. Argue with me. Treat me like you always do. Like your friend.

JULIE
You are my friend. You have a poison running through your arm right now, so no, I don't feel like having an argument with you. I'm telling you the truth about my life. This... right here... is my truth.

KRISTI
So you're going to sit there and pity me.

JULIE
Please.

KRISTI
It's insulting.

JULIE
I don't pity you, Kristi.

KRISTI
'Cause I don't want it.

JULIE
Ok, so why don't you make a list of all the things I'm allowed to do, to say, to feel and I'll work on it ok? Let me get you some paper so you can make sure to cover it all.

KRISTI
That would be helpful actually.

(JULIE pulls a pen and notebook out of her purse)

JULIE
Here you go.

KRISTI
Great. Great. *(starts writing)*

JULIE
Is this really how you want to spend today? Fighting with me over nothing?

KRISTI
I'm fighting for everything, Julie.

JULIE
If somehow you think yelling at me and making me feel like a shitty friend is gonna help, then have at it.

KRISTI
Thanks martyr Julie. That's kind.

JULIE
I'm angry too, you know.

KRISTI
I'm not angry

JULIE
Yes you are and thank god you are.

KRISTI
But I need you to see me because if you don't, nobody else will.

JULIE
Kristi. Look at me. I. See. You.

KRISTI
Because I feel like I'm disappearing. Really disappearing.

JULIE
You aren't.

KRISTI
I'm becoming one of those faceless statistics that meant nothing to me two months ago. That I'm losing every part of me and becoming that nameless number. Maybe somebody will do a walk with my name posted on their back, but I don't want that as my legacy.

JULIE
This is not your legacy.

KRISTI
If you start treating me like that person. If you start backing away from me and getting that look in your eye. If you start doing that, well then I've lost.

JULIE
I'm not looking at you like that. I'm just scared. Can I be scared? Is that on your list?

KRISTI
(looks at her sheet) Yes. It's number 2.

JULIE
Oh good. I don't want to screw this up. This is the most important thing I've ever done. And I don't want to let you down, Kristi. I want to be here all the way with you. I am here, but you know...

KRISTI
So why are you so concerned about screwing up?

JULIE
Because I don't know what I'm doing or how to make it better. Because... because... I love you.

KRISTI
You came with me today. That's all I needed. For now.

JULIE
And let me say this has been so much fun so far. I can't wait for next time.

KRISTI
There's my Julie.

JULIE
So do you want me to just shave your hair when we get home?

KRISTI
Yes.

JULIE
You could have just asked.

KRISTI
That's not much fun. *(pause)* God, this crap makes me so tired.

JULIE
So lean back.

KRISTI
I know. I might just try to shut my eyes.

JULIE
I got my ipod if you want.

KRISTI
No. No. I'll just listen to the sounds. What are you gonna do?

JULIE
Well, originally I wanted to read my magazine.

KRISTI
I did you a big favor if you thought that was reading

JULIE
Just lie back, dummy.

KRISTI
Let's pretend this is a spa day. Like that retreat I wanna go on.

JULIE
Spa day it is.

(They both lean back and JULIE and KRISTI hold hands for a minute, squeeze, and then move on)

(Lights change)

SCENE NINE

(TROUBADOUR starts to play "First Kiss" song and the chorus hums it)

WOMAN #1
Dear Diary, I am in love with Troy Wolf. Don't tell anyone. And if anyone is reading this diary you are totally violating my privacy.

WOMAN #2
When he walked in, I just knew. I knew before he said hello. My stomach did flips and I got so light-headed.

WOMAN #3
Every time he looks into my eyes, it's as if he sees all of me and still he smiles. At these moments, I've never felt more beautiful.

(Music and song starts)

FRANNY
(sings)
WILL I GIVE IT
WILL HE TAKE IT
IS IT HOT IN HERE
I WONDER IF HE SHAVES YET
WILL IT HAPPEN WHILE WE'RE HOLDING HANDS AND WALKING HOME
OR WILL IT HAPPEN AT MY DOOR
WHEN WE'RE ALONE

HIS HAND IS SWEATING
HIS CHIN IS SWEATING
HIS LIPS ARE SWEATING
AND TOTALLY GROSSED OUT I'M GETTING

IF I JUST RUN AWAY AND
NEVER EVER LOOK BACK
I CAN SHAVE MY HEAD AND
COP A PSYCHOTIC ATTACK

BUT I AM THE ONLY ONE WHO'S NEVER BEEN KISSED
THE ONLY ONE WHO CUPID HAS MISSED
AND I AM READY FOR MY
FIRST KISS FIRST KISS
I'VE WAITED FOR THIS DAY
SINCE I WAS BORN
FIRST KISS FIRST KISS
TODAY IS THE DAY
FOR MY FIRST KISS

ALL MY GIRLFRIENDS
THEY'RE IN THE CLUB NOW
THEY'VE ALL KISSED AND TOLD
ALONE I HAVE NO KNOW HOW

EVEN MAGGIE LOU WHO IS
NOTORIOUSLY SHY
SHE KISSED RICKY AT THE RINK
WHILE EATING FRIES,
MARY KISSED JOEY
HE BROUGHT HER CANDY
BRAD KISSED SUSAN
SHE SAID HIS TONGUE FELT CLAMMY

AND WHEN JANE THREW ICE
AT TOMMY LEROY'S HEAD
BLEEDING HE FELL DOWN SHE KISSED HIM
THINKING HE WAS DEAD

AND I AM THE ONLY ONE WHO'S NEVER BEEN KISSED
THE ONLY ONE WHO CUPID HAS MISSED
IT'S NOW OR NEVER
FIRST KISS FIRST KISS
I'VE PRACTICED WITH A PILLOW
SINCE THE AGE OF SIX
FIRST KISS FIRST KISS
TODAY IS THE DAY
FOR MY FIRST KISS

WILL I GIVE IT
WILL HE TAKE IT
WE'RE STANDING AT MY DOOR
WHAT IF I JUST FAKE IT

AWKWARD SILENCE FALLS
BETWEEN THE TWO OF US

FRANNY
(speaks) All I can hear is my heart trying to escape from my chest. I

can smell probably lamb chops cause it's Saturday. And the phone rings - my mother's picked it up. But we both jump at the sound of the phone. Now standing so close, face to face, I can count every freckle on your nose, and you are just a tiny bit shorter than me, but that's ok cause mom says boys take longer to grow and I can smell you, your sweat and watermelon gum. Breathing in your breath, tasting your air. Do you feel my heart? Can you see it pounding? You put your hands on my hips, pulling me toward you. This is it. Your head tilts to one side. You practiced this at home, I think. I've practiced too. And you are the most beautiful... I have ever and I am the most beautiful. Your lips have finally found mine.

ALL
(heavenly chorus)
FIRST KISS FIRST KISS
I'VE WAITED FOR THIS DAY
SINCE I WAS BORN
FIRST KISS FIRST KISS
TODAY IS THE DAY
FOR MY FIRST KISS

SCENE TEN

TROUBADOUR
(sings)
I'M JUST A FOOL IN LOVE...

WOMAN #3
He wrote me a song to tell me he loved me. He played his guitar and sang his song. I had no idea how little musical ability he had until that moment, but it was the sweetest thing I've ever heard. I got my own love song.

WOMAN #4
It's how my body reacts to her touch.

WOMAN #1
And the fact that he makes me laugh. Laugh so hard.

WOMAN #2
And is kind to my parents as they insult him to his face

WOMAN #3
And seems to accept that occasionally I do not make sense.

WOMAN #4
I know it is love when I curl up next to her in bed—she on her back and I on my side. The way my head fits perfectly on her shoulder and my curves somehow line up against hers. My leg wraps around hers. And we fit like jigsaw puzzle pieces. We fit and seem to have been made for this exact thing.

WOMAN #1
It's when I close my eyes, I want to see him. Always.

(Lights change)

SCENE ELEVEN

TROUBADOUR
(sings)
ERIN AND ANNIE
SITTIN IN A TREE
K-I-S-S-I-N-G
FIRST COMES LOVE AND
THEN COMES MARRIAGE
HERE COMES CHARLIE IN A BABY CARRIAGE

WOMAN
Thinking about becoming a parent? Spend an afternoon in a Chuck E Cheese. If you make it out alive, you've passed the test. And may God have mercy on your soul.

WOMAN #1
I want a baby.

WOMAN #2
I need a baby.

WOMAN #3
Adopt a baby.

WOMAN #4
Never ever want a baby

WOMAN #1
Can't have a baby.

WOMAN #2
No baby ever.

WOMAN #3
Maybe baby.

ALL
Baby, Baby, Baby

TROUBADOUR
(sings)
BABY BABY BABY BABY BABY...

WOMAN #4
I'd had a dream the night before. And I never dream. Ever. But that night I dreamt I gave birth to a bear in the middle of a forest surrounded by these huge black bears... mama bears. They just circled around and kept yelling, "Bear down. Bear down." I woke up before the baby bear actually arrived, but I knew it was a bear. It was one of those things you just know in dreams. I was so discombobulated when I woke up. I just sat up and thought... when was my last period.

(Lights change)

SCENE TWELVE

MAYA
I know what you mean when you say your kids come first - they have to. It's beyond a responsibility, it's a calling. At least that's been true in my case with my kids. After I got divorced - I was only married for barely a year - I wasn't interested in having that type of relationship anymore. I already had my two babies, Lucy and Claude. But I needed to find happiness, to find purpose and that's kind of how I fell into being a foster parent. I fell in love with them all though, every single one that I took in. But it was so hard, I couldn't stand to see them go to homes where I couldn't be sure they were safe. These people, I'm sure they were kind folk, but no, I couldn't do it week after week. My heart was constantly breaking and I felt that they needed my love, my protection. So I just started to adopt them and now I've got a full house and heart... it's better than I ever thought.

I've got 18.

I know. It's a shock, but yes. 18. 18 right now living with me although I've had more than 30 come through. But the house is pretty crowded with the ones I have now. There's Lucy and Claude like I said before, and then Clyde, Olive, and then Cheeto and Catherine. Then came Max, he was premature. Herbie, Pookey, Virgil, and Macaroni were next. Also I've got Goldie and Frenchy - they're sisters. Then Bubbles McFluffenstuff and Toodles J. McWhiskers. My most recent additions to the brood are Gordon, Thunderpaws, and Miss Puss—they are from the same liter. Is that 18? *(starts counting them out)* Yes, yes, that seems to be them all. Oh sure, my neighbors think I'm a loon. You're giving me that same look. I'm well aware that I've become the crazy cat lady; that lady everyone fears of becoming. I feared that status. Sounded too lonely and desperate. Nobody wants to be that, but you know what? I've stopped caring. I've got a full life. I have friends that aren't of the feline persuasion. Why do I even need to explain myself? If I had 18 human babies nobody would ask me if I'm lonely or wonder whether I get out of the house enough. My own family thinks I'm deluded, but my babies, and they are my babies, have personalities. Honestly. Frenchy is scared of thunderstorms. And Pookey, he cannot stand milk. Olive is blind, but it such a little love bug. And Lucy, she's the matriarch of the cats, very proper and a little cold. All of them have something. And they do give me so much love and affection. When I'm sick, my troops rally. All sticking by my bed in shifts to make sure I'm okay. When I have a bad day, I swear they are just a little sweeter, a little more tender. It's, I guess to the average person, it's a little unconventional… but we are a family, this is my family.

(Lights change)

SCENE THIRTEEN

SIAN
I tell him it's time for sleep. With his footy pajamas on, we climb into the rocking chair, with our book and bottle. Once story time is over and the bottle is emptied we just rock. He, wrapped up in his blanket, grabs onto my shirt gently and his head finds itself in the nook between my arm and my chest. Oh my god, I love this moment. Waiting for him to fall into a deep sleep. You know that sleep, when their head suddenly becomes 10 pounds heavier because his neck has finally relaxed.

This ritual, in the dark, in his room, to just be together. Even after those days when I feel like all I've done is fight with a 1 year old and somehow managed to lose, I cannot wait until this time of day.

So we rock and his eyes close and I'll wonder what he's thinking about. But sometimes I catch myself drifting away from him, from us. In that quiet moment, my head begins to reel and I start to think about everything else that there is to do, to say, to... Dishes, I've gotta put those away. Wait, did I pay the electric bill? I thought I did, but then that might have been last month. I gotta check that. Is Will putting the clothes in the dryer? Does he know to leave my sweater out? Crap, he is always shrinking my stuff. Oh my mother, I didn't call her back. I can do that while I get the dishes finished. I don't have enough milk though...Will can run out. He better. We've got to visit Grammie. Hope she knows who I am this time. Why is Will being so loud down there? He's gotta start to eat better.

And at this moment, my son moves uncomfortably to let me know that I've stopped rocking, that he's still here needing me. "Sorry, little man."

Be present. Be here.

I tell myself. Because one day in the not-too-near future this will go away. With that thought I look at his face. His flickering eyes. His leg twitching. I stroke his head... the same way I do when he's upset and needs to know everything is ok. This will go away one day.

I want to eat this moment. Burn this into my memory. This baby is almost a toddler and that toddler will soon be a boy and, while I get that this is the cycle of life, I just want to be here for a while. I don't want to think. Stop thinking!

Just be here. And so he and I rock and I listen to his breath become slow and steady. I close my eyes and feel him in my arms, memorizing it, and sense our hearts beat in time together. I almost lose my breath. And the only word that floats in my head, in this room, is Love.

(Lights change)

SCENE FOURTEEN

TROUBADOUR
(sings)
DO I TALK TOO MUCH
MAYBE NOT ENOUGH
WHEN YOU'RE HANGING WITH
YOUR FRIENDS
DO I WANT TOO MUCH
MAYBE NOT ENOUGH
WHEN ALL IS SAID AND DONE
I HOPE WE PART AS FRIENDS

YOU WILL ALWAYS BE
MY LITTLE SWEETIE PEA
LET ME HOLD ON FOR A WHILE
YOU MAY LIVE TO
A HUNDRED AND EIGHTY THREE
BUT YOU WILL ALWAYS BE MY CHILD

I KNOW I EMBARRASS YOU
WHEN I THROW I LOVE YOU
OUT THE WINDOW
AS YOU'RE RUNNING OUT TO PLAY
YOU KNOW AS MUCH
AS I THOUGHT I REALLY KNEW "LOVE"
I NEVER REALLY "KNEW"
UNTIL YOUR BIRTHDAY

YOU WILL ALWAYS BE
MY LITTLE SWEETIE PEA
LET ME HOLD ON FOR A WHILE
YOU MAY LIVE TO
A HUNDRED AND EIGHTY THREE
BUT YOU WILL ALWAYS BE MY CHILD

DO I WORRY TOO MUCH
OF COURSE I DO
BRUSH THOSE TEETH

LOSE THOSE FRIENDS
TIE YOUR SHOES
BUT IF ONLY THREE WORDS
THRU LIFE CARRY YOU

YOU ARE LOVE
YOU ARE LOVE
YOU ARE LOVE
YOU ARE LOVE
YOU WILL ALWAYS BE
MY LITTLE SWEETIE PEA
LET ME HOLD ON FOR A WHILE
YOU MAY LIVE TO
A HUNDRED AND EIGHTY THREE
BUT YOU WILL ALWAYS BE MY CHILD

(Lights fade)

END OF ACT I

ACT II
SCENE ONE

(Everyone on the stage as cheerleaders; cheers with pom-poms)

ALL
(cheer)
U
G
L
Y
YOU AIN'T GOT NO ALIBI
YOU UGLY
HEY HEY
YOU UGLY

(Change cheer beat)

ALL
LIPS
TEETH
NOSE
AND EYES
TUCK THAT TUMMY
ASS AND
THIGHS
YOU UGLY
HEY HEY
YOU UGLY

(Change cheer beat)

LILLY
(chanting)
This is me
as good as it gets
no shadow, no light
I look better yet
In the dark
Still
I am a beautiful woman.
a beautiful woman
I am

WOMAN
She's hot!

LILLY
Still
I am a beautiful woman
A beautiful woman
I am

ANOTHER WOMAN
She scares me.

LILLY
I heard that!

(Change cheer beat)

ALL
C
U
T
E
YOU GOT PERSONALITY
YOU CUTE
HEY HEY
YOU CUTE

COSMETIC PROCEDURE INS AND OUTS
PORCELAIN SKIN
IRRESISTABLE POUTS
YOU CUTE
HEY HEY
YOU CUTE

(Change cheer beat)

JUDY
DEFEAT THE FAT

ALL
YOU'RE FAT

JUDY
YOU CAN LOOK BETTER THAN THAT
DEFEAT THE WRINKLES

ALL
WRINKLES

JUDY
CROWS FEET LINES AND PIMPLES
YOUR TEETH ARE CROOKED AND YELLOW

ALL
YELLOW

JUDY
COMPLEXTION PALE AND SALLOW

ALL
SALLOW

JUDY
YOUR SKIN IS SAGGING
BEHIND IS WAGGING
YOUR LIBIDO IS LAGGING

(Change cheer beat)

EILEEN
(Military call)
LASERS BOTOX INVISALIGN

ALL
LASERS BOTOX INVISALIGN

EILEEN
SPEND THE MONEY
YOU'LL LOOK FINE

ALL
SPEND THE MONEY
YOU'LL LOOK FINE

EILEEN
SOUND OFF

ALL
NUTRA SYSTEM

EILEEN
SOUND OFF

ALL
WEIGHT WATCHERS

EILEEN
SOUND OFF

ALL
JENNY CRAIG
LYPO SUCTION
LYPOVOX
HOODIA

AUGMENT
CONTOUR
DYE
EXTEND
LIFT
TUCK
REDUCE
IMPLANT
INJECT
PEEL

(Change cheer beat)

SAMANTHA
EMBRACE NATURAL BEAUTY
BAKE IT FAKE IT TILL YOU MAKE IT
EMBRACE NATURAL BEAUTY
BAKE IT FAKE IT TILL YOU MAKE IT

(Change cheer beat)

AUDREY
(call)
GOD GAVE ME A BIG NOSE AND ASS

ALL
GOD GAVE YOU A BIG NOSE AND ASS

LILLY
YOU'RE UGLY HEY HEY YOU'RE UGLY

AUDREY
BUT I'VE GOT HAIR THAT'S GOR*GEOUS

ALL
YOU'VE GOT HAIR THAT'S GOR*GEOUS

LILLY
SO YOU'RE CUTE HEY HEY YOU'RE CUTE

(Change cheer beat)

JUDY
Gimme an H

ALL
H

JUDY
Gimme an A

ALL
A

JUDY
Gimme an I

ALL
I

JUDY
And R

ALL
R

JUDY
What does it spell?

ALL
HAIR

JUDY
Louder

ALL
HAIR HAIR

JUDY
Louder

ALL
HAIR HAIR

(Change cheer beat)

ALL
IT'S BROWN
IT'S BLOND
IT'S BLACK
IT'S WHITE
HEY HEY

IT'S RED
IT'S ORANGE
PURPLE
WITH HIGHLIGHTS

IT'S SPIKED
IT'S LONG
IT'S SHORT
IT'S GONE
HEY HEY

IT'S CURLY
PERMED
IT'S STRAIGHT
IT'S AN OAKLAND COUNTY BOB

BREAK IT DOWN

(They perform a cheer dance and cheer continues throughout)

IT'S DRY
IT'S WILD
IT'S COARSE
FINE AS CHILD'S
HEY HEY

IT'S STRINGY
IT'S BRITTLE
IT'S PARTED
IN THE MIDDLE

DO THE WAVE

(Women breathe rhythmically and do the wave in slow motion. Lights change)

SCENE TWO

JESSICA
I pass by that mirror in the hallway and I see only hair. The hair in that mirror is thin and white. But it's not mine. When I was young, I kept it very long with soft curls – the summer sun would streak the brown with honey colored stripes. We would string daisies and dandelions throughout our hair or coronate ourselves with a crown of ivy. After I had my first child, I kept it short as if I could no longer afford the naiveté and freedom that my long hair provided me. In my new role, I had to be practical. There was no time to fuss – children needing my attention. My hair was to get none. It would get colored, but only with bits of cupcake frosting, art projects, and the occasional food processor explosion. But now, when I pass by that mirror, I see my mother. She's the one who has the white hair… she is the crone. I'm the daughter whose hair is long and full of soft curls or the mother with two babies on her hip. But that mirror doesn't lie. Time has pushed my mother into a different place and I have now been crowned with the crone's hair.

(Lights change)

SCENE THREE

(BETH with a drink stands around looking at a bar, a little unsure of what she's seeing)

WOMAN
(kind of yelling) Hello? Hi! Can I get everyone's attention? Just for a sec! *(pause)* Thanks. Welcome everyone to CC's speedy dating bonanza. I know you are all eager to start and hopefully find that mate that's been missing. You'll have 5 minutes with your partner. At the sound of this: *(BUZZER)* That means ladies, you will move to the next table on your right. The most important thing is just to have fun. Alright, ladies and gentlemen, take your position. And— *(BUZZER)* GO!

(BETH begins to speed date)

BETH
Hi. I'm Beth. I'm sorry, what is your name? Diesel? Damon? I'm sorry; it's so loud in here. T – O- M? Oh, Tom.

Gotcha. *(silence)* Have you done this much? My girlfriends brought me here tonight. *(pause. She points)* Pink sweater. That's Kathy. Very pretty, yes. In the black shirt and blonde hair? Marcia, but she's married. She's only doing this as moral support. Really? Married people do this all the time? Are you married? *(pause)* Oh.

(BUZZER)

BETH

Hi. I'm Beth. Nice to meet you. Wow. That's a… a loaded question. Um… My last boyfriend and I split up about 1 year ago. Oh. I've dated, but nothing serious. It's hard as you get older to meet people. Don't you think? When was your last relation… Well your first love is hard to get over. What's a PPO? Within 250 feet of her? Wow. Yeah, girls don't like it when you show up to their house without calling first… Yeah, no. We don't like that either. Hiding in my bushes would scare me too.

(BUZZER)

BETH

I'm… You're not my type either. *(silence)*

(BUZZER)

BETH

Hello. Beth. I would love another drink. Yes. A vodka tonic, thanks. *(laughs)* Really? Hmmm, I'd have to think about it. What would you be? *(laughs)* An eagle? No. No. I get it. Patriotic, strong, sharp claws. That's a hard bird to get close to without getting a talon in your eye. Right? I think I'd choose a sea lion. They always seem rather carefree and enjoying themselves. I love to watch them at the zoo… No, I guess it's not very sexy. Neither is an eagle.

(BUZZER. BETH *just stares at him.* BUZZER)

BETH

Beth. *(pause)* You do retail? So that means… I love Target. I shop there pretty much every weekend. I'm a veterinarian. Well an associate vet. I'm doing my internship right now. I've always loved animals and I went to a little college in Albion. Where did you go to school? I meant college. Well, it's not for everyone. So it doesn't really… I'm not judging… I don't care… I've never been called intimidating. Well right now I am better than you.

(BUZZER)

BETH

(Louder with every sentence) Beth. I'm 27. Single. Straight. I don't swing. My spirit animal is the sea lion. I'm an associate vet in the area and am invested in my career. My last relationship ended a year ago after it was decided that we didn't light a spark for each other. I love my parents who are still married and my brother and I don't like each other. I came here tonight because my friends thought it would be a good way to meet people in a different way. The internet works, but I feel it's impersonal. I don't go to church, but that doesn't mean that I don't believe in God. I believe that religion and politics do belong at the dinner table. Yes, I want to have kids. No, I don't want them tomorrow. I don't sleep with guys on the first date… or the second. I secretly like romantic movies even though I make fun of the people that go and see them. I can cook, but only pasta. I get the occa-

sional pimple still, but that's normal. I don't have tattoos, but I smoked pot in college for a month. I drive an American car, but only because my uncle gets me the discount. I expect a guy to be nice to me, to like it when I laugh, to hold the door open for me, to tell me I'm pretty even when I'm sick, to not have untrimmed nose hair, to care about the world, to shower, to hold my hand, and to be comfortable with all my attributes. And this is just the beginning of what I expect because as the L'Oreal people say: I'm worth it. *(yells to the whole bar)* Kathy in the pink has my information for anyone interested. *(leaves)*

(All applaud. Lights change)

SCENE FOUR

(TROUBADOUR starts to play)

TROUBADOUR
SOMETHING PINK
A BEAUTIFUL BABY GIRL YOU HAVE
WITH TINY EARS
SHE LOOKS LIKE SHE'S DREAMING
JUST LIKE YOU
I WAS FATED FROM THE START
JUST LIKE YOU
AND STILL I AM DREAMING

LET ME IN DADDY
LET ME GET CLOSE TO YOU
I GOTTA KNOW HOW TO GIVE MY HEART
WITHOUT IT BREAKING IN TWO
WITHOUT IT BREAKING

(Instrumental continues)

WOMAN #1
Dad taught me to change my tire. It's saved my life more than once.

WOMAN #2
He never tried to teach me anything. He always let me find my way, but he was walking only three steps behind me just in case.

WOMAN #3
Every parade, I would get to watch from his shoulders. And I remember the smell of his hair, his shampoo I guess... as I laid my head on his.

WOMAN #4
We go to the movies every Sunday since I was 8.

WOMAN #1
My dad once farted so loudly he woke me up.

WOMAN #2
My dad taught me how to throw a football—it's all about the laces.

WOMAN #3
In my dreams, about once a month or so, he shows up, just to check in.

WOMAN #4
Always said he loved me.

WOMAN #1
Couldn't say he loved me, just a man thing. But when he choked up at my college graduation, well...

WOMAN #2
I can't tell you why I want him to be proud of me

WOMAN #3
But I do.

WOMAN #4
For him to approve

WOMAN #1
For him to know

WOMAN #2
For him to see

WOMAN #3
The real me

WOMAN #4
And think

WOMAN #1
That's my daughter.

ALL
And he does.

TROUBADOUR
Something blue
Beautiful baby boys I have
Look just like you
When they are dreaming
Don't want to
Break their hearts
And pick up the pieces down the way
Break their hearts
I want them to know me

Let me in Daddy
Let me get close to you
I gotta know how to give my heart
Without it breaking in two
Without it breaking

WOMAN #1
Do you know the power that you can hold over your daughters, Fathers. No matter how old we may be.

WOMAN #2
With one look we can be raised to the high heavens or dropped into the bowels of hell.

WOMAN #3
And no matter what we say, we always want your love unconditionally.

WOMAN #4
Because you are our dad.

(TROUBADOUR *begins transition into the next song*)

JOAN
The picture is framed
sits on my dresser
not to remind me
but to show me
to prove to me
that I made him happy.

The framed picture
I have no recollection of this day
but it is my father and me
Me, a baby
sleeping on his chest
His eyes look not at the camera
but at the person behind it
And the look - it's so unfamiliar
It is one of pure happiness

This is the only picture of just my father and me that is left.
Our life
Our relationship has been
full of large moments,
but it is this small one that seems most true
most honest
The picture is framed
sits on my dresser
to show me I made him happy.

TROUBADOUR
(*sings*)
I felt beautiful and strong
As we raced the sunset home
On our two wheeled steeds
"Fear us, Dragons, you cowards"
We fought and won for hours
Just my dad and me

Night fell hard and I fell harder
Into dreams of bloodied dragons
Felled within their bowers
From our weilding swords of power
Dad, it's us not them
Who are the cowards

He said
This is only make-believe

NOTHING, DARLING, IS WHAT IT SEEMS
ONE WORD, ONE THOUGHT, CAN CHANGE
THE WHOLE STORY
YOU ARE THE WEAVER OF THIS DREAM

BROKEN-HEARTED AND OUT OF BREATH
I WALKED THROUGH THE FIELD OF DEATH
FROM THE GAMES OF YESTERDAY
"FORGIVE MY MANNERS, DEAR DRAGONS
PLEASE COME TO MY HOUSE
IN THESE WAGONS
AND DRINK MOM'S LEMONADE"

NIGHT FELL HARD AND I FELL HARDER
INTO DISARMING DREAMS
OF FLOATING ARMOR
AROUND THE DRAGONS
DANCING IN THEIR BOWERS
DAD NO FIGHTING FOR ME
PEACE IS MY POWER

LIFE IS ONLY MAKE BELIEVE
NOTHING, DARLING, IS WHAT IT SEEMS
ONE CHANGE OF HEART
CAN CHANGE THE WHOLE STORY
YOU ARE THE WEAVER
OF YOUR OWN DREAM

I FELT BEAUTIFUL AND STRONG
AS WE RACED THE SUNSET HOME
JUST MY DAD AND ME

(Lights change)

SCENE FIVE

(Women sing and tap dance and hum TEA FOR TWO)

WOMAN #1
I like to play this game when the day goes by so quickly that I feel like nothing was accomplished. When I wish that time would be kind enough to pass by more slowly. When I wish I had just one more hour. *(pause)* Ideally with an extra hour, I'd meditate or do yoga.

WOMAN #2
Make myself a cup of tea and just sit, listening to the world.

WOMAN #3
I would go walking in the woods with our cat Charles and my husband, on the path that we created along the creek.

WOMAN #4
A hot, hot bubble bath. *(pause)* In reality.

WOMAN #1
Truthfully, I would probably sit with a bowl or two of popcorn and read some trashy magazine. Or nap.

WOMAN #2
Try to finish painting the house. Wash the bathroom floor. Organize my files. Rake the backyard. Read my book in time to return it to the library before it's overdue.

WOMAN #3
Shower. I smell.

WOMAN #4
I would waste it doing something that, in the long run, does not make my life any more fulfilling. You know, like reorganize my linen closet.

WOMAN #1
Just treasure it.

WOMAN #2
If we had an extra hour—

WOMAN #3
—we would do what we've always done:

ALL
Run out of time.

(Lights change)

SCENE SIX

TROUBADOUR
(as a LITTLE GIRL)
Where do babies come from?

ALL
What?

TROUBADOUR
Where do babies come from?

MOM #1
God.

MOM #2
The Stork.

MOM #3
I don't know.

MOM #4
My stomach.

TROUBADOUR/LITTLE GIRL
But how are babies made?

MOM #1
Well daddy and I got married and loved and prayed very hard for a baby and then you were born.

MOM #2
Fairies sprinkle fairy dust around the world and then I drank a magic potion and boom… there you were.

MOM #3
I don't know. How do you think they're made?

MOM #4
Well when a mommy and daddy love each other very much they hug and kiss. Mommies have got special parts and daddies have special parts and they fit together and make babies.

TROUBADOUR/LITTLE GIRL
Do I have special parts?

MOM #1
Um. No.

MOM #2
You are just special. Remember that.

MOM #3
Define special parts?

MOM #4
Yes, but it doesn't work yet.

TROUBADOUR/LITTLE GIRL
When will it work?

MOM #1
When you're married and want babies.

MOM #2
You need special batteries and you can't buy them until you are 40

MOM #3
(with hands over ears) La la la la la la la la la la…

MOM #4
When will it work? I ask myself that all the time.

(Lights change)

SCENE SEVEN

(In this scene, every beep is replacing an explicit word, but that word is next to it in brackets or you can replace the word with whatever you'd like. Outside, early morning on the rocks. JULIE and KRISTI are walking into an outside yoga class at a retreat)

KRISTI
Buck up.

JULIE
Only you would drag me on a girl's weekend where we're supposed to exercise.

KRISTI
This is yoga, mediation, technically not...

JULIE
It's six in the morning, I don't care.

(They stumble upon the class. SHANA and THERESA are currently in a yoga pose of some kind)

SHANA
So you want to clench those muscle for a tighter feel. *(to JULIE and KRISTI)* Good morning and many happy blessings to you both.

JULIE
I'm sorry we're late.

KRISTI
She wanted coffee.

SHANA
Oh, we are a caffeine free retreat.

JULIE
Another thing she forgot to mention to me.

SHANA
Let's open up our mind and release the negativity.

KRISTI
Yeah, Julie.

SHANA
Please join us. Find a spot where you feel comfortable and where your chakras are open to the energy from the earth.

(JULIE just looks at KRISTI. KRISTI finds her spot. THERESA is nearest to them)

KRISTI
(to JULIE) Just try to focus on the fact that we've got massages after breakfast.

SHANA
I'm Shana. Your names.

JULIE
Julie.

KRISTI
Kristi.

SHANA
Julie, Kristi, et me get you warmed up with some breathing. Let's get in lotus position.

(SHANA shows them a simple yoga position for meditation and breathing. JULIE and KRISTI get into that position)

SHANA
(to THERESA and the other "ladies") The rest of you—try another shoulder stand. Always good practice.

(THERESA starts to get in her pose)

SHANA
Remember to breathe. *(to JULIE and KRISTI)* Okay, Julie and Kristi, let's just get you up to speed with the breath. Ready? *(They nod, but then a fart sound is made and it comes from THERESA)* In through the nose, 1, 2, 3, 4, 5, Relax the body, 9, 10, *(THERESA farts again)* and now out through the mouth 1, 2, 3, 4—

(THERESA lets out a long and striking moan)

SHANA
(continues without pause) —5, silence that mental talk, 9, 10. Great. Great.

(JULIE and KRISTI are looking at each other and stifling laughter)

SHANA
And let's do that again.

(THERESA farts again)

SHANA
Calm the mind you two. In, 1, 2, 3—

(THERESA *again moans, louder, longer*)

SHANA
—4, 5, 6, 7, 8, 9, 10. And, out 1, 2, 3, 4, 5, 6, 7, 8, 9, 10. Great. How does that feel?

JULIE
Fine.

KRISTI
Good.

SHANA
Great. Friends, you are now ready. *(to THERESA)* Theresa, you're making great progress. But let's come out of it.

THERESA
Oh.

SHANA
You look a little flushed.

THERESA
I'm just wet

SHANA
Good. Good. Ok. Ok, sisters. We're going to move on to Sethu Bandhasan or the bridge pose. Let me show you how this will happen. First lay on your backs on the ground. You are going to bend your knees, bringing the soles of the feet parallel to the ground and close to the buttocks, like this. Then lift the hips up toward the sky. Are you watching? And next you'll want to interlace your fingers behind your back and straighten the arms, pressing them down into the mat.

JULIE
There's no way I can do that

SHANA
Okay. Let's have you all give this a try. Ready on the mat. Breathe and begin.

KRISTI
(to JULIE) Wow, you look great.

JULIE
Shut up. *(JULIE indicates to THERESA)*

KRISTI
I mean really good.

SHANA
Sisters, you are really going to need to focus when you do this at home.

KRISTI
(to JULIE, but a little louder than she notices) That's giving us a lot of credit isn't it?

SHANA
No. No. You can use this at home all the time. Your husband will love it.

KRISTI
Ha.

JULIE
Um, our husbands don't believe in yoga.

SHANA
They'll believe once…

(THERESA *is moaning again*)

SHANA
Easy, Theresa. Easy. Easy

THERESA
Shana, Shana. What's best for this pose?

SHANA
Beeping *[Thrusting]*.

THERESA
Oh. Beeping.

SHANA
Tell him to hold on to your beep *[buttock]* and beep *[thrust]* hard while keeping eye contact always.

JULIE
What?

SHANA
Alright, let go of the pose. And let's try it again with the image of beep *[entry/sex]*.

(JULIE and KRISTI look at each other)

JULIE
Kristi.

KRISTI
Um, Shawna.

SHANA
It's Shana.

KRISTI
Oh. Shana

SHANA
Yes, Kristi.

KRISTI
Julie and I are just a little confused about what you're talking about.

SHANA
Ok. What part is confusing?

THERESA
Are you guys throbbing? Because I'm throbbing?

KRISTI
This is a yoga pose, right?

SHANA
Yes.

KRISTI
So when you say beep and all that stuff.

SHANA
I'm talking about love making.

KRISTI
Oh. Ok.

SHANA
Alright. Let's try that again.

JULIE
(whispering) Kristi?

KRISTI
What?

JULIE
What do you mean what?

SHANA
Oh, this is also a great position if beep *[cunniligus]* is being performed on you.

JULIE
What type of yoga is this?

SHANA
Tantra. Julie, I'm sensing you're uncomfortable with this?

JULIE
Yes.

SHANA
This is a natural technique, poses that just happen to help make your beep *[sex]* life amazing and incredible. That's it.

JULIE
That's what makes me uncomfortable.

THERESA
Julie, Trust me. It's amazing. My husband and I were doing the forward bend and I...

SHANA
Allows for deeper beep *[penetration]*. Opens the beep *[vagina]* and the beep *[anus]* and allow for a divine expe-

rience.

JULIE
Disgusting.

THERESA
I had the most powerful beepasm [orgasm] ever.

KRISTI
Wait. Wait.

JULIE
No way.

KRISTI
(to SHANA) We might be back.

(KRISTI and JULIE on the side have a conversation)

JULIE
How dare you drag me to something like—

KRISTI
I'm just as shocked as you. I had no idea.

JULIE
Honest?

KRISTI
You think I would sign up for this type of thing?

JULIE
Yes.

KRISTI
Come on.

JULIE
Then let's get the hell out of here.

KRISTI
I'm freaked out too but now that we're here, we might as well...

JULIE
Are you crazy?

KRISTI
It might inspire some...

JULIE
I don't need inspiration.

KRISTI
You've been married 32 years and you don't need inspiration?

JULIE
That's none of your business. Haven't you punished me enough? I let you crone me...

KRISTI
But you had fun...

JULIE
This is vulgar.

KRISTI
But what about doing it for me?

JULIE
If you wanna stay, I'm not gonna judge you.

KRISTI
It's just you and me. Who's gonna know?

JULIE
Me.

KRISTI
We aren't committing a crime.

JULIE
That depends on who you ask. You know, things slow down as you get older. You know that right?

KRISTI
I know, but...

JULIE
Are you having trouble...

KRISTI
No. We have beep [sex]. It's great beep [sex].

JULIE
Ok.

KRISTI
But I've never... *(pauses)*

JULIE
You've never had...?

(Pause)

KRISTI
No.

EVERYONE BUT KRISTI
Oh.

KRISTI
I mean I still enjoy it quite a bit.

JULIE
I know but...

KRISTI
Come on, stay. We'll bond.

JULIE
Kristi.

KRISTI
I know, I know.

JULIE
I'm sorry. I'm going back to bed. Wake me up when you're done.

KRISTI
I'll just come with you.

JULIE
Stay if you want.

KRISTI
Now I feel weird.

(SHANA comes over)

SHANA
Can I interject something?

JULIE *(overlapping with KRISTI)*
No.

KRISTI *(overlapping with JULIE)*
Yes.

SHANA
I understand that this type of practice can be shocking at first.

JULIE
It's dirty.

SHANA
Yoga – Tantra yoga – isn't about beep. It's been an ancient eastern philosophy about connection to the mind and body and really the universe's energy at large. The interconnection is—

JULIE
Shana, you've lost me.

SHANA
Where?

JULIE
Does it matter? Listen, this is a private conversation.

THERESA
Can I share something? He finally found my beep *[clitoris]*!

SHANA
Right. Every woman's body is in a constant state of flux. We must learn from each other. Talk openly. Explore with an open heart and an open mind.

JULIE
(to KRISTI) This is where they make you look at your hoo-ha in the mirror.

SHANA
That's a different class. But Kristi, isn't it about time for a beepasm *[orgasm]*? Maybe you can't relax fully, maybe it's your breathing, or maybe it's that you are crushing your spine in a certain position. This practice gives you options, power. That's all and as for you Julie.

JULIE
Don't bring me into this.

SHANA
What's wrong with listening to your fellow sisters. Listening to your body. Your spirit. Maybe your love making can become making love.

JULIE
Or maybe this is just a bunch of pornographic mumbo jumbo.

SHANA
Then what's the harm?

THERESA
I saw Oprah talk about the beepasm being a necessity to age gracefully.

KRISTI
Really?

JULIE
Don't get me started on Oprah.

SHANA
It's been proven. Studies have shown…

JULIE
I'm encouraging Kristi to try it.

THERESA
(whispers to KRISTI) You'll think you went to heaven.

JULIE
But I don't need help. I'm fine.

KRISTI
It's just a beepasm. Let's go.

SHANA
Yes. Let go, Kristi. Let go. It is up to you to find your own beep – reclaim your beep. There is no shame in that. Let's own our beep and know our beep. Get that beep to beep your beep, and lick your beep, nibble, suck, caress your beep and end it all with an earthquaking beepasm.

(Silence)

JULIE and KRISTI
Oh my god.

KRISTI
I'm in.

(Lights change)

SCENE EIGHT

(TROUBADOUR starts to play)

TROUBADOUR
WE MET LIKE PERFECT STRANGERS
IN A NOT SO PERFECT WORLD
AND FROM MY FIRST BREATH ON THIS EARTH
YOU'VE GIVEN ME THE WORLD
OH MAMA, OH MAMA
OH MAMA, OH MAMA

AND THOUGH MY DREAMS MAY TAKE ME
MILES AND MILES AWAY
THE LOVE IN MY HEART FOR YOU
IS ONLY JUST A BEAT AWAY
OH MAMA, OH MAMA
OH MAMA, OH MAMA

WOMAN #1
I yearn to feel safe again
but she cannot hand that to me.

I can't jump into her bed
that took away the night monsters.
I can't ask her to kiss the hurt
and make it all go away.
I can't expect her to jump
to my rescue at every crisis.
I can't.

she can't rub my sick tummy.
she can't tell me what to do.
she can't perform magic on the bad.
she can't.

Maidens, Mothers, & Crones

I want to ask her if she went through
this loss when she was younger.
the mystery of childhood seems to
vanish into the adult air.
Mom is human
why didn't you explain earlier?

WOMAN #2
can you pick at me a little more?

yeah, I know my face is broken out.
I know I could lose some weight.
I know I don't have a job.
okay?
I guess I can do no right.

you're right,
I should quit smoking.
correct,
I should use better judgment.
sure,
I do have big issues with men.

anything else?

I don't let my kid eat chocolate.
I don't want to wear a more age appropriate outfit.
I don't want a more flattering haircut.
no,
no,
no,
I am not you.

don't keep throwing this stuff in my face
I know…
yeah, I have money trouble
but I…
so I know I have a pottymouth
the point is…
well yes you were right about my ex husband
what I'm trying…
uhuh, my decisions do suck and I'm usually wrong
but…

I know all of my flaws
perhaps I'm more aware
than you know
but they needn't be
a constant reminder
given by my mother.
I know it all
but I like to imagine
to pretend
so if you don't have anything nice to say,
just remember
I got it from somewhere.

WOMAN #3
if asked to name the one thing
I will always remember
it wouldn't be her face,
though I think she is beautiful.
it wouldn't be her mind,
although I know she is intelligent.
it would be her legs;
the legs
that make up half of her
five foot five frame.
the legs
that carried me to the hospital
when I cracked my chin.
the legs
that ran all over
from work to home.
the legs
which stand tall and
proud when I approach

i think of all the time
when I was little
when I was always clinging
to those legs
that prickled my skin
after she'd forgotten to shave.
those legs that kept
her near me
that kept me safe.
those legs
that have carried me far.

when asked about my mother
these words cross my tongue,
but never make a sound—
perhaps too much information
for a stranger
to know.

her legs,
the green and blue veins
that hold together her life
are visible
but barely noticeable
unless they are closely studied.
because they are protected
by a thick layer of skin,
her smooth, tanned skin
it cannot be broken through
unless you are part of
her life

TROUBADOUR & ALL
I JUST WANT TO
THANK YOU MOM
THANK YOU MOM
THANK YOU MOM
I WANT TO THANK YOU

THANK YOU MOM
THANK YOU MOM
THANK YOU MOM
I WANT TO THANK YOU

I JUST WANT TO
THANK YOU MOM
THANK YOU MOM
THANK YOU MOM
I WANT TO THANK YOU

(Lights change)

SCENE NINE

ALL
IF I KNEW YOU WERE COMIN'
I'D HAVE BAKED A CAKE...

TAMARA
Value is overrated unless you're talking about double coupon day at Kroger.

MARIA
My divorce lawyer asked me to figure out what my homemaking services were worth for the past twenty years. I laughed. I thought he was joking until the judge awarded me $400 a month in alimony. That's 4,800 dollars a year. I guess *he* didn't like my cooking either.

ERIN
It was just our typical monthly staff meeting, but I did notice the cake. Thought it was for another meeting. Then the director asked me to stand, presented me with a plaque and named me employee of the year for my dedication and hard work. Everyone clapped, everyone thought I was deserving. Plus I get three free days off! I didn't even know the director knew my name.

SUE
I know I have value because God told me during the 1982 Super Bowl game. *(smiles)* And I've never missed a game since. It's not that I didn't like football, it's just that Joel didn't think I was smart enough to understand it. I tried to watch it with him a few times, but I never could follow his rules: no questions, no talking, in fact no sounds from me. Any cheer I did provoked him and honestly, no one wants to provoke Joel. So Super Bowl Sundays found me in the kitchen while he and the boys watched the game. I provided

refreshments when called upon - my meatballs were always a must have - but otherwise, I was to stay away. That year it was the San Francisco 49ers and the Cincinnati Bengals. Joel's from Cincinnati so you can imagine his excitement, plus the fact that it was being played at the Silverdome - he pretty much took credit as if it were all his doings. Everyone was at our house that Sunday, but the rules remained in effect. I remained alone in the kitchen. Sometime during the second quarter, Joel yelled in for some more meatballs. "Meatballs! Meatballs! NEED MEATBALLS HERE!" I just sat there, I couldn't move. I didn't have any more. I hadn't made enough. If he had to get up and come in there... I don't know what would have happened. Nothing good, that's for sure. I remember closing my eyes and praying that I'd just die. That I would be better off dead. When I closed my eyes and as that thought floated across my brain, I heard this voice, this indescribable voice. I couldn't even tell if it was a man or woman. All it said was, "You want to die over meatballs? Really?" My eyes opened and suddenly I was filled with... with knowledge. I was warmed and I was loved. And when he screamed again for his beloved meatballs, the words and fear dripped off me and oozed onto the floor. I was me again, free, and before he could yell again I had made the decision to leave. Right then. And I promised myself that I would never let that happen again. How do I know it was God? The 49ers won.

(Lights change)

SCENE TEN

(This is a party and the word "crone" is being chanted. JULIE is wearing a red hat with purple ribbon and a t-shirt that says "Croning and Loving it". JULIE is definitely not loving it. KRISTI comes over)

KRISTI
You do realize this isn't called a curmudgeon ceremony, right?

JULIE
(drinks her wine) Ceremony? What do you expect me to say?

KRISTI
Well, your face says it all, but you should know everyone's here for you. Here to pass along their wisdom, let you borrow their chi, and...

JULIE
Watch me be embarrassed... I get it

KRISTI
This isn't embarrassing. This is enlightening.

JULIE
A croning party? And by the way I'm only 56, for Christ's sake.

KRISTI
Prime croning time, sister. Technically you're already a crone since you've finally entered menopause.

JULIE
Shut up.

KRISTI
It's not a bad word. Most everyone here has, you know, except me. But Tonight we are free... free to be crones, witches, sisters.

JULIE
But I just wanted a nice, quiet dinner

with our circle.

KRISTI
We can have that any old time. This... this is special, Jules. This is your rite of passage, your christening, your bat mitzvah. It's supposed to be fun.

JULIE
For who?

KRISTI
Can you fake it at least? You really need to stop railing against this phase in your life.

JULIE
I'm sorry but since when is it mandatory I celebrate my birthday on your terms.

KRISTI
Let me explain this croning thing to you. You aren't getting it. This is all about enjoying the best and last phase of womanhood with...

JULIE
I get what it is. I get that I'm getting older. I accept it. I'm not trying to recapture my youth—it wasn't that great to begin with. But I don't need to sing khumbaya around a damn campfire to celebrate the fact that I am getting older, entering my "last" phase and heading toward the grave.

KRISTI
Who told you about the khumbaya?

JULIE
(smiles) I hate you.

KRISTI
Don't you think it's important to embrace you, your age, your—

JULIE
Embrace it? I am it.

KRISTI
What? So we can't have fun. Hon, everyone always assumes that women like us are on downhill slope from here on out... I mean, we tend to disappear from the radar and lose importance in this screwed up society. Fuck that, I say. We are worth more now than 100 eighteen year-olds put together.

JULIE
Worth more to who?

KRISTI
To me. And hopefully to you and everyone here. Look at my warrior body, this made it through chemo... This pooch... your pooch... those are battle scars my friend. My crows feet, your laugh lines... We fought hard and earned those.

JULIE
I'm glad you are so comfortable. So serene with your mind and your body, but that is a daily struggle for me and...

KRISTI
It's a struggle. I struggle, but tonight this is a different world. The world we should live in 24-7. Here I love my grey pubic hair, varicose veins, and stretch marks. And maybe tonight that will help everyone start to truly understand the fact that we matter. We are beautiful. We are intelligent. We are!

JULIE
So then you call yourself a crone? Crone? That's a horrible word. I used that for the nun that taught us math in high school.

KRISTI
Well, we are reclaiming it. Strong older women. Wise. Beautiful. So quit your bitching. We are going to start.

JULIE
Start what?

KRISTI
The croning ceremony. *(yells to everyone)* Can I get everyone's attention just for two seconds? We are about to begin.

JULIE
You didn't tell me what's involved.

KRISTI
(to JULIE) I know. *(to the party)* Tonight is about celebrating Julie's new phase in the circle of life here on this plane. I ask that you all open your hearts and your minds tonight. Bring forth all of the love and glory from within yourself and share it with all of your sister crones here. Let's begin with the anointing of the crone.

("Crone" is chanted and laughed from the crowds)

JULIE
I still hate that word.

KRISTI
(to JULIE) Too late. *(louder)* Julie Heitman, tonight is the beginning of your most compassionate journey, the most illuminated adventure. You are now the full moon that the goddesses always intended woman to be. *(Takes out a white cotton necklace and puts it around JULIE's head)* This chain represents the beginning of your womanhood, as your moon began to wax.

JULIE
(looking at it) Um… oh my god, these are tampons.

KRISTI
I know.

JULIE
This is so gross

KRISTI
These gardening gloves. *(to JULIE)* Give me your hand. *(JULIE gives her hands to her)* These gloves represent the spirit of nurturing nature. The mother earth that lives in you. From the neighborhoods to your own backyard, you helped plant seeds that grew and continue to grow strong and bright.

(KRISTI grabs a bowl and fills it with water, then starts splashing JULIE)

JULIE
That's cold!

KRISTI
It's for purification.

JULIE
Of my—

KRISTI
Spirit. To open you up to what you are about to receive.

JULIE
Ok.

(KRISTI splashes her for a while around her abdomen and pubic region)

JULIE
You've been down there a while.

KRISTI
It's the area that needs the most work.

JULIE
Ok. I'm done…

KRISTI
Kidding. Kidding. *(takes the bowl)* And lastly— *(puts her finger in the bowl of red paint and marks JULIE's face as the*

natives did) The color red is for life... woman's life. The blood that begins the circle and will eventually end it. The first mark across the forehead represents the wisdom you as crone have. The two marks under your eyes represent the all seeing power your wisdom has brought to you. The circle around your mouth represents that your word, your voice is never to be silenced. Sisters, Crones, gather here today and celebrate Julie our newest crone.

(Crone chant. A crown of ivy is placed on her head. KRISTI forces JULIE to turn to the crowd and she looks horrible. Flashes from cameras explode)

JULIE
(laughing and making funny faces) Nice guys, real nice.

KRISTI
Alright, grab your granny panties *(she waves hers in the air)* and head outside—we are going to start the ritual burning of the cotton tents!

(Whoops and hollers from all the guests)

JULIE
Granny panties.

KRISTI
Look at these things. *(she holds them up)* Aren't they horrible?

JULIE
(pause) Whatever.

KRISTI
Are you wearing these?

JULIE
No.

KRISTI
Julie.

JULIE
Kristi

KRISTI
Julie

JULIE
Kristi

KRISTI
Pull up your skirt.

JULIE
You.

KRISTI
I'm not wearing panties.

JULIE
Oh my god.

(KRISTI comes for JULIE's pants)

KRISTI
Show me.

JULIE
Get off me.

KRISTI
Oh my.

JULIE
(slaps her hand) Get away from me. Let's keep going with the—

KRISTI
Just—

JULIE
Those panties happen to be very comfortable.

KRISTI
Well, then let's go get you some orthopedic shoes tomorrow and then we'll have dinner at Bob Evans at four.

JULIE
I didn't know we were having a granny panty burning party. I might have chosen different.

KRISTI
I should make you strip those off.

JULIE
I'd like to see you try.

KRISTI
Ok. Ok. But I can tell you are having a little better time now.

JULIE
This is all so silly.

KRISTI
Good.

JULIE
Thank you.

KRISTI
I love you, Julie Crone.

JULIE
I love you too, Bitch. Now let's go burn some panties.

KRISTI
After you. *(JULIE walks out and KRISTI yells to the crowd)* She's wearing the grannys! She's wearing the grannys! GET HER! GET HER! GET HER! GET HER!

(Lights change)

SCENE ELEVEN

(All the women form a circle and slowly move with the music)

TROUBADOUR
WE ARE THE LOVERS
THE SISTERS
THE MOTHERS
THE DAUGHTERS
TO OUR BROTHERS
OUR SISTERS
OUR CHILDREN
THE GREAT MOTHER
NEITHER MARY THE WHORE
OR MARY THE PURE
ARE WE ONLY
BUT ALL
WE ARE ALL
WE ARE ONE

WE ARE THE DAUGHTERS OF OUR GRANDMOTHER'S DAUGHTERS
WE HAVE THE SAME STRONG HANDS, SAME KNOWING EYE
WE THREE WADE
THRU THE MYSTIC WATERS
SEEDED WITH BLOOD, SWEAT AND TEARS
OF ALL THAT IS LIFE

OF ALL THAT IS LIFE

(Blackout)

END OF PLAY

VOICES OF THE MIDWEST

FLYOVER, U.S.A.

A PLAY BY
Dennis E. North &
Joseph Zettelmaier

THE VOICES FROM THE MIDWEST series of plays was created by the Williamston Theatre to explore and embrace what life is like in our part of the world. Directors and playwrights on the project developed questionnaires, and sent them all over the Midwest, inviting submissions from people of all walks of life. Those submissions were then taken and adapted into three evenings of theatre exploring the life of women, men, and families in the American Midwest.

FLYOVER, U.S.A. was written, in part, thanks to submissions from the following people: Jack Bates, Christopher Abraham, DE Alchin, Dean Atkins, Bruce Bennett, Patrick J. Brazil, David Briston, Steve Berglund, Dominic Caselli, Frank Caselli, Jake Christensen, Jim Daugherty, Ronald Dorr, Richard J. Enbody, Jay Fosgitt, Rick Foster, Edward J. Gillespie, Kurt Guter, Bill Haggerty, Bob Hanna, Gordon Hicks, Tobin Hissong, Frank J. Leahey, John Lepard, Timothy Lewis, Hugh Maguire, Clif McChesney, Scott Norman, Duane Reum, Kevin Schumacker, John Seibert, Marty Smith, Dr. Robert L. Smith, Todd E. Walter, John Zettelmaier, and many men who wished to remain anonymous.

FLYOVER, U.S.A.: VOICES FROM THE MIDWEST received its world premiere on May 21, 2009 at Williamston Theatre (Williamston, MI). It was directed by John Seibert. Set and Lighting Design by Daniel C. Walker, Costume Design by Melanie Schuessler. Stage Managed by Rochelle P. Clark. VOICES OF THE MIDWEST series concept by Tony Caselli.

The cast was as follows:

        GUY 1: Tobin Hissong
        GUY 2: John Lepard
        GUY 3: Scott Norman

For production rights, contact Williamston Theatre.

Flyover U.S.A.

ACT I
SCENE ONE

(The sound of a busy airport. Three travelers enter from different spots, all hitting the stage at the same time. All are on cellphones)

GUY 1
No, that's not what I said...

GUY 2
You're not listening to me. I didn't say that...

GUY 3
I need for you to stop and listen to me...

GUY 1
This trip was not my idea...

GUY 2
Then who's idea was it...?

GUY 3
No one's taking credit but me. This was all my idea.

GUY 1
This was not what I had intended.

GUY 2
I'm telling you, I didn't plan on this.

GUY 3
No, it's a good plan and we just need to stick to it.

GUY 1
All I'm saying is we're on a deadline here.

GUY 2
We're on a deadline here and time's running out.

GUY 3
Give me some options...

GUY 1
That's really not an option.

GUY 2
What do you mean we're out of options?

GUY 3
There is always another way.

GUY 1
What about a different direction?

GUY 2
A road less traveled.

GUY 3
Look, we need to stay on course here.

GUY 1
I think we're way off course here.

GUY 2
No, I'll meet him on the golf course.

GUY 3
Is that really the fair way to do this?

GUY 1
I'll need a driver then.

GUY 2
See, all we do is putter around the issue.

GUY 3
I can pick it up if you want?

GUY 1
No wait. This is not a gimmie.

GUY 2
Seriously, I'm off coffee now. Just tea.

GUY 3
We got too many balls in the air.

GUY 1
What happen to ours?

GUY 2
No, still in the bags.

GUY 3
Both of them?

GUY 1
I'm telling you, I can't find them but I'm willing to look.

GUY 2
Where? Where do you suggest I look?

GUY 3
I'm telling you, my hands are tied on this.

GUY 1
Are you listening to me? My hands are tied on this.

GUY 2
My hands are tied on this.

GUY 3
On this, my hands are tied.

(Airport announcement. They are all inaudible)

ANNOUNCEMENT *(short)*

GUYS 1,2,3
Hold on...

ANNOUNCEMNET *(longer)*

GUY 1
Ah great.

GUY 2
Perfect.

GUY 3
Just wonderful. We're delayed.

GUY 1
I'm going to be late.

GUY 2
I knew this was going to happen.

GUY 3
I had a bad feeling about this.

ANNOUNCEMENT *(short)*

GUYS 1,2,3
Hold on...

ANNOUNCEMENT *(longer)*

GUY 1
Alright, it's official. I'm stuck.

GUY 2
We're all stuck. It's official.

GUY 3
They said officially, nothing's moving. We're all stuck.

GUY 1
Well, what are you gonna do?

GUY 2
Alright, here's what I think we should

do.

GUY 3
We dominate the line of scrimmage.

GUY 1
It's fourth and long.

GUY 2
No way we're gong to punt on this.

GUY 3
We're going for the win.

GUY 1
It's a win, win.

GUY 2
Everybody wins on this.

GUY 3
Look, the Irish just need to play Notre Dame football, you know what I'm saying?

GUY 3
You get what I'm saying, right?

GUY 1
I think we are saying the same thing.

GUY 2
Enough said, but, what I'm saying is we can score from anywhere on the ice.

GUY 3
We can put that biscuit in the basket.

GUY 1
You go high on the top shelf good things happen.

GUY 2
It's crunch time.

GUY 3
It's gut check time.

GUY 1
The fat lady does not sing until we goose her in the butt.

(Slight pause as the two look at GUY 3)

GUY 3
We're a blue-collar team.

GUY 1
We got a blue-collar work ethic.

GUY 2
Grindstones, noses, let me tell you something; we don't even have noses anymore.

ANNOUNCEMENT *(short)*

GUYS 1,2,3
Hold on…

ANNOUNCEMENT *(longer)*

GUYS 1,2,3
No, they're just telling us that there's nothing to tell us.

GUY 1
We're going to make the best of it. That's what we're going to do.

GUY 2
As soon as I know, you'll know.

GUY 3
Yeah, I know.

GUY 1
Just keep looking on the bright side.

GUY 2
Just find the silver lining.

GUY 3
Yeah, whatever.

GUYS 1,2,3
Alright, I'll call. Bye.

(A nice pause as the guys look around. Simultaneously they all dial their cell phones)

SCENE TWO

(An announcer is heard as the lights slowly rise. GUYS 1, 2, & 3 are seated at an airport bar, glued to a football game on the TV. A scorpion in a glass is next to GUY 2)

ANNOUNCER
Now seating row D through H for Northwest Flight 136, non-stop to San Francisco. Please have your tickets...

(A fumble in the game. The 3 men react accordingly. 3 is by far the most intoxicated of all of them)

GUY 1
Oh come on!

GUY 2
Are you kidding me? Are you freaking kidding me?!

GUY 3
How hard is it to hold on to the ball?!

GUY 2
One game! Please! I'm begging you!

GUY 3
If that's how you're gonna run the trap, then just don't show up!

GUY 1
You're killing me! Honest to god, you're freaking killing me!

GUY 2
How much you put on 'em?

GUY 1
Two hundred bucks.

GUY 3
(Turning around) Please tell me you're joking. Or that I'm not as drunk as I think I'm drunk.

GUY 1
Hey. There's no law about putting money on the Lions.

GUY 3
Not yet.

(GUY 3's cellphone goes off)

GUY 3
Wonderful.

(He looks at the numbers, hangs his head in a moment of defeat, then picks up)

GUY 3
Malcolm! Buddy! What can I do you for?

(He talks in a corner as GUYS 1 & 2 chat)

GUY 2
So San Diego, huh? Was it a vacation or...?

GUY 1
Job interview.

(Beat)

GUY 2
Oh.

GUY 1
Human resources for Pfeizer.

GUY 2
What?

GUY 1
I'm saving you the trouble of guessing. I was in Human Resources for Pfeizer. Assistant manager. Got laid off 12 months ago.

GUY 2
I'm sorry.

GUY 1
Not your fault.

(GUY 3 notices the TV)

GUY 3
Malcolm.

GUY 1
I had an interview to run HR at Dolan Pharmaceuticals, San Diego Branch, so…

GUY 2
Hey, that's something.

GUY 1
Yeah, that's something all right.

GUY 3
Malcolm.

GUY 2
Better pay?

GUY 1
Better pay, more vacation time. And the freaking San Diego Chargers.

GUY 3
Gotta go, Malcolm. The game's back on.

GUY 1
So my options are, don't move and hope to God I can find another job. Or move my wife and kids to San Diego - where we know nobody - and try to make things work there.

GUY 3
Hey, man. You're cutting out.

GUY 1
But you know what really sucks? I got two boys… 10 and 12.. and we've got season tickets to the Lions. We're out there every damn game, screaming our heads off no matter how bad they lose. My dad did that with me and I just…

GUY 2
It won't be the same. Not with the Chargers.

GUY 1
Exactly. Exactly.

GUY 3
Yeah, I can barely hear you. Gotta go. Bye. Bye. BYE! *(hangs up, then goes right back to the game)* That's it. Run, baby, run.

GUY 2
A man's only really got one home, so he's only really got one home team.

GUY 1
What?

GUY 2
That's a Buckism.

GUY 1
A what now?

GUY 2
A Buckism. Something my dad used to say. He had hundreds of 'em. And his name was Buck. That's why we call them…

GUY 1
NO, I got it.

(Beat. GUY 2 offers his hand)

GUY 2
Archie Ruebens. You can call me Buck. That's what everyone calls me.

GUY 1
Rob Graff.

GUY 2
Nice to meet you.

GUY 1
You too.

GUY 3
Time out?! Are you kidding me?!

GUY 1
So I gotta ask… what is this thing?

GUY 2
Hmmm?

(GUY 1 points to the scorpion)

GUY 2
It's a scorpion. In glass.

GUY 1
It sure is.

GUY 2
They don't have these in Fargo.

(Beat)

GUY 1
They sure don't.

GUY 2
That's where I'm from. Fargo.

GUY 1
Got it.

GUY 2
I was down in Albuquerque and my son wanted a souvenir. I thought this was kina cool.

GUY 1
Albuquerque? That's worse than San Diego.

GUY 2
I hear ya. But I had to go. My sister had her first baby and...

GUY 1
Hey, congratulations.

GUY 2
Thanks.

GUY 1
Boy or girl?

GUY 2
It's a boy. They named him Buck.

GUY 1
What's his real name?

GUY 2
Buck.

(Beat)

GUY 2
Yeah, it's not a nickname.

(They sit in silence for a bit, with GUY 3 staring enraptured at the TV. GUY 1 raises his glass to GUY 2)

GUY 1
To fathers and sons.

GUY 2
Here, here.

(They clink glasses and drink. GUY 3 quickly moves towards them. His eyes are still fixed on the TV)

GUY 3
Hey, look. *(points to the TV. They look)*

GUY 1
Oh my god.

GUY 2
GO! GO!

GUY 3
Run, you magnificent bastard!

GUY 1
Dear lord in heaven please let him make it to the goal line. If it's your will.

(They stare in silence. A touchdown. The three men jump & shout excitedly. The ANNOUNCER speaks again)

ANNOUNCER
Northwest Airlines regrets to announce the cancellation of Flight 134 to scenic but inconsequential Flyover Country USA.

(Beat. Throughout the following, the announcer never loses her pleasant soothing tone)

Flyover USA

GUY 3
Did I hear that right, or am I just that drunk?

GUY 2
What did she say?

GUY 1
(Calling up at the voice) What did you...?

ANNOUNCER
Northwest Flight 134 to Indianapolis has been canceled.

GUY 3
That's not what you said.

ANNOUNCER
It is so.

GUY 2
No, you said something about scenic but inconsequential...

ANNOUNCER
I assure you, sir, I said nothing of the kind.

GUY 2
You did! You totally did!

GUY 3
(Looking around) Are we the only ones hearing this?

ANNOUNCER
If any of you gentlemen are supposed to be onboard Flight 134...

GUY 2
What the hell is Flyover Country?

ANNOUNCER
Come on. You know.

(Beat. All three just stare in the air)

ANNOUNCER
You know.

(Beat)

ANNOUNCER
The whole... you know... bunch of states that you... fly over. When you're flying between important places.

GUY 1
Am I to imply that these state are, therefore, unimportant?

ANNOUNCER
Actually, I'm implying that. You're inferring that.

GUY 2
And just what states constitute "Flyover Country?"

ANNOUNCER
You know. The Midwestern States.

GUY 3
Which are...?

(The ANNOUNCER says nothing)

GUY 3
You don't even know! You're the voice of the airport and have no idea...

ANNOUNCER
Oh please. You don't know then either.

GUY 2
Excuse me?

GUY 1
Illinois.

GUY 2
Indiana.

GUY 3
Iowa.

GUY 1
Kansa.

GUY 2
Michigan.

GUY 3
Minnesota.

GUY 1
Missouri.

GUY 2
Nebraska.

GUY 3
North Dakota.

GUY 1
Ohio.

GUY 2
South Dakota.

GUY 1
BAM! The Midwestern States! All 11 of them!

ANNOUNCER
There's twelve.

GUY 1
Come again?

ANNOUNCER
I just Googled it. There are 12 Midwestern states. You missed one.

(Beat. The guys come together and talk quietly to themselves)

GUY 1
Did we miss a Dakota?

GUY 3
I don't think so.

GUY 2
Was it one of the Great Lakes ones?

GUY 1
Which ones are the Great Lakes ones?

GUY 2
Michigan, Ohio,…

GUY 3
What about Indiana? Is that…

GUY 1
Wisconsin! It's Wisconsin!

ANNOUNCER
You got a gold star. Now if you'll excuse me, some of us still have jobs.

GUY 1
What?! Was that a crack at me?

GUY 3
"Flyover Country." Where does she get off?

GUY 1
I've heard it before. It's this BS term people came up with when they're working in the east and west coasts. They think the rest of the state are just this cultural wasteland.

GUY 2
Despite the fact that the third biggest city in the US is part of that wasteland.

(Beat)

GUY 2
It's Chicago.

GUY 1
City of Big Shoulders.

GUY 3
You got that right.

GUY 3
(Raises his drink) To the City of Big Shoulders!

(They drink)

GUY 2
Hey, to Wisconsin. Sorry we forgot you, baby!

GUY 1
To Wisconsin!

(They drink, GUY 2 laughs a little)

GUY 2
I can't believe I forgot Wisconsin. My dad went to school there.

GUY 3
Go Badgers!

GUY 2
If he was here, He would've torn me a new one.

GUY 1
That's what fathers are for.

GUY 3
Not mine. He didn't give a crap about sports. He liked… ballet. *(pause)* You heard me.

(Beat. They let that sink in. GUY 1 finally raises his glass again)

GUY 1
I said it before. I'll say it again. To fathers and sons.

(GUYS 2 & 3 raise their glasses)

GUYS 2 & 3
Here, Here.

(Lights fade)

SCENE THREE

TOBIN
My old man didn't worry about being "happy" in his job. It wasn't his "mission" in life… his family was. The job was just that, a job. And the hard work did not bother him.

JOHN
Dad was a salesman. At age 65, the time of his death, he was still the number one salesperson in his national company. He was in food packaging. I liked to walk the grocery store shelves with him where he'd point out products he helped design packaging for that allowed them to "jump off" t of the shelves and into people's carts. He constantly drilled into me the fact that I should never look at something for what it is, but rather what it can be. And that included people. Me as well.

SCOTT
My dad was working as a baker in this large bakery and one time they made a bunch of peach pies, but the pies didn't sell. So the boss tells my dad to throw them away but my dad asks if he could have them. His boss says yes. About two months later, dad presented his boss with a bottle of peach brandy he had made from all the peach filling in the pies. My dad used to say "have integrity… it doesn't cost anything and no one can take it away from you." I've tried to live by that.

TOBIN
My father was a disaster.

JOHN
My old man would say, "It's not the mistakes you make, it's how you respond to them."

SCOTT
"If you're waiting on me, you're wasting your time."

JOHN
"Give it away when you can. It was never yours to begin with."

SCOTT
"Don't be generous with my money. It's my money."

TOBIN
I have a haunting suspicion that my dad's best stories are the one's he hasn't told me yet.

(Lights change)

SCENE FOUR
JACK'S SANDBOX Pt. 1

(Lights up. JACK is walking with PETER)

JACK
I really appreciate this.

PETER
Not a problem.

JACK
I just… it was a whim, you know?

PETER
Sure. I've only been here maybe eight months. Haven't had the time to…you know.

JACK
What?

PETER
Clean up the place.

(JACK just stares at him, They arrived at their destination. They look out over the overgrown land)

JACK
Oh my god,

PETER
Just like you remember it?

JACK
Not at all. And exactly.

PETER
What was your name again?

JACK
Jack, Jack Santos.

PETER
Right. The Santos'. You guys had this place in the eighties, yeah?

JACK
Uh…'73-'83. My dad bought it, when it was… nothing. Just this old shell. It was built in the Civil War, you know that?

PETER
Yeah.

JACK
I mean… the Civil War. I can't even… the porch… he built that.

PETER
He did good work. Still level.

JACK
Yeah?

PETER
Yep. The damn kitchen's all up and down, but that porch. *(He draws his hand across, showing how level the floor is)*

JACK
(Staring off) Where is it?

PETER
Where is what?

JACK
There was… I had a sandbox out there. It was right there, by the shed. Wait. Where's the shed?

PETER
Maybe we're facing the wrong way.

JACK
No, it was right there. You step out on the back porch, and there's supposed to be a shed right there, and a big sandbox next to it.

PETER
Um, yeah. I don't know what to tell you.

JACK
Did you, like, tear it down, or…?

PETER
Nope, Nothing like that here when I moved in.

JACK
Seriously. You can tell me if you did.

PETER
Ok. But I didn't.

JACK
I won't get mad.

PETER
That's good. Still didn't.

(Beat)

JACK
Where the hell is my sandbox!?

PETER
Maybe it's underneath those bushes, I mean, it was sand right? Maybe the plants just kinda… grew over it. Or into it. Or whatever.

(JACK just stares out, sad and confused)

JACK
I think about this place. All the time. All the time. And when I drove through here… I never drove these roads myself. I was ten when we moved. But I remembered it all. As soon as I got to M-50, this thing in my brain just took over. Like a homing signal, taking me… well home. And I just… you see that tree there?

PETER
Yeah.

JACK
That's a Mulberry Tree.

PETER
I thought Mulberries grew on bushes. 'Cause of the song. With the weasel.

JACK
My brother and I… we'd eat right off the tree. And the berries… they stain everything purple and blue. I'm standing here right now, and I can remember it like I'm looking at it. I can tell you what we were wearing, how my mom cut our hair in these,, like, bowl-cuts. It's right there.

PETER
Yeah. OK.

JACK
I was happy here. Happier than I've ever been. But I don't know if I really was, or…

(JACK is lost in his own thoughts. Suddenly, he heads off towards the area where his sandbox once was)

PETER
Where are you going?

JACK
I'm gonna find my damn sandbox.

PETER
Look, I don't wanna be a jerk or anything, but this is my land now.

JACK
It was mine first!

PETER
Uh…ok. Except it's mine now.

JACK
Right. I know. But… look, I need to do this. OK?

(PETER just looks at him for a bit, then heads off in the direction JACK was going)

JACK
Wait. What…?

PETER
You wanna find this thing or don'tcha?

(JACK heads off after him. Lights fade)

SCENE FIVE

GUY 3
A man who cannot handle tools is not a man. Willy Lowman, Death of a Salesman.

GUY 1
You don't know me.

GUY 2
Oh, you may think you know me.

GUY 3
But you don't.

GUY 1
Not really.

GUY 2
You've lived with me for twenty years.

GUY 3
Or you've worked with me in the same office for five years.

GUY 1
Or I'm your husband. Or your son. Or that neighbor you only talk to when you want to borrow my damn snowblower.

(Beat)

GUY 1
Seriously. How hard is it to buy your own damn snowblower?

GUY 2
The point is, not all men are from Mars.

GUY 3
And why is it Mars, anyway? Mars is where the aliens live!

GUY 2
Mars - God of War. Venus - Goddess of Love.

GUY 3
Really?

GUY 2
Yeah. You know - *(sings)* I'm your Venus, I'm your fire, your desire...

GUY 1
I just wanna clear up some misconceptions is all.

(GUY 3 is now sort of singing to himself)

GUY 3
...She's got it. Yeah baby, she's got it...

(He realizes GUYS 1 & 2 are staring at him)

GUY 3
What? It's a good song.

GUY 2
No way. Give me Billy Jean any day of the week.

GUY 3
Michael Jackson? For real?

GUY 2
You have a problem with Michael Jackson?

GUY 3
I have a laundry list of problems with Michael Jackson.

GUY 1
Come on. Back on track.

GUY 3
One - He dangled a kid out a window.

GUY 2
That was taken out of context.

GUY 1
Enough with Michael Jackson already!

(Beat)

GUY 1
All I'm saying is, don't look at us and think you've got us all figured out. It's demeaning.

GUY 2
Seriously. I've been walking in my shoes my whole life, and I still surprise myself.

GUY 1
I like classical music. Yeah, that's right! Classical music! Not country, not mullet rock — Classical! Berlioz, Chopin, Stravinsky! This is what I'm listening to when I mow my lawn! How do your preconceived notions feel now?

GUY 2
Whoa, calm down.

GUY 1
No, I'm making a point here.,

GUY 3
We're all on the same side here.

GUY 1
Well, it pisses me off! Where is it written that a mechanic can't like classical music? Or watch Masterpiece Theatre? Or grow orchids? Beautiful, delicate orchids?

(Beat)

GUY 2
Seriously? You really don't like Michael Jackson?

GUY 3
Pasty-faced freak with a monkey.

GUY 2
You're just jealous 'cause you don't even have a monkey!

(Lights fade)

SCENE SIX

TOBIN
For my last birthday, my wife hands me a card that says, "pick something you want". Meaning, something from my daughters. My wife and I aren't... well; we're not talking too much at this point. But it's funny how you know what your mind, the rational part, after a lifetime of training, what that part should say... "a tie, dinner out, the girls could clean up their rooms"... your soul.... Blurts something out that's completely unexpected. Something needed to be heard. "I want a parachute jump". That's what came out. My oldest was scared to death, thought I was going insane. My youngest thought it was the coolest thing she'd ever heard and could she go with daddy. My wife... no opinion. *(pulls out a leather pilot jacket, circa WWII, from the carry on bag and puts it on)* So, for this milestone I was given one parachute jump. Tandem, because I really don't want to learn how to skydive, I just wanted to jump. The day comes and I'm strapped to Albert, my instructor, who's this retired tool and die guy that's been jumping forever and looks like a cross between Santa and a lifelong Grateful Dead follower and now for fun and extra cash, he ties himself to milestone birthday boys. We're up. People are trying to talk over the incredible din of the open door of the plane, trying to put words to their excitement or fear, their reasons for jumping or jumping again and me...? I'm just trying to breathe it all in. *(he takes a scarf from the bag and wraps it around his neck)* So, me and Al are strapped, tied,

screwed and glued together and he's yelling in my ear, explaining for the hundredth time, that I don't touch or pull anything until he gives me the high sign. Big thumbs up. Talk on Santa, I'm not hearing a thing. We're on our knees, moving in tandem toward the open door... and then Al asks the question... do I want to flip on the way down. "Easiest thing in the world. We tuck in a ball the second we start to fall and that's all there is to it." *(he takes out aviator glasses from the bag and cleans them with the scarf)* The rational part though, finally caught up and got a clue as to what was going on. I didn't do it. I did the jump but not the flip. How crazy is that? Eighteen thousand feet above the ground and I start to tell myself, I'm not coordinated enough for that, that's too dangerous. Albert yells, "your loss" and we're off like a prom dress and everything's a blur, Rushed and pounded by the sky and your kin is electric and freezing and you're alive and feeling... your soul. And I'm yelling to Santa that I've changed my mind and I want to do the flip. He's screaming in my ear, too late, we missed the chance and now we have to enjoy the ride. But, when Al gives me the sign, big thumbs up... I don't want it to end. If I can't do the flip, then lets just fly... Finally, Albert grabs my hand, forces it onto the ripcord and pulls for the both of us. We're floating and Santa's pointing out that a few more seconds and we might have been in real trouble. And it's so peaceful. And I'm so sad.

Next time. Next time I'll do the flip.

SCENE SEVEN
THUS ENDS THE LESSON

(GUY 1 picks up his newspaper and tries to settle in)

GUY 1
What is this? How'd you guys know?

GUY 2
I got a mole in Human Resources.

GUY 3
Blow out the candles, if you still have any breath left at your age.

GUY 1
Funny. You should take that on the road.

GUY 2
You do anything fun for your birthday? This was a big one, right?

GUY 1
In dog years, yeah but... no, nothing special. Girls cleaned their rooms.

GUY 3
Wow. You lead a life of excitement.

GUY 1
Don't you have work to do?

GUY 2
We're trying to stay out of the way of the movers.

GUY 3
Looks like we're going down to just two floors. Unbelievable, huh?

(Pause)

GUY 2
So, you and you're wife aren't talking?

GUY 1
Not right now... How'd you know that?

GUY 3
We were listening to your monologue.

GUY 2
Why?

GUY 1
Why what?

GUY 3
Why aren't you two talking?

GUY 1
Yeah, you know, I heard him. I was just deflecting the question because it's really none of your guys' business. I'm just trying to be polite.

GUY 3
Fair enough.

GUY 2
Fair enough and that was polite. *(pause)* Although…

GUY 1
What?

GUY 3
It just might be good to talk about it.

GUY 2
Let some if those feelings out.

GUY 3
You can come across a little emotionally closed off.

GUY 1
Is that a fact?

GUY 3
I don't know if it's a fact.

GUY 2
More like an observation.

GUY 1
I'm not all that comfortable talking with you guys, About things like this. Of this nature I mean. Understand? And no offense, right?

GUY 2
Absolutely not

GUY 3
None taken.

GUY 1
(He splits cupcake) I'm on the apology tour right now. It's nothing new for me, but I just don't want to talk about it. Alright?

GUY 2
Fine.

GUY 3
Yeah, no worries.

GUY 1
Thank you.

(A very long pause)

GUY 2
What'd you do?

GUY 3
Yeah. What'd you do? Had to be bad, right?

GUY 2
Had to be to get a guy on the tour, right?

Pause

GUY 1
I took a test and failed.

GUY 3
Like a math test, because those can be hard?

GUY 1
No.

GUY 2
Paternity?

GUY 3
That's easier than math.

GUY 1
No. I failed one of these stupid, rate your spouse, women's magazine tests. Those things are a death sentence.

GUY 2
What was the question?

GUY 1
It was a Menopause question.

GUY 2
Look out now.

GUY 3
Dead man walking.

GUY 2
Wow. There's a question for Menopause?

GUY 1
There's a question for everything and they're all sitting in a minefield. So be careful, because when you're on your hands and knees trying to make it across, and you feel that crunch or hear that ping, you know you've landed on one.

GUY 2
What was the question?

GUY 1
"When going through the change of life, will your spouse be: A. supportive, B. loving and supportive, C. loving, supportive, and open with his feelings as you experience a roller coaster of emotional ups and downs as well as unexplained mood swings that can make sexual desire a thing of the past or D., none of the above?

GUY 3
You said D.?

GUY 1
I said what do you mean, when? I'm living the dream now. She didn't see the humor either.

GUY 2
You know what's worse than those? My wife will do this to me... the visual test? She'll get a Victoria's Secret Catalogue. Find something drop dead sexy, then ask me if I think she'd look good in it... if you had that body, yeah. That's Victoria's real secret. You can buy it but you sure as hell ain't going to look like that.

GUY 1
Tell me you didn't say that out loud?

GUY 2
No. I think my education's coming along quite nicely.

GUY 3
What education...? *(GUYS 1 & 2 just look at him)* Oh, please, tell me you guys aren't afraid of your wives...?

GUY 2
You're not married are you?

GUY 3
No.

GUY 1
Then shut up.

GUY 2
Then shut up.

GUY 1
When you finally do get married, finally pull the trigger, she'll bring you up the way she wants but in the meantime... take this advice... ready?

(GUY 2 is onboard and they both educate GUY 3)

GUY 2
Ready?

GUY 1
She's always right. You're not.

GUY 2
She wants you to listen, not fix the problem.

GUY 1
Talking is a form of love.

GUY 2
Listening is a form of love.

GUY 1
Cuddling is a form of love.

GUY 2
I hate cuddling.

GUY 1
When asked to decide on jewelry… "They all make her look beautiful. It's her choice."

GUY 2
When asked to decide on nail polish… "They all make her look beautiful. It's her choice."

GUY 1
The time spent putting on make-up, fixing hair et cetera, prior to going out is proportionate to the time you need to spend acknowledging how beautiful she looks.

GUY 1
Never buy appliances as a gift. No matter what she says.

GUY 2
Never buy exercise equipment unless you disguise it as being for you.

GUY 1
If ever asked to offer an opinion on whether or not another woman is attractive, know that it is a trap.

GUY 2
Chew your own leg off if you have to but avoid the trap. The trap hurts.

GUY 1
Now this is important. Listen very carefully. If you're ever asked if any, and I do mean any, article of clothing makes her look in any way…fat… *(pause)* You. Must. Lie.

GUY 2
God will forgive you.

GUY 1
She will not.

GUY 2
Microsoft has nothing in the way of software that will match her memory potential.

GUY 3
Back up… you guys are scaring me.

GUY 2
It's a scary business.

GUY 3
I thought marriage was based on honesty. At least it's supposed to be. How is lying okay?

GUY 2
You are so young.

GUY 1
Two reasons. One, self-preservation, two and more importantly… because you love her with all of your heart.

GUY 2
And you'd give her your last breath…

GUY 1
And she not only sees, but represents the best parts of you… and you're life wouldn't be much without her.

GUY 2
Thus ends the lesson young Jedi.

(lights shift)

SCENE EIGHT
GARAGES

GUY 3
I'd been in Michigan for about two and a half years before I finally got invited to hang in another man's garage. Ladies, you don't know what that means for a man to hear.

GUY 2
Hey, some guys are coming over to my garage Saturday to watch the Pistons' game. Wanna join us?

GUY 3
Sure.

GUY 2
You like basketball?

GUY 3
Yes, I lied. I didn't want to blow my big chance at this rite of passage. That Saturday, in near freezing temperatures, we ambled out to his freestanding garage, threw some logs in a wood-burning stove, tuned an old TV to the Pistons' game, and fired up the grill. There were only three of us that night and between 8pm to 2am, we downed three large steaks and seven bottles of wine. I couldn't tell you if the Pistons won that night, but I can tell you, it was worth the hangover.

GUY 1
You know how every house has a junk drawer? Think of a garage as one big junk drawer for guys.

GUY 2
And it's up to each man to decide how that drawer should be organized.

GUY 3
I know ladies will say we have a room of our own somewhere in the house, but let's be honest… we don't, and we should stop that lie now.

GUY 1
The garage is our room.

GUY 2
And we love it because it's full of promise…

GUY 3
Full of dirt and grass clippings…

GUY 1
Solitude…

GUY 2
The smell of oil and gas…

GUY 3
And treasures in the way of tools collected or handed down…

GUY 1
Space for projects built…

GUY 2
Things fixed and tinkered with…

GUY 3
It's like a big wooden or metal or aluminum or vinyl sided wooby that protects our first love.

GUY 1
1965 Dodge Dart, three on the tree, bought it for a hundred bucks, sold it six months later for a hundred bucks.

GUY 2
My first car. A Buick Century that you had to climb through the windows like The Dukes of Hazzard.

GUY 3
A '62 VW, that was a hand-me-down from my brother when he went to college. In winter you had to use a credit card to scrape the frost from inside the window while you were driving.

GUY 2
Ever have one of these mechanical

marvels? The kind of car you had to park on a hill, let it roll down and "catch" it in gear to start the thing?

GUY 3
I had one like that, but no hill 'cause I lived in Nebraska, you had to push it, jump in and start it. Once after some friends had pushed my car for probably a quarter mile without it even starting, someone noticed I had forgotten to turn the ignition.. *(pause)* They stole my pants.

GUY 1
Had a blue '88 Ford Ranger. She was a great little truck I named Midnight. She allowed me to drive her 13 times across the country. She got to see Big Sur in California, the Grand Canyon, the lights of Vegas, and the Hoover Dam. She saw the sunrise in Key West and the sunset in San Francisco. She had a soul and she loved it when I talked to her. Her life ended quickly when a Chevy Astro smashed into her and she was declared a total. I said goodbye and actually shed a tear. To this day, I hate Chevys.

GUY 2
I had a little red, low to the ground TR7 and when he finally gave up the ghost after 250 thousand miles, the mechanics came out…it was like a scene from a doctor show, they came out and told me there was nothing they could do and at this point, it was best if I let him go. I donated him for parts to a Homeless Shelter but really what I wanted to do was take him out into a field or woods someplace and light him on fire. Give him a Viking send off. That just seemed right to me.

(Lights shift)

SCENE NINE
DREAMS DEFERRED

(GUY 2 sits by himself on stage. GUY 1 enters)

GUY 2
So…?

GUY 1
So what?

GUY 2
Come on, what did they ask you?

GUY 1
What do you think? They asked me what I was qualified to do.

GUY 2
And…?

GUY 1
And what? I said I'm qualified to work. That's what I told them. What do you think I told them? And then they asked about training and again I said… I'm trained to work. I'm trained to be an injection molder and have been for the last twenty odd years.

GUY 2
What about education… did they ask about that?

GUY 1
Again yes, and again, I'm educated in the field of injection molding.

GUY 2
Did they ask about degrees?

GUY 1
Yes, I told them I have two actually. All paid for, one in Elementary Education and one in Business, both from U of M. And they each have my daughters' names on them. Any more questions, Dr. Nosey?

GUY 2
No. She was nice though, huh? The woman trying to help us?

GUY 1
Yes, she was nice. I mean, don't get me wrong, I know she's trying to help us but what I was trying to explain is that I'm not looking for the perfect fit… I'd love to do what I know, what I'm good at, but what I'm really looking for is anything. Anything, get it? I'll do anything. I just need the work.

GUY 2
I hear that. You religious?

GUY 1
Sunday school boy from way back. Still am. You?

GUY 2
Like to think so. Was reformed Catholic but now I find I'm Catholic again.

GUY 1
Why do you ask? You turning this into a prayer meeting or something?

GUY 2
No, I do enough of that on my own. No, I'm only asking because it seems to me that we're paying for making greed our god.

GUY 1
You're quite a philosopher, aren't you?

GUY 2
You looking to hire one?

GUY 1
If you'll work for free, sure.

(GUY 3 enters)

GUY 2
There's our fearless leader.

GUY 3
Hello children.

GUY 1
So, anything for middle management and the skills that it requires?

GUY 3
Not today, but the assessment was fun.

GUY 1
Seriously?

GUY 3
Oh yeah. It's great to find out that if I were just ten years younger and not so educated… that's what they put down, "Overqualified", I just might have a shot at a job that doesn't even exist right now.

GUY 1
See, I got "Needs more" …education.

GUY 2
I got, "Does not apply." That would make my high-school consolers smile. That's all they ever preached… "You just don't apply yourself."

GUY 3
Never in my life have I ever been overqualified… for anything. Ask my wife. Seriously, I'll call her right now. You can ask her yourself. *(pause)* How did it get to this?

GUY 2
How indeed.

GUY 3
And this lady asks, after all the assessment, and data on my work history and experience and on and on and on…she's asks, what, if I could do it all over again, what would I want to do? What would I want to be…?

GUY 1
What'd you tell her?

GUY 3
Cowboy.

GUY 2
Right... You did not.

GUY 3
Oh, I most certainly did. What? Is she going to put on my permanent chart... "Does not take it seriously?"

GUY 1
You said cowboy?

GUY 3
Why not? She asked and I answered.

GUY 1
And she responded, how?

GUY 3
She wrote it down. It's now on my unemployment and re-training application form.

GUY 1
Why not put rock star down as well.

GUY 3
Don't want to be a rock star, I wanna be a cowboy. Yee-Haw. Always did. Ever since I was a kid and my old man and I kicked Grandma and Lawrence Welk off the TV and started watching Bonanza instead.

GUY 2
Well wait a second. I didn't know we could put down what we really wanted to be.

GUY 1
And what do you really want to be?

GUY 2
I don't know.

GUY 3
Sure you do. Go back, before mortgages and two car payments and cable and student loans that it takes you until your own kid is ten before you pay off.... go back there and what did you want to be...?

GUY 2
A priest.

GUY 1
You missed a good sermon earlier.

GUY 2
Did the alter boy thing, poured wine, took care of the Host. All of it. I loved it.

GUY 3
What happened?

GUY 2
Around 11 or so, I discovered that girls were more than just "pests".

ANNOUNCER
#60. #60

GUY 1
Scuba diver. I wanted to own my own dive shop.

GUY 3
Seriously?

GUY 1
Yeah. Me and water. I couldn't get enough of it. But you know...I just didn't allow myself to take it seriously. And my dad was brought up to believe that if work was "fun", it wasn't work.

GUY 3
You should go back in and have her put it down now.

GUY 1
Maybe I will.

GUY 3
First time I ever looked at a Playboy I thought, how do you get Hugh Hefner's job? That's an occupation I wanted.

GUY 1
Lion Tamer.

GUY 2
Mountain Climber.

GUY 3
Professional Bowler.

GUY 1
Professional Golfer.

GUY 2
Robin Hood.

GUY 3
Batman.

GUY 1
Superman.

GUY 2
Spiderman.

GUY 3
The Invisible Man.

(Nice long pause)

GUY 1
Well, you got that wish. I could always go back to my original, original dream job.

GUY 2
Which was?

GUY 1
Pumping gas. Seriously. I always loved the smell of petroleum.

GUY 2
Well there's seeing the bright side. Better do it quick though.

GUY 1
Why's that?

GUY 2
Two words… electric cars.

ANNOUNCER
#1,2,3,4

(lights shift)

SCENE TEN
VACATIONS, & THEIR DANGERS

GUY 1
When I was a kid, my folks bought this conversion van. It had this bubble top and a place for luggage and comic books, a couple of little windows, and if you were willing to sacrifice your body, you could crawl into it and pretend you were a pilot, flying really low over the ground. Muffled sounds from my parents and sisters made it sound like radio chatter. And it was my dad's idea that he was going to give his kids the gift of hitting every single state in the lower forty-eight. We were lead to believe Alaska and Hawaii didn't exist. So for about three summers in a row, we'd pack up the van with three kids, two parents, a grandma in summer, endless boxes of mac and cheese and we were off. And you know what…? We did it. Every state. Some of them we'd literally just back into and be on our way but my dad figured we weren't missing that much anyway. Sorry Vermont. Now that I'm older, with a kid of my own… I know what it means to give up the only two weeks you got all year long and spend them on your kids. Well done, Dad. Well done.

GUY 2
I got one. In the summers when I was young, we'd drive all the way

to Creston, Iowa to visit my grandmother. My only living grandparent. My dad would drive non stop, straight through. I was very young and needed to stop, which would just infuriate him so, he finally cut a hole in the floorboard so I could take a leak, through a hole, while he kept driving. Well done, Dad. Well done.

GUY 3
Anybody ever shot out the back window of a station wagon with a bb gun…? While the car was moving…? I still remember the way the pattern of the glass, in slow motion of course, just fell to the floor of the car. Maybe it was the Daniel Boone coonskin cap I got at Disney that trip and wore every waking second. Maybe it was because my dad and my Uncle Eddie, the Lewis and Clark of the Bible belt, had both checked the BB gun was empty and shooting nothing but air. Maybe it was because, after the initial shock, our two station wagons just screamed with laughter and even though we lost half a day in the Red Woods trying to find an auto repair shop to fix it… my dad laughed as well, until he cried. My dad laughed and I loved him for that.

GUY 1
My old man, would have this running commentary going wherever we went. Stuckey's, See Rock City, 130 miles to Flagstaff, Shell Station 1 mile, Check your gauge. I'm not sure if he just found his own voice comforting or if he knew it was driving us crazy and… now I do it. Thanks, Dad.

GUY 2
My dad would honk the horn every state line.

GUY 3
My dad would salute cops on the road and then give them a raspberry as we'd pass.

GUY 1
My dad's rule was the driver controlled the heat, radio, windows, everything. But the rule only applied when my dad was the driver.

(light shift)

SCENE ELEVEN
JACK'S SANDBOX, Pt. 2

(Lights up, JACK & PETER are digging or clearing plants in an attempt to find the sandbox)

PETER
You sure this is where it is?

JACK
Where it is. And yes.

PETER
I'm just sayin'.

JACK
What? What are you saying?

PETER
I've been clear-cutting around here. Know what I found? Weeds. And grass. And one time, a carburetor.

JACK
Wonderful. People were ripping apart cars on my childhood memories.

PETER
You and your dad never did that? I mean, the garage is right over there. This is a good spot for…

JACK
Living out a white-trash stereotype?

(Beat)

PETER
For restoring old cars.

(Beat)

JACK
I'm sorry about that.

(PETER digs in silence)

JACK
So you... you work on cars?

PETER
Yeah, when I'm not eating pig-knuckles or makin' moonshine in my still.

JACK
OK, OK. I was out of line. I get it.

PETER
You ever work on a car with your dad?

JACK
Ah... no.

PETER
Your loss. It's a hell of a thing.

JACK
Yeah?

PETER
One time, my dad found this old Plymouth 2-door in some guy's barn. Thing was a total pile. Suspension was shot, the tires were rotted all to hell. I mean, you could barely call this thing a car anymore. We must've spent four months on it. Hell, it took us a month just to find the right tires.

JACK
You get it up and running?

PETER
Nah. Didn't matter. It was just something we did together. I'll tell you, I can still put together a motor blindfolded.

JACK
I don't... I suck at cars.

PETER
Everybody sucks at something.

JACK
What about your dad?

(PETER stares at him, confused)

JACK
What did he suck at?

(PETER just stares)

JACK
I'm just curious.

(Beat)

PETER
I don't know. He... um... I don't think he could cook. At least, I don't remember him ever cooking.

JACK
My dad could do anything.

PETER
You think so?

JACK
That's how I remember him.

(They work for a bit. PETER smiles, remembering his own father)

PETER
You know what the thing about dads is? You never really know them. There's this part of them that just... theirs.

JACK
There's something he always holds back.

PETER
Yeah. I guess so.

JACK
And it's not necessarily something bad. Or good. It's just something you'll never know about.

(PETER sits down, tired)

JACK
You ok?

PETER
Yeah. Just gimme a minute.

(JACK stops working too, though he is less tired than PETER)

PETER
You could still keep going, couldn't you?

JACK
I'm a man on a mission,

PETER
If I told you the sandbox was over there, would you clear out the rest of the backyard for me?

(JACK laughs a little)

PETER
You have a house of your own?

JACK
Not yet.

PETER
Lemme tell you something. Something people don't tell you but they should. Homeownership is a ball buster. It's non-stop mowing and cleaning and worrying about every little thing. Are the pipes working right? Why is that board creaking when it didn't used to creak? God! I'm half-thinking about getting married again just so I don't have to do all this by myself anymore.

JACK
Then why did you buy it?

PETER
'Cause that's what a man does, right? He has a job, he buys a house, then someday, he has kids who get jobs and buy houses.

(PETER stands up. JACK just stares at him. PETER notices)

PETER
Kid?

JACK
Yeah?

PETER
Why are you staring at my ass?

JACK
You... you've got sand on your ass.

PETER
Um... yeah. I was sitting on the ground.

JACK
No. You don't have dirt on your ass. You have sand. On your ass.

(PETER cleans himself off, looking around. JACK immediately starts to clear away the area PETER is on)

JACK
Come on... come on, come on, come on...

(PETER helps him clear. Soon, they both back away)

PETER
I'll be damned.

(Lights fade)

SCENE TWELVE
MILITARY MEN

JOHN
My uncle Elliot.

TOBIN
My brother Tim.

SCOTT
My uncle Conrad.

ALL
Was a military man.

SCOTT
His favorite piece of advice... never forget the mission.

JOHN
Loyalty up and down.

TOBIN
Never take yourself too seriously, but do take chances.

SCOTT
Learn from your mistakes.

JOHN
Total integrity.

TOBIN
Always tell the truth because it's the easiest thing to remember.

ALL
Walk the walk.

(Lights shift)

SCENE THIRTEEN
AIRPORT 2

ANNOUNCER
Passengers of Flight 128 to Detroit, you may exchange your tickets at Delta Airlines. Delta Flight 346 to Detroit is accepting Northwest passengers from Flight 128.

(GUY 1 hurriedly grabs his bags)

ANNOUNCER
Please hurry, as seating is limited.

(GUY 1 is about to bolt)

ANNOUNCER
And Delta Flight 346 is now full.

GUY 1
Come on!

GUY 2
That's impossible!

GUY 3
You just announced it like...

ANNOUNCER
I suppose you should've been faster on the draw.

GUY 1
"Faster on the...?" I'm moving as fast as I can here!

ANNOUNCER
Well, then I guess it's true what they say.

GUY 3
What?

ANNOUNCER
Oh, it's just this thing people say.

GUY 2
What? What do they say?

ANNOUNCER
That Midwesterners are slow because they're so used to going nowhere.

(Beat. GUY 2 looks around the airport)

GUY 2
Come on. No one else heard that?

GUY 1
Why don't you come down here and say that to our faces?

GUY 3
Yeah!

ANNOUNCER
Wait. Let me check. *(Beat)* No.

(GUY 3 sits down)

GUY 1
Don't worry. They can't keep us here forever.

GUY 3
Are you sure about that? *(leans back, exhausted)*

GUY 1
You OK, pal?

GUY 3
Yeah. I just… yeah. I want to go home.

GUY 2
Don't we all.

GUY 3
I'm not a big traveler. I miss the way it feels. The way home feels.

GUY 1
Yeah? How does it feel?

GUY 3
Free. Like I'm free.

(GUY 2's cellphone rings. It plays the Metallica cover of Turn The Page. He sees who it is, then lets it go to voice mail. He sees the guys looking at him)

GUY 2
Freaking work. The minute you tell 'em you can't be reached, that's when they call.

GUY 1
Wait, is that Turn the Page?

GUY 2
Oh, yeah.

(Beat)

GUY 1
Your ringtone for work is Turn the Page?

(Beat)

GUY 2
Maybe.

(Beat)

GUY 2
It's my kid. He's really into Metallica.

GUY 3
That's not a Metallica song.

GUY 2
Right. I know. Metallica covered it a few years ago, and…

GUY 1
That's a Bob Seger song.

GUY 2
I know. I know. Trust me. I know. I was walking by my kid's room a couple years ago, and I hear this song. I just kinda start singing along and he can't believe I know the words. And I'm like "Hey, that's an old song." And then it hit me.

GUY 1
You're old.

GUY 2
I'm old. 'Cause I still remember when that album came out. The Seger one, not the Metallica one.

GUY 3
Back in '72.

GUY 1
God, that was an awesome album.

GUY 2
Stealer, Rosalie…

GUY 3
Midnight Rider…

GUY 2
But the really messed up thing... I started listening to my kid's Metallica albums... and they don't suck.

(Beat)

GUY 3
So you like Metallica?

GUY 2
Well, mostly Seger, but....

GUY 3
It's not a big deal.

GUY 2
I just... You know, I tell you I dig Bob Seger, and in your mind, I'm this good old boy with a chopper and a mullet.

GUY 1
That's kinda extreme.

GUY 2
But I'm not like that. Not totally. Sure I have a motorcycle, but...

GUY 3
You have a motorcycle?

GUY 2
Uh... yeah.

GUY 3
My dad has a chopper.

GUY 2
Really?

GUY 3
Yeah, I mean, he did. He can't ride it now. But he used to be the most straight-laced guy, you know? A science teacher. Never late, real nose-to-the-grindstone. But on the weekends, he'd hop on his Harley and raise hell. Except it's not his Harley now. It's mine.

GUY 1
He gave you his Harley?

GUY 3
Sure. He can't really ride anymore, so ...yeah.

(GUY 3 laughs a little to himself)

GUY 3
I'll say this. Next time I gotta fly. I'm gonna take the tickets, wipe my butt with them, then hop on that Harley. Might take longer, but it sure beats dealing with this BS.

GUY 1
Amen to that.

GUY 2
Just out there on the open road. God, that's so awesome.

GUY 3
Amen to that.

GUY 1
Yeah.

GUY 2
Yeah.

(They sit in silence, lost in their own thoughts. Suddenly, GUY 3 starts to sing to himself)

ALL
Say, here I am, on the road again.
There I am, up on the stage.
Here I go, playing star again
There I go, turn the page.

(Lights fade)

END OF ACT I

ACT II
SCENE ONE

(Lights up. Three men are standing on stage, facing the audience. DET is from Detroit, and holds a Coney Dog. He wears a Redwings jacket. CHI is from Chicago, and holds a slice of deep dish Chicago style pizza. He wears a Cubs jacket. CIN is from Cincinnati, and holds a bowl of Cincinnati chili. He is wearing an Ohio State jacket. They speak to the audience)

ALL
What I hold in my hands is perfection.

DET
A Coney dog, straight from Lafayette's.

CHI
A slice of deep-dish Chicago-style pizza.

CIN
A piping hot bowl of Cincinnati Chili, hand-made by yours truly over the course of three hours. 'Cause when you love something, really love something, you gotta do it yourself.

DET
There is a basic misconception about Coney Dogs that I feel I gotta clear up, right here, right now. You hear the word "Coney" and what's the first thing you think of?

CIN
Weak-ass Michigan chili spread over some poor hot dog.

DET
You shut up.
The Coney, or Coney Island Hot Dog, is not entirely a New York invention.

CHI
Oh come on.

DET
Yes, they have Coney's in New York, but they're a totally different animal than the delicious thing you see before you. A New York Coney Dog is a spicy white frank, or "White Hot", traditionally served with nothin' on 'em.

CHI
Lord. Only in New York.

DET
What most people across this great country think of as a Coney Dog was created in the streets of Detroit.

CIN
Sure as hell tastes like it.

DET
I swear to god, shut your hole. A real Detroit Coney Dog is a beef-casing frank, covered in all-meat chili, diced Yellow onion-YELLOW- and mustard. There is a reason why across the country, when one thinks of Coney Dog, it is the Detroit Coney that comes to mind. Detroit-Not where the Coney was created. But where it was perfected.

CHI
Created in 1943 by Pizzeria Uno, the Chicago-Style deep dish is a masterpiece of form and function. It begins with a unique dough, made of olive oil and cornmeal. You bake it up in a pan, then lay down a nice layer of mozzarella. Then you put down a layer of meat on top of that. Thick-cut pepperoni, prosciutto ham, and of course Italian sausage. And if you want, you can throw in some vegetables, but no one will think less of ya if you don't. Then you put the sauce on top of all that.

CIN
Good god. You eat one slice, you can't crap for a week.

CHI
(To CIN) No one's talking to you. *(to DET)* You may notice that this slice is on a plate. Now most pizzas, you can eat a piece in one hand, no big deal. But a Chicago-Style Deep Dish is such a force of nature that you've gotta take a knife and fork to it. Just like God intended.

CIN
God has nothing to do with that thing.

DET
People actually come to Chicago to eat this?

CHI
Yes. Chicago is a culinary Mecca. It doesn't matter where you come from. None shall be turned away.

DET
Yeah, there's plenty of room. 'Cause everyone's trying to get the hell out!

CIN
OK, Ok. It's my turn.

CHI
Oh, that's rich, coming from a Hoosier.

CIN
The thing about Cincin...

DET
Hoosiers are from Indiana, you moron!

CIN
(trying to speak over them) THE THING ABOUT CIN...

CHI
You wanna talk morons? Why don't you tell me how Kwame made it to the cover of Newsweek?

DET
Oh, that's it.

(DET closes in on CHI. CIN intercedes)

CIN
Shut the hell up already! I am trying to talk here!

DET
You hear what he just said?

CIN
Hey, was Kwame on the cover of Newsweek, or wasn't he?

CIN
The thing about Cincinnati Chili is, it's maybe not as famous as the Coney Dog or gutbuster pizza. But that's not a reflection on its quality. No, Cincinnati Chili is a working man's food. It doesn't want the spotlight. It wants to be there waiting for you, after a hard day at work. Each bite says "Hey, I know things are tough sometimes, so I wanna make things a little easier for you."

CHI
(creeping up behind CIN) What the hell is this?

CIN
I'm telling you. It's Cincinnati Chili.

CHI
Is this spaghetti?

CIN
Yes.

DET
(Joining them) What?

CHI
Check this out. This guy puts his chili on spaghetti.

DET

Man, that's just wrong.

CIN
You guys have so much to learn.

DET
That doesn't look like chili.

CIN
Oh, but it is.

CHI
It's all runny.

CIN
(to the audeince) Cincinnati Chili is utterly unlike any other chili served anywhere in the U. S. of A. The enticing aroma you're smelling is a unique mix of ingredients. Along with Worcestershire and allspice, throw in cinnamon, chocolate, and cocoa to cut into the saltiness.

CIN
Once the sauce is ready, you ladle it over some freshly made pasta.

CHI
This is the dumbest thing I ever heard.

CIN
Can I finish? Please?

(DET & CHI relent. CIN is about to speak)

CHI
Seriously? Pasta?

(CIN glares at him)

CHI
I'm done.

CIN
Now chili and spaghetti…that's called Two Way Chili. It's your basic staple. You can add different things to the mix, going all the was up to Five-Way Chili. *(takes an appreciative bite from his bowl)* This is Five-Way Chili.

DET
I'm almost afraid to ask.

CIN
Atop this heavenly creation are oyster crackers, cheddar cheese, chopped onions, and kidney beans. Mix all together and… *(Much to CHI & DET's shock and horror, he takes another bite)*

CIN
Delicious.

CHI
How do you eat that and not fart blood?

CIN
Oh please. It's no worse than the phony Coney over there.

DET
What was that?

CHI
I don't know, man. I mean, a chili dog's a chili dog. But this… it smells like chocolate covered rubber.

DET
I'll tell you this right now. No self-respecting Michigander would ever put that… monstrosity on a hot dog. I don't care how many "ways" there are.

CIN
Detroit's loss.

CHI
Heh, they're kinda experts at losing.

CIN
Oh! Burn! I mean, what're the odds? Not a single win all season?

DET
Hey, you got no room to talk, Cincinnati-boy. You've got two teams!

Two! No basketball, no hockey...

CIN
Hey! We made it to the Superbowl! Twice!

CHI
And lost!

DET
In Detroit!

CIN
(to CHI) Don't you start. You're the ones who gave us Al Capone. And Oprah!

CHI
Yeah, well at least we don't take a dump on a plate of spaghetti and call it food. Seriously, I can't imagine anything worse than chili on spaghetti.

DET
I can.

CHI
Oh yeah? Like what?

DET
Sushi.

CHI
I'll give it to you. You're totally right.

CIN
Sushi... Lord help me...

DET
Right? Raw fish? I mean, isn't that one of the things that separates us from the animals? We cook our damn food!

CHI
My lady made me try some this one time. It was octopus.

CIN
Come on!

CHI
Hand to God. Octopus. And as if that weren't bad enough, she smeared it with this green, I don't know, paste? It was like draino in my nostrils!

DET
God, what is that stuff called....

CIN
Wasabi. It's made from these peas grown in the bowels of hell.

CHI
You got that right.

DET
I'm totally serious here. I would eat a whole deep dish pizza, followed by that chili, before I ever put sushi in my mouth.

CHI
Agreed.

CIN
Absolutely.

DET
Because this food here... it was grown in the Heartland. By proud Americans who came together to form a more perfect dinner. We have faced war, we have faced depression. We have known hardship and suffering. But we are held together by one simple fact: We are men of the Heartland, and this is our food. It may be different in form and substance, but we are proud of our differences. They make us strong. For we live in a part of America that knows all four seasons, that sees our beloved land change from snow to sunshine and back again. We are made stronger by these changes and by this food.

CIN
Thank you

DET
No. Thank you.

(CIN notices DET eyeing his chili)

CIN
You want some?

DET
I gotta admit, I'm curious.

CHI
Whoa. You sure about that?

DET
Hand it over.

CIN
This will put hair on your chest.

DET
Mama didn't raise a coward. Hand it over.

(CIN hands the chili to him. DET stares at it for a moment, then takes the fork)

DET
Walk with me, Jesus.

(He takes a bite of the chili, chews it, and swallows. He is silent as CIN & CHI wait for him to react. He smiles a weak smile)

DET
Yeah. Yeah. Not bad. Yeah.

(He doubles over coughing)

DET
Oh god! Help me. It got in my nose.

(CHI & CIN go to him, patting him on the back. They start to laugh a little)

CIN
Yeah, it's an acquired taste. You guys are alright.

(Lights shift)

SCENE TWO
ADVICE FROM AND THEN TO...

GUY 1
Advice from my dad... be yourself, be honest, and be kind.

GUY 2
From my dad... Little kids, little problems.

GUY 3
From my mom.... Choose your battles.

GUY 1
My dad... follow your bliss.

GUY 2
From my mom... make it about her.

GUY 3
My dad.... nobody has ever really succeeded without failing first.

GUY 1
My dad... lead by example.

GUY 2
From my mom... best advice ever... The bridges you cross before you get to them, are over rivers that aren't even there.

GUY 3
Now, advice to my kids...

GUY 1
Be yourself, be honest, and be kind.

GUY 2
Little kids, little problems.

GUY 3
Choose your battles.

GUY 1
Follow your bliss.

GUY 2
Make it about her.

GUY 3
Nobody has ever really succeeded without failing first.

GUY 1
Lead by example.

GUY 2
The bridges you cross before you get to them, are over rivers that aren't even there.

GUY 2
Study nature. Love nature. Stay close to nature. It will never fail you. Frank Lloyd Wright. Richland County, WI.

GUY 3
The best thing about animals is that they don't talk much. Thornton Wilder. Madison WI.

(Lights shift)

SCENE THREE
FISHING SHOW

GUY 2
Anything else on?

Guy 1
You don't like fishing shows?

GUY 2
What's the expression... watching paint dry.

GUY 1
There you go, knock yourself out.

GUY 2
Thanks. Unless... were you watching this?

GUY 1
No. It's alright. They just ran the segment on wide-mouth bass. That's the one I was interested in.

GUY 2
Cool. Thanks. *(before he can change the channel, he sees a huge Marlin flying out of the water)* Whoa. What is that?

GUY 1
Marlin. That's deep-sea fishing.

GUY 2
Like the baseball team? *(GUY 1 nods)* Cool. You ever do that?

GUY 1
Tried it once. Didn't like it.

GUY 2
Seriously, see that's the kind of fishing I could get into. Out on the big powerboat, filled with buddies and beer. Yanking in one of those things... those Marlins. That would be great. So, what didn't you like about it?

GUY 1
The powerboat, the buddies, the beer.

GUY 2
Okay.

GUY 1
For me, it's always been about the relaxation of the thing. The quiet conversation with nature or yourself. See, when my mom taught me to fish, she taught me to enjoy the simplicity of it.

GUY 2
Your mom?

GUY 1
Yeah.

GUY 2
Your mom taught you to fish?

(GUY 3 enters as MOM with a basket of laundry. GUY 1 becomes a seven year old)

MOM
What do you look so sad for? *(no response)* Hey...? You don't answer your mother anymore?

GUY 1
Yes ma'am.

MOM
(Starting to fold laundry) Something happen at school today? After school? On the way home?

GUY 1
We were playing ball. I mean, pretending to pitch, seeing how far we could throw rocks.

MOM
Am I not going to like this story? Does this involve a rock going through anything breakable?

GUY 1
Nothing got broke.

MOM
Carry on then, but give me a hand here. *(She dumps the rest of the clothes and they fold them together)*

GUY 1
Timmy Cheeves threw his pitch a lot farther than mine. A lot. And he said it was because I didn't have a dad to teach me how to throw, and all the stuff I should know. I was probably never going to learn, and so I threw another rock and he threw another rock and he still beat me.

MOM
Isn't Timmy about a foot taller than you?

GUY 1
Maybe.

MOM
And wasn't he held back a grade?

GUY 1
So?

MOM
Nothing. It's just interesting. But listen, I'm sure by this weekend when you and tall, held back, intellectually slow Timmy and the rest of the squad are out playing ball, you'll strike him out and that'll show him. You, my young lad, are a great pitcher. You have a rocket for an arm.

GUY 1
Nobody's around this weekend. They're all on a fishing trip. Dads only.

MOM
Oh, I see. Well, we should put on our magic thinking caps and figure out what we're going to do this weekend then. *(Takes a pair of little underwear from the laundry basket and puts them on her head)*

GUY 1
My underwear mom, is not magic.

MOM
Well let's just see. *(MOM takes it off and examines the underwear)* Hmm. It's clean and there are no skid marks...in my book, that's magic. *(She puts them back on her head. GUY 1 smiles)* Oh, a smile. The magic must be working already. Here, you better put one on too and let's see what we can come up with.

(GUY 1 puts a pair on his head. MOM exits with a basket. GUY 1 takes off his magic hat. Back into the scene)

GUY 2
So, your mom knew how to fish?

GUY 1
She did. And from then on, every weekend that she could get off work,

we were out doing guy stuff.

(MOM enters, throws a sleeping bag to GUY 1)

GUY 1
What's this?

MOM
This, my dear is gear. And I only have one question… are you rough and tough and ready to bluff?

GUY 1
You bet. Where we going?

MOM
Where ever the trail takes us. *(exits)*

GUY 1
My pals could not believe that my mom took me camping. We built kites and entered them into a competition, soapbox derby's, she taught me how to clean a shotgun, lead a rabbit… I never knew it before, but my mom was like the petite Grizzly Adams of Southern Ohio.

(MOM enters covered in camouflage. She sits under the grass and weed blanket. GUY 1 joins her and they hide themselves onstage)

MOM
Now when it comes to blinds, and after you've found your field, concealment is the main focus. Geese aren't the brightest bulbs, kind of like Timmy, but they do get educated by the end of the season. So, Shake it up a bit. Late November, dig a shallow pit and get your blind lower. Save some of your best calls for later in the season too. That's when you can team up with someone who's worthy of your hunting time. *(She takes out a short reed goose call)* Ready?

GUY 1
Ready.

GUY 1
She could make a moose call out of a blade of grass, could predict the weather by what the leaves on the trees were doing. This was my mom.

GUY 2
I'm not buying any of this.

GUY 1
I'm not selling it. It's just fact.

GUY 2
No. No, see my mom would scream when she saw a spider.

GUY 1
Oh, mine too. She couldn't stand them. *(MOM scream as she runs across the stage)* Mom! It's just a bug, The woman could field dress a deer but was scared to death of spiders.

MOM
They have fangs and they're going to kill me.

GUY 1
They're not going to kill you mom. She loved nature and anything outdoors. But most of all, she loved fishing, Loved the simplicity of it. A string, a hook, and a worm. It was an even playing field and everybody had a chance and you know what? If they weren't biting, they weren't biting. And if they weren't biting… you might as well enjoy the stillness and the company.

MOM
(entering) Today… on this boat and in front of the ancient fishing gods of old, I declare that my son and I will catch a whopper of a wide-mouth bass. And this bass will bring us fame and fortune and when our faces are on

the cover of Time and People magazine...we vow on this sacred water to never forget the little people, the Timmy Cheevers' of the world. So let it be spoken, so let it be done. Worm please...

(They bait imaginary hooks and then cast)

GUY 1
Certain transitions that you don't know are transitions until way after the fact, happen in that wonderful stillness of those you love *(as a boy again...he looks at his mom)* Are we being quiet for the fish or just being quiet...?

MOM
What would you say if I invited a gentleman from work, over to have dinner with us some night, Think that would be alright?

(Pause)

GUY 1
Is he a nice man?

MOM
He's a very nice man.

(Pause)

GUY 1
Does he like kids?

MOM
With salt and pepper and the right BBQ sauce he does. *(Pause)* He does and he would very much like to meet you. But only if that's okay with you.

GUY 1
Do you want me to meet him?

MOM
Yeah. You know what, I do. *(exits)*

GUY 1
From then on, my mom was happy in a different way. A way that I didn't really understand until fate tapped me on the shoulder and said, "Here, let me introduce you to the love of your life." What'd they say Dad?

(GUY 3 enters, this time as GUY 1's older father)

GUY 3
They're telling me insurance is only going to take care of half, if I go with the surgery. And none of these office visits. Crooks.

GUY 1
Yeah, they are dad. You ready?

GUY 3
Just got to get the prescription down stairs.

GUY 1
Lets get there then.

(GUY 3 looks up and sees the TV)

GUY 3
This is a good show. Your mom loved to fish. Did you know that?

GUY 1
Yeah. I vaguely remember.

GUY 3
She loved it. Alright, let's go and I'll treat you to ice cream.

GUY 1
Deal.

(They exit. Lights shift)

SCENE FOUR
MAMALOGUE

SON

I hear these guys talking about "life on the farm" and I'm like... the hell? I mean, the country's nice and all but, gimme the city. I was born and raised in Detroit, and I wouldn't have wanted it any other way.

There were five of us living in a two-bedroom apartment. Me, my three sisters, and my mama. I know that sounds bad, but it wasn't at all. My dad left when I was thirteen. That was hard, and I'm not gonna pretend that it wasn't. You know how we got through it? Because we were living in a community. We came home, and my mama was at work. So Mrs. Davis took care of us. If Mrs. Davis was working, then Miss Neely took care of us. And if she wasn't around, then Mrs. Warshowski took care of us. And Mama took care of their kids too. It was like those Indian Tribes you hear about, where the children are raised by the whole tribe. And I'll tell you, I'm a better man because of it.

Now... I would've been seventeen... I got a letter. From Stanford University. I'd been accepted into their Journalism program. Mama was thrilled. And I was heartbroken. She saw the look on my face and lit into me. "What right do you have being sad? Do you know how many kids out there would kill to be in your position?" I told her that it didn't matter. There was no way I could afford to go. She sat me down and... Lemme tell you. It's hard to get anything through to a seventeen year old. But she said "Baby, there's a lot of people who will tell you that the world's out to get you. Don't you listen to them, not for a second? 'Cause it's real easy to talk yourself out of something good. But you're smarter than that. You know it. I know it. And Stanford University knows it. "

Yes, I went to Stanford. Yes, I've made a life for myself that I'm proud of. But that's not the point. The point is, there isn't a kid in my neighborhood who doesn't have a story just like that about mama.

Today is her 70th birthday. She has no idea what's coming. I've spent the last three weeks tracking down every kid my mama helped raise. Pictures, stories, their kids, their grandkids...Miss Neely has lined the street lamps with balloons. And when Mama comes home from the DMV, she's gonna see the faces of her many, many many children. She'll cry. I'll cry. There will be crying. And laughing. And bunt cake. And if she ever doubted it, Mama will know how much better the world is for having her in it.

I'm gonna introduce her to my boyfriend. And I'll tell you right now... you're never too old to be a little scared of your mother.

(Lights shift)

SCENE FIVE
FATHER'S & SONS

(The guys all put on Native American Headdresses and sit in a circle)

GUY 3
Howling Wolf... how goes job at car making plant?

GUY 1
Day at time right now, and the days seem to be getting shorter.

GUY 3
And you, Spotted Bear, how goes cubicle job?

GUY 2
Out of the seven floors in that building, we're down to two. Two floors. What about you?

GUY 3
Job suck'em. Suck'em bad. Wampum harder to come by, but as Great Father Spirit in sky say...

GUY 1
Will you knock it off please?

GUY 2
Seriously. Just use our regular names and skip the stereotype.

GUY 3
At least your kids gave you guy's cool Indian names. I got Soaring Penguin...? That doesn't even make sense.

GUY 1
I don't know but you need to let it go. *(Looking off)* Yo Will? William? Stay away from the fire. Do not throw that in. You hear me?

GUY 2
(Looking off too) Joey! You get back too! Get back from the fire. *(Back to the guys)* That kid's not going to be happy until he loses a limb.

GUY 3
I know. It's amazing...*(He stops, stands, and looks off)* Dion, you make me stand up again...! *(Satisfied, he sits back down)* It's amazing any of us are alive today. When I think about some of the crazy, stupid crap I did when I was his age.

GUY 1
Tell me about it. The first time I got my drivers license, I mean, like within a week, we're up-north and we're doing the back roads and it's like 11 at night, my family and a few other families are up for a couple of weeks for the summer, and I remember chasing each other in these two cars and Craig Ross, this kid I knew back then, he's in the car behind me, loaded with other kids and I'm in front and I'm loaded with kids and we're blasting down these country roads going close to a hundred. I'm not kidding. I look down at the needle and we're just touching it. And I'm so focused on making these turns right, that when I look into the rearview mirror, I don't see his headlights anymore. I'm thinking I won. Craig gave up. But then the guys in the back seat start cracking up and screaming and laughing their asses off and I look back again and this time, I can make out Craig and his buddies by their dashboard light. He was so close, going a hundred miles an hour, but so close that that's why I couldn't see his headlights. He's like, literally. Inches away from my car.

GUY 2
Ever shut off the lights and drive by moonlight?

GUY 3
Ever bumper ski in the winter?

GUY 1
Ever climb into somebody else's car while it's moving?

GUY 2
When I was a kid, we had a swimming pool and my brother and I would climb up onto the garage roof, get a running start and then leap off the roof, clear the cement, and make it into the pool.

GUY 3
M 80's down a toilet?

GUY 1
Did it.

GUY 2
Did it.

GUY 3
Egg cars?

GUY 1
Did it.

GUY 2
Did it until mine got egged. Makes a difference when you're paying for it, right?

GUY 3
You got that right. *(They all look off)* What is it with kids and fire? Dion! Hey! *(Back to the guys)* You ever take a can of aerosol and a lighter and make a flamethrower out of it?

GUY 1
Seriously?

GUY 2
Yeah. It's pretty cool.

GUY 3
I used to take my green army men, set 'em up on the battlefield and then just torch the hell out of 'em in the heat of battle. My mom would get so mad trying to figure out where all her hairspray was going. Used to take it out on my sister. It was great.

GUY 2
See, I was number one and I couldn't get away with anything.

GUY 1
I was the baby. I got away with everything.

GUY 3
I was number three out of four and they pretty much left me alone. If there was punishment, it was usually because one of my sisters would narc on me. I still remember getting spanked because she told them I was looking at naked natives in National Geographic. I mean, why did we even have it in the house if we're not going to look at it.

GUY 2
My old man boy, used to take it to me. A lot. *(Looking out)* That kid, I swear. Joey, you did not just put that in your mouth did you? Spit it out. I don't care if you cooked it...spit it out. *(To the guys)* You guys hit your kids? I don't mean hit, you know what I mean?

GUY 3
I'll give mine a smack on the bottom if he needs it.

GUY 1
Yeah, me too. Your kid, not mine, I mean. No, I will sometimes. They gotta learn.

GUY 2
No, I agree with that. I just don't

agree that a swat on the butt's the way to do it. That was one of the things I did learn from my dad... how to go too far.

GUY 3
Yeah, it's tough. There's no manual you know. "How to do your job as a dad."

GUY 1
There should be.

GUY 2
It's weird. I got a brother-in-law out east. The guy's a tool. He really is. Anyway, he and my sister have a kid and the kid's giving them trouble and don't get me wrong, the kid's a handful, but their solution is to ship him off to this prep school until he's twenty something and then they'll want him back. It's just wrong. I got a kid that age too. He's in high school now and it's like Satan moved in. And there are days when you just hate to go home. But you know what...? You do it anyway. You show up and you fight the fight because it's your job. And I have no patience for guys that won't do their jobs. And don't get me wrong, I'm mad at my sister too. She knows better that this.

GUY 3
Half the job is just holding on until that brain stem connects and they come back semi-normal.

GUY 1
I got one like that at home. My wife's kid from before. No, I don't mean to qualify it like that...he is my kid. Has been since he was four. But now... his name's Danny. Used to be.

GUY 2
What do you mean used to be?

GUY 3
What is it now?

GUY 1
Creepy D.

GUY 2
Creepy...?

GUY 1
D. Yeah, that's what he prefers now. Wears black constantly, even the nail polish, barricades himself in his room until after midnight and I swear, if I died today, fell off the face of the earth... he wouldn't care. Might not even notice.

GUY 3
That's not true.

GUY 2
All kids feel that way about their old man at some point. I know I did. It's his time. He's trying to find his tribe and you're supposed to be the bad guy. That's the way it works.

GUY 3
I don't know. I mean with my old man, I didn't worship the guy but I did respect him. I can remember every time I did something he was even remotely proud of. And it meant something to me that it meant something to him.

(Pause)

GUY 2
I'm sure Creepy loves you.

GUY 1
You know what it comes down to really...? What I really miss? Being his hero. It was like when he turned ten... it was his buddies he wanted

to be around. I miss my boy. *(They all look out)* Will! Yo pal.

GUY 2
Joey!

Guy 3
Dion!

GUYS 1,2,3
You guys ready for smores?

(Lights shift)

SCENE SIX
FATHER'S & DAUGHTERS

TOBIN
Many a man wishes he were strong enough to tear a telephone book in half-especially if he has a teenage daughter- Guy Lombardo. Or was it Vince Lombardi?

SCOTT
There was a snake in our basement once, I screamed bloody murder, and my daughter ran down the stairs, picked it up under its head, and said "Dad, you scream like a girl."

JOHN
God help me when my baby starts dating. And God help the poor kid she walks through the door. *(He mimes cocking a shotgun)*

TOBIN
When my daughter cries, I'll do everything short of buying a car to get her to stop. The problem is... I think she's starting to figure that out.

SCOTT
My 11 year old has decided she's... developing. She runs into the room, shouting, "Daddy! You wanna see?! You wanna...!?" I shouted "NO!" before she could finish the sentence.

JOHN
Patricia and I see eye to eye on... just about nothing. Politics, sports, food... nothing. We have the kind of fights you could sell tickets to. She just... she doesn't understand me. At all. Except for one thing. She knows that whatever she is, whatever she does, I'm right there next to her, and I'm proud as hell.

(Lights shift)

SCENE SEVEN
JACK'S SANDBOX Pt 3

(A while later, JACK & PETER are dirty but laughing)

PETER
I thought you were nuts.

JACK
I told you it was here.

PETER
No, I told you it was there.

JACK
What?

PETER
I said it was maybe buried underneath all that crap.

JACK
Yeah, but I was the one who said it was there. As in over there.

PETER
You got a hell of a memory, kid. I'll give you that.

JACK
Thank you. For letting me dig.

PETER
Ah, hell. I needed to get that area cleared out anyway. You wanna beer?

JACK
Nah, I gotta drive.

PETER
Well, I'm getting beer.

(PETER walks off. When he's gone, JACK pulls a small action figure out of his pocket. It's dirty, and missing a head. He just stare at it for a while, then begins to clean it off. Soon, PETER returns)

PETER
What'che got there?

JACK
This?

PETER
Yeah, that.

JACK
It's a GI Joe guy. I found it under the sand.

PETER
For real?

JACK
Yeah.

PETER
One of yours?

JACK
Yeah.

PETER
Jeez. What're the odds?

JACK
I know right? I can still... I was playing with my brother, in the sandbox. It was like a desert, and Cobra... Cobra was the bad guy in GI Joe...

PETER
OK.

JACK
Cobra set a trap. And this guy here, he was marching through the desert, and a boulder fell on him.

PETER
A boulder just fell on him? In the middle of the desert?

JACK
Yeah.

PETER
What the hell kind of army guy is he? There's all this empty desert, and he manages to find like the one boulder and get hit by it?

JACK
Well, it was a trap.

PETER
How the hell did he ever make it outta boot camp?

(Beat)

JACK
Yeah, he wasn't actually in the army. He's a toy.

PETER
I know. I'm just making a point.

JACK
So... he gets crushed. And his head just came right off.

PETER
You must've been pissed.

JACK
No, not really. Jon and I...Jon's my brother... we just started laughing. We didn't expect it to happen. I'm gonna have a baby. Well, not me. My wife.

PETER
Congratulations?

JACK
It wasn't... uh... planned. It just kinda happened.

PETER
Oh.

JACK
We found out two days ago. And it's like...look, we can do it. We wanted to have kids eventually. But...eventually, you know? And now it's just...

(Beat. JACK looks over his former home)

JACK
I think about this place, constantly. I was so happy here. YOU can't even imagine. I had a forest. And a sandbox. And we had animals here. It was just... idyllic. That's how I remember it.

PETER
You were ten. Things you remember then... that's not how they are. Look at this place.

JACK
I know. That's just it. I always thought that... if I was gonna have kids, I wanted to live in a place like this. In some farmhouse in some little town, in the middle of nowhere. Because then my kids would be happy, like I was. But I look at it now and... it still feels like home. And it really, really doesn't.

PETER
You sure you don't want a beer?

JACK
No, I'm good.

PETER
All right. *(realizes JACK is just staring at him)* Kid, I don't know what you want from me. I don't have any, like, homespun advice for you or anything. Things change, it's just what happens.

JACK
But... God! I'm gonna be a father! I need to give my kid something, to...

PETER
There isn't like a formula to being a dad, ok? You just gotta...be a dad. This place is a dump. How do you think I could afford it? You remember it better than that 'cause your family made you happy here. So just... wherever you live, make your kid happy there. Build him a sandbox.

(Beat)

JACK
I could build him a sandbox. *(He looks at the GI Joe toy)* Can I bury this?

PETER
Can you what now?

JACK
I want to bury him again. In the sandbox.

PETER
Why?

JACK
I want to leave something of mine here.

PETER
Jesus, haven't you left enough?

(JACK takes that in)

PETER
Why don't you take that home? Give it to your kid.

JACK
But it's broken.

PETER
It won't matter.

(JACK just stares at the toy)

PETER
Look, I gotta hit the head. You can stay out here if you want. Look around.

JACK
You sure?

PETER
Knock yourself out.

JACK
Thank you.

PETER
No problem. Just one thing.

JACK
OK.

PETER
If you find more stuff out there, take it with you.

JACK
OK.

(PETER heads back to the house. JACK just stares out at his old back yard, then heads out into it. Lights fade)

SCENE EIGHT
HEROES

GUY 2
My hero would be my kid. Don't get me wrong, he makes me crazy and of course I wish he'd get his act together and grow up and all the other things I'm supposed to say about my 22 year old musician. But deep down... I'm proud of what he's trying to do. And what he's trying to do is beat the system. It won't work...but I'm proud that he's trying. Living in his van with his dog, taking a month, maybe two, to drive down the California coastline and prolong his adolescence; trying to find a way to not be me. And I really mean that in a good way. He knows who I think he should be and now he's finding out who he thinks he should be... putting his upbringing to the test. But I do have faith in his upbringing. So, for now, I'll wait for the prodigal to return with stories of battles won and virtues lost. And yes... I am a little jealous.

(Lights shift)

SCENE NINE
FIRST KISS

(A TEENAGER sits down with a standardized test & a booklet. He is clearly distracted. Another ACTOR is onstage, occasionally speaking the teenager's thoughts)

TEENAGER
OK. OK. Focus up, Kevin. This is the S.A.T. Focus up. Focus up.

ACTOR 1
Boobies.

TEENAGER
No. No. Eyes on the prize. This test is the big one so just focus up.

ACTOR
I can't believe I kissed her.

TEENAGER
Shhh!

ACTOR
I kissed Lisa Spellman. Lisa Spellman kissed me.

TEENAGER
OK. Verbal section first. I can handle this. *(He reads)* Bird is to nest as A) Dog is to...

ACTOR
Boobies.

TEENAGER
Dammit! *(He realizes he said that out loud. He looks around at everyone in the room)* Sorry. Sorry. I'll just... very sorry. *(He goes back to the paper)*

ACTOR
I've known Lisa Spellman since 5th grade. She's been my friend longer than anybody. And now I know what her tongue feels like.

TEENAGER
B) Beaver is to dam.

ACTOR
We were just going to study. That's all. Her folks let us have the den.

TEENAGER
C) Cat is to... litter box?

ACTOR
It was such a flimsy excuse. I mean... I've liked her for... forever. God, she is hot!

TEENAGER
D) Book is to library.

ACTOR
We were watching the Simpsons, to unwind. We were laughing and she snarfed Pepsi out of her nose.

TEENAGER
Kevin. Stop reliving it and just focus up!

ACTOR
I wiped off her face and then... the look.

TEENAGER
It's A, right? It has to be A.

ACTOR
Her eyes stared to droop a little. Her head tilted like 23 degrees to the right.

TEENAGER
Stop thinking about her eyes

ACTOR
All of a sudden, six years of doubt and confusion vanished. I leaned in. And it happened. It really happened.

TEENAGER
It's gotta be beaver dam. That makes the most sense.

ACTOR
She tasted like Pepsi and lipgloss. I can still taste it.

TEENAGER
Bird is to nest and beaver is to beaver dam. That makes the most sense.

ACTOR
I wanted to touch her boobs so bad. But I didn't That was a good call. Yeah. Definitely. Yeah.

TEENAGER
OK. Next one. Cub is to bear as...
A) Puppy is to dog.

ACTOR
It was a good thing, and I didn't want to ruin a good thing. 'Cause everything's changed.

TEENAGER
B) Cat is to kitten.

ACTOR
She likes me. She totally likes me like I like her. Oh my God. Oh. My. God.

TEENAGER
C) Eagle is to predator.

ACTOR
Are we gonna be boyfriend and girlfriend? Is that what I want?

TEENAGER
D) Fork is to utensil.

ACTOR
What am I saying? That's totally what I want!

TEENAGER
E) Piano is to orchestra? What the hell?

ACTOR
I'm gonna ask her to homecoming. That's what I'm gonna do. And she'll say yes.

TEENAGER
Okay. OK. It's the puppy one or the cat one. Totally. 'Cause forks and pianos don't have babies.

ACTOR
But... there's a problem.

TEENAGER
Wait! No! No problem.

ACTOR
Can we still be friends? Or does this screw everything up?

TEENAGER
This screws nothing up. It's what I've wanted since...

ACTOR
Think about it. The big secret is out. She knows we're crazy about her. And yeah, she kissed us... but what does that say exactly?

TEENAGER
It says she's crazy about me too!

ACTOR
Not necessarily. Maybe she wanted to experiment. Maybe she did it 'cause Katy Donnell dared her to. Maybe she called Katy up as soon as you left and told her you were the worst kisser since Jabba the Hut!

TEENAGER
No! We were, like, in the zone! A make-out zone.

ACTOR
Maybe that's exactly what she wants you to think.

TEENAGER
No! No more maybes! *(He writes on the test)* Puppy is to dog. There.

ACTOR
She's got the power now. We have to accept that.

TEENAGER
Question 3. Tenet is to theologian as... wait, what?

ACTOR
Once a girl knows you're into her, it's aaaaaaalllllll over.

TEENAGER
What the hell is a theologian?

ACTOR
We've showed her all our cards. She's shown us... nothing.

TEENAGER
Please, I gotta get this question, OK?

ACTOR
Right. *(Beat)* A theologian studies religion.

TEENAGER
Right! Of course!

ACTOR
Just like we study every inch of Lisa Spellman's body.

TEENAGER
Dammit!

ACTOR
Let me tell you what happens next.

TEENAGER
A) Predecessor is to heir!
B) Hypothesis is a biologist!
C)...

ACTOR
She doesn't call. Because she doesn't have to.

TEENAGER
C) ARROGANCE IS TO PERSECUTION!

ACTOR
We'll sit at home, staring at our cellphone.

TEENAGER
D) Recluse is to rivalry.

ACTOR
It's not like she'll just call to catch up like we've done every day for two years.

TEENAGER
E) Guitarists is to.. is to...

ACTOR
Nope. We effed this up good buddy. We'll never kiss another woman again. Because we have tasted the forbidden fruit, the one thing man craves more than anything. Moths to a flame, man. The source of unbridled joy and ultimate destruction.

TEENAGER
Lisa Spellman.

ACTOR
Lisa Spellman.

TEENAGER
No, I mean... there she is.

ACTOR
What!?

TEENAGER
She got here late. She just walked in. She's sitting down...

ACTOR
Right in front of us.

TEENAGER
(whispering) Hey, Lisa.

ACTOR
OH MY GOD! Look at that!

TEENAGER
Am I seeing this?!

ACTOR
She smiled! She did that cute little hand-wavey thing!

TEEANGER
OH MY GOD!

ACTOR
Sweet salvation! Hallelujah!

TEENAGER
She likes me. It's all there. We're in

the zone.

ACTOR
Thank God that's over. Now we can get to work on this test.

TEENAGER
Forget the test.

ACTOR
Excuse me?

TEENAGER
I'm done stressing about everything. I'm just gonna answer what I think is right and just... not overthink it, you know.

ACTOR
I'm... not sure that's the best idea.

TEENAGER
Sure it is.

ACTOR
What if you don't know the answer?

TEENAGER
Oh, I know the answer. Kevin Wiley is to Lisa Spellman as... as... help me out here.

ACTOR
Sorry, I'm thinking about kissing her again.

TEENAGER
Yeah, that works too.

(Lights shift)

SCENE TEN
WIVES & OTHERS

GUY 3
One thing I wish my wife would understand about me... is my need to fix problems. It's what I do and if she presents me with a problem and explains the situation, I will put thought into the solution and present said solution. I know you just want to talk about it and I understand but you need to understand, I really want to try and fix it.

GUY 1
My wife doesn't understand my quest for adventure and a risk every once in a while.

GUY 2
I'd love my wife to realize that I don't cry because I can't It's not that I don't feel bad, it's just something I don't do and it's not because I'm blocking or hiding or whatever. Stuff just doesn't affect me that way.

GUY 3
Sometimes when I'm quiet, it actually mean I have nothing to say.

GUY 1
If I bring you flowers, it might mean I've done something stupid but it doesn't always mean that. Sometimes it just means I love you.

GUY 2
And if I don't tell you that enough, I'm sorry.

GUY 3
My wife doesn't understand why filling up the house with "stuff" drives me crazy. There is absolutely no space left. Please stop it!

GUY 1
The reason we laugh at farts is because they're funny.

GUY 2
They're free.

GUY 3
And we made them.

GUY 1
Oh yeah, your cat really does hate me.

GUY 2
They say such lovely things at funerals that it makes me sad I'm going to miss mine by a few days. Garrison Kieler, Anoka, MN.

(Lights shift)

SCENE ELEVEN
FUNERALS AND FINAL WORDS

GUY 1
It's strange sometimes when you see, maybe just notice, the continuum of life in the little things. Big things too of course, funerals, etc., but the little things that lead up to the big ones. Keys. I fly down to Florida to bring my folks back and I'm driving their RV, just a medium sized one, nothing too fancy, but we're on a four lane, going through some mountains right outside of Chattanooga, going about seventy and my dad had spotted me for a bit so I could eat. And I'm reaching back to take a plate of food from my mom when all of a sudden… boom. And I have no idea what we hit, all I know is my dad is starting to lose control of the thing at this point., so, I reach over and grab the wheel and now we're pulling off to the side of the freeway. Cars blasting past. And I realized we had just traded paint with a semi. Going seventy. Now we're off to the side and I'm telling my dad to put the RV in park. He's ready to climb out and see what's what but he's forgetting to put the thing in park and I'm thinking, oh yeah, there's absolutely no potential for disaster here. The truck driver's out of his cab, looking understandably pissed, mom and my wife are in the RV, looking worried and I get to the driver before my dad and start to explain that he just looked down for a second, reaching for something and pulled the wheel with him. I calm the guy down and he's fine. He's very cool about the whole thing. Damage was on our end. And I don't mean just the RV. My dad was so angry and embarrassed that he had actually, completely lost focus and hit this guy. So embarrassed that he made that kind of mistake. My wife, quietly, wants me to drive again at this point but I'm not going to do that to my dad. Not going to take away that from him. All I ask is, "you okay?" We've only got another half hour to go before we fill up anyway. And I'm telling him, "you know dad, we've go to focus and get rid of whatever's a distraction at this point." Sure, sure. And my dad's a proud man. That's one of the things I've never faulted him for and actually, always respected about him because in my opinion, he was justified in being proud. He'd been a strong guy all his life and he took care of his family and protected the ones he loved and he was kind to the ones who couldn't do the same. And now, he was one of these little old men behind the wheel that I would personally bitch about on my own

familiar freeway. So, the keys. We stop for gas and my wife is giving me the look like- please, you're not really going to let him drive anymore are you? And I'm thinking of what to do, even though I know what to do but...but my dad hands me the keys and asks, if I'm ready to take over? "Love to", I said. "That's why I'm here." And that little exchange stuck with me, in my mind, as we're driving down the road, getting my folks back to my childhood home...That's why I'm here...to take over for the man who's lost his strength. And as my dad was napping in the passenger seat, it was so clear in my mind's eye...so clear and I could see when I was sixteen and begging him for the car keys, or fifteen and begging for him to drive with me since I had my permit, or thirteen when he would sneak us out into a parking lot somewhere and was teaching me to drive so I'd already know and know it right, or six when I was sitting on his lap out in the country and he would let me steer and pretend I was doing it all on my own. And it was so clear now, that I needed to take the keys and keep them. The man is still my hero though.

GUY 3

My dad was not what you'd call a "church guy" but never said a word against it when mom would take me and insist that we went as a family. An entire family. And one of my favorite stories about my dad and his being in church involves confession. Apparently, the warm and sunny day turned dark and violent as a storm raged while my dad was in the confessional. Moments after he came out, the storm passed away and the sunny skies returned. Mom just looked at him and said "I don't want to know."

GUY 2

What to say huh? Okay, I'm 5, brother's 7. Sister's 8 , and it's just after Halloween. Dad calls the 3 of us into the kitchen..."I told you kids not to touch the 3 Musketeers bar and now it's gone. Which one of you ate it?" Silence. "Well, somebody did. It didn't just walk away, did it?" Silence. "Alright." He then proceeds to the drawer and takes out a paring knife. He turns the gas burner on the stove and starts moving the knife blade in and out of the flame. "In Mexico when prisoners are lying, the police will heat a knife and touch the tongues of the suspects. The ones telling the truth won't be burned because their tongues will be moist but the one lying will have a dry tongue and the knife will burn them, terribly. So, I'll ask you one more time...who ate the 3 Musketeers bar? Although I had absolutely no knowledge of the missing candy, I also had no knowledge of medicine or physics and so I burst into tears and admitted my crime. Many years later, my sister confessed. We will miss you, dad.

(Lights shift)

SCENE TWELVE
THE END

(All three guys are asleep at the airport. Late night, early morning. One of their cell phones starts to ring)

SCOTT
(Still asleep) Not it.

(SCOTT turns over and goes back to sleep. TOBIN mumbles something but is out again. JOHN, sits up, realizing it's his phone that's ringing)

JOHN
Yeah, what, hello? *(looking at the number to see who called, still waking up)* Hello?...Yeah, yes. Speaking... really...? No, that's fine. Gosh, what time is it?... Not at all, I'm just still stuck at the airport so I haven't made it home yet to check e-mail... No, I, absolutely will and uh, thanks. Thank you. Very much... As soon as I get home and thank you again. *(He closes his phone. Pause. He dials a number)* Did I wake you...? I know, I don't sleep well without you either...everybody okay? ...Okay, so here's the deal. They want me. They just offered me the job... Yeah, just called... Really early but they hadn't heard from me and wanted to give me first shot before they moved on to choice number two... Yeah. That's something huh?... I don't know... Yeah, no, the money's right. Not great, not what it was, but right... Forget all that. What do you think we should do? What so you want us to do?... I guess I'm thinking that too. I mean, I've been stuck here all night and all I want to do is get home. But that's what's sinking in, I don't want to leave our home... you sure? Did I mention I love you? Good, just wanted to clear that up. So, why don't you try and go back to sleep and I'll be in and then you can take me out to breakfast and we can figure out what's next?... Love you too. *(He hangs up)*

ANNOUNCER
May I ask you something?

JOHN
Whoa! Scared me. You shouldn't do that. That's heart attack stuff. What's your question...?

ANNOUNCER
Simple. Are you nuts? Are you crazy? Insane?

JOHN
Even though they're similar, that's technically three questions and judging by their nature, I guess I should assume you're "inferring" that I am.

ANNOUNCER
Why would you stay? You're giving up a great chance to actually flyover, Flyover Country. This is your way out.

JOHN
Okay, you know, here's the thing. Some folks, view the Mid-West as a little bit boring maybe. Not as cultured, not as trendy and willing to wear black all year long or substitute tofu for everything that even remotely tastes good. But here's what those folks don't understand... we really don't care what you think. Our job is not to impress you. We don't work so hard to be different, we just work hard.

It's not our purpose in life to be noticed... our purpose in life is to live. And do I have crappy season tickets for our losing football team? Yes, absolutely, but they're with my sons. And do I have an ugly, god awful pink paisley tie hanging in my closet? Yes, but it was made to match the pink paisley dress my daughter will be wearing next month to the daddy daughter dance at her school. So to me, it's a pretty beautiful fashion disaster. I hate road construction but put up with it because I love the change of seasons. I may complain about mayors in nearby big cities, but not because I want to see them fail, no, it's because I believe in what these great cities have to offer and will again. I believe in the middle class and you know what? I'm okay with being part of it. I love to travel, to see what the rest of the world has to offer but I also love coming back home. And that's what keeps me going, see...? Getting back to the things I love... the things that mean the most to me. It's home. And it tells me I belong.

(Pause)

ANNOUNCER
Ladies and gentlemen, Northwest Airlines is pleased to announce that our nasty weather system has cleared and we will now begin re-seating all cancelled flights.

JOHN
Thank you.

ANNOUNCER
Please return to you original departure gates and wait for further instructions and once again, thank you for choosing Northwest.

TOBIN
We're going home? Is that what I'm hearing?

JOHN
That's what you heard. You guys have a good sleep?

TOBIN
Awful. But at least the bench was really uncomfortable.

SCOTT
Ah man. I fell asleep on my arm. Ah come on now. Wakey wakey.

(The guys collect their stuff)

JOHN
Well, gentlemen, it's been a slice.

SCOTT
Yeah, you too. It was nice sharing a beer.

TOBIN
It was and good luck with... well, whatever the day brings. See you boys.

SCOTT
Unless we see you first.

JOHN
Good one.

(SCOTT's arm is still asleep)

SCOTT
Somebody hit redial for me, will you? *(JOHN hits it, SCOTT balances the phone between his ear and shoulder)* Thanks.

(TOBIN and SCOTT are on their phones again and exiting)

TOBIN
Malcolm buddy, hey, I was sleep-

ing on this and I think I got it all figured out...

SCOTT
No, I got a scorpion instead... take a breath, it's under glass.... take another breath...

JOHN
(Looking up to the ANNOUNCER)
Thanks again.

ANNOUNCER
Safe trip home.

(He exits)

END OF PLAY

It Came From Mars

A PLAY BY
JOSEPH ZETTELMAIER

Cast of Characters

QUENTIN FARLOWE - 40s-50s, director/writer/actor
MAUDE MYRTLES - 30s-40s, secretary
WERNER KREILIG - 20s, sound effects technician
GEORGE LOOMIS - 40s, actor, former soldier
DOLORES BRECKINRIDGE - 20s, actress
JULIA CRANE - 40s, actress

TIME
October 30, 1938

PLACE
The rehearsal room of WHQN Studios, New York

IT CAME FROM MARS received its world premiere on Feb. 18, 2010 as a co-production between The Performance Network Theatre (Ann Arbor, MI) and Williamston Theatre (Williamston, MI). It was directed by Tony Caselli. Set Design by Janine Woods Thoma, Lighting Design by Daniel C. Walker, Costume Design by Sally Converse-Doucette, Sound Design by Will Myers, Prop Design by Charles Sutherland. Stage managed by Rochelle P. Clark.

The cast was as follows:

QUENTIN FARLOWE: Wayne David Parker
MAUDE MYRTLES: Morgan Chard
WERNER KREILIG: Jacob Hodgson
GEORGE LOOMIS: Joseph Albright
DOLORES BRECKENRIDGE: Alysia Kolascz
JULIA CRANE: Sandra Birch

For information about production rights, visit www.jzettelmaier.com

It Came From Mars

ACT I

(Lights up. MAUDE is carving a pumpkin onstage, listening to the radio. The door flies open and QUENTIN enters dramatically. He has coffee with him, clearly agitated)

QUENTIN
Maude. We're doomed. *(downs the coffee)*

MAUDE
I beg your pardon?

QUENTIN
How does he expect me to do it?! That's what I'd like to know! Damn you, Jerome Albertson! Damn you straight to the very bowels of hell!

MAUDE
What did Mr. Alberts…?

QUENTIN
The man's a damned fool, that's what he is! One rehearsal?! If he wants to bend me over, he could at least buy me dinner first! It's not enough that I'm trying to put on a quality program with a skeleton crew. Now he expects me to perform a miracle, and gives me no time to do it! What did I do to deserve this, Maude? THAT'S what I'd like to know.

MAUDE
I'm sure it's nothing pers—

QUENTIN
I was on Broadway, Maude. Did I ever tell you that?

MAUDE
You may have mentioned it, yes.

QUENTIN
It was glorious. The resources, the adoration… and now this. Left to rot in the soulless vacuum of radio, alone.

MAUDE
You're not alone, sir. You've got a fine company of…

QUENTIN
Of what? Actors? I have no actors! I have a debutante who barely qualifies as an idiot. A sound-effects man with almost no grasp on the English language.

MAUDE
What about George?

QUENTIN
Between you and me, Maude, the man has one voice and two volumes: Loud and Louder. He's as subtle as an epileptic chimpanzee. No, the only two actors in this ragtag lot are me and Agnes.

MAUDE
Oh! Mr. Farlowe! I almost forgot! Agnes...

QUENTIN
Of course! Agnes! The jewel in my crown. I tell you, if it weren't for her, I'd drive this whole company into the Hudson. If we are to pull off Mr. Albertson's miracle, it will be because of her brilliance.

MAUDE
That's lovely. But...

QUENTIN
She brings a sort of untamed sexuality to every role she plays. A smoldering intensity that forces you to hang on her every word, wouldn't you agree?

MAUDE
Oh. Um. I suppose so?

QUENTIN
Yes, she is a creature of great passion. If you get my drift. Maude.

MAUDE
I get it, sir.

QUENTIN
By god, you're right! We can do this!

MAUDE
What?

QUENTIN
With my words and Agnes' talent, we may yet prevail! Thank you, sweet Maude. Thank you.

MAUDE
But I didn't...you're welcome?

QUENTIN
My god, I want to fuck something! *(notices the jack-o-lantern for the first time)* Maude, there's a jack-o-lantern in my rehearsal space.

MAUDE
Yes, I'm sorry. I was just carving it for the children.

QUENTIN
I thought you were barren.

MAUDE
No, sir. My Dominic and I just...

QUENTIN
Fascinating. Make it go away.

(She puts the pumpkin on her cart)

QUENTIN
Doesn't trick-or-treating happen tomorrow? Not on the eve of All Hallow's Eve?

MAUDE
It's a community program, sir. A lot of parents are concerned about their children running into hooligans on Halloween proper.

QUENTIN
Well, there's church-folk for you.

(MAUDE starts setting up the space)

QUENTIN
Just keep those urchins out of the building.

MAUDE
I'll just greet them at the doorway.

QUENTIN
See that you do. I'll not have them interrupting my rehearsal with their trick-or-treatery.

MAUDE
I'll keep them out of your hair.

(Beat. QUENTIN runs his hands through his thinning hair)

MAUDE
I'm so sorry.

QUENTIN
Out.

MAUDE
Mr. Farlowe, I...

QUENTIN
Out, damn you! OUT!

(She bolts. He takes out a flask and takes a long drink. He puts it back in his jacket)

QUENTIN
Maude. Come back.

(She does so)

QUENTIN
I'm sorry about that. I don't mean to shout.

MAUDE
It's all right.

QUENTIN
You've the patience of a saint.

MAUDE
I don't know about all that.

QUENTIN
I'm not an easy man to work for. I know that.

MAUDE
With. *(Beat)* I work with you. I work for WHQN.

QUENTIN
I am WHQN.

MAUDE
I'm not sure the Board of Directors would agree. Sir.

QUENTIN
I gave this station art, I gave it legitimacy.

MAUDE
Good thing for Mr. Welles then, hmm?

(QUENTIN glares at her)

MAUDE
I just mean... because that's where the station got the idea for your show. From Orson Welles' Mercury Theatre of... the umm... Air.

QUENTIN
Our work is completely different. They do trash! Dracula, Treasure Island...

MAUDE
I like Trea....

QUENTIN
What I give people are original stories! Plucked from my own mind and painstakingly put to paper. I create, Maude. Orson Welles merely... re-creates.

MAUDE
I suppose you're right. His program's just as bad off as yours.

(Beat)

QUENTIN
Where is Agnes? She's always early.

MAUDE
OH! Mr. Farlowe, I'm sorry. I forgot that...

QUENTIN
What? What is it?

MAUDE
Agnes phoned.

QUENTIN
Ah. Is she going to be late?

MAUDE
She just said to phone her back.

QUENTIN
And...?

MAUDE
And I'm staying out of it.

QUENTIN
You're a credit to your profession, Maude.

(He storms out, calling Agnes from the reception desk. MAUDE begins laying out the printed scripts and otherwise setting up for the rehearsal. WERNER is heard offstage)

WERNER
(offstage) Good evening, Mr. Farlowe.

QUENTIN
(offstage) Yes, yes. Move along.

(WERNER enters. He is a young man from Germany who serves as the company's sound effects technician. His English is good, but not perfect)

WERNER
Hello, Miss Myrtles.

MAUDE
Oh! Hello, Werner.

WERNER
You are good on today?

MAUDE
I'm very well, thank you. And it's MRS. Myrtles, remember?

WERNER
Oh. Yes. I am sorry, I...

MAUDE
It's fine, dear.

WERNER
I will get it.

MAUDE
I know.

(WERNER begins putting a piece of candy on everyone's scripts)

MAUDE
What's that you're doing?

WERNER
Candy.

MAUDE
I can see that.

WERNER
For Halloween, yes? *(He gives her a piece of candy as well)*

MAUDE
You got all of us candy.

WERNER
Yes.

MAUDE
Werner! You're such a dear.

WERNER
Danke.

MAUDE
This is so thoughtful.

WERNER
My mama say tomorrow is a wicked day. That it teaches children to beg. But I like it.

MAUDE
How is your mother, dear?

WERNER
Good. She goes to see a movie tonight.

MAUDE
So she doesn't have to give out candy?

WERNER
Yes.

MAUDE
Well, don't be surprised if you have soap on your windows when you get home.

(He stares at her, confused)

MAUDE
That's what the children do, dear. If they can't treat, they trick.

(He's still confused)

MAUDE
Just harmless pranks. Throwing eggs at doors, rubbing soap on the windows.

WERNER
Oh.

MAUDE
Except those Bowers boys. They like to start fires.

WERNER
I should go home.

MAUDE
I'm not sure Mr. Farlowe would appreciate that.

WERNER
I must protect my house.

MAUDE
Werner, it's nothing. Really. Just children being children.

WERNER
Mama will be angry. And then she will drink.

MAUDE
I'm sure everything will be fine. It's the day before Halloween, after all. What's the worst that could happen?

WERNER
But...

MAUDE
Besides, you don't want to leave before Dolores gets here, do you?

(WERNER smiles, becoming self-conscious)

MAUDE
Just get your machines, dear. The others will be here soon.

(WERNER goes to the closet, and begins pulling out various sound-effect devices. He sets them on one end of the table)

MAUDE
Ooo. What's that one?

WERNER
For making thunder. *(He shakes the thunder sheet)*

MAUDE
Oh, that's just wonderful.

WERNER
This is my favorite. *(He pulls out a wind machine and cranks it. MAUDE is clearly impressed)*

MAUDE
My goodness.

WERNER
I listened to Frankenstein on Witch's Tale. My friend say this is how they make the wind, so I build myself.

MAUDE
Aren't you clever?

WERNER
It is not so difficult. You wrap the cloth around the...

MAUDE
You used it in The Monster of Dr. Monstroso.

WERNER
Yes! For the storm, when the Doctor brings his metal man to life. *(Getting excited, he begins acting out the scene. When he speaks the lines, his accent almost entirely disappears)* "Let the gods tremble in fear this night, for I have stolen from them their secrets. I have

improved upon their designs, for where they crafted with soft and fragile flesh, I have made a man...OF STEEL!"

(MAUDE *claps*)

MAUDE
Werner! That was wonderful!

(WERNER *smiles and bows*)

MAUDE
You should audition for Mr. Farlowe. He'd hire you on the spot.

WERNER
I am no actor. I make noises.

MAUDE
If you say so. Oh! I saw this in the weekend paper. The Invisible Ray is playing at that little theatre down on Fourth.

(*He goes about, resetting his machines*)

WERNER
I do not know that one.

MAUDE
It came out a few years ago. Boris Karloff and Bela Lugosi discover light rays in outer space that allow them to see into the past.

WERNER
Karloff and Lugosi? Together?

MAUDE
Oh yes.

WERNER
And there is a monster?

MAUDE
That would be telling.

(GEORGE *enters. He is in his forties, strong, a former military man. He walks with a slight limp. He speaks as he enters, checking his watch*)

GEORGE
Look at that. Seven thirty on the tick, and I'm the only actor here on time. Imagine that. Maude, where's...

(GEORGE *notices* WERNER)

GEORGE
What's the goose-stepper doing here?

MAUDE
George...

GEORGE
Honestly, Klaus...

WERNER
Werner.

GEORGE
...shouldn't you be out massacring women and children in Belgium?

MAUDE
George Loomis!

GEORGE
Relax. Klaus knows I'm just giving him a hard time. Don't you, Klaus?

WERNER
My name. Is. Werner.

(WERNER *goes back to setting up equipment*)

GEORGE
See? No harm done. (*He takes his seat at the table*) Oh for fuck's sake. Where is everyone else?

MAUDE
Mr. Farlowe's on the phone with Agnes.

GEORGE
Found out about that, did he? (*setting his leg up on one of the chairs and rubbing his knee*)

MAUDE
About what exactly?

GEORGE
I saw Agnes having lunch over at Ogilvy's... oh, this must've been last Thursday. You know Ogilvy's? They've got this beef brisket that...

MAUDE
To the point, George.

GEORGE
No, honestly. Heinrich, you ever had beef brisket?

WERNER
I know you know what my name is.

GEORGE
I once had beef bourguignon, in Normandy... must've been back in '18. Ate it right off the bare back of a French farmgirl. Ogilvy's beef brisket is the only thing I've ever had that comes close.

MAUDE
Back to Agnes.

GEORGE
Right. I saw her having lunch.

MAUDE
At Ogilvy's.

GEORGE
Right.

MAUDE
Last Thursday.

GEORGE
Right.

(Beat)

MAUDE
So why is Quentin on the phone with her now?

GEORGE
Why do you think? Because of Welles.

WERNER
Orson Welles?

GEORGE
No, wishing wells. Of course Orson Welles.

MAUDE
George.

(He looks back to her)

MAUDE
Bring it all together for us, would you?

GEORGE
Who do you think Agnes was having lunch with last Thursday at Ogilvy's?

WERNER
Orson Welles?

GEORGE
No. Wishing wells. Of course....

WERNER
We did this already.

MAUDE
Agnes was having lunch with Orson Welles?

GEORGE
Didn't I just say that?

WERNER
Not really.

GEORGE
Oh yes. Yes, yes, yes. And they were looking very cozy.

MAUDE
Lord help us.

GEORGE
Lord help her. Five on the barrelhead says that Quentin is tearing into her like the German infantry tore into those poor souls in Antwerp.

(WERNER storms out. MAUDE glares

at GEORGE)

GEORGE
What? I took three bullets to the leg. You don't see me crying to mein mater.

MAUDE
I'm not talking to you.

GEORGE
So I pick on him. I'm an ass. I admit it. I'm just trying to give the kid a thick skin. There's worse than me out there, and you know it.

MAUDE
That's debatable at best.

GEORGE
You're not fooling anyone, you know.

MAUDE
Hmmm?

GEORGE
All that hostility towards me. The fancy airs. Everyone knows.

(MAUDE stares at him, uncertain if she should ask)

MAUDE
Against my better judgment, I'm going to ask what exactly you mean.

GEORGE
It's just you and me, lamb. You can admit it.

MAUDE
Oh dear god...

GEORGE
You're not the first to fall under old George's spell.

(She looks slightly ill)

GEORGE
After all, you know what they say about actors.

MAUDE
They killed Lincoln?

GEORGE
Don't try to deny it. There's a heat between us, and you know it.

MAUDE
George.

GEORGE
Yes?

MAUDE
It would be difficult for you to be more wrong than you are this very second.

GEORGE
(closing in on her) Oh, I think I could find a way.

MAUDE
Stop it.

(He smacks her bottom)

GEORGE
All right then. Just having some fun. *(He notices the candy on his script)* Well, well, well. What's all this then? (He picks it up, showing it to her)*

MAUDE
They call it candy.

GEORGE
Sweets for your sweet, hmmm?

MAUDE
It's not from me.

GEORGE
How's that?

MAUDE
It's from Werner. You know, the nice German boy you've been demoralizing all night.

GEORGE
Demoralizing? How does a sweet little thing like you learn a big old word

like that?

(Finally, MAUDE closes in on him)

MAUDE
Listen to me, you deplorable skunk of a man. I've been privately tutored since I was five years old. I attended Vassar, I speak three languages, and I wouldn't even be in this pitiful job if my father...a drunken military man very much like yourself, I might add... hadn't put our family's money in beet farms. That's just something for you to think about while my husband pounds you into the ground like a tent post. Are we clear?

(Beat)

GEORGE
Having our monthlies then, are we?

(MAUDE comes at him, and he bolts out of the room, laughing. DOLORES enters as he does, nearly getting run over)

DOLORES
Oh my!

GEORGE
One side, Wiggles!

(He's out. DOLORES is a pretty young woman, fashionable and, to all appearances, a little vapid. She just stares at MAUDE)

DOLORES
Did he just call me "Wiggles?"

MAUDE
I believe so.

DOLORES
Why?

MAUDE
Why does that man do anything?

(Beat)

DOLORES
Inbreeding?

MAUDE
Rhetorical question, dear. *(DOLORES just stares at her)* It means I wasn't expecting an answer.

DOLORES
Then why did you ask? *(notices the candy)* Ooooooo! Candy! *(She takes it off her script, eating it)* Mmmmmmm. Chocolate. Maude, you're so thoughtful.

MAUDE
Thanks. It wasn't me.

DOLORES
Beg pardon?

MAUDE
It was from Werner.

DOLORES
Werner got me candy?

MAUDE
He got everyone candy, dear.

DOLORES
Oh. How is your husband's leg?

MAUDE
Better, thank you. Dr. Haverstock thinks he'll be back on his feet soon.

DOLORES
When I was seven, my horse Duchess broke her leg. Daddy said he took her to a special farm, but I think they shot her. *(She takes a look at the script)* Have you read it?

MAUDE
No.

DOLORES
I don't know how you do it. If I had to do your job, I'd be so bored I'd read anything I could get my hands on. But

I guess that's why you do what you do, and I do what I do.

(Beat)

DOLORES
What is it you do, exactly?

MAUDE
I'm a receptionist.

DOLORES
My daddy has a receptionist. She's colored. I hope we don't go too long tonight. I've got the most wonderful party to go to. Do you know Chester Wolcott?

MAUDE
Can't say that I...

DOLORES
He's in oil. Texas oil. I met him at the Hartford ball. He's so big and...Texan. Anyway, he's having the most wonderful party. A masquerade. Couldn't you die?

MAUDE
I really, really could.

DOLORES
So if you could tell Quentin to keep it snappy, that would be lovely.

MAUDE
Quentin... Mr. Farlowe doesn't listen to me.

DOLORES
Oh, he doesn't listen to anyone. He just goes on and on and on. Don't you just hate people who go on and on and on?

MAUDE
As a matter...

DOLORES
There's no getting a word in edgewise with that man. He starts going on about his theatrical career...that show he wrote...

MAUDE
The Stain Upon My Soul.

DOLORES
You'd think he was the toast of Broadway, the way he talks. I'd almost call him erudite if he wasn't so myopic. (Beat) Where is Quentin? Chop-chop and all that.

(WERNER enters)

DOLORES
Hello, Werner.

WERNER
Hello, Ms. Breckinridge.

DOLORES
Werner, you can call me Dolores.

WERNER
Dolores.

DOLORES
"Ms. Breckinridge." He's so proper. Couldn't you die?

WERNER
Someone is dying?

MAUDE
It's an expression, dear. How's Mr. Farlowe doing?

WERNER
He is red-colored. And yelling.

DOLORES
Why?

MAUDE
Agnes was meeting with Orson Welles.

DOLORES
Oooooooooh. I bet he didn't like that. Quentin, I mean. Not Orson.

MAUDE
Safe bet.

WERNER
You look very pretty.

DOLORES
Why, thank you. I've been invited to a party tonight.

WERNER
Oh.

DOLORES
That's assuming we get out of here at a reasonable hour. Who holds rehearsals on Halloween, anyway?

MAUDE
Halloween's tomorrow, dear.

DOLORES
Either way. It's unpatriotic.

(GEORGE re-enters)

GEORGE
Well, they can only afford one rehearsal. Let's take what we can get, eh?

DOLORES
Hello, George.

GEORGE
Wiggles.

WERNER
What do you mean?

GEORGE
Hmmm?

MAUDE
They can only afford one rehearsal, so we should take what we can get.

GEORGE
When I said "we", I was referring to the talent, Maude.

MAUDE
George, what are you talking about?

GEORGE
Did you notice that there's no broadcast tonight? Any thoughts as to why, little Miss Vassar?

WERNER
We have no money?

GEORGE
Yavohl. WHQN lost three sponsors this week, including Listerine.

MAUDE
But... but Listerine was our biggest sponsor! We've been running their commercials for years.

GEORGE
I know! It cleared my dandruff right up. But now...

MAUDE
Oh dear.

DOLORES
We have no money?

GEORGE
And the last horse crosses the finish line.

WERNER
But...I need this job!

DOLORES
So do I!

GEORGE
Please. You can just dip into daddy's trust fund. But what about an old warhorse like me? Or a spinster like Maude?

MAUDE
Spinsters aren't married, you idiot.

GEORGE
And what about poor Wolfgang here? He's lucky enough to land a job with Quentin, but most employers... they're not exactly eager to hire krauts, hmm?

WERNER
I am a hard worker! I do good work!

DOLORES
No one's denying that. George, stop panicking everyone.

GEORGE
I'm just telling you what I heard.

MAUDE
From whom?

GEORGE
Quentin. It's amazing what happens when you talk to someone rather than about them.

MAUDE
Don't you high-horse with me. You're the biggest gossip in eight city blocks.

GEORGE
What about those old Irish biddies next door?

(Beat)

MAUDE
Neck-and-neck.

DOLORES
Maybe I can ask daddy to donate again.

GEORGE
Quentin already tried. The old skinflint drew up his purse strings like that.

(GEORGE snaps)

DOLORES
Don't call my daddy a skinflint.

GEORGE
I wouldn't if he didn't give me such a damn good reason.

WERNER
Mr. Breckenridge already give us money last month.

GEORGE
Yes, yes. Times is hard all over.

MAUDE
We can't... I need this job... we have a mortgage. Dominic's laid out for another two weeks...

GEORGE
What's the matter this time?

DOLORES
Broken leg.

MAUDE
Oh god. We need my paychecks.

(In a fit of frustration, WERNER takes a small magazine out of his pocket and throws it across the room)

DOLORES
Oh my!

WERNER
Why!? Why did I buy this? I am indulgent. I think I have a good job, but...

MAUDE
Calm down, dear.

DOLORES
(retrieving the magazine) Astounding Science Fiction. I didn't know you read this.

MAUDE
He loves space stories. He's a very imaginative boy, aren't you, Werner?

WERNER
Twenty-five cents! That is what I paid, and now it is gone! What will I tell mama?

(DOLORES begins flipping through the magazine. GEORGE looks over her shoulder)

GEORGE
Treasure Asteroid? Are you serious?

DOLORES
Hush. This is a good issue.

GEORGE
You read that trash?

WERNER
Not trash!

DOLORES
Daddy has a subscription. I flip through it now and then.

WERNER
I am at Gimbel's and I see it on the rack. A new story by D.B. Pennyworth. So I think "Is alright, Werner. You have worked hard. Go ahead and buy the magazine."

MAUDE
Pennyworth's his favorite.

DOLORES
Really?

WERNER
My poor mama. I have failed her.

(The door swings open. QUENTIN enters, a ball of barely-contained rage)

QUENTIN
Maude, to me.

(MAUDE goes to him)

QUENTIN
I need you to go to Weybridge Apartments. You know where that is?

MAUDE
Two blocks south.

QUENTIN
I need you to get Julia.

GEORGE
Good god, man!

QUENTIN
Tell her I need her.

MAUDE
Are you sure about this?

GEORGE
(grabbing QUENTIN's shoulders) Think about what you're doing. I'm begging you.

QUENTIN
I don't have any other goddamn options.

MAUDE
But why send me?

QUENTIN
Because if I ask her, she'll say no. But she likes you. Beg. Plead if you have to. Explain to her that it's a part only she can play. Appeal to her ego.

GEORGE
Lord knows she's got enough of it.

QUENTIN
Promise her anything. Anything but money. But get her over here. Immediately.

MAUDE
I... alright.

QUENTIN
Now go. Go, go, go.

(She hurries off)

GEORGE
(calling after her) Run like your job depends on it!

(QUENTIN glares at GEORGE)

GEORGE
Oh. Right. I told them they might be losing their jobs.

QUENTIN
Why... would you do that?

GEORGE
Hmm. That's an excellent question.

DOLORES
Is it true? Is the station going to close?

QUENTIN
No, no, no. The station's not going to close. *(Beat)* But they may cut loose our program.

WERNER
What?!

QUENTIN
It's a possibility. That's why we have to rehearse on the sly.

WERNER
"On the...?"

GEORGE
It means WHQN doesn't know we're here.

QUENTIN
I can't afford to rent their rehearsal space.

DOLORES
But...but...

QUENTIN
Don't worry.

QUENTIN
No one's going to be here but Maude. She was kind enough to let us rehearse while she tends to the trick-or-treating. Bless her soul, she never asks questions. Oh! Dammit! *(He pulls some bills from his pockets and heads towards the door)*

DOLORES
Quentin, where are...

QUENTIN
Maude! Wait! *(He runs off after her)*

GEORGE
Five on the barrelhead says he's making her pick up scotch.

WERNER
And so it has come to this.

DOLORES
All because of Agnes.

GEORGE
Not all because of Agnes.

DOLORES
The drinking is because of Agnes.

GEORGE
Fair enough.

DOLORES
I for one never knew what Quentin saw in her.

(Beat. Both GEORGE & WERNER laugh at that)

DOLORES
What?

GEORGE
Come on. Even you aren't that dim.

DOLORES
I'm not dim!

WERNER
He means that... well, Agnes is... and she has large...

GEORGE
They were going at it like Italian sailors on shore leave.

(Beat. DOLORES just stares at them)

GEORGE
Oh for Christ's...when a man and a woman love each other very much...

DOLORES
I understood the reference, George.

GEORGE
You sure? Because it was pretty clever.

(DOLORES goes to the door, looking for QUENTIN)

DOLORES
I swear, Quentin only got into directing to get the attention of women who wouldn't normally give him the time of day.

GEORGE
Well! Wiggles has an opinion! Or is it something you just picked up from Daddy?

WERNER
Do not talk to her that way.

GEORGE
Now, now, children. We have to present a united front when Julia arrives.

DOLORES
George.

GEORGE
Hmmm?

DOLORES
Who is Julia?

(QUENTIN returns)

QUENTIN
Julia Crane. My ex-wife.

DOLORES
You were married?

QUENTIN
I was on Broadway once, too. But no one wants to talk about that.

DOLORES
You talk about it.

(Beat. QUENTIN stares at her)

DOLORES
All the time.

(Beat)

QUENTIN
All I will say about Ms. Crane is this. She is a fine actress, who will...with some cajoling... take over Agnes' part.

WERNER
You were married?

QUENTIN
Yes, dammit! Do we have to trample the subject into the ground?

GEORGE
Steady, Quentin.

WERNER
I am sorry! I ask only because...

QUENTIN
Fifteen years! Fifteen years we were together, and I caught her shtuping another man! (grabbing WERNER) Are you happy now, Werner!? You've dragged it out of me!

WERNER
I just...

QUENTIN
What?

WERNER
I was just...

QUENTIN
What, damn you!? Out with it!

WERNER
...I just wanted to know if she liked chocolate.

QUENTIN
(releasing him) What?

DOLORES
Werner got us all chocolate. He's trying to be nice.

QUENTIN
Oh. I see. I... my apologies, Werner. I

have no idea what came over me.

GEORGE
Oh, I have an idea.

QUENTIN
Quiet, George.

GEORGE
That hussy always brought out the worst in you. Even when she wasn't in the room.

QUENTIN
I know. Of course I know. But what choice do I have? Welles has fucked his way through just about every other actress in this city.

WERNER
Not Dolores!

DOLORES
Darn right not me. Not to say he didn't try.

(They all turn and stare at her)

DOLORES
What?

GEORGE
Orson Welles tried to bed you?

DOLORES
Well, maybe not all that. He did ask me out to dinner... oh, about a year ago.

QUENTIN
WHAT?!

WERNER
You... went to dinner? With Orson Welles?

DOLORES
Oh, it was nothing. He tried to get me drunk.

QUENTIN
Can we stop talking about Orson Welles for two fucking minutes?!

(Beat)

QUENTIN
We have a rehearsal to prepare for. Werner, set up your machines.

(WERNER looks around. All his machines are already out. Beat)

WERNER
All right.

QUENTIN
Dolores, could you put a pot of coffee on? It's going to be a long night.

DOLORES
All right. *(Beat. She stops, having no idea how to make a pot of coffee. QUENTIN catches on)*

QUENTIN
Werner, go show Dolores how to make a pot of coffee.

WERNER
All right.

(He exits. QUENTIN sits, holding his stomach)

GEORGE
Ulcer acting up?

QUENTIN
What do you think?

GEORGE
I think your ulcer's acting up.

QUENTIN
You're smarter than you look.

(Both men smirk at the joke, a ribbing between friends)

GEORGE
You're going to be all right.

(QUENTIN stares at him, unsure what he means)

GEORGE
You survived Julia Crane for fifteen years. You can survive her for one rehearsal.

QUENTIN
Let's hope so.

GEORGE
Remember. You're the director. She's working for you. You don't have to take any of her bunk.

QUENTIN
She's bailing us out at in our moment of desperation. And she knows it.

GEORGE
Don't worry. She starts to lip off, I'll give her some of this.

(GEORGE shadow-boxes. QUENTIN smiles sadly. GEORGE catches on)

GEORGE
It's not Julia, is it? It's Welles.

QUENTIN
It's both, I think. Just hearing his name...

GEORGE
Look at it this way. Could Welles have written The Stain Upon My Soul? Not in his wildest dreams. That play redefined theatre! You've told me so lots of times.

(Beat)

QUENTIN
That's what I like about you, George. Loyalty.

GEORGE
Nothing more important in the world.

QUENTIN
I...I'm sorry that I ever chose him over you.

GEORGE
Water under the bridge.

QUENTIN
George, I...

GEORGE
He was your protégé. I understood that.

QUENTIN
It wasn't enough that he turned his back on me. He took everything I'd work so hard to build, everyone who...

GEORGE
Not everyone.

(Beat. GEORGE can tell who QUENTIN is really thinking about)

GEORGE
Quentin, you've only made two mistakes in your entire life. One was trusting Welles. The other was marrying that loud-mouthed cellar smeller.

(QUENTIN laughs a little at that. GEORGE laughs as well)

GEORGE
Remember when you took her flask before opening night? I walked into my dressing room, and she was trying to drink my benzene!

(They both laugh louder)

GEORGE
You have absolutely nothing to fear from her, old top.

QUENTIN
You know what? By god, you're right.

GEORGE
Almost always.

QUENTIN
Who the hell is she? No one! Some

washed-up actress living in some third-rate apartments!

GEORGE
Yes!

QUENTIN
And who am I? I'm Quentin Melville Farlowe! I'm the goddamn writer and director of the finest radio theatre in this proud country!

GEORGE
Yes!

QUENTIN
Let the rapacious harpy rain down her foulness upon me! I'll shake it off like... like... help me, George.

GEORGE
Like...um...like a cherry cordial shaking off its wrapper.

QUENTIN
Like a cherry cordial shaking off... WHAT?! *(stares at GEORGE)*

GEORGE
I was looking at the candy.

(WERNER & DOLORES return)

DOLORES
The coffee's on. I feel so... domestic.

WERNER
She did well. No burns.

DOLORES
Not with my Teutonic knight watching over me.

WERNER
I'm not... I was just...

QUENTIN
All right, all right. Let's try to put on a professional face, shall we?

(QUENTIN motions to their seats. They all sit down, going to their scripts.

WERNER preps his machines)

GEORGE
So what's the story this time, old top?

DOLORES
(reading the title) The House That... Hell Built? Oh please.

QUENTIN
You have a problem with the title, missy?

DOLORES
Well, come now, Quentin. That Hell Built? What does that even mean?

QUENTIN
It means the house was built by a coven of Devil-worshiping witches in Colonial times.

DOLORES
Another ghost story?

(WERNER rolls some thunder. GEORGE flips through the script, underlining his lines)

QUENTIN
Thank you, Werner. Yes, it's a ghost story. People love ghost stories.

GEORGE
....bullshit... bullshit... me... bullshit... me...

DOLORES
Who talks like this?

QUENTIN
What? What was that?

GEORGE
...bullshit... bullshit... what's that word...

DOLORES
Nothing. Nothing at all.

GEORGE
...Egom... egonimom...

QUENTIN
Do you think you could do better?

DOLORES
Well, if you're open to some constructive...

QUENTIN
Dolores, let's make one thing perfectly clear, shall we? I am the director here. I am the writer. And you are here because you can read lines with something resembling emotion without tripping over your words. Understand?

(Beat. DOLORES is cowed)

DOLORES
I'm very sorry.

GEORGE
Egomaniacal!

(They all stare at GEORGE, who is very pleased with himself for figuring out the word)

GEORGE
It's egomaniacal.

QUENTIN
All right. It's the standard breakdown. Dolores, you're playing Lily, and I'm playing John. Newlyweds on their way to the coast for their honeymoon. George, you'll be playing...

GEORGE
Mr. Krenshaw, the mysterious man at the gas station.

QUENTIN
Yes. You'll also be playing Inspector VanHorn, the policeman who finds their bodies at the end. Werner?

WERNER
Ja?

QUENTIN
I'm going to need creaking doors and floorboards, wind, chains and...

(WERNER shakes the thundersheet again)

QUENTIN
Exactly. The story is a classic, but compelling nonetheless. John and Lily are...

DOLORES
Newlyweds on their way to the coast for their honeymoon.

QUENTIN
And they stop off at this little, run-down gas station. In the middle of a thunderstorm.

GEORGE
(reading the script) Mm-hmmm.

QUENTIN
Mr. Krenshaw warns them about the old house up the road...

GEORGE
Oh! This is golden. *(reads aloud, with a character voice)* "They say no one lives there now... except evil. And evil always sets the table for guests."

QUENTIN
Very nice reading. Now the couple get a flat tire...

DOLORES
On their way to the coast for their honeymoon.

QUENTIN
And will find their only sanctuary from the storm is in... The House that Hell Built!

(No one responds to his moment. QUENTIN glares at WERNER. He rolls the thunder again. JULIA has entered,

and stands in the doorway. She is very confident, knowing that she is in control. MAUDE is with her)

JULIA
And people say theatre's a dying art.

QUENTIN
Julia.

JULIA
Quentin.

QUENTIN
You're looking well.

JULIA
I am, aren't I?

QUENTIN
May I assume that Maude has explained our situation?

MAUDE
I...

JULIA
She told me that you need me to pull your proverbial fat out of the fire. I was feeling nostalgic, so here I am.

MAUDE
Here's your... um... package.

(She hands QUENTIN a bag with a bottle in it. The sound of knocking and trick-or-treaters at the door)

MAUDE
Mr. Farlowe. If you... can I just...

QUENTIN
Yes, yes. Tend to the rabble.

(She heads out. An awkward moment)

QUENTIN
Julia, this is Dolores Breckenridge, our ingénue.

DOLORES
It's a pleasure.

JULIA
Of course it is.

QUENTIN
Werner Kreilig, our sound effects man.

(WERNER offers her a chocolate)

JULIA
A cherry cordial? Aren't you sweet. And strapping.

QUENTIN
And, of course, you remember George.

JULIA
Yes, yes. How's the leg, George?

GEORGE
Just fine. How's the great empty hole where your heart should be?

JULIA
It grows at the mere sight of you.

QUENTIN
And now that we're all acquainted, let's get started, shall we?

JULIA
Just a moment, Ducky.

QUENTIN
We're a bit pressed for time, Julia...

DOLORES
I have a party to get to.

QUENTIN
So if you'll just take a seat...

JULIA
I'm not taking anything.

QUENTIN
Beg pardon?

JULIA
Maude asked me to come. I've come.

QUENTIN
Yes, and that's lovely. Let's...

JULIA
But I haven't agreed to anything. *(He just stares at her)* Oh, come now. After everything that's gone on between us, do you really think I'd come running back like some schoolgirl? You broke my heart.

QUENTIN
You slept with...

JULIA
Be that as it may. I've not even heard a peep from you in over a year now. But suddenly, you come calling at my door.

GEORGE
Well, Maude came calling.

JULIA
Let the grown-ups talk, George.

QUENTIN
All right, all right. What is it you want? If it's money, you've made the trip for nothing. I can't offer more than scale. But...

JULIA
Oh, I think you know what I want.

QUENTIN
No. I don't.

JULIA
Yes. You do.

QUENTIN
Haven't the foggiest.

JULIA
Don't make me spell it out to you.

QUENTIN
Just tell me. The clock is ticking.

JULIA
I remember you being more fun than this. What I want, my dear Quentin, is for you... to beg.

(Beat)

QUENTIN
You must be joking.

JULIA
Oh, must I?

GEORGE
Don't do it, man. We can find someone else...

JULIA
At this late hour? Of my caliber? I doubt it.

DOLORES
Can we please just get going?

JULIA
Come along, sweet. Say those words that you swore you'd never say again, and I'm all yours. Of course, if your pride means that much to you, please remain silent. Perhaps this little biscuit could do the role.

DOLORES
(shocked, to WERNER) Did she just call me a biscuit?

(Long beat)

QUENTIN
I need you, Julia.

JULIA
How badly?

QUENTIN
Oh come on!

JULIA
Have a lovely evening, all....

QUENTIN
Badly. I need you. Very badly. Please, rescue us in this, our darkest hour.

JULIA
(smiling, taking it all in) My god... you spend so much time imagining what

this moment will be like, and then it happens and… delicious.

QUENTIN
All right. Let's get going.

JULIA
Like honey on my lips.

QUENTIN
Are you quite finished?

JULIA
Oh, I haven't even started. So tell me, Ducky…

QUENTIN
Don't call me that.

JULIA
What's the plan for this evening, hmm? I was ready to settle in before Maude came begging at my doorstep.

QUENTIN
It's a meaty character roll, just like the old days.

JULIA
Mm-hmm.

QUENTIN
It requires an actress of great range and…

JULIA
What's it called?

QUENTIN
Well, the title of the piece is…

JULIA
(takes a script and reads) The House That… well, that's just terrible.

DOLORES
I knew it!

JULIA
And what's my part? Wealthy socialite? The mysterious but alluring foreigner?

QUENTIN
You'll be playing the witch.

GEORGE
Ha!

QUENTIN
The ghost of a witch, actually.

JULIA
(rubbing her eyes) I'm going to need a drink. Werner, is it?

WERNER
Ja?

JULIA
Be a dear and fetch me…

(QUENTIN sets his booze in front of her)

JULIA
Well, what the wait staff lacks in manners, it makes up for in timing. *(She drinks, then leafs through the script)* So when do we go up?

QUENTIN
Sunday.

JULIA
How many rehearsals?

QUENTIN
One, including tonight.

JULIA
God. Well, at least it's one of your scripts.

(Beat)

QUENTIN
What exactly does that mean?

JULIA
That it's short. And that it won't require a great deal of depth.

GEORGE
You don't know. You haven't even read it yet.

JULIA
Well, they're all variations on the same theme, aren't they?

QUENTIN
Don't start.

JULIA
A couple meets their untimely end at the hands of some sort of spook.

QUENTIN
You must sleep so soundly under your blanket statements.

DOLORES
Well, she's... um...

QUENTIN
Let's just rehearse, shall we?

DOLORES
I mean, I've played basically the same character for three months. *(Beat. She looks to JULIA)* That's how long I've been here.

JULIA
Well, my dear, get ready for many months of the same.

GEORGE
That's enough!

WERNER
...not if we lose our jobs...

GEORGE
Oh, now look what you've started.

QUENTIN
No one's losing their... let's start on page one.

JULIA
What is he talking about?

QUENTIN
Absolutely nothing. Let's begin. *(as the narrator)* Tonight's tale takes us on a dark road, one rarely traveled. Those who know of it avoid it, for this road does not lead to sunny shores or scenic venues. When this road ends, it simply... ends.

(DOLORES stifles a snicker. QUENTIN glares at her)

DOLORES
I'm sorry.

QUENTIN
On this twisting road, we...

JULIA
How many times are you going to say "Road"?

QUENTIN
Excuse me?

JULIA
It's just, you've already used it... let's see... four times. And we're only a few sentences in.

QUENTIN
The story begins on a road.

DOLORES
Five times.

QUENTIN
AND the road also serves as a metaphor for...

JULIA
Here we go.

GEORGE
We are trying to rehearse here!

JULIA
Everything's a damn metaphor for you, isn't it?

GEORGE
Why don't we take it from the gas station?

(WERNER scans the script, trying to determine where they are. He starts to

shake the chains as he reads)

GEORGE
(reading MR. KRENSHAW) Well, what brings you nice folks to my old station?

DOLORES
Where are we?

GEORGE
Next page.

DOLORES
All right. Let me just... *(She finds the page. As LILY)* Well, it looks...

QUENTIN
It's my line, Dolores.

DOLORES
Sorry.

QUENTIN
(As JOHN) Well, it looks as though our tire's gotten itself a flat.

JULIA
Very original.

QUENTIN
(as JOHN) And I was wondering if you might have a spare.

GEORGE
(As KRENSHAW) Well, let me just...

QUENTIN
Werner! Enough with the damn chains!

(WERNER stops, then slowly reaches for the thundersheet)

QUENTIN
No thunder either! Just sit down.

WERNER
(sitting next to DOLORES, he speaks to her quietly) I do not know where I am.

DOLORES
(showing him in the script) Right...there.

(GEORGE glares at them)

DOLORES
Please go on.

GEORGE
(As KRENSHAW) Well, let me take a look. I think I might just have something for you lovely newlyweds.

JULIA
How does he know they're newlyweds?

GEORGE
...FOR YOU LOVELY NEWLYWEDS. Just wait here a moment.

DOLORES
(As LILY) Oh John, can't you just imagine it? Soon we'll be basking in the beauty of Shell Beach.

QUENTIN
(As JOHN) I certainly hope so, Lily. But those foreboding storm clouds give me pause.

DOLORES
(as LILY) Oh, John. Must you be so gloomy? I'm sure they will pass long before we arrive at our honeymoon destination.

JULIA
When do we get to my part?

(They set down their scripts)

JULIA
I'm sorry. I just assumed that, since I was called here in the midst of a panic, I might actually get a chance to rehearse. Tonight.

QUENTIN
Julia, we're trying to...

GEORGE
Let me handle this, Quentin. *(To JULIA)* I know you've been out of

the game for a while, but those of us who still work believe in following the protocol. And that protocol is to rehearse whatever the director says. And the director is the gentleman sitting right there who somehow found it in his heart to bring you back into the fold. So why don't you shut those ever-flapping lips of yours and try to behave like a goddamn professional?

(Beat)

JULIA
So it looks like I come in on page nine…

QUENTIN
We're not there yet, dammit!

JULIA
You watch your tone, Ducky.

GEORGE
My GOD! The ingratitude…

JULIA
I completely agree! I haven't even heard a single 'thank you' since I got here.

QUENTIN
Excuse me!

WERNER
Why is there yelling? Why don't we….

QUENTIN
Thank you?

DOLORES
Everyone just…

QUENTIN
THANK YOU?!

JULIA
You're welcome. See? Was that so hard?

(DOLORES reads from script, trying to get things on track)

DOLORES
(As LILY) If only I had known…

QUENTIN
You're lucky to get any work at all at this point!

DOLORES
…that this road…

WERNER
Six times.

GEORGE
Shut your gob, Fritz!

JULIA
Oh! Is that a fact?

DOLORES
(To herself) That's not very good, is it?

WERNER
You call me 'Werner', or do not talk to me at all!

QUENTIN
It is the very definition of a fact!

DOLORES
(to herself) …maybe if I were to use the subjunctive…

GEORGE
Toughen up, you Bavarian creampuff!

QUENTIN
Need I remind you…

JULIA
No! You needn't!

WERNER
What did you call me?

QUENTIN
…of your shining performance as Kate in Taming of the Shrew?

GEORGE
I'm sorry. "You whiney sausage-eater Werner."

JULIA
How dare you!

QUENTIN
What was it the critics said…

DOLORES
(to herself) …had I known that the…

WERNER
Enough!

QUENTIN
"Even in the fifth row, I could smell the liquor wafting off of Julia Crane."

WERNER
I cannot work with this oaf!

QUENTIN
"In the end, the Shrew won out…"

GEORGE
Tough talk, sweinholt!

QUENTIN
"…at the expense of every ticket-holder in the theatre."

JULIA
You memorized it. I'm touched.

WERNER
Why don't you hobble over here and say that into my face?

DOLORES
Quiet, please! I'm trying to…

GEORGE
WHAT?!

QUENTIN
And still you think yourself worthy to judge my genius!

GEORGE
Was that a crack about my leg?

JULIA
Oh! That's rich!

WERNER
Come over here, and I will crack it.

DOLORES
Werner!

JULIA
You sit here in your petty little kingdom, telling yourself you're actually creating art!

GEORGE
Oh, that's it.

(GEORGE gets up too quickly, and falls)

DOLORES
George!

JULIA
But somewhere deep inside, you know you're just so much balloon juice!

QUENTIN
How dare you!

GEORGE
Stay there, Franz. Let me just…

JULIA
You surround yourself with these boobs, because that's all you are!

GEORGE
(managing to right himself) And I'm up!

JULIA
King Boob himself!

(WERNER starts to come at GEORGE. DOLORES stops him)

WERNER
Ich töte Sie, verkrüppelte Esel!

QUENTIN
Get out! Get out of my rehearsal!

DOLORES
Now just hold on!

JULIA
Gladly! I leave you to your sinking ship!

GEORGE
This is for the fighting 35th! *(lunges at WERNER. They struggle)*

DOLORES
Maude! MAUDE!

JULIA
And maybe one day you'll realize you don't have the talent God gave a cheap hairpiece!

(QUENTIN grabs JULIA by the shoulders)

QUENTIN
Leave my hair out of this!

DOLORES
MAUDE! HELP!

(The door swings open. MAUDE enters, shocked and terrified)

DOLORES
Maude?

MAUDE
Oh... oh god...

(The fights stop as everyone notices the visibly-shaken MAUDE)

WERNER
Mrs. Myrtles? What is it?

(She looks at them, too scared to speak)

QUENTIN
Maude, we're in the middle of something here.

JULIA
Quiet, Ducky. Something's wrong. *(goes to MAUDE)* What is it, dear?

MAUDE
I can't... oh my god... it's... it's horrible.

GEORGE
What's she blathering about?

MAUDE
I was just listening to... to Ramon Raquello. On the radio. Stardust, I think. And then... they said that...

DOLORES
What? What did they say?

(MAUDE looks at all of them, unable to really form the words. She goes offstage)

QUENTIN
What the hell's gotten into her?

GEORGE
She's having her monthlies.

DOLORES
What if something's happened to Dominic?

(Beat. DOLORES looks at JULIA)

DOLORES
Dominic is her husband.

JULIA
I know who he is.

(MAUDE enters, rolling in the radio with her)

MAUDE
There was music... and then they interrupted the music.... a reporter... first, it was at Princeton.... they were talking to a professor... something happening in space... and then.... *(She fiddles with the radio, trying to get the station back)* It crashed in New Jersey.

WERNER
What crashed?

MAUDE
They thought it was a meteor... but it wasn't.

DOLORES
What was it?

MAUDE
They said it was a cylinder. A huge metal cylinder that fell from the sky.

GEORGE
My god. Have the Germans invaded?

MAUDE
No. Worse. Much worse.

QUENTIN
The cylinder... Where did it come from?

(MAUDE *manages to get the radio station*)

MAUDE
From Mars.

(*The Radio Interviewer,* CARL PHILLIPS, *is heard*)

CARL PHILLIPS
Ladies and gentlemen, this is the most terrifying thing I've ever witnessed.

Wait a minute.

Someone crawling out of the hollow top. Someone... or something... I can see, peering out of that black hole two luminous discs... are they eyes? It might be a face, might be almost...

Good heavens. Something wriggling out of the shadows like a grey snake.

Now it's another one, and another one, and another one. They look like tentacles to me, or...

I can see the thing's body now. It's large, large as a bear. It glistens like wet leather.

But that face, it's... ladies and gentlemen, it's indescribable. I can hardly force myself to keep looking at it, it's so awful. It's eyes are black, and they gleam like a serpent's. The mouth is a kind of v-shape, with saliva dripping from its rimless lips that seem to quiver and pulsate. The monster, whatever it is, can hardly move. It seems weighed down by... uh... possibly gravity or something. The thing's rising up now, and the crowd falls back. They've seen plenty.

The most extraordinary experience, ladies and gentlemen. I can't find words... uh.... I'll pull this microphone with me as I talk. I'll have to stop description until I can take a new position.

Hold on will you please. I'll be right back in a minute.

(*Music plays. They all look to* MAUDE, *equally terrified*)

MAUDE
It's the Martians. They're here.

BLACKOUT

END OF ACT ONE

ACT II

(Lights up. The cast has gathered around the radio, mesmerized and terrified)

ANNOUNCER
We now return you to Carl Phillips at Grover's Mill.

CARL PHILLIPS
Ladies and gentlemen... am I on...? Ladies and Gentlemen, ladies and gentlemen, here I am at the back of the stone wall that adjoins Mr. Willman's garden. From here, I get a sweep of the whole scene. I'll give you every detail as long as I can talk, and as long as I can see. More state police have arrived, they're drawing up a cordon in front of the pit. About 30 of them. No need to push the crowd back now, they're willing to keep their distance. The captain's conferring with someone... can't quite see who... ah yes, I believe it's Professor Pearson. Yes, it is. Now, now they've parted and the professor moves around one side, studying the object, while the captain and two policemen advance with something in their hand. I can see it now. It's a white handkerchief tied to a pole. Flag of truce. If those creatures... know what that means... what anything means.

(A strange sound is heard in the background)

CARL PHILLIPS
Wait a minute... something's happening...

A humped shape is rising out of the pit.... I can make out a small beam of light against a mirror.

What's that?

A jet of flames springing from the mirror. It leaps right at the advancing men! It strikes them head on! Oh lord, they're turning into flames!

(Men are heard screaming over the radio)

CARL PHILLIPS
Now the whole fields, followed by the woods... the fires!... there's gas heading everywhere... coming this way now, about 20 yards to my right...

(The broadcast is cut off. All wait in terror what seems like an eternity. Finally—)

ANNOUNCER
Ladies and gentlemen, due to circumstances beyond our control, we are unable to continue to broadcast from Grover's Mill. Evidently, there's some difficulty with our field transmission. However, we will return to that point at the earliest opportunity. In the meantime, we have a late bulletin from San Diego, California. Prof. Endelcoffer, speaking at the California Astronomical society, expressed the opinion that the explosions on Mars are undoubtedly nothing more than severe volcanic disturbances on the surface of the planet.

GEORGE
Idiots.

ANNOUNCER
We continue now with our piano interlude.

(The broadcast continues underneath the following dialogue)

QUENTIN
Turn it off.

DOLORES
I want to hear this.

JULIA
He's right. Turn it off.

WERNER
People are dying out there!

JULIA
And what are we supposed to do about it?

MAUDE
Dominic...

QUENTIN
We're safe for now. I haven't heard anything about New York yet. Just New Jersey.

MAUDE
New Jersey is practically next door!

GEORGE
Goddammit!

DOLORES
We're all going to die!

(The music stops)

GEORGE
Wait, shhh.

ANNOUNCER
Ladies and gentlemen, I've just been handed a message that came in from Grover's Mill by telephone. Just one moment please. *(Beat)* At least forty people, including six state troopers, lie dead in a field east of the village of Grover's Mill, their bodies burned & distorted beyond all possible recognition.

DOLORES
Oh my god...

WERNER
No...

ANNOUNCER
The next voice you hear will be that of Brigadier General Montgomery Smith, Commander of the State Militia at Trenton, New Jersey.

GENERAL
I have been requested by the Governor of New Jersey to place the counties of Mercer & Middlesex, as... as far West as Princeton and East to Jamesburg under Martial Law....

(QUENTIN turns off the radio. Most of the others react badly)

MAUDE
Quentin!

QUENTIN
I'm sorry! Were you planning to make a trip to Middlesex tonight?

DOLORES
We need to know what's going on!

JULIA
Haven't you figured it out!? We're under attack. Those things have come down and...

GEORGE
They're conquering us.

(All look to GEORGE)

GEORGE
That's what this is. A war. An invasion. And we don't stand a snowman's chance in Hell.

JULIA
Steady, George.

(GEORGE pulls a gun from his jacket. All jump. He grabs MAUDE, kissing her deeply. She is too stunned to respond)

GEORGE
In another time, I could have loved you. *(He bolts for the door)*

QUENTIN
George?! Where are you going?

GEORGE
There are soldiers out there, dying for

the cause. Probably. And they need my help. Good-bye, friends. Shed no tears for me. Tonight, I go to my destiny.

QUENTIN
You can't leave!

GEORGE
(quickly pulling QUENTIN aside) Quiet, you're ruining my exit. *(Immediately to the others)* And so, with head held high, I go...

QUENTIN
Stop! We need you here!

DOLORES
We do?

QUENTIN
Yes, you dolt! George has military experience. *(To GEORGE)* Please, just stay the night. Help us survive. Tomorrow, you can... I don't know... re-enlist?

MAUDE
Dominic... I need to get to Dominic.

(As they talk, MAUDE has crept to the door. She's about to leave when—)

JULIA
Maude! Where are you going?!

(GEORGE gets in the way)

QUENTIN
You're not going out there.

MAUDE
The hell I'm not!

GEORGE
If you ever loved me, listen to me now. Those cylinder things could be here any minute.

DOLORES
Which is why we should be listening to the radio!

MAUDE
I want to be with my Dominic!

WERNER
Let her go!

DOLORES
We need to listen to the radio! *(pushes past QUENTIN)*

QUENTIN
Hey! *(He staggers backwards, bumping into the radio. It crashes to the ground, loudly. They all stare at it for a moment)*

QUENTIN
Well. That was helpful.

WERNER
No! The radio-box!

DOLORES
Maybe it still...let me just...

(DOLORES rights it, tries to get a station. Nothing)

JULIA
Turn the knobs. No, the other knobs.

DOLORES
I'm turning every damn knob this thing has! It's not working!

JULIA
It's not working because you broke it.

DOLORES
I didn't break it. He broke it! *(She points at QUENTIN)*

QUENTIN
I did what now?

DOLORES
You're the one who knocked it over.

QUENTIN
You're the one who pushed me into it!

GEORGE
Shut up! All of you!

(Beat. MAUDE makes another dash for the door)

QUENTIN
George! Stop her!

(GEORGE grabs her by the arm, pulling her into a bear hug)

MAUDE
Let me go!

GEORGE
There you are...shhh...shhhh....everything's going to be all right.

MAUDE
Take your hands off me.

GEORGE
Don't you worry, lamb. George is going to...

(MAUDE stomps on his foot. He drops her)

GEORGE
Ow!

MAUDE
I'm coming, baby!

DOLORES
Oh my God, Oh my God...

(GEORGE tackles her. A struggle ensues. QUENTIN & JULIA end up in it, too)

GEORGE
Ow! My corns!

MAUDE
I'm coming!

QUENTIN
Maude, stop!

JULIA
We need to stay together!

MAUDE
DOMINIC!

QUENTIN
Listen to her! She's right!

JULIA
I know I'm right!

QUENTIN
I'm agreeing with you! Shut up already!

WERNER
We need to think of something!

MAUDE
I WANT MY LOVEY-BEAR!!!

(GEORGE manages to pull free, then points the gun at the group)

GEORGE
Now, why don't we all stop behaving like Frenchmen and calm down.

JULIA
George.

GEORGE
Julia.

JULIA
Please don't shoot us.

GEORGE
I have no intention of shooting you. I just needed to get your attention. Now. All of you. Sit down.

(He motions to the chairs with his gun. MAUDE sits, but appears to be in shock. GEORGE paces the room, as though briefing the troops)

GEORGE
All right. Those things are in Mercer County. That means they could be here any minute. Agreed?

(They all ad-lib agreements)

GEORGE
Good. Now, from what we've heard, I think it's safe to say they have us at

a serious tactical disadvantage. That heat-ray is a nasty piece of business.

DOLORES
And if those machines could survive space travel and entry into our atmosphere, we can assume that whatever they're made out of is incredibly durable.

(They all stare at DOLORES, again surprised at her insight)

GEORGE
So what do we know? Definitively?

QUENTIN
These things aren't from Earth.

JULIA
Obviously, they're from Mars.

QUENTIN
George asked what we know definitively. And we don't know that definitively, do we?

JULIA
They were just talking about disturbances on Mars!

QUENTIN
That's not definitive!

JULIA
Oh for fuck's… Do you want me to go out there and ask them?

GEORGE
We can't take them on. Do we all agree on that at least?

(Again, ad-libbed agreement)

QUENTIN
So. What is it we can do?

(Beat)

GEORGE
We can hide.

JULIA
Hide?

GEORGE
Hide.

JULIA
I'm sorry, but.. hiding? That isn't a plan. That's what you do in the absence of a plan.

GEORGE
Wrong. Sometimes, hiding is the very best thing one can do. We stay here for the night. We become invisible. Let them pass right over us, and then…

WERNER
I want to call mama.

GEORGE
No phone calls, you fool! They could be listening. We can't do anything that will bring the slightest attention to us. That's step one.

QUENTIN
What's step two?

(JULIA raises her hand)

QUENTIN
Julia?

JULIA
I move that we try to fix the radio.

DOLORES
Second.

QUENTIN
This isn't the goddamn Chamber of Commerce. You don't have to nominate things.

WERNER
Second.

JULIA
Look, let's just try to fix this thing. It's our only chance to find out what's going on out there.

GEORGE
Fair enough. Werner.

(Beat)

WERNER
You... you called me Werner.

GEORGE
Can you fix it?

WERNER
Let me take a... can I get up now?

GEORGE
Yes.

WERNER
I will look. *(Examining the broken radio)* There is torn wiring. I am maybe able to splice it.

GEORGE
Then get to it.

WERNER
I should say, without proper tools, if I can get it working, the signal will be... *(He makes the "so-so" sign with his hands)*

QUENTIN
Just do your best, lad.

WERNER
All right. *(WERNER sits down with the radio and starts working)*

GEORGE
We should lock this place down. Nail boards over all the doors and windows.

QUENTIN
I'm not sure we have hammers. Or nails.

GEORGE
Then we barricade. Any large furniture... desks, bookshelves, cabinets... drag them to the doors and windows.

Then we need to break up into teams of two.

JULIA
Oh dear god.

GEORGE
What?

JULIA
We're not going to... repopulate, are we?

GEORGE
Keep dreaming. No, we need to explore the building. Take anything we can find that might be of use.

DOLORES
Define useful.

GEORGE
Food. Kindling. Anything that might be used as a weapon.

QUENTIN
Go through all the desks, see if anyone has a gun hidden in a drawer somewhere.

DOLORES
I don't like guns.

GEORGE
Know what I don't like?! Bear-sized aliens bursting down the door and incinerating us!

JULIA
Stop scaring her, George.

GEORGE
She needs to be scared. For all we know, they can kill us from miles away, just with the power of their minds!

WERNER
AHH!

(Everyone jumps at WERNER's cry of pain. DOLORES screams a little)

DOLORES
What happened?

WERNER
I cut my finger.

GEORGE
Back on track, people. The plan is, we break up into three teams of two, and explore the building. Once we've gotten everything we can use, we barricade ourselves into this room until we come up with a long-term plan.

DOLORES
Why in here? There's a lovely view of the bridge from Mr. Albertson's office.

GEORGE
(rubbing his eyes) Wiggles, I can't tell if you're truly dense, or just putting me on.

DOLORES
Don't call me dense, you...

GEORGE
We're going to hole up in here because it has no windows, and only one way in or out. If those things try to force their way in here, we can pick them off as the come through the door. Understand?

WERNER
Wait! Wait!

DOLORES
What is it?

WERNER
I think I... let me just... *(He adjust the knobs on the radio. It sparks to life just for a moment, though the sound is full of static)* Got it!

ANNOUNCER
This is Newark, New Jersey. This is Newark, New Jersey. Warning: Poisonous black smoke flowing in from Jersey marshes. Reaching Ball Street. Gas Masks useless. Earth population, move into open spaces. Automobiles use Routes 7, 23. 24. Avoid congested areas. Smoke now spreading over...

(Static overtakes the transmission)

QUENTIN
No!

WERNER
Verdamt machine!!! *(WERNER whacks it. The signal cuts out entirely)*

DOLORES
Did... did he say poisonous smoke?

QUENTIN
That heat-ray wasn't enough. Now they're gassing us like damn cockroaches.

JULIA
This isn't an invasion. It's an extermination.

(MAUDE begins to laugh, born more out of hopelessness than humor. They all turn to her, waiting for her to speak)

MAUDE
I mean... my god... this is it? This is how it ends? Gassed to death with you...you...people? Everything I did... everything I wanted to do... I was going to be a linguist... I was going to live with the Tatungalung people of Australia... learn their ways... marry their chieftain... discover the cure for measles from their native remedies... I would return to America a heroine... a heroine... not a secretary. This isn't what I wanted to be. Who would want this? To spend every day harangued and belittled by a washed-up fraud with delusions of significance? My god, it's

all so ridiculous, isn't it? Just utterly... *(She stops, as if in deep thought. Then she bolts out the door)*

QUENTIN
Maude!

GEORGE
Dammit, woman! *(GEORGE takes off after her. The others go to the door)*

QUENTIN
George! Get back here!

JULIA
Look at her go.

DOLORES
She could've been a sprinter.

JULIA
He will not catch up to her, not on that bad leg.

QUENTIN
I wouldn't count George Loomis out. That man is nothing if not persistent.

JULIA
If there are aliens out there, they're going to see those two tearing down the street. Then they'll interrogate them and then the four of us are as good as dead.

QUENTIN
Well, what do you suggest we do?

JULIA
Don't ask me. Our master strategist just went limping into the wild blue yonder.

QUENTIN
Stop cutting us down and do something useful!

JULIA
Useful? Oh, that's rich, coming from you.

WERNER
I...I will work on the radio.

JULIA
You may talk a big talk, Quentin Farlowe, but you are easily the most useless person I've ever met. I know it, these two know it... your mother certainly knew it.

QUENTIN
My mother was a saint!

JULIA
Then why didn't you marry her!?

QUENTIN
Maybe I should have!

(Long, awkward pause)

DOLORES
Why don't I go look for guns?

WERNER
Me too.

QUENTIN
No! You sit there and fix that radio.

WERNER
I'm not sure it can be fixed.

QUENTIN
(glaring at WERNER) Fix. It. Dolores, go find guns.

DOLORES
(looking at WERNER, clearly wanting to stay with him) I... all right.

(DOLORES is about to exit. GEORGE walks back in, a look of shock on his face)

QUENTIN
George, did you...?

GEORGE
I lost her.

JULIA
Lost her? What do you mean "lost

her?" Did she...?

GEORGE
She was like a damn jackrabbit. I was right on her the whole time, then... woosh.

DOLORES
I'm sure she'll be all right. Really. She knows this town better than anyone.

GEORGE
No... I don't think she'll be all right. Not at all.

(Beat)

QUENTIN
Why do you say that?

GEORGE
As soon as I got to the front door... I turned to my left and... people. In the street. Panicking. Not many, but...

(QUENTIN smacks GEORGE)

GEORGE
Ah! Dammit!

QUENTIN
Pull yourself together.

GEORGE
I am together!

JULIA
Maybe I should hit him.

GEORGE
No one's hitting... Just let me explain!

QUENTIN
Go on.

GEORGE
These people... they were running.

WERNER
From what?

GEORGE
Black smoke. All over the place.

JULIA
You mean...?

DOLORES
Black smoke? Poisonous black smoke?

GEORGE
They're here.

(Beat)

DOLORES
Oh god! We're all going to die!

WERNER
No! I will protect!

JULIA
Maybe we should try to surrender!

GEORGE
The hell you say! I'll kill myself first!

QUENTIN
Everyone calm down.

DOLORES
Oh god! I don't want to die! I DON'T WANT TO DIE!

JULIA
Surely they won't kill all of us, right? Maybe they can be reasoned with.

GEORGE
Tell that to those poor bastards in New Jersey.

QUENTIN
Enough! This doesn't change anything. We still proceed as planned.

DOLORES
No, maybe Julia's right. Maybe we should...

GEORGE
We're not surrendering!

QUENTIN
No, we can still go ahead with the plan. Barricade ourselves in here, and

wait for the threat to pass.

WERNER
But Mrs. Myrtles…?

GEORGE
She's gone! I know it's hard, but you have to let her go. She… would've wanted it that way.

WERNER
I'm sorry. I…

QUENTIN
So. We're splitting up into groups, right now. We scour the building for anything remotely useful. Then we meet back here in twenty minutes.

DOLORES
I just want to go home.

GEORGE
NO! We do as he says! There is poisonous fog out there, and I'm not letting any of you go out into it. Not even her. *(points to JULIA)*

JULIA
How sweet.

QUENTIN
George?

GEORGE
Yes, sir.

QUENTIN
You and Dolores take this floor, and the basement.

DOLORES
Why do I have to go with George?

QUENTIN
It's George, or me.

DOLORES
Why can't I go with Julia?

QUENTIN
Because we're going in man-woman teams. Dolores, you search all the desks, drawers… anything at all. George, you start barricading.

GEORGE
Got it.

QUENTIN
Julia, you and I will take the top two floors. The highest level is storage space, but there might be something useful up there. I'll barricade while you search.

JULIA
Or, we could barricade first, then search together.

QUENTIN
What do you know about barricading?

JULIA
Exactly as much as you know.

QUENTIN
Werner.

WERNER
Ja?

QUENTIN
You'll stay here. It's imperative that you get that radio up and running.

WERNER
Try to find strippers.

GEORGE
Find what now?

WERNER
Strippers! For stripping wires.

GEORGE
Oh. I… yes, of course. Wait. *(pulls out a pocket knife and tosses it to WERNER)* This might help.

WERNER
Thank you.

GEORGE
If, in the course of our searches, the Martian's break the perimeter...

DOLORES
Oh god.

GEORGE
Do not try to engage them. We clearly don't stand a chance against them.

JULIA
Clearly.

QUENTIN
Just retreat back to this room as quickly as possible. George and I will protect you as best we can. Understood?

(They all nod in agreement)

QUENTIN
All right. Twenty minutes.

(DOLORES, JULIA and GEORGE all exit. QUENTIN turns to talk to WERNER)

QUENTIN
All right, Werner. We're relying on you to...

JULIA
(Offstage) Are you coming or not?!

QUENTIN
Give me a minute, woman!

WERNER
I know what I need to do, Mr. Farlowe.

QUENTIN
Good man. We're counting on you. *(exits)*

(WERNER is alone, working on the radio. He works for a while, testing periodically. Finally, he manages to get a signal)

WERNER
So. It is down to you. And to me.

RADIO VOICE
2X2L, calling Say-Q. 2X2L, calling Say-Q. 2X2L, calling Say-Q, New York. Isn't there anyone on the air? Isn't there anyone on the air? Isn't there anyone? 2X2L....

WERNER
I am here! I am...

(WERNER realizes he's yelling at a radio. He lifts it up, trying to get a clearer signal. It cuts out entirely. He continues to try to get a signal, but fails. It doesn't work, getting him more and more frustrated. He sits down for a bit. The total silence begins to make him nervous)

WERNER
He...hello?

(No answer. He takes out the knife to defend himself)

WERNER
Is anyone outside of here?

(The sound of crashing and breaking. WERNER tries to hide. GEORGE & DOLORES can be heard fighting)

DOLORES
(offstage) Goddammit, George!

GEORGE
(offstage) What?!

DOLORES
(offstage) You nearly broke my neck!

GEORGE
(offstage) Oh please! I missed you by at least half a foot!

QUENTIN
(offstage) Stop yelling, you two!

GEORGE
(offstage) She's the one yelling!

JULIA
(offstage) You're going to bring the whole damn Martian... OH! (The sound of JULIA falling down stairs. GEORGE laughs)

DOLORES
(offstage) Are you all right?

JULIA
(offstage) That wasn't funny, George!

GEORGE
(offstage) From where I was standing, it was funny.

QUENTIN
(offstage) Get back to work! All of you! And be quiet.

(WERNER goes back to working on the radio. He still can't get a signal. Soon, GEORGE re-enters, laden with machine parts. WERNER jumps a bit)

GEORGE
Sorry. Didn't mean to scare you.

WERNER
I was not scared.

GEORGE
Here you go.

(GEORGE dumps the parts in front of WERNER)

WERNER
Vas ist das?

GEORGE
I found a few more radios, and gutted them for parts. Thought you could use them.

(Beat)

WERNER
You found radios.

GEORGE
Yes.

WERNER
Then tore them apart?

GEORGE
Think nothing of it. (exits)

(WERNER works in silence for a bit longer, clearly getting nervous. He hears movement offstage. He starts to pace and panic. He overturns the table, then hides behind it. After a few seconds, DOLORES enters. WERNER leaps up with the knife drawn, yelling loudly)

DOLORES
AH! (She leaps back, almost running out of the room. WERNER calms down. DOLORES has a bowl of candy with her) What in god's name are you doing?!

WERNER
I thought you were a Martian.

DOLORES
Do I look like a Martian?

(Beat)

WERNER
I do not know what a Martian looks like.

DOLORES
Bear-sized. Leathery. Tentacles.

WERNER
Yes. Of course. I apologize.

(She leans against a wall, relaxing. She begins to laugh. WERNER laughs as well)

DOLORES
You scared the hell out of me.

WERNER
I think you do not have so much hell in you.

DOLORES
Well, if I did, I'd have less of it now.

WERNER
Where is George?

DOLORES
Probably making his way to the basement. I ditched him.

WERNER
Why?

DOLORES
Mostly because he's George.

WERNER
I understand.

DOLORES
Dammit, I need a smoke.

(WERNER *takes a pack out of his pocket and gives it to her*)

DOLORES
Thank you.

WERNER
Of course. (*He lights her cigarette, then lights one for himself as well. They sit in tense silence for a bit. WERNER points to the bowl of candy*) What is that?

DOLORES
Oh. Maude's candy. For the trick-or-treaters. I thought we might need something to eat.

WERNER
Oh.

DOLORES
Of course, it didn't look like there'd be any trick-or-treaters tonight.

WERNER
You went outside?

DOLORES
Just looked out the window.

WERNER
Did you see anything? Anything bad?

DOLORES
I saw some smoke.

WERNER
Are you all right?

DOLORES
I just saw it, Werner. I didn't breathe it in.

WERNER
Still, it is Martian Smoke. We do not know what it can do.

DOLORES
I love you.

(*Beat*)

DOLORES
I think there's a very good chance we're not going to make it through the night. And I wanted you to...

(*WERNER grabs her and kisses her*)

DOLORES
Oh. My.

WERNER
I love you also. Since the day I saw you.

DOLORES
I know.

WERNER
You know?

DOLORES
Well, for a while. You get... nervous around me.

(*WERNER takes their cigarettes and puts them out*)

WERNER
I am not so nervous now.

(*They kiss again. WERNER breaks away*)

WERNER
Wait. I know what this is.

DOLORES
What?

WERNER
You are here, with me, because it is the end.

DOLORES
I'm not following.

WERNER
If Texas man was here, and I was here, you would choose Texas man.

DOLORES
Oh my lord...

WERNER
Three months you have been here. You are always going to parties.

DOLORES
Do you really care about that? This might be our last night on earth.

WERNER
You think they might take us to Mars?

DOLORES
Ah... actually, I meant that they're going to kill us.

WERNER
I see.

DOLORES
So let's stop talking. All right?

WERNER
When you kiss me, do you think of kissing Texas man's face?

DOLORES
Werner! Maybe they do things differently where you come from, but what you're doing, right now, is killing the moment.

WERNER
I am only...

DOLORES
I love you. And I want to be with you. Isn't that enough?

WERNER
But I...

DOLORES
Let me put it this way. You can either make love to me tonight, or wait for the Martians to turn you into a flaming pile of... Werner.

(Beat)

WERNER
I see your point.

(They kiss again, beginning to remove each other's clothing)

DOLORES
Wait. *(She closes the door. She turns to go back to him, then stops)* Werner, you're right... I haven't been entirely honest with you.

(Beat)

WERNER
You have been lying to me?

DOLORES
Yes.

WERNER
I knew it. I was a fool. Why would you want to be with me?

DOLORES
Wait.

WERNER
You come from good family, good American family. I live in a tiny place with my Mama. We can barely afford it. We wait for my Papa to return from Munich.

DOLORES
Werner, you're not...

WERNER
I read stupid little space stories, I watch monster movies. My Mama yells at me, that my head is always in clouds. I could not give you a good life.

DOLORES
Werner. Stop talking.

(He stops talking. Pause)

DOLORES
Those parties... they aren't what you think. The man I was meeting there... Chester Wolcott... he's a publisher with Astounding Science Fiction. We've been meeting at these parties so no one would suspect. My father would have a stroke if he knew what I was doing.

WERNER
You are together with a publisher?

DOLORES
Not exactly, no.

WERNER
Then why...?

DOLORES
Because... because I'm D.B. Pennyworth.

(Beat. He just stares at her)

DOLORES
I'm D.B. Pennyworth.

WERNER
No you're not.

DOLORES
I am. I really am.

WERNER
D.B. Pennyworth is a man. He writes space stories for...

DOLORES
Astounding Science Fiction.

WERNER
I am confused.

DOLORES
How many female science fiction writers can you think of?

WERNER
(staring, unsure) Is Isaac Asimov female?

DOLORES
No.

WERNER
Then none.

DOLORES
That's because we write under fake names. When people see a story by a woman, they think "romance" instead of "robots." That's what Chester says. So we have to be kind of... sneaky.

WERNER
But you and this Chester aren't...?

DOLORES
I think you're more his type than I am. If you get my meaning.

WERNER
I don't.

DOLORES
Never mind.

WERNER
So you are...?

DOLORES
Dolores Breckenridge Pennyworth.

(She kisses him. He smiles at her)

WERNER
I just kissed my favorite writer.

DOLORES
How does that feel?

WERNER
Very confusing.

DOLORES
I'd imagine.

WERNER
All this time... you knew I was reading your work... but said nothing?

DOLORES
I didn't want anyone to know. Kind of pointless now.

WERNER
You pretend to not be smart so people won't suspect.

DOLORES
You're very clever.

WERNER
Yes, well... I am not so...

DOLORES
And you're adorable when you can't take a compliment.

(He's about to respond, but just smiles)

WERNER
My favorite story is The Spheres of Saturn, when... when...

(They stare at each other for a moment)

WERNER
Why are we still talking?

DOLORES
I have no idea.

(They kiss, then move behind the table. Suddenly, QUENTIN and JULIA enter. QUENTIN's head is bleeding. JULIA has a handkerchief on his wound)

JULIA
Stop squirming. You'll make it...

(WERNER and DOLORES jump up in states of partial-undress)

QUENTIN
What's going on? I've got blood in my... *(He removes his handkerchief, staring at DOLORES & WERNER)* Oh for Christ's sake.

WERNER
We weren't... I mean... I just... she fell.

(They start putting their clothes back on)

DOLORES
Are you all right?

QUENTIN
No!

JULIA
He got hit by one of Mr. Albertson's awards.

DOLORES
What?

JULIA
We were moving a bookcase in front of the window. This five pound sterling monstrosity came tumbling off the top, and brained him.

(DOLORES giggles a little. JULIA gets the bottle of alcohol)

QUENTIN
Yes, yes. It's a goddamn riot. Never mind that I'm about to bleed to death. Werner, please tell me you got the radio working before you two went horizontal.

WERNER
It was... no.

QUENTIN
Damn it all to hell! What did I tell you to do? Fix the goddamn radio! And Dolores! Why aren't you with George?

DOLORES
I wanted to be with Werner.

QUENTIN
This is... I just... For fuck's sake!!!

JULIA
Calm down.

QUENTIN
What is so hard about...

(JULIA dabs alcohol on QUENTIN's wound. He lets out a girlish cry. As the scene continues, WERNER attempts to work on the radio, with DOLORES' help, but they have difficulty keeping their hands off each other)

QUENTIN
How bad is it?

JULIA
Not too bad.

QUENTIN
It's going to need stitches, isn't it?

JULIA
Don't be dramatic.

QUENTIN
I'll be whatever I want. I'm the one who had a fucking civic trophy lodged in his skull.

(JULIA can't help but laugh at the remark)

QUENTIN
You think that's funny?

JULIA
I do, actually.

QUENTIN
(chuckling at it himself) You're not helping, you know?

JULIA
Forgive me. I'll call for a nurse.

QUENTIN
I mean... you're undermining my authority.

JULIA
Is that what I'm doing?

QUENTIN
It's what you've always done.

JULIA
You might be right about that. Which is shocking, considering how rarely you're right about anything.

QUENTIN
My god, do you ever get tired of castrating me?

JULIA
Well, you make it so easy.

QUENTIN
I used to think you just liked to make a show in front of others, but no. The fact is, you're just a heartless bag of bile.

JULIA
(stops tending his wound, looks down, thinking) You might be right about that too.

(Finally, WERNER & DOLORES' fooling around gets to be too much)

JULIA
Dolores!

DOLORES
What? I wasn't...

JULIA
Go find George.

DOLORES
But I...

JULIA
Werner, go help her find George.

DOLORES & WERNER
All right.

QUENTIN
Werner, fix the goddamn radio!

JULIA
Let them go help George. I'm sure they'll only need...what...ten minutes?

WERNER
Fifteen would be better.

JULIA
Fifteen minutes. The radio can wait till then.

QUENTIN
No! I'm giving the orders around here and...

(DOLORES & WERNER have exited)

QUENTIN
They're gone, aren't they?

JULIA
So it would appear.

QUENTIN
You know they're not going to look for George.

JULIA
I had an inkling.

QUENTIN
Well at least someone gets to enjoy the end of the world. *(noticing JULIA is off in her own world)* What is it?

JULIA
The end of the world. *(Beat)* How do you fight the end of the world?

QUENTIN
I suppose we'll have to fight it together.

(He offers her his flask. She drinks. She looks at him, her expression unreadable)

QUENTIN
I thought I knew all your faces. But this one's new to me.

JULIA
It's gratitude.

QUENTIN
Oh. Well. Isn't that something. *(He takes another drink, and passes the bottle back to her)* I'm glad you're here. *(She stares at him)* If this is the end... and I'm not saying that it is... but if it is, I'm glad you're here.

JULIA
Are you going to get romantic on me, Ducky?

QUENTIN
I'm not all that drunk yet. So it's doubtful.

(They both laugh at that. QUENTIN goes to the radio)

JULIA
Don't muck around with that. Just wait 'til Werner gets back.

QUENTIN
That'll be fifteen minutes.

JULIA
Not very likely. At their age, they'll be done in a flash.

QUENTIN
Were we ever that young?

JULIA
Speak for yourself, Ducky. I'm still that young. Perhaps younger.

QUENTIN
Still, I'm glad for them. They've been mooning over each other for months. There's something... hopeful about it, don't you think?

(They smile, enjoying each other's presence. Suddenly, JULIA's mood turns)

JULIA
Stop it.

QUENTIN
Stop what?

JULIA
Stop being charming. It's not going to work.

QUENTIN
You've lost me.

JULIA
I'm not sleeping with you.

QUENTIN
I wasn't aware I'd made the offer.

JULIA
Oh, don't be coy. I was Mrs. Farlowe for fifteen years. I know this side of you. You make glib jokes, you smile your sweet smile, and the next thing I know, I'm grabbing the headboard. Well, those days are done.

QUENTIN
Julia, I'm not...

JULIA
We come in, see the two children going at it, and we get ideas. But that's not...

QUENTIN
We get ideas?

JULIA
What?

QUENTIN
You said "We". "We get ideas."

JULIA
I most certainly did not.

QUENTIN
You most certainly did.

JULIA
If I did, it was a slip of the tongue.

QUENTIN
Oh? And just what ideas did your tongue get?

JULIA
Stop! I said no, and I meant it.

QUENTIN
I heard you. And I wasn't asking you to say yes. I was just trying to fix this goddamn radio.

JULIA
Of course. Yes, of course. I'm sorry. I just...

QUENTIN
What? You just what?

(Beat)

JULIA
Do you wonder where we went wrong?

QUENTIN
Oh Jesus...

JULIA
It's a simple enough question.

QUENTIN
Why on earth do you want to talk about this?

JULIA
Because for all I know we'll be dead in the morning!

(Beat)

QUENTIN
Of course I think about it. But it doesn't matter now.

JULIA
Of course it matters. It was our last fight, Quentin. And we never finished it.

QUENTIN
Funny. I thought the divorce papers were pretty damn final.

JULIA
God, you never listen.

QUENTIN
To what? To your constant criticism? Forgive me, lamb, but it got a bit monotonous.

JULIA
I'm monotonous? Me?

QUENTIN
Your stabs at my writing, at my acting...

JULIA
Quentin! The last two years of our marriage, you'd turned into this bitter, angry... thing. How was I supposed to stay supportive in that?

QUENTIN
I made it to Broadway. That's better than...

JULIA
Two performances, Quentin. The Stain Upon My Soul ran two performances. The backers couldn't back out fast enough.

QUENTIN
They weren't ready for what I was trying to say.

JULIA
You didn't say anything! You just stood on stage washing a stained shirt. For two hours. And then you shouted "Mother!" at the top of your lungs. And then blackout.

QUENTIN
I was pushing the boundaries of the medium.

JULIA
You were so damn busy reinventing the wheel that you didn't even notice that it had stopped rolling.

QUENTIN
And that's just cause for fucking another man behind my back?!

(Beat)

JULIA
I didn't want to sleep with Orson. I mean, I did, but it's not...

QUENTIN
Don't.

JULIA
I just... I wanted out. And I did it all wrong.

QUENTIN
Yes! You did! Of all the people in the world...

JULIA
I know, and I'm sorry.

QUENTIN
Was it his youth? Was that it? Were you trying out the new model?

JULIA
He didn't look at me the way you looked at me. That's what it was.

QUENTIN
I loved you.

JULIA
No. You worshiped me. And so you couldn't see me for what I really was.

QUENTIN
You're the greatest actress of a generation!

JULIA
I'm not! I never was! You saw this woman, this wreck of a woman, and made her into Mary Magdalene. Orson saw me for what I was. A woman. Not a goddess. A woman.

QUENTIN
The boy is a fool. He wouldn't know talent if it had its mouth around his...

JULIA
I've always wondered if you hated him for sleeping with me, or because he had the gall to be your better.

QUENTIN
What?!

JULIA
No need for histrionics, Ducky. You know it just as well as I do. He's a genius. He's a genius, and you're...

QUENTIN
Why are you doing this!?

JULIA
Because if you can't face the truth on your last day on Earth, then when?

QUENTIN
And what truth is that, Julia? I'm dying to hear your take on it.

JULIA
That being a good artist has become more important to you than being a good man. So you've become neither.

(He rises, looking as though he might strike her. He does not. He looks into her eyes for a long time. She touches his cheek)

JULIA
God, I'm so sorry. I am. But it's the truth.

(His anger melts away, and he lowers his head, defeated. She holds him to her)

JULIA
I've missed the way you smell.

QUENTIN
(chuckling a little) What?

JULIA
You smell nice. Cologne and pipe smoke. I didn't realize I'd missed it 'til just now.

(He smiles at that. She smiles back. She leans in, kissing him gently. He takes her hand)

QUENTIN
You know, when you walked through that door, when George told me to let you go rather than beg, I thought about it. I said "He's right. I can have Dolores read the other part. I don't need Julia." But I decided to beg anyway. Because I wanted to see you again.

JULIA
You don't have to say that.

QUENTIN
I know I don't have to. I want to, because it's the truth.

JULIA
Would you... I mean... if you want to, you...

QUENTIN
What?

JULIA
You know what.

(He stares at her, then smiles. He goes to her, stands behind her, putting his arms a around her waist. He then quacks in her ear a la Donald Duck. She laughs)

JULIA
There's my sweet Ducky.

QUENTIN
At your service, ma'am, as always.

(They stay there, enjoying the moment)

QUENTIN
Do you really think I've fallen so far?

JULIA
Well, if so, then I can't think of a better time to start over.

QUENTIN
As a good artist? Or as a good man?

JULIA
Try being a good man first. It's easier. *(The door flies open. WERNER and DOLORES enter, looking scared)*

JULIA
My god. Has it been fifteen minutes already?

(GEORGE enters behind them, gun drawn)

QUENTIN
George, what are you...?

GEORGE
Who stands to benefit?

(Beat. DOLORES & WERNER stand with JULIA & QUENTIN)

QUENTIN
What?

GEORGE
Who. Stands. To benefit? My old Sergeant taught me that. He'd been a policeman in.... I want to say Iowa... and he told me "George, if you want to solve a mystery, the first thing to ask yourself is 'Who stands to benefit?'"

DOLORES
He's gone crazy.

GEORGE
Shut the hell up!

(All fall silent)

GEORGE
The last hour, something's been buzzing around in the back of my brain. "Why now?" "Why did the Martians decide to attack now?" Our allies are trying to fight back the German war machine yet again. America is ripe for the picking. And suddenly... Boom! Martians. Their timing was so perfect... so very, very perfect. *(He lights himself a cigarette)* So I've been walking around out there, wondering where Dolores has run off to, and trying to figure out why this whole invasion seems so odd. And then, I hear this... thumping sound in the bathroom.

WERNER
It's not what...

GEORGE
I think "Oh god. The Martians have gotten in, and they've taken Dolores." Well, turns out I was half right. Someone was taking Dolores.

DOLORES
You're a pig.

GEORGE
And you're a floozy! And... I don't know why, but for some reason, seeing the two of them there, pantsless and vulnerable, it hits me. Who stands to benefit?

(Beat)

JULIA
Who?

(GEORGE points his gun at WERNER)

GEORGE
The Germans.

JULIA
What?

GEORGE
Don't you see? It's perfect! We already know the damn Krauts are hellbent on taking over the planet. They proved that twenty years ago. But we pounded them back to the Stone Age. Their ambition might have survived,

It Came From Mars

but they had no way to act on that ambition. Until... now, go with me, because it takes a little imagination...

QUENTIN
Just put the gun...

GEORGE
Let's suppose Hitler's scientists make contact with something... out there. Something like Martians. Communication is established. A dialogue, if you will. The Martians want to invade, but they don't know the planet. They don't know who to strike, or if the strike would even be successful. Then suddenly... *(snaps his fingers. They all jump)* ...the Martians have someone on the inside. A country giving them the lay of the planet. A country with a rather sizable grudge against... anyone?

(QUENTIN is about to say something)

GEORGE
Against the United States of America!

QUENTIN
George. I need you to listen to what you're saying.

GEORGE
Think about it, Quentin! How has Germany been able to go from a smoking crater in Europe to an industrial warmonger in the space of a few years?

WERNER
Please, just let me get the radio...

GEORGE
The Martians have been helping them. Giving them technology, teaching them the art of alien warfare. My god, it's all so obvious!

JULIA
It is?

GEORGE
This has probably been going on for years! Years, I tell you! YEARS! The Market Crash... Martians! I'd wager they have infiltrators everywhere!

DOLORES
What in god's name are you talking about?!

GEORGE
Don't you see? There's a pattern here! A conspiracy set into motion years ago, to weaken their greatest threat. I mean, have you heard about the Martians invading anyone else? No!

DOLORES
Of course not! The radio's broken!

GEORGE
Right! And it's still broken! And who was supposed to be fixing it? The German!

(Beat. GEORGE looks at the table and equipment WERNER had been hiding behind)

GEORGE
What the hell is all this?

WERNER
I built a little fort.

GEORGE
Someone set it back up.

(WERNER and QUENTIN both go towards it. GEORGE points the gun at WERNER)

GEORGE
Not you.

(JULIA and QUENTIN right the table)

QUENTIN
So. George. What is it you... um... think we should do?

GEORGE
Oh, you leave that to me. Werner, why don't you have a seat?

(WERNER *sits at the table. GEORGE walks behind him, trying to intimidate him*)

GEORGE
Out of respect for the 6 months we've been working together, I'm going to give you this one chance to tell us everything you know about the German-Martian Alliance.

WERNER
I know nothing about the German-Martian...

GEORGE
I thought you'd say that.

(*GEORGE grabs DELORES*)

DOLORES
Hey!

WERNER
Leave her alone!

QUENTIN
George!

GEORGE
I don't want to hurt her. I really don't. But I guess that's up to you.

WERNER
Please. Please. Don't do anything crazy. Or more crazy.

GEORGE
How long have you been living in this country?

WERNER
A year. Wait. Thirteen months.

GEORGE
Just you and your mother, yes?

WERNER
Yes.

GEORGE
And where is your father?

WERNER
In Munich.

GEORGE
And what does your father do in Munich?

WERNER
He makes shoes.

GEORGE
He makes....! Wait, I thought you said he was a corporal.

WERNER
I said he was a cobbler!

DOLORES
George, this is utter nonsense.

GEORGE
You're not off the hook either, Missy. You've been fraternizing!

DOLORES
That has nothing to do with anything!

GEORGE
Oh, doesn't it? What about your thing earlier? Something about their machines surviving space travel and what-not?

JULIA
I'm sure she just...

GEORGE
How did she know something like that? Methinks our dear Dolores has been playing us all for fools.

QUENTIN
I'm sure there's a perfectly reasonable explanation for that.

GEORGE
Like what?

(Beat)

QUENTIN
Dolores, give him a perfectly reasonable explanation.

DOLORES
I... I'm a science fiction writer.

(GEORGE laughs)

GEORGE
Of course! And Julia's the Virgin Queen!

JULIA
Excuse me?

DOLORES
It's true. I write under the name D.B....

WERNER
She pretends to not be smart so that no one will find out she is smart!

GEORGE
Please. That's just ridiculous.

DOLORES
Everything you've just said is ridiculous!

GEORGE
Spoken like a German-Martian Double Agent!

DOLORES
Let me go!

GEORGE
Quentin, you're with me, right?

QUENTIN
I'm sorry, George. But I'm... unconvinced.

GEORGE
Oh god. They've gotten to you, haven't they? *(He raises his gun towards QUENTIN)*

JULIA
Wait! Don't do anything stupid!

QUENTIN
All right, George. Let's say you're right.

GEORGE
I am right!

WERNER
He's not right!

QUENTIN
Let's say for a second that you are. What do you think we should do?

GEORGE
Hmm. Good question. Very good question.

(Beat)

QUENTIN
Have you considered...?

GEORGE
Oh! I've got it! We send Werner out into the streets. If the Martians don't kill him, then he's obviously in league with them.

WERNER
WHAT?!

QUENTIN
Alright, alright. Now what if they do kill him?

GEORGE
Than I'm willing to concede that I might have been mistaken.

DOLORES
You bastard!

WERNER
I am not going out there!

JULIA
The smoke will kill him!

GEORGE
Doubtful. I'm sure the Martians designed the stuff so it wouldn't affect Germans.

QUENTIN
George, there's a problem with your plan.

GEORGE
There is?

DOLORES
Yes! It's completely insane!

QUENTIN
If we lose Werner, then no one can fix the radio. And you agree we need to fix the radio, don't you?

GEORGE
(thinking on that) You're right.

QUENTIN
Good. So let's just...

GEORGE
Yes! Let's send out Dolores.

DOLORES
What?!

QUENTIN
No.

WERNER
No!

GEORGE
That way Werner can still fix the radio... To prove his loyalty.... and if the worst should happen, we don't lose anyone of importance.

DOLORES
WHAT?!

(WERNER finally snaps. He lunges at GEORGE, knocking him to the ground.

The two wrestle for a bit, as JULIA pulls DOLORES out of the line of fire. GEORGE finally manages to get WERNER on the ground and levels the gun at him)

QUENTIN
George! Stop!

GEORGE
He attacked me! What more proof do you...?

(Suddenly, a loud crash is heard outside. Everyone freezes)

JULIA
What was...

(More crashing)

GEORGE
Quentin, take a look. Carefully.

(QUENTIN quietly peeks outside, then shuts the door behind him. He speaks in a whisper)

QUENTIN
They're here.

DOLORES
What?

QUENTIN
One of them is pushing its way through the front door.

JULIA
Oh god no!

DOLORES
What do we...?

(GEORGE grabs WERNER, getting behind him & pointing the gun at his head)

QUENTIN
George!

GEORGE
They're not taking me! You hear me!

Call them off, Kraut!

WERNER
I can't! I am not...

DOLORES
Let him go!

GEORGE
You call them off now.

(More crashing outside)

DOLORES
Please, George. Please! Don't hurt him. I'm begging you.

GEORGE
I'm trying to save us all! Why can't you see that!?

WERNER
Let me go!

GEORGE
Now or never, boy. One... two...

(QUENTIN closes in, getting GEORGE's attention)

QUENTIN
GEORGE!

(GEORGE doesn't shoot, but remains ready to do so)

QUENTIN
Give me the gun.

GEORGE
You want to shoot him?

QUENTIN
No. I don't want him shot at all.

GEORGE
They're going to be here any second! That's why he attacked me!

QUENTIN
He attacked you because you were threatening the woman he loves.

WERNER
Yes.

QUENTIN
What more proof do you need that he's one of us?

GEORGE
They've gotten you all turned around, Quentin. But don't worry. I'm still on your side. I'll protect you.

QUENTIN
I don't need protection. I need you to give me the gun.

(GEORGE just stares at him, gun still pointed at WERNER)

QUENTIN
You're a good man, George. You've just been pushed to the edge.

GEORGE
No, I...

QUENTIN
Give me the gun, and trust me. As your leader. As your friend.

(GEORGE still doesn't give in)

QUENTIN
You're not a killer, George. You're a soldier. You fight other soldiers, not innocent civilians. Look at us. No one here means you any harm. We're all on the same side.

(GEORGE looks at everyone. The reality of what he was doing sinks in on him. He gives QUENTIN the gun)

GEORGE
I'm so sorry. I just...

(WERNER leaps up and punches GEORGE on the chin. DOLORES runs to WERNER)

WERNER
You never touch me again!

GEORGE
I deserved that.

(*WERNER is about to go after him again. A crash right outside the door. Everyone freezes. They whisper to each other*)

JULIA
They're here.

GEORGE
We need to barricade. Quietly.

DOLORES
Oh my God, oh my God...

(*They all begin building a barricade in front of the door. Once it's built, Dolores, Julia, George, and Werner try to hide in the closet*)

QUENTIN
Everyone. Hide. Spread out. Spread out of the closet. If it comes in here, I don't want to present a single target.

(*They all go to different corners. DOLORES goes with WERNER, JULIA with QUENTIN. The sound of more crashing outside*)

GEORGE
Quentin?

QUENTIN
Yes?

GEORGE
Still have the gun?

QUENTIN
Yes.

GEORGE
Good. Don't shoot until you have a clear target.

(*The sound of crashing grows closer. Soon, the door starts to slowly push open. QUENTIN slowly rises, taking aim at the door. MAUDE can be heard as she pushes the door open*)

MAUDE
Hello? Are you in here? Hello?

QUENTIN
Maude?

(*She turns on the light. Everyone is visibly relieved. GEORGE embraces her*)

GEORGE
Oh thank god. I thought I'd never see your sweet face again.

MAUDE
George... please... your hands...

JULIA
Maude! (*embraces her as well*) How did you survive?

WERNER
Did the Martians see you come in?

MAUDE
Yes. About that.

QUENTIN
Quickly, get behind the barricade. They may still be out there.

MAUDE
Wait. Just listen.

WERNER
(*grabbing a piece of debris & hands it to MAUDE*) If the Martians come, you can hit them with this until they...

MAUDE
There are no Martians.

(*Beat*)

QUENTIN
What?

GEORGE
Did we beat them? Did the Army chase them off?

MAUDE
They didn't have to. There are no

Martians. It was all a hoax.

(Beat)

GEORGE
So the Martians convinced people that...

MAUDE
No. George. Listen carefully. There are. No. Martians.

DOLORES
You can't be serious.

MAUDE
I'm afraid so. I'm sorry I didn't get here sooner. Honestly, I forgot you didn't have a working radio. I just assumed you'd heard. And then Dominic says "Maudy? Should you check on...."

QUENTIN
Maude.

MAUDE
Mr. Farlowe.

QUENTIN
I need you to explain just what the hell you're talking about.

MAUDE
All right. Let me just...Oh! Did you get the radio working?

WERNER
Almost.

MAUDE
Try to turn it on. And then tune in the CBS.

(They stare at her, uncertain)

QUENTIN
Go ahead.

(WERNER turns on the radio. He splices some wires from the other radios, and it sparks to life. He tunes it to CBS. MAUDE speaks as they wait for the signal. GEORGE goes to help him)

WERNER
Do not touch me, crazy man.

GEORGE
All right. I just... I'm so sorry. And to you too, Dolores. I...

DOLORES
I'm not talking to you.

GEORGE
Fair enough.

MAUDE
When I got home, my neighbor Morrie told me all about it. Apparently, there was an announcement at the beginning of the broadcast that we'd missed. It explained...

GEORGE
Shhh! It's on!

(ORSON WELLES can be heard over the radio)

ORSON WELLES
This is Orson Welles, ladies and gentlemen, out of character, to assure you that the War of the Worlds has no further significance than as the holiday offering it was intended to be. The Mercury Theatre's own radio version of dressing up in a sheet and jumping out of a bush and saying, "Boo."

QUENTIN
Orson fucking Welles.

ORSON WELLES
Starting now, we couldn't soap all your windows & steal all your garden gates by tomorrow night, so we did the best next thing. We annihilated the world before your very ears and utterly destroyed the CBS. You will be relieved, I hope, to learn that we

didn't mean it. And that both institutions are still open for business. So goodbye everybody, and remember please, for the next day or so, the terrible lesson you learned tonight: That grinning, glowing, globular invader of your living room is an inhabitant of the pumpkin patch, and if your doorbell rings & nobody's there, that was no Martian. It's Halloween.

(*The radio music plays. QUENTIN shuts off the radio*)

MAUDE
So. There it is.

JULIA
Son of a bitch.

GEORGE
Is that even legal? Playing with people's fears like that?

DOLORES
I swear to god, I'll kill that man myself.

GEORGE
It doesn't seem legal, does it?

MAUDE
I'm so sorry I started this...

WERNER
He is a bad man. A wicked, bad, wicked, bad man.

MAUDE
If it makes you feel better, it sounds like lots of people were fooled. Not just us.

JULIA
But there was smoke! In the streets!

MAUDE
Turns out it was the Bowers boys. They set fire to that abandoned tenement down on Second.

DOLORES
So it wasn't Martian smoke?

MAUDE
No.

DOLORES
It was just... smoke smoke?

MAUDE
Yes.

GEORGE
That mean-spirited, pompous son of a...

(*QUENTIN, who has been sitting quietly, begins to laugh. Quietly at first, but it grows in volume. They all just stare at him*)

QUENTIN
He's a goddamn genius.

GEORGE
What?

QUENTIN
My god, it's brilliant. To use his program like this... he didn't break the fourth wall. He blew it up!

DOLORES
He just terrorized thousands of people.

QUENTIN
And he'll get off scot free.

WERNER
How?

QUENTIN
He had disclaimers. He told everyone it was a joke. My god, the CBS is going to get more free publicity than it knows what to do with.

GEORGE
He's a bastard!

QUENTIN
The most brilliant bastard in America.

He's just made himself a millionaire.

DOLORES
The public will never forgive him. And the police...

JULIA
Quentin's right. The CBS wouldn't have put this on if they didn't know what he was going to do. I'd wager they have a team of lawyers ready to jump at this.

GEORGE
So... what? He just made saps of the entire nation and walks away smelling like a rose?

QUENTIN
That would be my guess.

(QUENTIN *begins to laugh again. JULIA & GEORGE join in*)

DOLORES
I don't know why you think this is so funny. We could've gotten killed.

WERNER
And we tore apart the offices.

QUENTIN
Dammit. I forgot about that.

JULIA
How bad can it be? *(She looks out the door)* Oh.

QUENTIN
You'd best get out of here. Right now. If anyone from the station were to come in...

DOLORES
Go home? We can't just go home!

QUENTIN
I'll have Maude get in touch with everyone tomorrow to reschedule our rehearsal.

WERNER
What about the mess in the...

QUENTIN
I'll take care of it. Now go on. All of you. You still have something of an evening left. Go enjoy it.

GEORGE
Quentin.

QUENTIN
What?

GEORGE
We might not even have jobs tomorrow.

QUENTIN
Are you serious? Welles just tripled the demand for radio theatre in a single broadcast. I think we'll be fine. *(They all just stare at him)* What do you want to do? Hmmm? Sit here and discuss how we were all victims of the greatest trick in Halloween history? How we were all played for saps by the goddamn Mercury Theatre of the Air? Or would you rather go home to your loved ones? *(They all just stare at him)* Go! Go, go, go!

(MAUDE, DOLORES & WERNER *speak as they leave. JULIA also exits*)

MAUDE
Good night, Mr. Farlowe.

QUENTIN
Good night, Maude.

DOLORES
I've missed my party.

WERNER
If you would like, there is a movie playing down on Fourth. The Invisible Ray. It has Karloff and Lugosi.

DOLORES
Ooo!

(GEORGE remains)

GEORGE
So I guess I'll just go then.

QUENTIN
Good night, George.

GEORGE
Again...very sorry about the whole...

QUENTIN
Water under the bridge.

GEORGE
No, Quentin. I need you to understand...

QUENTIN
George. Water under the bridge.

GEORGE
Really?

QUENTIN
Really.

GEORGE
Well... good night then.

QUENTIN
Night.

(GEORGE leaves. QUENTIN is alone for a bit. He sits and touches the wound on his head. It still stings. Suddenly, the door creaks open, and the jack-o-lantern appears, held by JULIA. She makes a silly, ghostly sound)

JULIA
Ooooooooo!

QUENTIN
Very funny.

(JULIA enters, fully)

JULIA
I found this on the front step.

QUENTIN
It's Maude's.

JULIA
I thought trick-or-treating happened tomorrow.

QUENTIN
It's a community program.

JULIA
Well. There's church folk for you. *(She hands it to him, then starts to go)*

QUENTIN
Julia?

JULIA
Yes?

QUENTIN
If I... that is... If I were to call on you tomorrow, would you answer?

(She smiles)

JULIA
Why don't you call on me tomorrow and find out?

(She is about to leave, then looks back at him)

JULIA
Oh hell. Why wait?

(They laugh, take each other's hands & kiss. Lights fade. Blackout)

END OF PLAY

VOICES OF THE MIDWEST

HOME

A PLAY BY
ANNIE MARTIN & SUZI REGAN

Cast of Characters

This play was originally cast with 2 women and 2 men with a troubadour, but it can be performed with as many as 39 actors: 18 women and 21 men. Songs indicate whether a male or female should sing it.

TROUBADOUR

MARIA: Mother to HENRY and SUZI; wife to JACK
JACK: Father to HENRY and SUZI; husband to MARIA
HENRY: 13-15 year old boy
SUZI: 13-16 year old girl

JOHN: 83 year old man

LITTLE GIRL #1
LITTLE GIRL #2
LITTLE BOY #1
LITTLE BOY #2

SAM: 40ish husband to THERESA; father to LINDSAY and BRENDAN
THERESA: 40ish wife to SAM; mother to LINDSAY and BRENDAN
LINDSAY: teenage daughter of SAM and THERESA
BRENDAN: teenage son of SAM and THERESA

DAD: Father to TOM
TOM: 17 year old son

DAVE: late 20s-early 30s; AMY's husband
AMY: late 20s-early 30s; DAVE's wife

ROE: elderly woman
STEVE: late 20s-early 30s; married to MARGO
MARGO: late 20s-early 30s; married to STEVE

SARAH: 16-17 year old girl; babysitter to TOMMY
TOMMY: 7 or 8 year old boy

HELEN: late 30s-early 40s; TIM's sister
TIM: late 30s-late 40s; HELEN's brother

WOMAN #1
MAN #1
MAN #2
WOMAN #2

CHARLEY: 5 year old girl

BILL: father of SARAH, ex-husband of OLIVIA
OLIVIA: mother of SARAH, ex-wife of BILL
SIMON: OLIVIA's date

SETH: 24 year old bartender; Jim's boyfriend
NANCY: late 50s-early 60s; mother of Jim

PETE: retiring teacher

COACH
HAZEN: little boy
SANDY: little girl
MAGGIE: little girl

SETTING and TIME
The set is a house; almost looks like a dollhouse.
Upstairs is a bedroom and bathroom.
Downstairs is a kitchen with working oven and table and a living room.
Next to the bedroom stands a tree and a tree house,
in which sits the troubadour with his guitar.
He narrates and plays from his perch (can sing some songs).

The time is here and now.

THE VOICES FROM THE MIDWEST series of plays was created by the Williamston Theatre to explore and embrace what life is like in our part of the world. Directors and playwrights on the project developed questionnaires, and sent them all over the Midwest, inviting submissions from people of all walks of life. Those submissions were then taken and adapted into three evenings of theatre exploring the life of women, men, and families in the American Midwest.

HOME was written, in part, thanks to submissions from the following people: Fran Ahern, Norma Baker, Sandra Birch, Christine Boesen, Judith Bridger, Dennis Brunzell, Julie Brunzell, Megan Buckley, Eileen Burns, Tony Caselli, Erin Clossen, Linda Kay Clossen, Hazen Cuyler, Ron Dorr, Llewellyn Drong, Brian Jones, Edmund Alyn Jones, Kaliandra Jones, Patti Kenney, Kate Koshnick, Frank J. Leahey, John Lepard, Danielle Lobdell, Spencer Lyons, Annie Martin, Margaret Martinelli, Theresa Martinelli, Margaret Meyer, Jane McChesney, Trever McTaggart, Margaret Miller, Patricia P. Miller, Sidney Miller, Helen Murray, Patty Nolan, Gina Phipps, Erin Roth, Abbie Scott, Danna Segrest, Cheyenne Shemwell, Carolyn Swanson, George H. Swanson, Toby Ten Eyck, Gloria Watson, Kathryn Wildfong, Louis Wildfong, Liz Wright, Emily Zimmer, and many people who wish to remain anonymous.

HOME: VOICES FROM FAMILIES OF THE MIDWEST received its world premiere on May 13, 2010 at Williamston Theatre (Williamston, MI). It was directed by Suzi Regan. Set and Lighting Design by Daniel C. Walker, Costume Design by Amber Marissa Cook, Music by Suzi Regan. Stage managed by Erin K. Snyder. VOICES OF THE MIDWEST series concept by Tony Caselli.

The cast was as follows:

Sandra Birch
Hazen Cuyler
John Lepard
Maggie Meyer
and Nick Hinz as the Troubadour

For production rights, contact Williamston Theatre.

HOME

ACT I
SCENE ONE
FAMILY TREE SONG

(Cast moves slowly from each room singing with the TROUBADOUR)

ALL
DEEP ARE THE ROOTS
HIGH IS THE TREE
WIDE ARE THE BRANCHES
FRAGILE THE LEAVES
THOUSANDS UPON THOUSANDS
-ONE SEED
THOUSANDS BY THOUSANDS
HOLD FAST IN THE BREEZE

THRU GALE WIND AND STORM
HEART WOOD REMAINS STRONG
LULLABIES OF SPRING TIDE
US THRU WINTERS LONG
GNARLED AND FLAWED
OUR BARK, BITING TONGUES
HUMBLED AND HOPE FILLED
WE TURN TO THE SUN

WE
CLING TO THE FORTRESS
BLIND IS THE SEARCH
BELOW AND ABOVE
WE
ENCIRCLED BY THE ELDERS
WE
RETURN TO THE CENTER
LOVE

SOMETIMES MY ENEMY
AT TIMES MY ALLY
ALWAYS THE THICK LIFE BLOOD
BETWEEN YOU AND I
BUT I WILL HOLD YOU UP
WHEN DAY FALLS TO NIGH
ROCKING YOU GENTLY
TIL MORNING SKY

WE
CLING TO THE FORTRESS
BLINDLY WE SEARCH
BELOW AND ABOVE
WE
ENCIRCLED BY THE ELDERS
WE
RETURN TO THE CENTER

TAKE ROOT
RAIN FALLS
GROW A LITTLE
SUNSHINE
GROW A LITTLE MORE

LIVE A LITTLE
RAIN FALLS
GROW A LITTLE
SUNSHINE
GROW A LITTLE MORE

FORGIVE A LITTLE
RAIN FALLS
GROW A LITTLE
SUNSHINE
GROW A LITTLE MORE

GROW A LITTLE
GROW A LITTLE
GROW A LITTLE
GROW A LITTLE MORE

WE
CLING TO THE FORTRESS
BLIND IS THE SEARCH
BELOW AND ABOVE
WE
ENCIRCLED BY THE ELDERS
WE
RETURN TO THE CENTER
LOVE

DEEP ARE THE ROOTS
HIGH IS THE TREE
WIDE ARE THE BRANCHES
FRAGILE ARE WE

(Lights change)

SCENE TWO

TROUBADOUR
The Lyons Home. Wayne, MI

(DAD is setting up the camera and tripod. MOM is directing)

MOM
Henry! Suzi!

DAD
Where do you want me to aim this thing?

MOM
I want to start on the couch and then maybe try the stairs. *(yells)* Henry!

HENRY
Yep. Comin. *(runs down the stairs)*

MOM
(to HENRY) You look so handsome. Let me just— *(licks her hand and tries to flatten his hair)*

HENRY
Mom.

MOM
Go sit on the couch. *(yells)* SUZI! NOW!

SUZI
This is ridiculous!

MOM
No it's not. *(to DAD)* Can you do something?

DAD
What do you want me to do?

MOM
Anything.

DAD
Fine. *(goes to SUZI)* Come on.

SUZI
Dad, this is so stupid.

DAD
It's not stupid. Do we look stupid? Maybe. But it's not stupid, it's memories.

SUZI
Why does she make us...

DAD
Because time flies by before you know it. You're gonna go off on your own

sooner than we think and... it's 10 minutes Suzi. Come on. We'll look back and laugh at these.

SUZI
Fine. *(walks over to the couch)*

MOM
(to SUZI) You look beautiful.

SUZI
Thanks.

MOM
(to SUZI) Do you want to run a brush through your hair?

SUZI
God. I'm sorry if I don't look the way you think I should.

DAD
(to MOM) Honey.

MOM
I was trying to help.

SUZI
Uh-huh.

HENRY
(whispers to SUZI) I think it looks good.

SUZI
Thanks.

HENRY
Not.

(SUZI punches HENRY)

HENRY
Mom!

(MOM ignores them)

MOM
Henry stop whining.

SUZI
(interrupting) Yeah, Henry.

MOM
(to HENRY) I need you on that arm of the couch. And Suzi I want you on the other one.

HENRY
(interrupting; to SUZI) I wonder if she'll be able to fit your fat butt in the picture.

MOM
(to DAD) Babe will you go sit so I can see what this looks like.

(DAD sits. MOM looks through the camera lens)

MOM
This looks good. Really good.

DAD
Hon, do you remember how to program it? You have to...

MOM
Yes. Yes. I remember. *(tinkers then sits down)* When the red light shines we have 5 seconds, ok? *(pause)* Ok?

DAD, HENRY, and SUZI
Yes.

MOM
There it is. And...

(Click. MOM and HENRY were the only ones smiling. MOM gets up and checks the camera)

MOM
A couple more. Let me just get it re-set. *(looks at the shot)* Jack!

DAD
What?

MOM
You and Suzi aren't smiling.

DAD
I look like an idiot when I smile.

SUZI
Me too.

HENRY
(to SUZI) Yeah. You do.

(MOM stares at DAD with that look)

DAD
Fine. *(Looks at SUZI)* We'll smile, right?

SUZI
Sure.

(MOM runs back over to the couch)

MOM
Get ready. Get ready. Red... Cheese!

(Click. They all blink. MOM back up)

MOM
Hold on. No one move. *(Tinkers with the camera)* Darn. Blinked. Ok. Let's do this again.

(MOM runs back to the couch)

MOM
Alright. Smile guys.

(SUZI gives the finger and HENRY sees)

HENRY
She just gave the finger, Mom.

(Click)

SUZI
No I didn't.

MOM
Are you kidding me?

DAD
(laughing) Suz.

MOM
You know, I just want one nice picture of us all and it's like I'm expecting the world from all of you. So all of you zip it and smile before I lose it. Now get up and get on the stairs. The couch isn't working anymore.

SUZI
Calm down, Ma.

(They move to the stairs. DAD goes to MOM and gives her a kiss)

MOM
(to DAD) Don't start.

DAD
I'm sorry.

MOM
Uh-huh. Go sit on the top stair will you. *(to HENRY)* Henry sit beside your dad. Suzi below Henry. *(They move)* Closer please. *(tinkers with the camera)* Ok. Now smile and we can be done. *(runs to the stairs and sits)* Red light and...

(Everyone smells something bad. Click. MOM gets up quickly and runs to the camera)

HENRY
It wasn't me?

SUZI
Dad?

DAD
That wasn't me.

(They all look at MOM)

MOM
I didn't think it would be so foul.

(They all start laughing)

MOM
Oh this picture is horrible.

(HENRY gets up)

HENRY
I wanna see.

MOM
Fine. Here.

(HENRY *laughs. SUZI gets up and comes over*)

HENRY
That's awesome!

SUZI
Oh my god. Mom, you're the only one smiling.

MOM
Stop it.

HENRY
This is a keeper.

(*DAD gets up*)

DAD
Now I gotta see this.

(*Everyone is laughing*)

MOM
I'm deleting this.

SUZI
No way!

HENRY
(*at the same time*) Mom.

DAD
It is a memory, Sweetie.

MOM
(*trying not to laugh*) I won't delete it if I can just get a normal one of us. One more. Get back there.

(*They get back on the stairs as MOM resets the camera*)

MOM
Ok. Let's do this. (*MOM runs back to the stairs*)

HENRY
Mom, let us know if you're gonna drop another one.

SUZI
Yeah, right.

(*They all smile. Click. Lights change*)

SCENE THREE
HOMEBODY

TROUBADOUR
The Harpster Home. Bloomington, IN.

(*JOHN sits on the bed and works to get up and down to make a couple of tea*)

JOHN
Still standing after 83 years,
Weathered the storms
Soaked in the sun
A new part needed here or there.

The lights are still on
    sometimes too much
    and the plumbing still works
    with an occasional leak.

The roof has thinned out,
    but it's still all mine.

Walls are cracked, bubbled, and uneven
    and the paint is the color
    of faded paper

A sweater is needed
    since the thermostat barely works
    and sometimes there is a faint
    smell of must.

But the windows still open
    seeing what the new day brings.

And the foundation,
    even after all this,
    has never faltered.

May not look like much now
    but in my day, I could
    lift 3 kids and still

carry the groceries.

Trapped inside me is an unending slide-show
    of senses and their memories.

Taste that double decker burger
    blood in the mouth
        cherry chapstick on Sally's lips

Smell the dinner
    baby
    illness

Hear booming laughter
    nagging voices
    Daddy, Daddy

See her wink
    him sleep
    those tears

Feel a nail in my heel
    hands on her body
    ache in my heart

Feel all the anger
    Pain
    Laughter
    Sorrow
    Loss
    Joy

Feel all that Love
Love wanted
Love needed
Love given.

Still standing after 83 years,
My home body.

(Lights change)

SCENE FOUR
ALIENS

TROUBADOUR
Earth. Midwest, U.S.A

(Four kids are outside with tin cans as telephones, a paper towel roll for a telescope/binoculars, and a big box that's dressed up like a radio or something)

LITTLE GIRL #1
(looking through the paper towel at the sky) I think I saw something. I saw them.

LITTLE BOY #1
Where? Where?

LITTLE GIRL #2
I saw'em too.

LITTLE BOY #2
Should we wave?

LITTLE BOY #1
Time to make contact. Come on.

LITTLE GIRL #1
Warm up the Alien talker.

LITTLE BOY #2
Me?

LITTLE BOY #1
Me. *(steps forward and pushes LITTLE BOY #2 out of the way)*

LITTLE GIRL #2
We're gonna lose them. Come on.

LITTLE GIRL #1
Go! Go! Go!

LITTLE BOY #1
Hazen, go put the antennae in the tree.

LITTLE BOY #2
Me?

LITTLE GIRL #1
This is serious. Really serious, guys.

LITTLE BOY #2
Do I have to climb up?

LITTLE GIRL #2
They better not eat brains.

LITTLE GIRL #1
They'll be friendly, I think.

LITTLE BOY #2
Brains?

LITTLE GIRL #2
(to LITTLE BOY #2) Yep. Gooey brains.

LITTLE BOY #1
They're not gonna eat you.

LITTLE GIRL #1
They might let us on their ship.

LITTLE BOY #1
Or their planet.

LITTLE GIRL #1
Yes, and they'll have magic medicine that will make people all better like Katie.

LITTLE GIRL #2
What's wrong with her now?

LITTLE GIRL #1
Nothing is wrong with her.

LITTLE BOY #1
She's got awesome.

LITTLE GIRL #2
Oh.

LITTLE GIRL #1
She's autistic. Not awesome.

LITTLE GIRL #2
Yeah, John.

LITTLE BOY #2
Will eating her brains help?

EVERYONE
NO.

LITTLE BOY #2
Stop yelling. I gotta be home by 8 or my mom...

LITTLE BOY #1
It's ready. We're ready.

LITTLE GIRL #1
Ok. Guys. This is it. I'll talk.

LITTLE GIRL #2
What makes you get to talk to them?

LITTLE GIRL #1
It's my box. *(turning pretend knobs and stuff like that)* Hello? Hello?

LITTLE GIRL #2
I can do it better.

LITTLE BOY #2
Do I have to keep holding this?

EVERYONE
YES!

LITTLE GIRL #1
Hello out there. This is Maggie. Maggie on Earth. In Michigan. We are friendly people.

LITTLE BOY #2
Don't mention the brains. It'd be rude.

LITTLE GIRL #2
(taking over the mic) I'm Sandy. And the leader of this planet.

LITTLE BOY #1
No. She's not.

LITTLE GIRL #1
SANDY!

LITTLE BOY #2
Don't confuse the aliens.

LITTLE GIRL #1
(into the mic) Can you hear us? If so, say something. Talk to us even if it's not English.

LITTLE GIRL #2
They don't speak English?

LITTLE GIRL #1
No. Clicks. They talk in clicks.

(LITTLE BOY #1 looks through the telescope)

LITTLE BOY #1
I see lights.

LITTLE BOY #2
What?

LITTLE GIRL #1
(into the mic) We see you. We see you!

LITTLE GIRL #2
HI! HI!

LITTLE BOY #2
I can't see them. Are them coming?

LITTLE BOY #1
Oh it's a plane.

LITTLE GIRL #1
Are you sure?

LITTLE GIRL #2
I knew it.

LITTLE BOY #2
Thank god.

LITTLE GIRL #1
Hello? Hello? This is Maggie from Earth. From Michigan. Come in. Come in. We are friendly. Hello?

(Lights change)

SCENE FIVE
I DON'T WANNA GO TO WORK TODAY

(Song originally performed by two men and two women)

I DON'T WANT TO GO TO WORK TODAY
I WANNA HANG AROUND WITH YOU
I DON'T WANT TO GO TO WORK TODAY
I WANNA HANG AROUND WITH YOU

SUNSHINE IS CALLIN MY NAME
IF I STAY INSIDE I WILL GO INSANE
WANNA RUN ON THE BEACH HOLDIN' HANDS
WANNA FEEL MY TOES IN THE SAND

CAUSE I DON'T WANT TO GO TO WORK TODAY
I WANNA HANG AROUND WITH YOU
I DON'T WANT TO GO TO WORK TODAY
I WANNA HANG AROUND WITH YOU

WANNA FEEL THE SUMMER HEAT
OF PEOPLE DANCING TO A SUMMER BEAT
KICK OFF YOUR SHOES AND DANCE IN BARE FEET
COME ON LET'S HIT THE STREET AND SING

LA LA LA

OH NO IT LOOKS LIKE RAIN
I WISH IT'D GO AWAY AND NEVER COME BACK AGAIN
WELL IF THE SUN'S GONNA HIDE
WE CAN PLAY INSIDE

I DON'T WANT TO GO TO WORK TODAY
I WANT TO HANG AROUND WITH YOU
I DON'T WANT TO GO TO WORK TODAY
I WANT TO HANG AROUND WITH YOU
AROUND WITH YOU
I WANT TO FOOL AROUND
AND ROUND AND ROUND AND ROUND AND ROUND
I WANT TO FOOL AROUND WITH YOU

(Lights change)

SCENE SIX

TROUBADOUR
The Gruber Home. Muskegon, MI

(Morning. Alarm clock goes off. THERESA gets up from bed with SAM beside her)

SAM
Hey babe. *(kisses her head)*

THERESA
Morning. Don't forget about Brendan's—

SAM
Game. I know.

(THERESA goes to the bathroom, looks at herself in the mirror, maybe weighs herself)

THERESA
Are you showering?

SAM
Uh-huh.

THERESA
I need to get in before you.

SAM
Ok. But I need to—

LINDSAY
(enters) I need the bathroom.

THERESA
We're in here.

LINDSAY
But I gotta go.

SAM
Good morning to you too.

(LINDSAY goes and shuts the door)

SAM
I gotta go after her. Then the shower's yours.

THERESA
Just go while I'm in there.

SAM
I've gotta take a dump.

THERESA
How old are you?

SAM
Shut up.

THERESA
You gotta wait Sam. I don't want to end up smelling like your poop... it lingers.

SAM
What do you want me to do?

THERESA
Go outside.

(A shower has started)

SAM
I don't want to—

THERESA
(pounds on the door) LINDSAY!!! NO WAY! YOU GET THE SHOWER AT 7:10. GET OUT OF THERE!

SAM
OPEN THIS DOOR!

THERESA
RIGHT THIS MINUTE!

LINDSAY
(from inside) I'll be five minutes.

SAM and THERESA
NO.

THERESA
(opens the door) Get out!

LINDSAY
HEY!

THERESA
I've got a meeting and you will not—

SAM
Not cool, Linds.

LINDSAY
We need another bathroom.

THERESA
Well, I need a more respectful daughter.

LINDSAY
Yeah, well I need a realistic mother.

SAM
Hey. Enough.

THERESA
I'm tired of this.

LINDSAY
I'm late almost everyday.

SAM
Don't care. We work. It's what pays for all your—

LINDSAY
I can't help it. Mom takes forever. Why do I get penalized for—

THERESA
Then get up earlier.

LINDSAY
Why don't you?

SAM
Watch it! *(pause)* Good. Both of you get out—

THERESA
Light a match.

LINDSAY
GROSS! Dad, please let me shower before. Please!

THERESA
(to Sam) Maybe you can hold it?

LINDSAY
Come on, Dad. Please.

SAM
Why am I made to feel bad—

BRENDAN
(smiling) Morning! *(they look at him)* I just need my toothbrush. (Grabs his toothbrush)

THERESA
Morning.

LINDSAY
Brendan, don't you think it's unfair that—

BRENDAN
I shower at night.

THERESA
Exactly.

LINDSAY
Well, I care about what I look like.

THERESA
Your brother cares.

LINDSAY
I'm not gonna brush my teeth in the sink.

THERESA
Nobody asked you too.

SAM
Your brother is resourceful, so move out and—

LINDSAY
It's gross.

THERESA
Wait. Does he brush his teeth in the kitchen?

SAM and LINDSAY
Yes.

THERESA
Why did I not know that?

SAM
It's fine, now move.

THERESA
Just try not to—

(SAM slams the door)

LINDSAY
Open the window, Dad.

THERESA
And light a match.

SAM
GET AWAY FROM THE DOOR!

LINDSAY
Why can't we build another bathroom in the basement?

THERESA
Because it costs money. Stop complaining. This isn't so bad.

LINDSAY
Yeah, well Brendan is using your dish rag on his pits.

THERESA
(looks over) BRENDAN!

(Lights change)

SCENE SEVEN
SEX TALK

TROUBADOUR
The Baker Home. Sylvania, OH.

(Living room sofa. TOM and his DAD are sitting on the sofa watching basketball)

DAD
Get it to Summers. Get it to Summers. God.

TOM
Another turnover. Come on.

DAD
Why are they taking a time out?

TOM
TV time out.

DAD
Ah, right.

(Silence except for the television. They both are watching TV and never look at each other)

DAD
So how are things with you and Christina?

TOM
Good.

DAD
Good.

(Silence)

DAD
Things getting serious?

TOM
I don't know. I guess.

DAD
Hm.

(Silence)

DAD
So your mom wanted me to talk to you.

TOM
Uh-huh

DAD
She found some condoms.

TOM
Oh.

DAD
And she thought we should talk.

TOM
Uh-huh.

DAD
So.

(Silence)

DAD
Anything you want to talk about or you know anything?

TOM
Not really.

(Pause)

DAD
Well you know if you do...

TOM
Yeah.

DAD
Good. Good. *(to the TV)* His house is made out of beer cans. Ha.

(TOM starts to get up)

DAD
(grabs his arm) Where you goin...

TOM
Bathroom?

DAD
You're being safe, right?

TOM
In the bathroom? Yeah.

DAD
With Christina.

TOM
Uh-huh.

DAD
It's important to be... safe all the time.

TOM
I know. Trust me.

DAD
Yeah. Ok.

(Silence)

DAD
So, if you have any questions...

TOM
(starts to leave) Ok.

DAD
You might want to keep those things in a different place. Where mom doesn't go. *(TOM nods and leaves. DAD looks at the screen again)* That duck always gets hurt.

(Lights change)

SCENE EIGHT
BABY TIME

TROUBADOUR
The Barsch-Shuler Home. Marquette, MI.

(DAVE is upstairs in the bed. AMY is in the kitchen cleaning up. DAVE is waiting)

AMY
(singing softly)
For Love I'd travel mountains steep
Deserts dry, oceans deep
Without I'd never wake or sleep
My sun sets and rises in your eyes

DAVE
(calling out)
Amy! Amy! What are you doing?

AMY
What?

DAVE
Come up here!

AMY
In a minute.

DAVE
Come on.

AMY
In a minute.

(DAVE comes down into the kitchen and starts to nuzzle her)

DAVE
(mumbles) I love you.

AMY
I love you too.

(Kissing)

DAVE
God, you're sexy.

(AMY laughs and they continue to fool around on the kitchen table)

DAVE
Let's make a baby.

(DAVE kisses her, but AMY has stopped)

AMY
What?

DAVE
(kissing her) I'm ready.

AMY
Ready?

DAVE
I'm just letting you know.

AMY
Ready for sex or a baby?

DAVE
(stops) Both, I guess.

AMY
You wanna have a baby?

DAVE
Well, yeah. I thought you wanted to—

AMY
And you feel like now, right now, is the perfect time to let me know this?

DAVE
Are you getting mad at me?

AMY
It's like you're trying to slip something by me.

DAVE
(kisses her) Well yeah, something like that.

AMY
(pushes him back) Wait, you can't just drop this and…

DAVE
I thought you wanted to start trying.

AMY
I did. I do.

DAVE
Then let's not make a big deal about this.

AMY
Big deal? Babies… big deal.

DAVE
You know what I mean.

AMY
Where's this coming from? I'm confused.

DAVE
Yeah. Me too.

AMY
So you want to start to try, right? That is what you are saying?

DAVE
Yes.

AMY
And this isn't about wanting sex more?

DAVE
Are you kidding me?

AMY
I'm serious. I realize I haven't been in the mood…

DAVE
I'm not using children as an excuse to have sex. I just want to have sex.

AMY
I wanted this a year ago.

DAVE
I know.

AMY
You weren't ready.

DAVE
I remember.

AMY
And?

DAVE
And, now I am... or I should say, was.

AMY
(pointing) See, you can't change your mind.

DAVE
Joking.

AMY
It's not funny.

DAVE
I'm not laughing.

AMY
This is going to change everything. Everything.

DAVE
Ok.

AMY
Ok? That's it.

DAVE
Amy, I...

AMY
So you really want kids now?

DAVE
I've always wanted them.

AMY
Because a year ago you said...

DAVE
That was a year ago. I just changed jobs, remember. We bought this house and couldn't afford the mortgage.

AMY
But.

DAVE
It was too much. I told you that then.

AMY
Well you know babies are stressful.

DAVE
What? They are? Babies aren't all rainbows and sunshine?

AMY
I'm just saying they change everything. Keep you up all hours of the night, they need constant attention, love. And what if we have a sick kid? I mean the financial burdens are tenfold, have you considered that? Children, everyone says, they change a relationship. Men can have very bad reactions to not coming first anymore.

DAVE
When did I come first?

AMY
Have you thought about this? I mean really thought about it.

DAVE
Yeah.

AMY
This will change us. Forever. We can't take this back.

DAVE
Do you not want to...

AMY
No. No. I do, I do

DAVE
Honey, people dumber than us have raised fairly normal families. I think we can handle it.

AMY
Really? You really think we can?

DAVE
Come on. I don't want to try to pass your crazy test.

AMY
I want to talk about this and you are acting like I'm putting you out. Like I can't ask a question about how your mind got changed. I can't read your mind. I don't know how you got to this place. I don't know what you're expecting. You have to talk instead of making declarations.

DAVE
Well I don't know what else to say. I've always wanted to have kids with you... even with all your issues. My hesitation earlier was about being able to provide for you and them.

AMY
Well I provide too.

DAVE
I know you do, but as a man... I... it's just... I'm supposed to provide... it's an ingrained thing or something. I want to make sure I can give our kids everything they need. Make sure I can be a good father and not just a sperm donor who maybe sees their kids on the weekend for 2 hours, aka your father. And now I'm feeling a little better about my abilities and honestly I don't want to be 50 when I have a kid. Jerry at work, his wife can't have kids and they've been trying for 6 years. So, you know times ticking away and that's really it. No hidden agenda.

AMY
Oh.

DAVE
Did I pass?

AMY
Yes.

DAVE
I only have one concern.

AMY
What?

DAVE
I don't want to look at this kid coming out. Don't make me look.

AMY
Ok.

DAVE
I'm serious.

AMY
Ok. *(pause)* I love you.

DAVE
I love you too. Let's get to work

(They kiss)

AMY
You know, we should probably wait until Wednesday. I think I'll be ovulating then. Is that okay?

(Lights change)

SCENE NINE
AUNT ROE

TROUBADOUR
The MacAdam Home. Madison, WI.

(ROE, an elderly woman, is onstage watching out the window with a phone in her hand. We see her get pissed and dial the phone)

ROE
Yes. This is Mrs. Rose MacAdam at 1056 Pembroke. I need you to send an officer over here immediately. *(pause)* People are trespassing on my lawn and destroying property. *(pause)* I have asked their parents to keep them away, but they are back again graffiting my sidewalk. *(pause)* I don't know. I can't tell. It's either spray paint or chalk. *(pause)* No, it is my sidewalk, not the city's. *(pause)* What is your name? *(pause)* Well Officer Polish-ski or whatever it is, I want to speak with your supervisor. *(pause)* Not in? Hm. Some slick department you're running over there. I'll be writing to the mayor about this. And I'll expect to see an officer in 5 minutes or I'll be calling again. *(hanging up, ROE goes to the door and yells out)* Get off my lawn, Hooligans! I just called the police and you're going to jail. GET! *(goes to sit and look out the window again)*

(STEVE and MARGO knock on the door)

ROE
Who is it?

MARGO
Mrs. MacAdam? It's Steve and Margo Bailey.

ROE
Who?

MARGO
Margo from next door.

ROE
I can't hear you.

STEVE
IT'S STEVE AND MARGO FROM...

(ROE opens the door)

ROE
Stop yelling; you look foolish.

MARGO
Morning, Mrs. MacAdam. We haven't seen you out and...

ROE
Are you spying on me?

STEVE
No. No. Margo brought you some of her famous chocolate chip cookies.

ROE
I can't eat those anymore. Upsets my stomach and gives me diarrhea.

MARGO
I'm sorry I didn't know.

ROE
(cuts her off and takes the plate) Maybe I'll just feed them to the squirrels and birds in the back. *(throws them out)* Thank you.

STEVE
Mrs. MacAdam, I noticed the shrubs on the side of your house are a little overgrown.

ROE
Is there a law against that?

MARGO
He'd like to help.

STEVE
Trim them back if you'd like.

ROE
Well that would be fine, but don't put yourself out.

STEVE
Ok.

MARGO
Is there anything you need?

ROE
Do I look like I do?

MARGO
Well, we won't take up anymore of your time.

ROE
Well you're already here, so come in for a minute.

MARGO
Um… well, we can stay just for a few minutes.

STEVE
Ok.

MARGO
I just love those roses outside. And this year, they are just beautiful.

ROE
My husband Randall planted those the first year we moved in here. Used to say "Every woman named Rose deserves roses in the yard."

MARGO
How sweet.

ROE
It was. He was a good man. I wish you both would have known him. But…

MARGO
Yes.

ROE
He would have had some things to say about this neighborhood going downhill like it has.

STEVE
I don't think it's going downhill, Mrs…

ROE
How would you know?

MARGO
Well, we love it here.

STEVE
Hon, we should probably get going.

ROE
My bathroom upstairs… the toilet keeps running.

MARGO
Oh. That's too bad.

ROE
It keeps me up at all hours.

STEVE
Maybe you should call a plumber.

ROE
I'm on a fixed income. I can't. I'll just have to deal with it. I sleep with a pillow over my head, but sometimes I wake in such a panic thinking I'm suffocating. I wouldn't be surprised if this actually caused me to die.

MARGO
That's horrible.

ROE
I'm just stating facts.

(MARGO looks at STEVE)

STEVE
I could look at it if you'd like.

ROE
What do you know about plumbing?

STEVE
Not too much, but a toilet running like that is common and…

ROE
Fine. But don't make the problem worse unless you're willing to pay for the repairs.

STEVE
Let me just go assess the situation.

ROE
It's up the stairs. First door on the left.

Don't touch anything else.

(STEVE just goes upstairs)

MARGO
He's handy.

ROE
Randall thought he was handy too, but he wasn't.

(Silence)

ROE
Did you see those kids trashing my lawn again?

MARGO
(pause) Who? Oh no. They're just doing sidewalk chalk.

ROE
(cuts her off) They're little rats, leeches... little punks of the neighborhood.

(Silence)

MARGO
Well we're going to be adding to it.

ROE
What?

MARGO
Steve and I have exciting news. I'm pregnant.

ROE
Why?

MARGO
Excuse me?

ROE
Why do you want children?

MARGO
We've always wanted a family.

ROE
I hope you plan to raise them responsibly and with morals and respect.

MARGO
(interrupting) Of course.

ROE
(keeps going) These children today, they get away with anything. I hear the way they talk to their parents. It is appalling.

MARGO
I hope we'll be able to...

ROE
You need to be strict.

MARGO
Well...

ROE
They need rules and supervision.

MARGO
Yes. Yes.

ROE
(looking her over) I think you'll be capable.

MARGO
I hope so. It's a little nerve racking.

ROE
How are you feeling? You don't look well. I didn't want to say anything when you walked in, but your color...

MARGO
I've had some morning sickness.

ROE
(Pulls out some tea) You need to drink this. It will help.

MARGO
(reading the box) Ginger tea?

ROE
Three cups a day, at least. Helps with the nausea.

MARGO
I haven't seen this before. Thank you. I

don't want to take your box though...

ROE
I insist. I'll make you a cup right now.

MARGO
Oh, you don't have to.

ROE
You've got to take care of yourself. I hope your husband is being understanding and supportive.

MARGO
Steve is wonderful.

ROE
He doesn't seem so wonderful at fixing my plumbing. *(yells up)* Boy, you better not be touching anything but my toilet.

MARGO
I'm sure he's working on it.

STEVE
JUST GIVE ME A MINUTE!

(ROE grabs one of her cookies out of the trash and gives it to MARGO)

ROE
What does your mother think about your expecting?

MARGO
My mother passed.

ROE
She did?

MARGO
Yes.

ROE
Sisters?

MARGO
Just me.

ROE
That doesn't seem right.

MARGO
It's just life, I guess.

ROE
I'm sorry about your mother.

MARGO
Thank you.

ROE
Girl needs a mother going through such a big change.

MARGO
Do you have any children? I...

ROE
No. It wasn't meant to be.

MARGO
Oh.

ROE
You know what else you need. Some Ensure. My doctor gave me some, but I think you need to drink it. It's like a strawberry milkshake. It'll boost up your immune system. *(yells up)* Boy, Go in the attic and get my case of Ensure!

MARGO
Mrs. MacAdam, please. I can go buy some.

ROE
No. No. I want you to have this.

STEVE
ENSURE?

ROE
Is he deaf? *(yells up)* YES! Open your ears.

(STEVE is rummaging through the attic)

MARGO
I really couldn't. That's for you.

ROE
Gives me gas. So I'd rather have it used then... What is your husband

doing up there?

MARGO
He's...

ROE
He's taking to long. I've got valuables up there.

MARGO
Ok. Ok. *(calls)* STEVE!

STEVE
WHAT?

ROE
Get out of there!

MARGO
Come on down here, honey. Mrs. MacAdam doesn't want you...

(STEVE walks down the stairs with the case of dust covered Ensure)

STEVE
I found it.

ROE
You didn't find anything. I told you where it was.

STEVE
Ok. Here it is. Where would you like it?

MARGO
That's for me, Sweetie.

STEVE
Really?

ROE
Your wife needs to nourish herself. Look at her. She looks horrible. This pregnancy will take a toll on her.

STEVE
(to MARGO) You told her?

MARGO
It just kind of...

ROE
She didn't have too. It's obvious.

STEVE
Uh-huh. The toilet's all fixed

MARGO
Good job, babe.

ROE
What do you mean?

STEVE
The chain was just tangled. It's an old toilet.

ROE
It's the original.

STEVE
Well, it's working now.

ROE
It was working before.

STEVE
I mean it's not running anymore.

ROE
We'll see about that.

STEVE
Ok. Let me know if it happens again. It wasn't too hard.

ROE
Could have fooled me. *(to MARGO)* I wanna give you something else.

MARGO
No. Please.

ROE
Just let me. It'll make me feel good. *(to STEVE)* Go back to the Attic and grab the box labeled Junk.

STEVE
There's a lot of boxes up there.

ROE
You can read, can't you?

STEVE
Yes.

ROE
Then look for the box labeled Junk. Can you handle that?

STEVE
Yes. *(to MARGO)* But then honey, we need to go. *(goes back up the stairs)*

ROE
And be careful. I think I've heard bats or squirrels up there. I don't want them loose.

MARGO
Babe, be careful.

ROE
There's a lot of good stuff you'll be able to use.

MARGO
You are too generous. I don't know how to thank you.

ROE
No need. But you know, Margo, you should come over later this week. I'd like to see how you're doing. If the tea is helping.

MARGO
Yes, I'd like that.

ROE
Good. Good.

(STEVE comes down with a large box that's very overflowing with clothes and a lamp)

STEVE
We've gotta go.

MARGO
Wow. That's so much.

ROE
It is, yes.

STEVE
(walks out) Have a good day, Mrs. MacAdam.

MARGO
Well, thank you again.

ROE
(yelling after STEVE) Don't forget to trim my bush.

MARGO
It was good to see you.

ROE
Oh. You're welcome. *(they hug)* Is he going to make you carry that? *(indicates the Ensure)*

MARGO
I'm alright. Bye Bye.

ROE
Be careful now.

(They leave and ROE walks back to the window and talks to somebody unseen)

ROE
She's a sweet little thing, isn't she, Randall? I'll keep my eye on her.

(Lights change)

SCENE TEN
BYE (Song)

(Originally performed by one woman a capella)

THIS LOSS
OF YOU
IS MYSTIFYING
A MASTER RIDDLE
A RUBICS CUBE
MY HEAD IS SPINNING
DID I LET YOU
SLIP THRU THE CRACKS

I SHOULD OF
HAD YOUR BACK
FAMILY OF MISFIT TOYS
LAST CHANCE OASIS
FOR HOPEFUL GIRLS AND BOYS

I'M JUST BETTER
FOR HAVING KNOWN YOU
I'M JUST BETTER
HAVING BEEN LOVED BY YOU
AND I'M PICKING UP THE PIECES
BEFORE THE NEXT MOVE

SMILIN' PERCHED
AT THE BACK OF THE HOUSE
WATCHIN US DUKE IT OUT
LIFE IMITATES ART
IMITATES LIFE
AS WE PLAY OUR PART
THERE IS NO COMEDY
WITHOUT FIRST TRAGEDY
IT SEEMS TO ME
YOU WERE ONE FUNNY FUCKER, RANDY

I'M JUST BETTER FOR HAVING KNOWN YOU
I'M JUST BETTER FOR HAVING BEEN LOVED
BY YOU
AND NOW I'M PICKING UP THE PIECES
BEFORE THE NEXT MOVE

IS IT HOME IF THEY KICK YOU OUT
IS IT HOME IF THEY CHANGE THE LOCKS

THE KINGS HORSES AND MEN ARE FALLING
BUT THE EMPEROR IS STILL STANDING

NOTHING RINGS TRUE ANYMORE
HOW CAN ANYTHING RING TRUE AGAIN

THIS LOSS THE LOSS OF YOU IS STUPEFYING
YOU WERE TIRED
I'M TIRED TOO
I'M SICK OF BLAMING
AND STILL I FEEL YOU RIGHT HERE
SMOKING, DRINKIN A BEER
YOUR OPTIMISTIC CYNIC VOW
  SINGING "I LOOK AT LIFE FROM SIDES
FROM BOTH SIDES NOW"

I'M JUST BETTER FOR HAVING KNOWN YOU
I'M JUST BETTER FOR HAVING BEEN LOVED
BY YOU
I'M JUST PICKING UP THE PIECES
BEFORE MY NEXT MOVE

(Lights change)

SCENE ELEVEN
STARVING

TROUBADOUR
The Burns Home. Detroit, MI.

(TOMMY, maybe 7 or 8, runs around the room in a superhero cape like he's flying and fighting bad guys. SARAH, the babysitter, calls to him from the kitchen)

SARAH
Tommy, you want macaroni or grilled cheese? *(silence, running)* Tommy? *(silence, running)* Tommy? *(trying to stop him)* Tommy? Can you answer me? What's up?

TOMMY
I'm not hungry.

SARAH
You gotta eat something. Gotta be a little hungry.

TOMMY
Nope.

SARAH
Your mom said you liked both these.

TOMMY
No I don't. I hate 'em.

SARAH
Ok, so then what do you want? I'll make you whatever you want.

TOMMY
Sheppard's pie.

SARAH
Huh?

TOMMY
Sheppard's pie.

SARAH
I don't even know what that is. What is that?

TOMMY
My dad makes it.

SARAH
Oh.

(Pause. TOMMY slows down and crashes on the couch. Turns on the TV)

TOMMY
It's really good. Potatoes, meat, carrots. It's a man's meal.

SARAH
Well, um... I don't know how to make it.

TOMMY
No you don't.

SARAH
Name something else. I can make something...

TOMMY
I don't want anything else.

SARAH
You sure you won't eat anything. What about some cookies?

TOMMY
No.

SARAH
Ok. Ok. *(pause)* You'll tell me if you get hungry though. Ok? *(sits down next to him)* What are you watching?

TOMMY
Batman and Robin.

SARAH
Cool. *(she starts texting someone and TOMMY just watches TV. A few moments pass)*

TOMMY
My dad is dying.

(Silence)

SARAH
Yeah. I know.

TOMMY
I don't want him to die.

SARAH
Of course you don't.

TOMMY
When he dies, I'm gonna die.

SARAH
No you won't.

TOMMY
Yes.

SARAH
That's not how it works.

TOMMY
I'm gonna starve to death.

SARAH
Tommy.

TOMMY
My dad's food – he is the best cook ever.

SARAH
Well, your mom will cook for you. She'll make you lots of yummy...

TOMMY
YUCK!! She can't cook, it's horrible. Even dad says so. It's so gross.

SARAH
What about your grandma? She makes those really good cookies that...

TOMMY
It's not the same, Sarah. It's not the same. She can't cook like him. I only like what my dad cooks. And when he dies, I won't be able to eat anything. And then I'll die. Just like him.

SARAH
I won't let that happen.

TOMMY
You can't do anything.

SARAH
But I can...

TOMMY
Nobody can do anything. It's just the way it's going to be. *(he keeps watching TV)*

(SARAH scoots up next to him and puts her arm around him)

SARAH
I'm sorry.

(TOMMY leans his head into her)

TOMMY
Thanks. *(pause)* Maybe I could eat a little ice cream.

(Lights change)

SCENE TWELVE
I THOUGHT I HAD IT ALL FIGURED OUT (Song)

(Originally performed by one woman a capella)

THOUGHT I HAD IT ALL FIGURED OUT
FELL IN LOVE FOUND A DOG BOUGHT A HOUSE
WORE HIS NAME FOR A WHILE
LIKE THE DRESS DOWN THE AISLE
NEVER REALLY FIT
IN THE BOX
NEVER REALLY FIT

SO
I GOT LOST
DUE WEST RACING DOWN THE HIGHWAY
NOT GONNA STOP TIL IT ENDS
WANNA HOLD THE SINKING SUN IN
MY OUTSTRETCHED HANDS
TEACH THE CHILDREN OF DEEP STILL WATERS
REDISCOVER THE GREAT I AM
WANNA START AGAIN
WHERE I BEGAN
HOME
HOME

SERVED THE PAPERS WISHED HIM LUCK
PACKED MY KIDS, MY WHOLE LIFE IN A TRUCK
AND NO I'M NOT ANGRY PLEASE JUST HELP
ME UNDERSTAND
HOW LIFE WITHOUT PASSION
IS WORTH A DAMN
HOW LIFE WITHOUT PASSION
IS WORTH A DAMN

DUE WEST RACING DOWN THE HIGHWAY
NOT GONNA STOP TIL IT ENDS
WANNA HOLD THE SINKING SUN IN
MY OUTSTRETCHED HANDS
TEACH THE CHILDREN OF DEEP STILL WATER
REDISCOVER THE GREAT I AM
START AGAIN
WHERE I BEGAN
HOME
HOME

MAMA ALWAYS SAID WALK THE TALK
DADDY ALWAYS SAID KEEP IT SIMPLE STUPID
WISH I HAD EM HERE TO BOUNCE THIS OFF
WHEN I GREW UP
THE SMARTER THEY GOT
I GREW UP
AND THE SMARTER THEY GOT
WHEN I GREW UP
AND THE SMARTER THEY GOT

DUE WEST RACING DOWN THE HIGHWAY
NOT GONNA STOP TIL IT ENDS
WANNA HOLD THE SINKING SUN IN
MY OUTSTRETCHED HANDS

TEACH THE CHILDREN OF DEEP STILL WATER
REDISCOVER THE GREAT I AM
START AGAIN
WHERE I BEGAN
HOME
HOME

(Lights change)

SCENE THIRTEEN
ARMY

TROUBADOUR
The Synder Home. Iowa City, IA.

(HELEN's cleaning the house manically. Spays air freshener)

HELEN
(smelling) I've been airing out this house for 3 days now. I quit smoking. About 5 minutes ago actually, but I quit. I promised my mother I would as soon as he got home. If Tim knew I was… he would have a fit. And honestly I just want everything to be easy for him, to be perfect when he gets here. It's the least I can do. 18 months in Afghanistan and to come home and find that things are different… well they aren't. Tim - or Major Pooper as I call him - has been in the Army doing Civil Affairs stuff… all I know is they go door to door and talk to the people in villages. You know, the people that could be terrorists. But that's over with now. I think. He's home for good when he walks through the door.

TIM
(outside smoking a cigarette) This is my last one. Never thought I'd start… they're disgusting… but sometimes you just need something… something to do really. Something that doesn't have to do with… you know, it doesn't matter.

HELEN
We wanted to have a party. Have all the family and friends over to welcome him back, but he said…

TIM
Hell no.

HELEN
(to the oven and takes out cookies) He's uncomfortable being the center of attention, I think. So it's just gonna be me and Mom. I made his favorite.

TIM
I didn't want some fucking party with people asking me questions about something they can't even understand.

HELEN
He never wants to talk about it. He'd get to make phone calls every other week or so and he'd e-mail when he could. When I've asked him what was going on, he just told me to—

TIM
Read the newspaper.

HELEN
(getting cookies off the sheet and onto a plate) Only thing he wanted to hear about was the most banal details. Like what my new haircut looked like or what I was eating. He actually wanted to hear the family gossip. That in itself was bizarre. One time when I was talking about Mom's birthday, he wanted a full description about the cake.

(Lights change. Flashback)

TIM
Yellow or chocolate?

HELEN
Marble with white frosting.

TIM
Square or...

HELEN
Round with blue and red flowers. Little green leaves around them.

TIM
What'd you write on it?

HELEN
Happy Birthday, Mom. In blue.

TIM
Candles?

HELEN
Of course. Can we talk about...

TIM
Was it from Holiday bakery?

(Lights change back)

TIM
I could only think about getting home. That's what motivates pretty much everyone over there. Do your job quick, but well and get the hell out. And now I'm here and hmmm... I don't know. I'm a little... I feel like... I don't know.

HELEN
I can't help but wonder how much he's changed. I mean, he's said he lost a bunch of weight. Says he'd highly recommend it as a weight loss program for me. Dick. But you come back changed right? I mean, how can you not? I've read these stories about... you know people having trouble readjusting. Mom says we shouldn't treat him any different, but what if we should.

TIM
We were outsiders over there and the idea of belonging... I was grateful everyday for what I had back here. Every day. For it just being normal. My normal. But now that I'm here, ever since that plane landed I feel like an outsider again. Maybe home was just a mirage. Maybe normal doesn't live here. Maybe when I walk through that door, everything that I dreamed about on those horrible nights, will be nothing like I thought or I won't be what I thought. Am I even making sense? Jesus. I sound like the goddamn base's shrinks.

HELEN
For the last week, I just had a feeling something bad was going to happen. Like he wouldn't make it home. I didn't tell Ma. Oh my god, are you kidding me? She'd lose it. But I just haven't wanted to believe he was gonna come home because if I got too excited, too hopeful, he wouldn't make it. The whole time he's been gone, I've just worried. It's been a constant and if I thought differently then I just felt like I wouldn't see him ever again. So until I get to see him, until he steps foot in this house, I won't believe it. I can't.

TIM
Maybe when I see them, when I see my sister Helen, maybe then it'll be normal. *(puts out his cigarette and goes inside)* Hello?

(HELEN just stands there)

HELEN
Hi!

TIM
Hey.

(Neither move toward the other)

HELEN
I made your favorite cookies.

TIM
Snickerdoodles. I haven't had those in forever.

HELEN
(interrupting) Chocolate chip

TIM
No. Snickerdoodles are my favorite.

HELEN
No they aren't.

TIM
I know what my goddam favorite cookie is.

HELEN
You're an idiot.

TIM
You got fat.

(They look at each other and start to laugh)

TIM
I'm home.

HELEN
You're home.

(They hug for a long time. Then they both start to sniff each other)

TIM & HELEN
(to each other) Have you been smoking?

(Lights change)

SCENE FOURTEEN
HOME FOR THE HOLIDAYS (Song)

(Song originally performed by the full cast)

GOING HOME
FOR THE HOLIDAYS
BEEN GONE SO LONG
THINK I LOST MY WAY
GOING HOME
FOR THE HOLIDAYS
I WILL NOT
IF THEY ASK ME TO STAY
GOIN HOME
I GOT THE
HOME FOR THE HOLIDAY BLUES

I'M CRYIN LIKE A BABY
WHEN I PULL UP THE DRIVE
I FEEL JUST LIKE A KID AGAIN
THE STOMACH FLU AT FIVE
THERE'S MY OLD DOG GUS
A FRIEND TRIED AND TRUE
HE GREETS ME WITH A YOWL
A BEAGLE HOW DO YOU DO
I'M HOME
OH YES, OH YES I'M HOME
LORD, I AM HOME
GOT THE HOME FOR THE HOLIDAY BLUES

MAMA'S COOKIN IN KITCHEN
DADDY'S STOKIN THE FIRE
UNCLE PAULY IS DRUNK AGAIN
CALLIN SOMEONE A LIAR
COUSIN JOE TALKIN SHOP
JUST LIKE HE ALWAYS DO
HE'S BEEN WEARIN THE SAME SUIT
SINCE 1982
HOME
OH YES, OH YES I'M HOME
LORD, I AM HOME
GOT THE HOME FOR THE HOLIDAY BLUES

NOW
THE FOOD AND THE TALK
PLAIN AND SIMPLE
ENOUGH LAUGHIN TO WAKE THE DEAD

WE THANK THE GOOD LORD
REACH CROSS THE TABLE

FOR ONE MORE YEAR
AND ONE MORE CHANCE

TO COME HOME
FOR THE HOLIDAYS
BEEN GONE SO LONG
THINK I LOST MY WAY
THANK GOD I'M HOME

FOR THE HOLIDAYS
I WILL NOT
IF THEY ASK ME TO STAY
I HOME
I GOT THE
HOME FOR THE HOLIDAY BLUES

(Lights change, but as the cast leaves the stage a member says: BANDS TAKING A BREAK. WE'LL BE BACK IN TEN)

END OF ACT I

ACT II
SCENE ONE
DINNER TABLE

TROUBADOUR
Midwest dinner tables. Anywhere, USA.

(Dinner table scene. Actors are setting the table as they sing)

ALL
(singing) Dinner Time. Dinner Time. Dinner Time.

(Lights change. Family of four around the table eating dinner)

MAN #1 (DAD)
Son, how's school?

MAN #2 (SON)
Great. I got an A on my Math test.

WOMAN #1 (MOM)
Way to go.

WOMAN #2 (DAUGHTER)
Congrats, Bro.

MAN #1
I'm real proud of you. And Sweetie, what about you?

WOMAN #2
Billy asked me to Homecoming.

WOMAN #1
Oh my, we have to get you a dress.

MAN #1
Billy? Billy Smith, quarterback.

WOMAN #2
Yeah.

MAN #1
Well I'll wanna talk to him before.

WOMAN #1
Oh honey.

MAN #2
He's a good guy, dad. Trust me. No funny business,

MAN #1
Ok. He's gonna have the best looking date.

WOMAN #2
Ah, dad.

WOMAN #1
It's true. *(to DAD)* Darling, was work...

MAN #1
The meeting was terrific and we've gotta meet Joe at the club on Friday. The wives and the head honchos.

WOMAN #1
Oh, ok. I haven't seen Phyllis in forever.

MAN #1
How was your day?

WOMAN #1
Well, you'll never guess. Cindy and Bill are talking D-I-V-O-R-C-E.

(Stunned silence and a beat)

MAN #2
Mom, this sauce.

MAN #1
Honey, so great.

WOMAN #2
Good job, Mom.

WOMAN #1
Martha Stewart knows how to use a tomato.

(They all laugh. Lights change)

ALL
Dinner Time. Dinner Time. Dinner Time.

(MAN #1 exits. MOM putting food on the table)

WOMAN #1 (MOM)
(yelling) Joel! Kali! Dinner! Now!

(JOEL comes in with his back pack)

MAN #2 (JOEL)
I'm late.

WOMAN #1
You have time to eat.

MAN #2
No I don't.

WOMAN #1
Yes you do.

MAN #2
Mom.

WOMAN #1
Five minutes.

MAN #2
The guys.

WOMAN #1
Eat.

(JOEL eats standing up)

WOMAN #1
(yells) KALI!

WOMAN #2 (KALI)
(yells back) What?

WOMAN #1
(yells) Dinner!

WOMAN #2
(yells) OK.

WOMAN #1
Now!

WOMAN #2
God. *(comes out of her bedroom and to table)*

WOMAN #1
Joel, you've got a 4:30 Dr. Bowman appointment tomorrow.

MAN #2
(mouth full of food) Ok.

WOMAN #2
I hate spaghetti.

MAN #2
(again with mouth full of food) I'm going to study at Matt's after the game.

WOMAN #1
What?

WOMAN #2
You're disgusting.

(JOEL opens his mouth at KALI revealing food)

WOMAN #1
Joel.

WOMAN #2
This is why you don't have a girlfriend.

MAN #2
(to KALI) Bitch.

WOMAN #2
Mom!

WOMAN #1
(to JOEL) Hey.

MAN #2
(starts to leave) I'm studying after the game.

WOMAN #1
Home by 10:30.

MAN #2
11?

WOMAN #2
If he gets to stay out until 11 then I…

WOMAN #1
10:30. You've got school.

MAN #2
Ok. *(kisses her)* I might be a little late, but I'll call. Love you. *(runs)*

WOMAN #2
We gotta go.

WOMAN #1
You didn't eat.

WOMAN #2
I'm on a diet.

WOMAN #1
Eat.

WOMAN #2
I ate at Hilary's after school. Come on.

(Lights change)

ALL
(chant again) Dinner Time. Dinner Time. Dinner Time.

(WOMAN #1 exits, MAN #1 reenters. DAD's in the kitchen and his son and daughter sit at the table waiting)

MAN #1 (DAD)
We've got another 3 minutes, ok?

MAN #2 (RYAN)
Ok.

WOMAN #2 (MEGAN)
Ok.

(DAD puts ketchup on the table)

MAN #2
Do you have barbeque sauce?

WOMAN #2
Yeah.

MAN #1
No.

MAN #2 and WOMAN #2
Oh.

MAN #1
Sorry guys. I haven't really shopped this week, it's been crazy. But we'll go to the grocery store tomorrow, ok? You can pick out whatever. I'll put barbeque sauce on the list. Ok?

WOMAN #2
I'm hungry.

MAN #1
You want some fishy crackers.

WOMAN #2
Yeah.

(DAD grabs a little bag)

MAN #2
Can I have some toast?

MAN #1
Toast?

MAN #2
Yeah.

MAN #1
But I've got chicken nuggets coming.

MAN #2
I know, but toast would be good with it.

MAN #1
Well buddy, I guess you can, but your old man doesn't have a toaster yet, so...

WOMAN #2
We can't have toast?

MAN #1
We can put it in the oven though

MAN #2
That's not toast.

MAN #1
No. It is. Sort of. In college, that's how Jim and I... *(oven beeps)* See chicken nuggets are ready.

MAN #2
Can I call mom?

MAN #1
Mom?

MAN #2
Yeah.

MAN #1
But it's my weekend.

WOMAN #2
I wanna talk to her too.

MAN #1
Ok. Ok. But after dinner. Let's eat first.

MAN #2
I wanna go home.

MAN #1
This is your home too.

WOMAN #2
Dad, can you please take us back to our house?

MAN #1
Let's just eat first. Ok? Let's just eat and... *(burns his hand in the oven)* Dammit.

(Lights change)

ALL
(chanting) Dinner Time. Dinner Time. Dinner Time.

(WOMAN #1 enters. Grammie's table. Family dinner. PAMMY, the granddaughter, is just about to start eating)

MAN #1 (GRAMMIE)
Pammy, will you say grace, please?

WOMAN #2
Really, Grammie? Me?

MAN #1
With everyone here, I think it would be nice.

WOMAN #2
Okay.

MAN #1
(a little loud) Alright everyone. Everyone. Pammy is going to say grace. OK, Pammy.

WOMAN #2
Ok. Alright. Well, it's been a while. Let's see. Dear God. Thank you for this food and all that you do. It's appreciated. Amen.

(Pause)

MAN #1
That's it?

WOMAN #2
Yes?

MAN #1
Okay. AMEN

WOMAN #1 & MAN #2
AMEN.

(Everyone starts to eat)

MAN #1
That was interesting.

WOMAN #2
Oh.

MAN #1
I think an eight o'clock service this Sunday would benefit you.

WOMAN #2
Service?

MAN #1
Church.

WOMAN #2
Eight in the morning?

MAN #1
Jesus never sleeps.

WOMAN #2
Okay.

MAN #1
You'll be my escort. It'll be just like when you were little.

WOMAN #2
But I never went to church with...

MAN #1
(looking PAM dead in the eye) Never too late to start.

WOMAN #2
Sounds great. Okay.

(Lights change. MIKE, KRISTI, LUCY, and JOHN are all toasting and laughing)

ALL
Dinner Time. Dinner Time. Dinner Time.

WOMAN #1 (KRISTI)
To Friends.

(They clink and drink. The rest might say, "Cheers" or repeat the toast)

MAN #1 (JOHN)
To Thanksgiving with my true family.

(Again they drink)

WOMAN #2 (LUCY)
To the Lions losing.

(Again they drink)

MAN #2 (MIKE)
To not watching my uncle eat those nasty giblets.

(Again they drink)

WOMAN #1
To, um, to the turkey that gave its life.

ALL
(laughing) What?

WOMAN #1
Well, we ate him.

(Again they drink)

MAN #1
To the butcher.

(They drink)

MAN #2
To the pilgrims and Indians. Those Indians gave us corn.

(They all laugh and drink)

WOMAN #2
To boats?

(Everyone laughs)

WOMAN #2
You know they brought the people here so they could eat together and... forget it.

(Lights change)

ALL
Dinner time. Dinner time. Dinner time.

(JIMMY has brought home his girlfriend to dinner with his parents. Middle of dinner. JESSICA is continuously eating throughout the scene and her mouth full)

WOMAN #1 (MOM)
Jessica, Jimmy didn't mention what you're studying.

MAN #2 (JIMMY)
Yes I did. She's studying Bowling Industry Management.

MAN #1 (DAD)
Jim, we would have remembered that.

MAN #2
(to JESSICA) I've told them.

WOMAN #1
Well that seems very unusual and specialized.

WOMAN #2 (JESSICA)
mm-hmm.

MAN #2
It's a growing industry.

MAN #1
I'm a bit of a bowler myself.

MAN #2
No you're not.

MAN #1
(to JESSICA) So are you hoping to open a business of your own?

WOMAN #2
(Mouth full of food) Uh-uh.

MAN #1
So what exactly do you want to do with that degree?

(WOMAN #2 shrugs)

WOMAN #1
But you must be quite a bowler?

WOMAN #2
Uh-uh.

MAN #2
Her program is really difficult to get into. So much competition.

MAN #1 and WOMAN #1
Really?

MAN #2
You should hear her talk about the pinsetter machines. It's incredible. I mean this is like the biggest sport of all times.

MAN #1
Sport?

MAN #2
Dad.

MAN #1
It's not a…

MAN #2
In 10 years, Dad, bowling will be larger than football, baseball, soccer, or basketball. It's the fastest growing industry.

MAN #1
I don't think so.

WOMAN #1
Excuse him. I think he doesn't understand how it's exercise. You know like curling.

MAN #2
Her dad was an Olympic curler.

WOMAN #2
mm-hmm.

WOMAN #1
I'm sorry. I just… We certainly are having our horizons broadened tonight.

MAN #1
Uh-huh.

MAN #2
I'm even thinking about making it my major.

WOMAN #1 and MAN #1
What?

(Lights change)

ALL
Dinner time. Dinner time. Dinner time.

(Nobody is around the dinner table. Son is playing a hand held video game. DAUGHTER is texting. DAD is on his laptop. MOM puts the food on the table and is talking on the phone)

WOMAN #1 (MOM)
(to the phone) I'm putting dinner on the table. So… *(pause)* Yeah. Let me call you back. *(pause)* You're kidding me. He said that? *(pause)* Well yeah, he's an idiot. *(pause)* Well… you know, let me call you back in a little bit. *(pause)* Yeah. *(pause)* Alright. Bye. *(hangs up the phone but puts it by her plate)*

MAN #1 (DAD)
(not looking up from his computer, but eating) Who was that?

WOMAN #1
Penny.

MAN #1
Hmm.

WOMAN #1
Sam, put the game down.

MAN #2 (SON)
Just a sec. I gotta get through this level.

MAN #1
(to JENNY) Jen, how was your day?

(JENNY, daughter, isn't listening)

WOMAN #1
Jenny?

WOMAN #2 (DAUGTHER)
(texting) Yeah. Fine.

MAN #1
Great.

WOMAN #1
Greg.

MAN #1
Huh?

WOMAN #1
Computer?

MAN #1
Just a minute.

(Phone rings. MOM picks it up)

WOMAN #1
Hello? *(pause)* Hi. Nothing. *(pause)* I'm in the middle of dinner can I… *(pause)* Yeah, I'll call you right back. *(pause)* Ok. Ok. Bye. *(hangs up)*

(MOM looks around the house and at the empty table)

WOMAN #1
Let's put everything down. Ok? Greg, computer. Jenny, no phone. Sam…

MAN #1, WOMAN #2, MAN #2
Just a minute.

(Phone rings and MOM picks it up)

WOMAN #1
Hello? *(pause)* Hi. What's going on? *(pause)* Just eating dinner. *(pause)* Wait. Let me see if I have that. *(gets up from the table)* No. No. It's no problem. *(goes into the kitchen)*

(Silence except for clicking and MOM laughing and mumbling)

ALL
Dinner time. Dinner time. Dinner time.

(Lights change)

SCENE TWO
MAGIC BED

TROUBADOUR
The Perez Home. St. Paul, MN.

(A parents' bedroom. Something under the covers is moving and out pops a little girl)

CHARLEY
Oh. Hi. I thought you were my mom. You aren't. Good. *(goes back under the covers. And then peeks out again)* Don't tell her I'm in here ok? Ok? Ok. *(pause)*
I'm hungry. Daddy grilled steak. BLECH! Do you know that steak is cow? A real cow? Disgusting. Daddy said if I didn't eat it, it just means more for him. That's ok with me. *(turns quickly)* She's coming! *(hides. Then peaks out)* Is she coming? I'm not supposed to be in here. Not unless I'm sick. I can come lay in here when I'm sick because it makes me feel better. She says it's got magic powers to help me sleep when I got a temperature or I'm coughing too much. Dad is really really good at rubbing my tummy when I feel like throwin up. They have better pillows too. I wanna get the better pillows, but Dad says I have to wait until I get my own place. I don't want my own place. This is my place. Dad is sometimes too weird. I don't get him. Mom says that's normal; she doesn't get him either. Then we laugh and dad says no fair. He's always saying he's outnumbered. But he's a pretty big guy. Big round tummy like he's got a baby in there. But mom says only girls have babies. I'm not ready for a baby. I'm supposed to be in my own big girl bed. But I do not like my bed. I'm lonesome in my room. It's lonely

in the dark. They got me a ladybug nightlight that's also a flashlight. It is so cool. Isn't it cool? I love it. It's mine and I don't have to share it. But it makes shadows. Really scary scary shadows. And it looks like a monster that wants to eat me. Isn't that scary? Dad says it isn't real, but it kind of is. It is real looking even if I am making it up. Mom tried making me sleep with the light on, but I told her I thought I should just sleep in her bed. We can all sleep together because we are a family and I'll sleep better. She smiled and then kissed me and said no. I don't like it when she says no. It's not fair. Man. I would say that it sucks but I'm not allowed to say sucks. Dad says sucks is inappropriate. But he sometimes says shit which mom says is worse. I'm really not allowed to say shit. That's big trouble. *(cuddles up with the blanket)* It's not scary in here. It's warm and bouncy. I'm a really big cuddler. A cuddle monster really. Dad's pretty good at cuddling, but if he falls asleep, his arm gets really heavy and he snores and he's much better when he's awake and cuddling. Mom is really the best. She says she learned from her mom. You know what? Why do they get to sleep together, but I have to sleep alone? I have to ask about that. You know, why do they get the magic bed and I don't. Hmmm. I have to ponder that. *(goes under the covers)* I really like it here. *(starts to close her eyes)* It makes me happy. And it's good. You should try it. *(pause)* But not in here... there's not enough room for you in here. Night.

(Lights change)

SCENE THREE
TOOLBOX

TROUBADOUR
The Martinelli Home. Ann Arbor, MI.

(BILL walks into the kitchen with a gigantic old tool box and goes toward the sink. He looks down into it and then puts his hand down)

BILL
I've told her a thousand times to stop putting rice down the disposal. Clogs the frickin drain. *(sighs)* Could be worse I guess. Her mother used to put banana peels in the disposal. Banana peels. Jeez. Who does that? Not my problem now. *(pause)* I need to teach her how to do this. SARAH! SARAH!

SARAH
Dad, I'm on the phone.

BILL
OH. Sorry. *(pause)* Never off that phone. That would be odd to see her ear unattached. *(pulls the tool box to him)* I should really teach her how to do this though. How to fix somethings by herself. There's no need to rely on some cockeyed SOB. Trust me, nothing is better than when a woman can do for herself. And Sarah, well she's old enough and capable enough. Hell, my dad started teaching me to hammer and use a screwdriver by the time I was four. She's sixteen though and... forget it. *(pause)* "You can't fix everything in life, so just fix the stuff you can." That was my dad's motto. When I didn't make the baseball team, he wasn't there with any words of wisdom... really what could he say. Instead, he fixed the chain on my bike that kept coming off track.

I always loved that. Don't try to fix what you can't control, just worry about the little things. I try to make that my motto too, but 'course my ex-wife would tell you different. Tell you that I'm "uncommunicative" or "unresponsive". But well...

(Lights change. Flashback)

BILL
(turns to OLIVIA) So you're sure "peachy keen" is the color you want?

OLIVIA
I don't think you're happy. Are you happy?

BILL
I don't know. I'm...

OLIVIA
Because I don't think you are.

BILL
OK.

OLIVIA
We're not making each other happy.

(Silence)

BILL
Well, let me go to the store to get this. I wanna finish painting by tonight.

OLIVIA
I don't want you to paint. Put the paint chip down.

(Lights change back. BILL turns back to audience)

BILL
Some times it's just not worth the fight. And sometimes there is no way to fix it. *(pause)* Where's my... here. *(pulls out a plumber's wrench)* My dad's. In fact, the toolbox was his. A man is only as good as his toolbox, his tricks, as my dad said. His dad gave it to him, I took it when he died, and one day... well, I don't know if I'll give it to Sarah. Maybe a grandson if I'm alive that long. I don't know. If Sarah would just let me... ah, she's a teenager. You'd think her world was falling apart on a daily basis. Her and her mother, her friends, boys... just punch someone and get it over with. I'm about as useless around her as a... as a... forget it... *(goes under the sink with a huge wrench. Is on his back)*

(Lights change. Flashback. SARAH enters, upset)

BILL
Sarah is that you?

SARAH
Yeah.

BILL
You gotta stop putting rice down the disposal. This is getting crazy.

SARAH
(crying) I'm sorry ok. I'm really sorry dad. I'm a horrible person

BILL
Sarah?

SARAH
What can I do? What do you want me to do?

BILL
(pause) Hand me a screwdriver.

SARAH
Here. *(it's the wrong tool)*

BILL
A screwdriver.

SARAH
Here. *(wrong tool again)*

BILL
Sarah, I said a screwdriver. Come on.

SARAH
(hands him a bunch of tools) Fine.

BILL
Thanks.

(SARAH tinkers in the kitchen for water. Bill is silent)

SARAH
He said it wasn't me, it was him. Can you believe that?

BILL
Sounds like something a boy would say.

SARAH
Exactly.

BILL
Who is this again?

SARAH
Mike.

BILL
Did I meet Mike?

SARAH
Oh my god. I can't talk to you. I can't...

BILL
Mike the guy with the sneer?

SARAH
He broke my heart, Dad. He broke my heart and all you can do is talk about rice. I'm in pain. I'm in real pain and you're just like mom. You could care less. I loved him. I loved him and now I have nothing. Nothing. I'm humiliated. And... forget it.

(SARAH walks out)

BILL
Well that's just part of life, but—

(comes out from under the sink) Sarah? Sarah?

(Lights change back)

BILL
I've never pretend to be something I'm not. Although I shouldn't, I occasionally wish this toolbox held a few more tricks just to help, but then again, you can't fix everything in life, so just fix the stuff you can. Sarah has been asking for a full length mirror in her room... True Value carries those... I think I can handle that.

(Lights change)

SCENE FOUR
LEFT HOME (Song)

(Originally performed by the TROUBADOUR with harmony by an actor)

I'M DONE GET OUT
UPSTAIRS THEY'RE SCREAMING
KID I'M SORRY OUR
EYES MEET , I AM EATING
PEAS AND MEATLOAF
FELL ON THE FLOOR
ROLLED OUT THE DOOR
STUCK INTO THE SOLES OF HIS TENNIS SHOES AS HE WAS LEAVING

MY DAD LEFT HOME TODAY
I DON'T THINK HE'S COMING BACK
I THINK I WANT HIM TO STAY
BUT HE'S NOT COMING BACK
NO WAY

MOM RAN DOWN THE STAIRS
TO THE KITCHEN
SHE'S SORRY I HAD TO HEAR THAT
I'M TRYIN TO LISTEN

FOR THE CAR
MY BIG BROTHER'S
OUT SOMEWHERE DRIVIN
HE'S SIXTEEN AND HE'S NEVER HERE
WHEN I NEED HIM

MY DAD LEFT HOME TODAY
HE'S NOT COMIN BACK
I REALLY WANT HIM TO STAY
BUT HE'S NOT COMING BACK, NO WAY

MIDNIGHT, I KEEP AN OPEN EYE
ON THE CARS, ONE BY ONE
AS THEY PASS BY
OUR HOME
WHISPER TO THE STARS IN THE SKY
WHY

STAR LIGHT STAR BRIGHT
MAKE THIS ALRIGHT
STAR LIGHT STAR BRIGHT
MAKE THIS ALRIGHT
STAR LIGHT STAR BRIGHT
MAKE THIS ALRIGHT
STAR LIGHT STAR BRIGHT
MAKE THIS ALRIGHT

MY DAD LEFT HOME TODAY
I DON'T THINK HE'S COMING BACK
I THINK I WANT HIM TO STAY
BUT HE'S NOT COMING BACK
MY DAD LEFT HOME TODAY
HE'S NOT COMING BACK
I THINK I WANT HIM TO STAY
BUT HE'S NOT COMING BACK
NO WAY

(Lights change)

SCENE FIVE
CATCHING MOM

TROUBADOUR
The Peterson Home. McHenry, IL.

(OLIVIA and SIMON make out as they make their way into the house and straight for the kitchen table with a lot of awkwardness. SARAH, OLIVIA's daughter, walks in the front door and flips on the light)

SARAH
Mom!

OLIVIA
Oh, um, Hi Honey. *(gets off SIMON)* Um, how was your night?

SARAH
Uh. Uh. Uh.

OLIVIA
Cookies? We made cookies.

SIMON
They're tasty. *(to OLIVIA)* Where's the loo?

OLIVIA
(points up the stairs) This is my friend, Simon. Simon, this is Sarah.

(SIMON goes up the stairs)

OLIVIA
Sarah. Honey.

(SIMON can hear the entire conversation)

SARAH
That is so GROSS! Gross!

OLIVIA
What?

SARAH
What if my friends were with me?

OLIVIA
We were just baking.

SARAH
I'm not stupid.

OLIVIA
You're reading too much into this.

SARAH
Your bra, mom.

Olivia
Huh? *(looks)* Oh. *(starts to fix it)*

SARAH
I'm gonna throw up.

OLIVIA
Calm down.

SARAH
I hope you're gonna burn that table.

OLIVIA
Stop it. You know I caught you with that guy just last...

SARAH
Ben? That's normal mom. You and Match.com dude... not normal.

OLIVIA
Well, you're early. Curfew's 11:30

SARAH
So I should never come home early again?

OLIVIA
Sarah.

SARAH
I don't ever want you complaining about me and Ben or...

OLIVIA
Excuse me. I'm an adult, a parent. This is my house. My rules.

SARAH
Whatever. I'm gonna go poke my eyes out now. *(goes up the stairs and runs into SIMON. They both head back to where they came from)*

OLIVIA
Grow up. I have needs.

SARAH
Ugh, I have a need never to see that again.

OLIVIA
Sarah.

SARAH
What, mother?

OLIVIA
Let's not make this weird or you know...

SARAH
Impossible.

OLIVIA
I'm sending him home, ok?

SARAH
Don't make me be the reason.

OLIVIA
We were just kissing. He's very nice and... it wasn't anything. It's not. It's just...

SARAH
I don't need to know.

OLIVIA
Your father can go out with whomever he wants but I have to be a nun?

SARAH
Well he doesn't flaunt it in my face.

OLIVIA
He doesn't have too—you don't live with him. What do you think he's doing when you're not there?

SARAH
Is Match guy spending the night?

OLIVIA
Of course not.

SARAH
Because Dad never has anyone...

OLIVIA
I said no. I wouldn't ever have a man sleep over with you here.

SARAH
Fine.

OLIVIA
And you can't use this against me later...

SARAH
(smiling) Ok.

OLIVIA
My behavior doesn't mean that this is ok for a teenager.

SARAH
Yeah, right.

OLIVIA
Go to bed. I'm sending him home. Go. Now.

(SARAH goes up to her bedroom as SIMON come down)

SARAH
It was a pleasure meeting you, Simon!

SIMON
Yes! Yes! Pleasure, Sarah.

SARAH
(to OLIVIA) Night mother. *(goes to her room)*

OLIVIA
(to herself) Shit.

(SARAH makes a phone call as OLIVIA and SIMON meet again in the kitchen)

OLIVIA
Sorry about that.

SIMON
I think I'll head out.

(They kiss)

OLIVIA
I can't... sorry.

SIMON
No. No. It's fine.

SARAH
(to her phone) Jessie, you will never guess what I just saw?

OLIVIA
I'm so embarrassed.

SIMON
I've got a daughter too. I know.

OLIVIA
Can't wait for this therapy bill.

SIMON
(kisses her cheek) Thank you for a lovely evening.

OLIVIA
Yes. It was lovely, wasn't it?

(They kiss again. And then it becomes even more passionate and they head back to the kitchen table trying to be quiet, but they can hear the overly loud SARAH)

SARAH
It was like watching the two oldest, ugliest animals trying to mate. Horrible. Like manatees trying to go at it. I'm never gonna sleep again. Ever.

(OLIVIA and SIMON stop kissing)

SIMON
Nite.

OLIVIA
Yeah. *(closes the door)* SARAH!!

(Lights change)

SCENE SIX
THE OTHER WOMAN (Song)

(Performed by two women and a man)

WOMAN
I MUST CONFIDE
I CANNOT HIDE
I WILL NOT ABIDE
THESE FEELINGS WON'T SUBSIDE
THERE IS ANOTHER WOMAN

I LOVED AND MARRIED THE MAN
AND NOW THE PROBLEM
IT'S SIMPLY OUT OF HAND
I HOPE YOU UNDERSTAND
I DON'T LOVE MY STEP DAUGHTER

GIRL
I HATE HER
I REALLY HATE HER
CAN'T BELIEVE HE'D EVEN DATE HER
AND NOW SHE'S HIS WIFE

DAD
MY GIRLS GET ALONG SO WELL

GIRL
I HATE HER
SHE'LL NEVER BE MY MOTHER
I ONLY HAVE ONE MOTHER
SHE'S ONLY HIS WIFE

DAD
MY GIRLS GET ALONG SO WELL

WOMAN
I FEEL SO GUILTY

GIRL
NOT ME

WOMAN
ALMOST DIRTY

GIRL
PLEASE

WOMAN
MUST HANDLE GENTLY
I KNOW 14
IS NOT EASY

GIRL
I JUST STARE AT HER BLANKLY
I KNOW THIS DRIVES HER CRAZY
AND THAT IS FUN

DAD
MY GIRLS GET ALONG SO WELL

WOMAN
SHE'S SLY AS CAN BE
TRANSPARENT IS SHE
WELL NOW WE HAVE SOME RULES
CHORES YOU HAVE TO DO
THIS IS MY HOUSE TOO

GIRL
SHE CALLED ME A SPOILED
BRAT. THIS CLINCHED IT
SHE CALLED ME A ROYAL—

WOMAN
(talks not sings) She wanted $100 for some class trip and honestly, we couldn't afford it.

GIRL
(talks not sings) She told me to get some of my dad's money from my mom.

WOMAN
(talks not sings) I told her she can't only come to us for money. She's got a mother too.

GIRL
(talks not sings) My mom doesn't have that kind of money.

WOMAN
(talks not sings) Your mom needs to get a real job.

GIRL
(talks not sings) Like your boob job?

(WOMAN looks at GIRL in shock)

DAD
MY GIRLS GET A LONG SO WELL

WOMAN
SHE'S NOT HERE ALL THE TIME
OUR VOWS WOULD NOT SURVIVE
HE WILL NOT TAKE A SIDE
I'LL TAKE HER FOR A LONG WINDING DRIVE

DAD
MY GIRLS GET ALONG SO WELL

GIRL
AT THE START IT WAS A DIFFERENT SONG
YOU FAKED AND GOT A LONG
YOU TRIED TO BE MY BEST FRIEND
AND NOW YOU WANT CHILDREN

WOMAN
YES, NOW LATELY
I WANT A BABY
SOMEONE OF OUR OWN
TO BLESS OUR HAPPY HOME

GIRL
MY DAD DOESN'T WANT A BABY
NOT REALLY
TELL HER DADDY
THAT SHE'S CRAZY

DAD
MY GIRLS GET ALONG SO WELL

(Music stops for a moment)

GIRL
(speaks) Daddy.

DAD
(speaks) Maybe.

(Music starts again)

GIRL
I HATE HER
BOY, I REALLY HATE HER
CAN'T BELIEVE HE'D EVEN DATE HER
AND NOW SHE'S HIS WIFE

WOMAN
I MUST CONFIDE
I CANNOT HIDE
I WILL NOT ABIDE
THESE FEELINGS WON'T SUBSIDE
THERE IS ANOTHER WOMAN

DAD
MY GIRLS GET ALONG SO WELL

(Lights change)

SCENE SEVEN
GAY SON

TROUBADOUR
The Schaberg and Wilson Home, Kalamazoo, MI.

(SETH in the kitchen cooking. NANCY walks in and surprises SETH)

SETH
(jumps) Jesus! Oh, hi. Hi.

NANCY
Hello.

SETH
You're here.

NANCY
The door was open.

SETH
Well hi. Hi. Welcome. I'm Seth.

NANCY
Jimmy's friend.

SETH
Yep. Mrs. Schaberg, it's so nice to meet you. Jim talks about you all the time.

NANCY
Well that's nice to hear. Thank you.

SETH
Do you know Jimmy's running behind at work? He said he's going to...

NANCY
(interrupting) Yes. I know. He called me.

SETH
Oh. Good. Good. He wanted to pick you up, and I couldn't... I'm sorry. But...

NANCY
(interrupting) It doesn't matter. Metro car was fine.

SETH
And your flight was ok?

NANCY
Sure. Long, but ok. I left my bags in the hall. They were a little heavy.

SETH
(cuts her off) Oh, yeah, let me grab 'em. *(goes out into the hall and drags in two huge bags)*

(NANCY is looking around and finds her way into the kitchen)

SETH
(as he drags the bags upstairs) Jim's really been looking forward to your visit.

NANCY
I have too.

SETH
(comes downstairs and finds her in the kitchen) Is there anything I can get you?

NANCY
I can find my way around. You don't have to stay. I'll be fine until he gets home.

SETH
I'm staying for dinner.

NANCY
You are?

SETH
Yes.

NANCY
Oh. Ok.

SETH
What about something to drink?

NANCY
Actually, yes. That would be wonderful.

SETH
We have...

NANCY
I'll take some wine. Red. I know he got me some. Always has it.

SETH
Yes. Yes. Of course.

(SETH gets out the bottle and the wine opener)

NANCY
Something sure smells good.

SETH
Dinner. I'm finishing it for Jim.

NANCY
I recognize that smell... *(opens the oven)*

SETH
Oh it's..

NANCY
Yep. Garlic chili chicken—that's my recipe.

SETH
Oh. I didn't know. Wonderful. It's delicious.

NANCY
Looks like you forgot the breading on top.

SETH
It's on there.

NANCY
Oh. Why don't you just let me tinker with it? That's what I do.

SETH
You just got off a...

NANCY
I insist. You're a guest.

SETH
At least let me help do something. Why don't I...

NANCY
(interrupting) You can keep me company and tell me more about yourself. *(fiddles with the bread crumbs)* Now a little more crumbs and ooh... onion. Yes. Onion... *(she fiddles in the kitchen cutting up some chilis and garlic)* So what do you do?

SETH
For work?

NANCY
Yes. Jim may have mentioned something about sales.

SETH
Oh, well not really. I'm a bartender.

NANCY
Oh.

SETH
Yep.

NANCY
Couldn't afford college?

SETH
No. I actually have a degree in business from Western.

NANCY
Hmm. And you're a bartender.

SETH
Well, I'm young still and...

NANCY
Yes. I noticed that. You're much younger than Jim.

SETH
I guess.

NANCY
He calls you a friend, but I'm assuming it's more than that.

SETH
Yes. It is.

NANCY
And so you met through...

SETH
The bar.

NANCY
Oh. And you've been together . . .

SETH
A year.

NANCY
That follows his pattern I guess. He tends to stay with someone for about a year, year and a half and then... well to be honest, I'm not sure he's really that happy with his lifestyle choices. It never sticks really. Speaks volumes really. I hope that doesn't offend you.

SETH
No. It doesn't. But I think he's happy. We both are.

NANCY
That's good. Important. Can you chop some of these tomatoes? *(give them to him and they chop together)* Do you talk to your parents?

SETH
Yes.

NANCY
And they are ok with your... your choices?

SETH
You know, it was an adjustment at first, but...

NANCY
Because Jim's father would have died if he hadn't already died. Cut those smaller please.

SETH
Oh.

NANCY
And your father is...

SETH
Ok with me? Yes. He loves me.

NANCY
Still must be difficult.

SETH
Well... I don't know. I've always had their support.

NANCY
Aren't you lucky? And do you have siblings?

SETH
Yes. Two older sisters.

NANCY
Well that's nice. Your parents will get to be grandparents, right? Have weddings and all that? You know, Jim's my only child.

SETH
He's mentioned that

NANCY
So, I feel it's natural to mourn in a way.

SETH
Mourn?

NANCY
Mourn. I don't get to have what every mother wants for their child and for themselves. Your parents... maybe that's why they are ok with your...

SETH
But you know things are changing all the time. It's all becoming possible now.

NANCY
You still can't give birth to my grandchild can you?

SETH
No.

NANCY
And you can't get married yet, right?

SETH
Not here, no.

NANCY
There you go.

SETH
But we can adopt and get married legally in Iowa or...

NANCY
Not really the same, however, I'm trying to understand that it's not my life. That's my mantra. Not my life. I just keep my nose out of it and just pray for... well I just pray. So are you two serious because you know, he hasn't really mentioned you all that much? I mean he's private, but usually...

SETH
He hasn't?

NANCY
Not until a few weeks ago.

SETH
Oh. Well, we are serious. A year. That's serious, I think.

NANCY
Well you know relationships, no matter the nature of them, they are

still complicated.

SETH
We're monogamous and committed.

NANCY
But it's not like you want to get married or live together..

SETH
Actually...

NANCY
What?

SETH
We already do.

NANCY
You do?

SETH
We do.

NANCY
You do?

SETH
We do.

NANCY
Both of you?

SETH
Yes.

NANCY
Oh.

(Pause)

SETH
I'm sorry. I didn't want to lie to you.

NANCY
Yes. Well...

SETH
Jim was going to tell you tonight.

NANCY
How long?

SETH
About a year.

(Silence again)

NANCY
I was here six months ago. Where were you?

SETH
I stayed at a friend's.

NANCY
You didn't wanna meet me?

SETH
No I did, but Jim likes his time alone with you. You're both very close and he wasn't ready.

NANCY
Seems like he was ashamed.

SETH
He's not ashamed of me.

NANCY
Did I say that?

SETH
No, but...

NANCY
Can you tell me what I did? What did I do wrong?

SETH
Nothing.

NANCY
I did something wrong because he's lying to me and you're here at this table instead of a daughter-in-law and I'm just wondering if you can explain this to me so I can understand what I did to cause all this.

SETH
You didn't do anything wrong.

NANCY
Well of course you'd say that.

SETH
I mean he's gay, you didn't cause him to be that way.

NANCY
I took him to musicals as a young boy. I loved musicals and he had a love for them too. 'Annie', 'Into the Woods', you name it, we saw it.

SETH
Not all gays love musicals.

NANCY
He was obsessed with 'Xanadu'. Obsessed. Olivia Newton John on roller skates. That's all he wanted to be for Halloween when he was 5 and 6 and 7… I think every year until he was in 5th or 6th grade.

SETH
Really?

NANCY
I would not let him go out like that, but around the house, I didn't think it would harm him.

SETH
Mrs. Schaberg…

NANCY
Nancy, please.

SETH
Ok, Nancy, he's just who he is. He's a good person.

NANCY
I know that.

SETH
He's just…

NANCY
I've tried to be ok with it all. I've tried to make sure he knows I love him, but…

SETH
I think that's probably why he didn't tell you about me. Wanted to make it easy on you.

NANCY
It'll never be easy on me. I will never really like you Seth because you represent everything I don't want in my son's life or in mine.

SETH
Oh.

NANCY
That came off mean, but… well, I can tell you're a kind person. I can tell you have feelings toward my son. And while I wish you had a better profession, I think under different circumstances I really could like you.

SETH
That's ok.

NANCY
That's ok?

SETH
Well I'm hoping at some point you might change your mind, but yeah it's ok. You don't have to like me, but you should also know I'm not going anywhere.

NANCY
Do you think maybe I should go to a hotel? Make everyone more comfortable?

SETH
Jim would be hurt I think. But you do what you need to do.

NANCY
You can understand why I'm upset right?

SETH
Uh-huh. I told him to tell you what

was going on, but it's not my place to interfere.

NANCY
Maybe he doesn't want me here, maybe he *(spills her wine)* Ah…

SETH
(rushing to clean it up) Hold on. Hold on.

(They are wiping it up)

NANCY
Sorry.

SETH
Oh, no problem. I just worry about the table. I'm so protective. It's an antique. Jim's had it forever.

NANCY
I know.

SETH
You do?

NANCY
This was our family table.

SETH
He never told me that. Just said it was his prized possession.

NANCY
He did?

SETH
Yes.

NANCY
This was my mother's table. Her father, my grandfather, built it for her as a wedding gift. I ate almost every meal of my life at this table. Did my homework on this table, got engaged over this table. And then when I got married, my mother gave it to me to put in my home so that my children could continue the tradition. So Jimmy learned to eat, color, study at this table and it seemed only right that he use it when he started his adult life.

SETH
Oh.

NANCY
The table's sacred. It's been a home for Jim, a home for me.

SETH
I didn't know any of that. Wow.

NANCY
So you like it?

SETH
Yes. Very much. I love it.

NANCY
That's good. That's really good.

SETH
I hope you'll stay until at least you and Jim can talk. Then…

NANCY
I think I can wait until then.

(Lights change)

SCENE EIGHT
KEYS

TROUBADOUR
Dublin Coffman High School, Dublin, OH.

PETE
I've worked in this building for what seems like forever and technically speaking 40 years in one place is forever. I've taught over 11,000 students how to read and analyze 'Of Mice and Men'. And spent almost 70,000 hours in these walls and that's a rather conserva-

tive estimate. In one hour, when that 7th hour bell rings, I will be officially done. I'll just be another old teacher running into former students at CVS or the grocery store They may need to jog my brain a little, but I always remember something about them. Always. It makes them feel special and to be honest, it makes me feel good to know that I was worth the stop to say hello. *(pause)* At 4pm, they are throwing me a party. A depressing, bad sheet cake retirement party at Jack's, the bar down the street where the adults congregate off school ground with alcohol. These parties.... they give them for every retiree. They'll say a few kind words, put a lei around me, buy me a drink or two, and then we'll eat the cake. And everyone will come. Even those I don't like. But they will come and celebrate the fact that I made it. I've spent more time with them than I have with my own family. Oh my god, they are my family. Would I have hired these people if it was my choice? No. Are you kidding me? But together we've made a school. That's something, don't you think. A fairly productive school. Hmmm. *(pause)* This will be the last time I see any of these people. None of us will keep in touch because it takes too much energy. Sounds horrible. It's not my world anymore. Can't be. I'll be replaced and forgotten in time. And I'll replace them with golf, or boating, or some hobby I haven't even considered yet. That's just the way the machine works. This party is kind of like a funeral. The death of my career, my life work. Huh, never thought about it like that. Jesus. *(pause)* Everyone will know this feeling when their time comes, but right now I'm wondering if... well maybe I'm not ready. Maybe this is a mistake. I could easily last a few more years. *(pause)* But I know. I'm burnt out. I know I need to go. Linda's ready for us to start the next phase. She's so excited and I am too. I really am. But retiring is like I'm admitting I'm old. I feel old when I look around here, but never coming back...that means I really am old... *(pause)* Sarah Benson gets this room now. She's finally getting a room with windows. She's been counting down the days just like me. *(pause)* I'll lock up one last time. Shut the door to Room 110. This has been my classroom for the last twenty years. It's heard me give some of the best lectures, seen me lose my temper and call a kid an asshole, watched a whole class grieve over a loss. I've watched young love bloom and die, seen that click when a young person finally understands the author's meaning, and I've watched the kindness of the human spirit. But I've also seen meanness. I tired to stop it, offer shelter, encouraging words to those that needed it most, but there was truly little I could do. High school is an animal kingdom and you just want to make it out in one piece. *(pause)* So I'm supposed to turn in the last of my paperwork and this part I will enjoy the least. Because I know they will ask me to turn in my keys. The keys to the door and the teacher's lounge. I've given this school everything of me, all I want is to keep my keys. The keys which unlocked the door to my day for all these years. These are mine and I'm not passing them down. I will walk past the front office and go directly to my car. I've earned the right to keep them. *(pause)* So I'll get in my car and drive to Jack's. Brag about our trip to Hawaii for three weeks. We leave tomorrow. Then I'll be home by 5:30 and Linda will have dinner waiting. A special meal, maybe a steak. I'll tell her about the party, about saying good-bye, and then I'll tell her I kept my keys. She'll nod and smile—maybe shake her head at my silly notion—she'll touch my head so gently to let me know that it's all ok. I won't be able to talk. I'll just look down at my meal and grieve the loss.

(Lights change)

SCENE NINE
WHO WILL KEEP WATCH? *(Song)*

(Originally performed by just one woman)

WOMAN
HE LOVES DANCING BEARS
AND THE GRATEFUL DEAD
SAW EM 5000 TIMES
THEY'RE RINGING IN HIS HEAD
NOW HE LOVES JINGLE BELLS
TREES WITH LIGHTS
CAROLS ALL YEAR LONG
O HOLY NIGHT

HE'S HIS PAPA'S
FIRST BORN AND ONLY CHILD
GOD, I LOVE THAT BOY
HE'S A GOOD HEART
GONE WILD
DAMN NEAR BURNED THE HOUSE
RIGHT TO THE GROUND

LIT A CANDLE WAITIN FOR THE BAND
AND UNCLE JOHN

AND WHO WILL KEEP WATCH WHEN I GO
WHO WILL PULL HIM FROM
HIS DARK NIGHT OF THE SOUL
DREAMIN OF HIM ON HIS OWN
IN SLOW MOTION
WHO WILL CATCH HIM
WHO WILL BREAK THE FALL

A FATHER OFF TO FIGHT
HE'S A PEACEFUL MAN
BUT THE PRICE IS RIGHT
DOES WHAT HE CAN
TO KEEP HIS FAMILY OF FIVE SAFE
BOTH HERE AND THERE
EVIL HE SAID IS
EVERYWHERE

AND WHO WILL KEEP WATCH WHEN I GO
WHO WILL WITNESS
MY DARK NIGHT OF THE SOUL
DREAMIN OF THEM ON THEIR OWN
IN SLOW MOTION
WHO WILL CATCH THEM
WHO WILL BREAK THE FALL

ITS COME BACK BEEN 10 YEARS
ITS NOT FAIR
SHE BEAT ONCE AND NOW ITS EVERYWHERE
HOLD ON DEAR CHILDREN
TAKE IT DAY BY DAY
A BROKEN HEART IS LOVE'S
PRICE TO PAY
CAUSE
WHO WILL KEEP WATCH WHEN I GO
WHO WILL WITNESS
AS THEIR BRIGHT LIGHT UNFOLDS
DREAMIN OF THEM ON THEIR OWN
IN SLOW MOTION
WHO WILL CATCH THEM
WHO WILL LOVE THEM ALL

(Lights change)

SCENE TEN
COACH

TROUBADOUR
The Little Tigers, Toldeo, OH.

(The dugout of a little league team, the Little Tigers)

COACH
Alright everyone. Huddle up. Huddle up.

(The three players get around him)

COACH
Ok. Ok. Come on, Sandy. *(She comes in)* Come on in. Alright Alright you guys. I can tell you're all really trying out there. You all need to realize that you've got the skills to win this. I've seen your talent in practice. But right now you guys need to watch each others back. We need to come together and play as a team. Teamwork—remember we've talked about this. You wouldn't let your family fall would you?

HAZEN
I pushed my sister down.

(Everyone giggles)

COACH
Well, I wouldn't do that and I'm sure you didn't really want to hurt her. But come on. Focus. Focus. We are a family. We help and work together. We protect each other. That's the only way we can win this.

(MAGGIE's hand is raised)

COACH
When Maggie missed the ball, where were you Sandy, Erin, Nick? You've got to be there in case she misses it. You're her backup.

SANDY
She always misses it.

COACH
Then that's even more reason to expect that you'll need to be there. This is a thinking game as well. Maggie, what?

MAGGIE
I gotta go potty.

COACH
You've gotta hold it. Hazen, finger out of your nose. You guys, I don't want you to think about the score. Don't worry about that. We've got the advantage here, do you know that? This is our turf. Our home field. These little panthers don't belong here. This is our place. And we are going to show them how we do it.

HAZEN
Is the game almost over?

COACH
Hazen, come on buddy. We have to believe we can win in order to actually win. *(SANDY's waving)* Sandy, what are you doing?

SANDY
There's my mom.

COACH
Well you need to pay attention. Before you guys go up to bat, remember eye on the ball. And just run to home plate. The tee is on home plate. And that's what you need to run to. Not the bleachers or the fence. Home plate. Ok. That's a run. That's how we score. But first you gotta run to first, second, third and then home. Everyone got that?

MAGGIE
I still gotta potty.

SANDY
You can hold it.

HAZEN
You can do it.

MAGGIE
Ok. I'll try.

COACH
Ok. Ok. Hands in. Hands in. *(everyone's hands come in)* On three. One, Two, Three.

EVERYONE
Go LITTLE TIGERS!!

COACH
Alright, Hazen you're up. Get up there and hit that ball.

HAZEN
Ok. Dad... Coach.

TROUBADOUR
John, I'm supposed to stop the game at this point. It's a mercy. 25 to 0... we don't want the kids to feel bad.

COACH
Just give us a chance. It's only the 2nd inning. COME ON, SANDY!!!!

(Lights change)

SCENE ELEVEN
FORECLOSURE

TROUBADOUR
The Lyons Home. Wayne, MI.

(The same family as the one in the original scene at the top of the show)

MARIA
Look at this place. Look around. My voice is echoing through here. That's never happened. An empty house—a box really - that was once our home. Everything that used to fill it fits into that medium size U-haul out in the street. All our possessions. Almost 20 years worth into a truck. But there are so many things I'm not allowed to take. I wanted to take those stairs. Henry fell down them when Suzi convinced him that he could fly.

(HENRY walks onto the stage and sits on the stairs like in the opening scene)

HENRY
I'm super... *(crying)* MOMMY!!!! MOMMY!!!

MARIA
Suzi fell down 'em all dressed up for her 8th grade graduation wearing her first serious pair of heels.

(SUZI walks onto the stage and sits on the stairs where she was in the opening scene)

SUZI
Mom, this dress looks horrible. It should be shorter. Why couldn't you... AH!!!!!

MARIA
Jack fell down them carrying the dog... don't ask.

(JACK walks onto the stage and sits on the stairs where he was in the opening scene)

JACK
SON OF A BITCH!

MARIA
And me... I broke my ass while yelling and chasing my children after they broke my... doesn't even matter. *(pause)* I wanted to take the doors too. The old fashion glass knobs—those aren't easy to find these days. I saw'em and knew I wanted to buy

this place. If you listen really closely. I mean really really closely. Do you hear it? That's the reverberation of all the doors that have slammed shut.

HENRY
You are so mean!

(Everyone stomps their feet on the steps like a door slam)

SUZI
I'm so sick of this family

(Everyone stomps their feet on the steps like a door slam)

JACK
Join the club.

(Everyone stomps their feet on the steps like a door slam)

MARIA
I wanted to take the floor. Not that crappy tile in the bathroom. That can stay. But the hardwood. Jack spent a whole summer refinishing it.

JACK
What do you think? I don't think it looks bad.

MARIA
And then we hired a professional to fix it. *(pause)* Right there on that spot… there's where Suzi took her first step. Her first step. And Henry, he would skate across the floors in his socks trying to play hockey. I wanted to take the walls. These old plaster walls full of lead and all those other toxic chemicals you read about. Look at those holes and those monstrous chips. There's gotta be at least eight different colors under there. I could never figure out the right one. Man these walls hold all our secrets. All of them.

JACK
(to MARIA) I don't want another kid. I can't handle the ones we've got.

SUZI
(on the phone) Yeah, French kissed him. It was gross.

HENRY
I picked the lock to her diary, so boring but she has a crush on Mr. Kamoo.

JACK
(hugging SUZI) Sweetie, Your hair cut is beautiful. Very mature

SUZI
Where's mom? I need her.

JACK
STOP COLORING ON THE WALLS!

HENRY
Please tell me I was adopted!

JACK
You are my world. You know that right?

SUZI
Dad, I love you.

HENRY
She just gave me the finger.

JACK
Do we look stupid? Maybe.

SUZI
Oh my god, Mom, you're the only one smiling.

MARIA
I love you so. *(pause)* I wanted to take pretty much everything. Everything but that mailbox. Never anything good in it. Electric, gas, water, phone, cable, mortgage, insurance, doctors,

visa, mastercard, taxes. That damn mailbox and its attraction to bills. First warning, second warnings, the red letter with the last warning. For a while I feared the mailbox, but now... well now you can just keep it. You can keep this house. *(honk. She turns to the truck)* I'm coming. *(to us)* This place can have our past. We'll find a new floor, new walls, new doors... we'll find our future. Together. Because... *(she sits in her position from the opening scene, arms around her family for a photograph)* This is our home.

(They are in the pose from the beginning of the play)

SUZI
(singing)
DEEP ARE THE ROOTS
HIGH IS THE TREE
WIDE ARE THE BRANCHES
FRAGILE ARE WE

(Flash of a camera and blackout)

END OF PLAY

A PLAY BY
SOPHOCLES

ADAPTED BY
ANNIE MARTIN &
TONY CASELLI

Cast of Characters

OEDIPUS

JOCASTA
CREON
TIRESIAS

MESSENGER
ALEC THE HERDSMAN

DRUNKEN SERVANT
TELLER

MAN #1
MAN #2
MAN #3
WOMAN

CHORUS
CELLIST/NARRATOR

OEDIPUS received its world premiere on January 27, 2011 at the Williamston Theatre (Williamston, MI). It was directed by Tony Caselli. Set Design by Daniel C. Walker, Lighting Design by Dana L. White, Costume Design by Holly Iler. Stage managed by Erin R. Snyder.

The cast was as follows:

OEDIPUS, MAN #1: John M. Manfredi
JOCASTA, TIRESIAS, WOMAN: Sandra Birch
CREON, MAN #2, DRUNKEN SERVANT, HERDSMAN: Barton Bund
MAN #3, MESSENGER, FORTUNETELLER: Brandon Piper
CELLIST/NARRATOR: Jamie Weeder

There is no intermission.

For information about production rights, contact:
Tony Caselli at tony@williamstontheatre.com.

ACT I

(Lights are on and only the CELLIST is there, playing in the corner)

CELLIST
This is a story about darkness.

(Lights go out. CHORUS then enters with candles)

MAN #3
A city in darkness.

MAN #1
Cursed.

MAN #2
Famished.

WOMAN
A town of death

MAN #3
Plagued.

MAN #1
A town begging to be saved.

MAN #2
By a hero.

CELLIST
Oedipus.

MAN #3
Oedipus.

WOMAN
Oedipus.

MAN #1 and #2
Yes, Oedipus.

MAN #1
So this is really the story of a King.

MAN #2
No. This is the story of a man.

WOMAN
And his fall.

MAN #3
This is a story of dark versus light.

WOMAN
A story about the dangers of being human.

MAN #1
Of being flawed.

MAN #2
Of having the best of intentions.

CELLIST
This is a story about truth.

CHORUS
This is the story.

(Lights alter. MAN #1 becomes OEDIPUS)

CELLIST
Thebes, for reasons unknown, had always had the attention of the Gods, who showered the city with their love or their anger. When Oedipus first arrived on the outskirts of town, the gods anger was apparent.

CHORUS
The sphinx.

CELLIST
The sphinx had made her home on the border of Thebes waiting for those who sought passage in or out of Thebes.

CHORUS
The riddle.

CELLIST
She would ask only one question

CHORUS
One riddle.

CELLIST
It seemed so simple.

MAN #2
Wrong.

WOMAN
Wrong.

MAN #3
Wrong.

CELLIST
Men, women, children disappeared. Killed, eaten, vanished into the sky. All at the hands of the sphinx and a wrong answer.

CHORUS
Terror reigned.

CELLIST
The answer came.

(OEDIPUS has been stopped by the sphinx and has heard the riddle)

OEDIPUS
(to the Sphinx) You leave me very little choice, dear Sphinx. I am sure to die if I run, right?

CHORUS
Correct.

OEDIPUS
And I may die if I don't try.

CHORUS
Correct.

OEDIPUS
Then my only way to survive is to answer your question. Your riddle.

CHORUS
Correct.

OEDIPUS
Hmm. It is a good riddle, if I may compliment you so. So, what has four legs at sunrise, two at midday, and three legs at sunset? I can see from your healthy and happy appearance that this question has kept you well fed.

CHORUS
Correct.

OEDIPUS
Does man really fascinate you so much? He must. For man starts his life crawling on all fours, but then we learn and grow... walking on our own two feet, yet age demands much of our bodies. So much so that the last years of our life are spent using a cane, a third leg as you call it. The answer, dear sphinx, is me. Me and all humanity.

(Sphinx screams - the cello's screech)

CELLIST
Upon hearing the right answer, the Sphinx collapsed and died for all to hear. Oedipus was surrounded by all and offered adoration and gratitude.

WOMAN
Embraces and cheers.

MAN #2
Blessings and gifts.

MAN #3
A crown.

(A crown is placed on OEDIPUS)

CELLIST
A humble young man lead Thebes to its most prosperous times, and for nearly twenty years the Gods did shine down their love. Until the darkness came…

CHORUS
(echoes multiple times) Darkness, plague.

(The CHORUS becomes citizens and they pray silently in the courtyard. OEDIPUS walks to his people)

OEDIPUS
Citizens. We are all one in this nightmare. I know you are all ill, as am I. I see the pain every day and night as do you; it follows us all. It is important that every one of you know that I do not sit above you. I sit with you. I not only see the effects of this plague, I feel it deep within me. You have all entrusted me as your king and I suffer not just as an individual, but as a King I suffer for the entire city. When you weep, my soul weeps with you. When you lose hope, when you suffer, I too feel it. Your pain is mine. We are all brothers. And as your brother, I promise you, I am doing everything I can. EVERYTHING. I have not, will not, cannot sleep or eat with Thebes in such pain. You are my only concern. But countrymen, I am not without hope. I have hope, people of Thebes. I have hope and I continue to press forward for resolution.

WOMAN
But what are you going to do?

OEDIPUS
I have been…

MAN #3
My family is starving

OEDIPUS
I hear you.

MAN #2
My family has died.

OEDIPUS
I have seen the daily funerals.

MAN #3
Then my family will be next.

OEDIPUS
Brothers, remain calm. Stay with me. Answers are being sought this very moment: I sent Queen Jocasta's brother, Creon, to Apollo's temple many days ago to see what he could learn. I hoped to have had word from him sooner, but I expect him back at any time. And when he gets here, we will follow all that Apollo commands of us until the city is well once again.

WOMAN
Bless you.

MAN #2
Thank you.

MAN #3
Bless you, King.

OEDIPUS
You have not been forgotten. Not at all. Your Queen prays every morning and night for resolution as do I. Let me see if perhaps we can get you some drink and bread. For strength as we wait for Creon's return.

(Citizens become the CHORUS once again)

CELLIST
So the city continued to pray and thanked the Gods for Oedipus. They suffered and hungered for two more days until Creon returned.

(MAN #2 changes into a vest and becomes CREON)

CREON
Oedipus? Are you here?

OEDIPUS
Creon!

CREON
I need to talk to you.

OEDIPUS
(to unseen guards) Tell the Queen her brother has returned. Finally. *(hugs CREON)* We've been waiting.

CREON
Yes. I see. I need to...

WOMAN
(interrupts) Do you bring good news?

CREON
Well...

MAN #3
It is bad.

CREON
No. It's...

OEDIPUS
Tell us, brother. What did you learn?

CREON
(quietly to OEDIPUS) Let us go inside where I can talk to you in...

MAN #3
Speak Creon. Share your news with us all.

OEDIPUS
(loudly) Yes. Yes. This is news we all need to hear. Let there be no secrets between countrymen in despair. Tell me you brought good news.

CREON
There is good news, yes: I know why we are being plagued.

CHORUS
Tell us! Tell us!

OEDIPUS
You heard them. Come. We are waiting with bated breath.

CREON
The darkness is upon us because there is evil within the city limits.

WOMAN
Evil?

MAN #3
Of what nature?

WOMAN
How do we get rid of it?

OEDIPUS
You're being cryptic. Evil in Thebes? What does that mean?

CREON
(whispers) There is a murderer...

OEDIPUS
Murderer? Creon, we have had murderers before.

CREON
Never one that murdered a king.

(CHORUS gasps)

CREON
I have been told that the person who spilled this blood must either leave town - by coffin or their own accord.

OEDIPUS
Which King was... *(CREON whispers into OEDIPUS' ear and then to himself)* Laius. Are you sure?

MAN #3
(overlap; to a citizen) Did he say Laius?

WOMAN
(overlap; to another citizen) King Laius?

CREON
Yes, Jocasta can help us with this.

MAN #3
(to CREON) This is about the death of King Laius?

WOMAN
May he rest in peace.

CREON
Does it matter who it was? A victim is a victim. When one of our own is murdered, we all suffer. Is that not correct?

OEDIPUS
(to the citizens) Forgive me. I am a little stunned.

MAN #3
Sir, is this about King Laius? Please tell us!

OEDIPUS
Yes. It is

CREON
Oedipus.

OEDIPUS
(to CREON) They deserve to know. They could help. Yes. It seems Creon has found out that we are being punished for the former king's death, his murder.

WOMAN
He was murdered years ago!

MAN #3
He was not even in the city when he was struck down.

OEDIPUS
Creon, speak truth. He was gone when I arrived and I have little knowledge of ...

CREON
He was traveling to Delphi on matters of state when he and his guards were killed. We only found out when the lone survivor returned to tell his story. He was disturbed and deeply affected by what he saw, barely able to relate the story to us. However, we did manage to learn that they all died. But the killer was never found.

OEDIPUS
Could the survivor have been the killer?

CREON
No. Beside the fact that he no longer resides in Thebes, he would never have been able to kill those men. He was loyal to a fault and if you saw his eyes upon his return from the bloodbath, you would know his soul was murdered as well that day.

OEDIPUS
I have seen that look before in a man.

CREON
Robbers seemed the likely source since the bags and site had been picked through by the time we arrived. But...

OEDIPUS
What?

CREON
If they were indeed killed by robbers, then it was not a single person as the Gods would have us believe. Perhaps the...

OEDIPUS
Perhaps this is not an act of random violence. Perhaps it was an attack from a city looking to increase their power? Who were his enemies? Was there trouble with one of our neighbors and perhaps a price was put on his head?

CREON
It is possible, yes. But this was years ago and the murderer is here, in Thebes now.

OEDIPUS
Gods, Creon.

CREON
What?

OEDIPUS
How could you not try to solve your king's murder?

CREON
I did try...

OEDIPUS
Were you not in charge after his death?

CREON
Not officially, but yes. I was quite young and...

OEDIPUS
I do not understand how you would not make this a priority.

CREON
It was.

OEDIPIUS
Jocasta, I understand. She lost her husband. But you were his right hand...

CREON
I know. I was trying to...

WOMAN
Creon, sir, did you not want to find out the truth about his murder?

MAN #3
He was your king as well.

CREON
There was not time.

OEDIPUS
Was not time?

CREON
Do not attack me if you do not understand what was going on. *(to the crowd)* Do not you remember what was happening!? It was mayhem! The Sphinx had lain siege to the city, she was destroying Thebes! Children were disappearing. No one could enter or leave our city without being challenged and attacked by that monster! *(to OEDIPUS)* I had my hands full here trying to keep the people safe. You solved her riddle, you saw the terror we'd been living under! *(to the crowd)* I could not allow myself to be consumed with his murder, not when there were other problems and deaths to deal with right in our city. I had to look ahead for all of us. *(beat)* That may have been the wrong decision. It was what I thought was best and if I was wrong, I am sorry.

(A moment)

OEDIPUS
I am sorry. We are all sorry, Creon. You have served us well and with our best interest at heart. We know that.

WOMAN
Please forgive us.

MAN #3
We did not know.

CREON
There simply was never an opportunity. After you defeated her, there was so much to do to put the city back together... and you became King... and

perhaps I moved on too easily. I should have...

OEDIPUS
No more of this. Creon, brother. By helping to bring justice to Laius' death, we bring life back to the city. I do not like to think about what these villains could be planning, but it is in my best interest, as well as all of yours, to find these killers. Who knows what they could be planning next? They seem to be rather interested in the throne, which I will never give up easily. Now we know and now we will act. Will you help me?

CHORUS
Yes.

OEDIPUS
Will you help me?

CHORUS
Yes.

OEDIPUS
Then come. *(to CREON)* Brother, let us draw up our plans.

(OEDIPUS and CREON exit or take off their crowns. CHORUS returns)

CELLIST
Plans were pursued, but people were growing desperate.

MAN #2
Patience was growing thin.

MAN #3
Very thin.

CELLIST
And so they waited.

MAN #3
Waited.

WOMAN
And hoped.

MAN #3
Hoped.

MAN #2
And prayed.

WOMAN
Prayed.

MAN #3
For their King.

ALL
For Oedipus.

CELLIST
The bells rang out for the city to gather.

MAN #3
The wait—

CHORUS
—was over.

(OEDIPUS arrives and gives a state of the union type speech to the entire city on the raised stage)

OEDIPUS
Thank you all for coming tonight. Nothing makes me feel more at home than being all together like this even with the difficulties we face. Our great city, Thebes has had its times of growth and prosperity, it also had times of sadness and despair. However, through all times, what always remains is our strength and resilience. It is why we do not leave, but stay and persevere. Thebes runs through our blood and we are all family. Although I was not born here, I have been accepted as a true citizen and I thank you all for that. This city has given me my reason to live, my wife and children, and I have a purpose. It is an honor to serve you all and to honor the faith you have shown in me as a king. And so, I

come to you tonight to answer your questions and clear up the rumors that have been running rampant throughout. Here is what we know. The plague and darkness hovering over our city has been caused by the murder of your former King, Laius. To restore order and prosperity to the city, we must find the killers and punish them as only murderers should be punished. Simple enough. I need your help though. Someone has information on the murder. In fact someone in this crowd tonight may be the murderer. And I am speaking directly to that person now. I'm not here to judge the choices you've made. I do not want to know the circumstances and I do not need to know the details. What I do need you to do is to step forward and take responsibility. You can save this city from ruin. If you come forward, your only punishment will be to leave Thebes and never return. I will reward your courage with your life. So for the sake of your fellow citizens, step forward. If you do not, you will be hunted down.

People of Thebes, you have a responsibility to turn this person in and let the swift arm of justice deliver punishment. Someone in this city knows something. Come forward.

The offer to turn yourself in will last only one day. A good man, a King, is dead. Murdered. Many more are suffering now. So let me be clear: if you are the killer, or are harboring the killer, and do not come forward, your life will be a series of miseries, each greater than the other. No one will be exempt from this curse, from the humblest of servants to the highest members of the court – banishment awaits you, suffering will haunt you, and your life will be spent alone, agonizing in miserable darkness. As Apollo punishes this city, so will I punish you.

My quest is for the truth. I do this not only in the name of Laius, but in the name of Jocasta, his wife and mine, and our children. I do this in the name of all Kings that have been wronged and mostly I do this in the name of the people of Thebes who have suffered greatly. The truth will set us free.

I will never give up on our great city. We will rise again, better than before, like the phoenix from the ashes. Hold your children tight tonight and let them know that the end of their suffering is near. That is my promise. Good night and God bless you and God bless our great city.

(OEDIPUS *bows to the crowd and steps aside*)

CELLIST
For that moment,

CHORUS
A glimmer of hope.

CELLIST
But no one came forward.

CHORUS
Not one person.

CELLIST
No confessions were made.

CHORUS
No information.

CELLIST
Oedipus walked...

CHORUS
Walked again

CELLIST
Among his people.

CHORUS
Offering comfort.

CELLIST
With little to offer but empty words.

(OEDIPUS *appears as the citizens kneel and pray*)

OEDIPUS
We have discovered nothing yet, but we're not giving up.

CELLIST
The glimmer faded.

OEDIPUS
We will overcome. I have summoned old Tiresias to me.

MAN #2
Tiresias.

MAN #3
Tiresias.

OEDIPUS
As Creon has sworn by her visions, I have agreed to try anything and everything.

CELLIST
Some called her a prophet. Others chuckled at her old world ways. But nobody ever denied that the blind old woman was something other worldly. And so she came in her blindness to show Oedipus the light.

CHORUS
Tiresias.

(CHORUS *becomes citizens again. The* WOMAN *has transformed into* TIRESIAS *with a walking staff and robe covering her eyes. She enters, led by one of the* CHORUS)

TIRESIAS
(*grabbing a citizen's hand*) Bitter tea leaves, a piece of birch bark and three drops of fish oil.

MAN #3
Ma'am?

TIRESIAS
Your wife's stomach. Tell her.

MAN #3
Thank you.

(TIRESIAS *looks to another as if right in the eye*)

TIRESIAS
Carrots. Give them carrots. (*to another person*) Let her go. She will return. Let her go.

OEDIPUS
Thank you for coming, Tiresias.

TIRESIAS
I cannot help you.

OEDIPUS
But we are in need...

TIRESIAS
We are all in need. (*to the crowd*) Trust that the world will right itself.

OEDIPUS
Your King needs you. Your city needs you.

TIRESIAS
How are your children, sir? Not sleeping well.

OEDIPUS
None of us are sleeping well.

TIRESIAS
Belladonna. Just a dab.

OEDIPUS
We need your answers.

TIRESIAS
They will need their strength.

MAN #2
You can help us, Tiresias.

MAN #3
Who is the murderer?

MAN #2
Death and darkness are infecting Thebes.

TIRESIAS
Death infects all who are human.

OEDIPUS
Old woman, we seek your cure. Your oracle tells us that our freedom will come when...

TIRESIAS
I know what it said.

OEDIPUS
We place our trust, our fate, in your wisdom, and your knowledge. So speak freely.

TIRESIAS
I should not have come.

MAN #2
Do not desert us.

MAN #3
Not now.

TIRESIAS
I would never desert you.

OEDIPUS
Then tell us what you see.

TIRESIAS
I see a city exhausted, full of sadness. A King at his wit's end.

OEDIPUS
Then help us.

TIRESIAS
I can offer remedies. Counsel those in need.

OEDIPUS
I did not bring you here for that.

TIRESIAS
That is all I can offer.

OEDIPUS
You refuse to help these people?

TIRESIAS
No.

OEDIPUS
You mock them.

TIRESIAS
Never.

OEDIPUS
I order you to tell me what you see.

TIRESIAS
That woman over there. I feel the pain of her lost child. From just days ago. I see that she is slowly being driven mad. And that man over there, is thinking of killing his entire family to enter a heaven all together.

OEDIPUS
But who murdered Laius? Are they here?

TIRESIAS
The Oracle said they were

OEDIPUS
You are being insolent.

TIRESIAS
I am being evasive, but not insolent.

OEDIPUS
I could be murdered next.

TIRESIAS
You will not.

OEDIPUS
Do you see that?

TIRESIAS
You will live.

OEDIPUS
What else did you see?

TIRESIAS
Enough to know that this path is not the one you want it to be

OEDIPUS
The oracle is wrong?

TIRESIAS
Wrong? No. Incomplete. Yes.

OEDIPUS
I need the truth!

TIRESIAS
The truth is that you must offer your kindness and love to your people. *(he stomps off)* Do not let this break you. Do not turn on each other.

OEDIPUS
Why will you not share your visions with us?

TIRESIAS
Your burdens are yours and mine are mine. I will not add to their grief, do not ask me to.

OEDIPUS
These people are dying.

TIRESIAS
We are all dying.

OEDIPUS
They are dying before their natural time.

TIRESIAS
Who is to say?

OEDIPUS
Damn you. I am a fool.

TIRESIAS
If you say.

OEDIPUS
I have had enough of this.

TIRESIAS
Then I will go home.

OEDIPUS
Do not walk away from me! I may never allow you to return home. I can bring chaos and ruin onto you.

TIRESIAS
I have seen what you are able to do.

OEDIPUS
Witch!

TIRESIAS
I refuse your anger.

OEDIPUS
You are in no position to refuse me.

TIRESIAS
And yet, here we are. *(to a citizen)* Young man, please help me home.

(OEDIPUS begins to circle TIRESIAS)

OEDIPUS
I understand you. I understand all that you are. You are a traitor.

MAN #2
Traitor?

MAN #3
A traitor!

OEDIPUS
You are protecting someone. That is why you will not speak—because you are guilty.

TIRESIAS
Oh, Oedipus.

OEDIPUS
You were here when Laius was

murdered, and did you use your "powers" then? Did you reveal his killers then? Of course you did not, because you WANTED him dead!

TIRESIAS
To see a King grasp at nothing is difficult for all.

OEDIPUS
Oh yes. Yes, yes, yes. If you were not blind I would say you acted alone, but no - no, this was a conspiracy! But with whom? Who killed Laius?! Answer me, traitor!

TIRESIAS
You are beginning to insult me.

OEDIPUS
Then allow me to continue.

TIRESIAS
Oedipus, do not follow this path.

OEDIPUS
You address me as if we are friends, but it seems that you would rather see this city fall than to help it rise. With whom do you conspire?

TIRESIAS
Only the Gods.

OEDIPUS
As if they would use a vessel such as you. You are a traitor!

TIRESIAS
Look no further than yourself, your highness. *(touches his heart with her palm)* You. It is you. Has always been you. In your own reflection, Oedipus, will you find the man you swore to punish. Will you keep your word, oh King?

OEDIPUS
(throws her hand from his chest) Me? How dare you!?

TIRESIAS
I have seen your family's shame.

OEDIPUS
Who put you up to this?! Who stands to benefit? Whose situation improves? *(a dawning realization)* Is it Creon?

TIRESIAS
You have your answer.

OEDIPUS
Is it my wife's brother?

TIRESIAS
You said you seek the truth - but you are not prepared for it.

OEDIPUS
I have tried, but this woman is nothing but a fraud. A charlatan! Get her out of my sight. I will find the traitor Creon.

TIRESIAS
(stomping her stick loudly and all is silent) You asked me what I saw. Oh pitiable King, I saw you. You have eyes, but cannot see. You live in a house that is yours, was yours, but will not be yours any longer. You are an enemy to what you love; love what you should not; and today you will gain a mother, a father, and a curse. The man you seek will be found. He is here, and his tale will be remembered with horror. This will happen. And when you have nothing, remember the kindness I tried to show you. You the murderer. *(exits)*

OEDIPUS
CREON! *(storms off)*

CELLIST
Her words rang throughout the minds of all the citizens.

CHORUS
Oedipus a murderer?

CELLIST
But truth is never easy

CHORUS
Creon a traitor?

CELLIST
Truth is always complicated.

CHORUS
Oedipus raged.

CELLIST
Within hours, news of the confrontation spread through the city.

WOMAN
People knelt in prayer.

MAN #3
Uncertain

MAN #2
Afraid.

CELLIST
And the darkness choking the city grew even stronger when Creon returned to the square.

(CREON enters and walks among the people. Sits and prays with them. They all stop and stare)

CREON
May I pray with you all?

(Silence)

WOMAN
You are here?

CREON
Where would I be? I suffer with you, I should pray with you.

MAN #3
Have you not spoken with the King?

CREON
I hope to soon – I am anxious to hear what news he learned from the Prophet.

WOMAN
(to the MAN) He does not know.

MAN #3
(to the WOMAN) How can he not know?

CREON
Know what?

WOMAN
Creon, kind sir, you must leave. Leave Thebes just for a bit. It is not safe...

CREON
Me?

MAN #3
King Oedipus... he...

CREON
Out with it.

MAN #3
I don't want to repeat it. Not here, sir.

WOMAN
The accusations, the rage.

CREON
Someone needs to tell me NOW. If only in a whisper, in my ear. But tell me now.

(The man approaches CREON and whispers the tale in his ear. A cello plays as the WOMAN continues to chant)

WOMAN
(chants) Dear Apollo, please hear our prayers. Dear Apollo please hear our prayers. Dearest Zeus, please hear our prayers.

(We see CREON's face fall. We hear him interrupt the MAN telling him what has occurred)

CREON
He said that?

(More whispers, more chants)

CREON
No. No. He wouldn't.

(More whispers. More chants)

CREON
Where did Tiresias go? Did she leave? *(to the crowd)* It is true? All that I have been told? *(silence)* Speak. *(No one can look at him)* Some of you are my friends. Known me since birth. And now... now none of you can bear to look at me. Does this mean you think I have done these horrific things? That I am capable of lying, cheating, murder? Am I? Look at me and speak to my face.

MAN #3
He was so angry.

WOMAN
Yes.

MAN #3
So full of rage.

CREON
I can hardly believe my ears. Believe what you have told me. *(to the man who whispered in his ear)* Why did no one come find me?

WOMAN
We were shocked as well.

MAN #3
Unable to move.

WOMAN
To blink.

MAN #3
The King has been deeply affected by this dark cloud.

WOMAN
Yes.

MAN #3
Circles under his eyes. He is growing gaunt.

CREON
I have always put this city first. You all know me. We have laughed and cried together for many years. I would never harm any of you. I am Thebes. Thebes is in my blood and I would never betray blood. I am no traitor.

MAN #3
No. No.

WOMAN
He spoke in anger.

MAN #3
Creon, he was confused.

CREON
Confused? Was he mad? Foaming at the mouth? Or was he emotional but his speech remained in tact?

WOMAN
He was not mad.

MAN 3
He had his wits about him.

CREON
Is it wrong that I wished he was mad? That those words crossed his lips, but his mind was not aware of the meaning?

WOMAN
We were all frightened, sir. If you—

(OEDIPUS enters)

OEDIPUS
(sees CREON) You must be joking me? Apollo, are my eyes deceiving me or is the lying murderous traitor standing in front of me, in front of my people?

CREON
Oedipus, let us speak in private about—

OEDIPUS
(grabs CREON's arm and twists it behind his back; very painful) The crown still sits on my head. Does it irk you to see that

it did not work? That your plan was surprisingly easy to foil?

CREON
(does not fight him back) I had no plan. Please let us...

MAN #3
Perhaps you should listen to him, King.

OEDIPUS
(ignoring all) I think what surprises me most is that you thought so little of me. That I seemed like such easy prey to you.

CREON
That is not true. Let us go inside, in private—

OEDIPUS
I would have respected you more had you been open with your intention to pry the crown from my head

CREON
Never.

OEDIPUS
(continues) But this... How did you think this would actually work, you scum of the earth, you boil of the gods?

CREON
Allow me the right to talk to you in private

OEDIPUS
(laughing, lets him go) Now you want to talk. *(to the crowd)* Now he wants to talk.

CREON
Allow me to defend myself.

OEDIPUS
That time has past.

CREON
You are being blinded by your stubbornness.

MAN #3
Please, sirs. Please.

OEDIPUS
(to crowd) No man is above the law. Not even the Queen's brother. Am I wrong? Can one man be above us all.

MAN #3
You are correct, but maybe...

OEDIPUS
There is no "maybe". It is either right or wrong.

CREON
Stop your posturing and tell me what I have done. How have I wronged you so much that I deserve this black mark on my name?

WOMAN
Tell him, King Oedipus. Explain to him what you think.

OEDIPUS
Did you advise me to seek out that fraud, that sham of a seer?

CREON
Tiresias? She is our most revered prophet!

OEDIPUS
I did not ask your opinion. I asked you yes or no, did you tell me...

CREON
Yes. I did.

OEDIPUS
And did you...

CREON
I stand by that advice.

OEDIPUS
(smiles) Of course you do. And did King Laius consult Tiresias? Did the King seek her out?

CREON
Yes. Often.

OEDIPUS
Was this based on your advice as well?

CREON
He thought quite highly, as I do, of the old woman.

OEDIPUS
But did you advise him to call on her?

CREON
I cannot be sure. He did not look to me for such advice.

OEDIPUS
Smart man. So you alone decided to leave unsolved the murder of your king?

CREON
We all did what we could, but found nothing. Then we were under siege by...

OEDIPUS
The sphinx. I know this part, Creon! I remember it well!

MAN# 3
Bless you King Oedipus.

MAN #3 and WOMAN
Bless you, our King.

OEDIPUS
(to the townsfolk) I will end this plague as I ended that one.

CREON
You have always had our gratitude.

OEDIPUS
I have had theirs. *(indicates to the people)*

CREON
You have had mine. I celebrated as you were anointed King. I rejoiced when you married my sister. As a city, we put the dark times behind us and moved forward!

OEDIPUS
And yet the darkness has returned, Creon. And it is obvious who is to blame.

CREON
Me? Honestly?

OEDIPUS
I cannot help but wonder why you never sent for Tiresias when your King was missing. Why did she not come to help you? *(to the WOMAN)* Can you understand that? Because, would you not, dear lady, if you knew something, step forward to help your kinsmen?

WOMAN
I would.

CREON
I do not answer for Tiresias. I cannot remember...

OEDIPUS
You cannot?

CREON
If I knew anything, I would not hold back. Not with such accusations thrown at me.

OEDIPUS
Of course you would. *(whispering into CREON's ear)* You are the reason that hag dared to accuse me of being the murderer.

CREON
She said that?

OEDIPUS
I can only assume you put her up to it.

CREON
You assume wrong. I have no idea what

has prompted her to say such things, but since she did, let me ask you something.

OEDIPUS
(to CREON) I did not kill Laius.

CREON
Just a few questions, King. You are not afraid to let me clear my name?

OEDIPUS
Oh this should be fun. Ask me whatever you will Creon. Should I stand or sit here next to my fellow man? Oh, I think next to this fine gentleman full of reason and morals.

CREON
I am your brother-in-law.

OEDIPUS
(to the MAN) Is that a question?

CREON
You are married to my sister.

OEDIPUS
Is there a question yet?

CREON
Is that correct?

OEDIPUS
Even he can answer that. *(indicates to the MAN)*

MAN #3
(to CREON) Yes he is.

CREON
And you consider her your equal in responsibility and reign over Thebes?

OEDIPUS
I do. She is smart and beautiful and I would be a fool not to give her everything and anything I am.

CREON
And in your circle have I not had a place? Have you not given me responsibility and given me freedom to act in the best for the country?

OEDIPUS
I considered you my own brother.

CREON
And you are mine. This does not make sense. Think about it.

OEDIPUS
Reason makes no sense to a liar.

CREON
Oedipus, think about who I am. Who I have been to you, to Jocasta. I have seen two men, friends, brothers as King.

OEDIPUS
Begging does not become you, Creon.

CREON
This is not... Stop. Think. Why would I want to be King?

OEDIPUS
Why would you not?

CREON
Being King means that you have the world on your shoulders. Anxiety beating down on you. I have seen how this plague has affected you. Why would I want that? You have given me the power to help the people, to be kingly in a way that allows me to work with the citizens, to be respected by our neighbors, to be loved by those who love you... I have done all this without the true responsibility of being a King. Oedipus, I enjoy all the benefits with none of the hardships that you as a true king must encounter daily.

OEDIPUS
(to the crowd) That is true, he has never been one who can make hard decisions.

CREON
If you admit that, if I admit that… then why would I ever want your crown? Why would I risk treason when I have been happy in my role? Have any of you heard me say otherwise?

MAN #3
No.

WOMAN
Never.

OEDIPUS
Do not prey on the loyalty of my people.

CREON
Then go ask the oracle of Delphi. Ask the priestess if all you say is true.

MAN #3
She will tell you, King. She will tell you all.

CREON
If they tell you I am guilty of it all, then kill me. I beg of you. Kill me over and over again. But if, if they tell you that you have been confused then—

OEDIPUS
I do not need the priestess to confirm my story.

CREON
A story. That is it exactly. You have no proof.

OEDIPUS
Proof?

MAN #3
Sir, that is true.

CREON
All you have are guesses!

WOMAN
He is right, your highness.

CREON
Can you so easily succumb to paranoia? After years of friendship together? I urge you to confirm your suspicions, and not act so rashly that you regret your decisions!

MAN #3
(to OEDIPUS) He offers a reasonable plan. To satisfy all parties.

WOMAN
(overlapping Man #3) We cannot act too quickly.

OEDIPUS
(to the crowd) You want ME to wait for him to murder me and destroy Thebes?

MAN #3
No. No.

OEDIPUS
You want me to act slowly and watch him usurp my throne? No. I will not.

CREON
Then I will leave. I will leave the city. Would that make you happy?

MAN #3
That would work.

OEDIPUS
(in CREON's face) You dead would make me happy. You with my knife in your gut. Since I have had to dig yours from my back.

CREON
I have betrayed no one!

OEDIPUS
You have betrayed me and my city.

CREON
This is my city too.

(*A fight begins between OEDIPUS and CREON. JOCASTA runs out and sees the scene*)

JOCASTA
What are you doing!?! OEDIPUS! CREON! STOP THIS! *(to MAN #3)* Help stop this. What has happened?

(MAN #3 helps to break up the fight)

JOCASTA
(to CREON and OEDIPUS) HOW DARE YOU EMBARRASS OUR CITIZENS IN THEIR TIME OF NEED! SHAME! SHAME ON YOU BOTH! You must be JOKING! NOW?! NOW is the time for this?!

(The fight is broken up and the men are out of breath. JOCASTA leans over OEDIPUS and whispers)

JOCASTA
Get back in the house.

OEDIPUS
Jocasta.

JOCASTA
Now.

OEDIPUS
I need to tell you…

JOCASTA
And do not let these people see that look of madness in your eyes.

OEDIPUS
Do not speak to me like…

JOCASTA
(turns to the crowd) I must apologize for these grown men who have let their disagreements bubble over so easily in these troubled times. They are shamed I'm sure.

OEDIPUS
Do not speak for me.

CREON
Or me.

JOCASTA
When you both can speak rationally and act like adults, I will be happy to let you handle your business yourselves.

(She walks to CREON and whispers to him)

JOCASTA
Get out of here and go home.

CREON
He wants to kill me.

OEDIPUS
No. He wants to kill me and take the crown.

JOCASTA
What?!

CREON
He has gone insane, Jocasta. I do not know what has happened!

OEDIPUS
He is trying to ruin us. Ruin everything we have built.

CREON
(overlapping) I swear to God, I swear on everything, on my life that I would never take part in overthrowing him. I swear. I swear on all that is holy.

OEDIPUS
Do not listen to him.

CREON
(overlapping) Do not believe him. Please.

OEDIPUS
He is evil.

JOCASTA
(in CREON's face) You swear to me?

CREON
I have never lied to you.

(A moment)

JOCASTA
(sits next to OEDIPUS and speaks softly and calmly to him) I do not know what has happened.

OEDIPUS
Because you are not listening.

JOCASTA
Do not speak to me like that.

OEDIPUS
You take his side over mine?

(CREON stalks the stage)

JOCASTA
I am not taking a side. But Creon would never harm you because he would be killing me. He knows this. And I know him. Better than anyone. If you do not believe him, then believe me. I have never misled you. Have I ever lied to you?

OEDIPUS
No. But...

JOCASTA
I love you, Oedipus. I love you. I see that fire in your eyes. I see it, but do not let it blind you. Not now.

OEDIPUS
Then believe me, Jocasta. Believe what I am telling you. He is trying to destroy us.

JOCASTA
Then let us go in and discuss it. But not here. You are scaring your people.

OEDIPUS
No. I'm making them accountable. They have witnessed it all. If my own wife cannot believe me, will you believe them?

JOCASTA
I did not say...

OEDIPUS
(to MAN #3) You. Friend. Come here. You saw what happened?

MAN #3
You know I think highly of you.

OEDIPUS
And I, you. Not every man has the strength to break up such a fight between a King and a traitor.

MAN #3
Thank you.

OEDIPUS
What do you think? Be honest. Tell the Queen what you saw.

MAN #3
You do not need my opinion.

OEDIPUS
I want you to tell her what you saw.

CREON
Yes, tell her what you saw.

MAN #3
I... I have a great respect for both you men.

JOCASTA
You do not need to answer sir.

OEDIPUS
Yes, he does.

CREON
Tell us. And do not fear your answer.

OEDIPUS
Just the truth. That is all I am interested in.

MAN #3
I think you both have a point, but I... I... I cannot believe Creon would try to destroy the city like this just so he can be King. That doesn't mean that I do not have respect and...

OEDIPUS
And do you all feel like this? Feel that Creon would never harm you or me? *(he looks and sees that they are all agreeing with MAN #3)*

JOCASTA
Please let us not bother the people with such family issues. Let us go inside for a drink and...

OEDIPUS
(to the crowd) So you pick him? Him over your King?

MAN #3
No.

OEDIPUS
Choosing him is choosing my death.

JOCASTA
Do not say that. That is not true.

MAN #3
No. No it is not.

JOCASTA
They are not picking him - They are asking you to spare him. That is what they are saying.

MAN #3
Yes. Yes. Exactly.

OEDIPUS
Then I pity their blindness.

CREON
(to OEDIPUS) See, Brother.

(OEDIPUS gets up to go toward CREON)

JOCASTA
(to CREON) Go. Now.

CREON
Fine. I'm leaving. *(goes toward the crowd)* These are the people that know me. Believe me. *(to the crowd)* Thank you my friends. *(CREON exits)*

OEDIPUS
That is what he is doing to me. Do you see? Do you understand?

JOCASTA
Let us go inside.

OEDIPUS
I will go when I am ready

JOCASTA
Do not pull rank on me.

OEDIPUS
Jocasta.

JOCASTA
I want to talk with you. Find out what started this.

OEDIPUS
Tiresias.

JOCASTA
I heard she came.

OEDIPUS
And left.

JOCASTA
Tell me more.

OEDIPUS
She said I murdered King Laius.

JOCASTA
What?

OEDIPUS
She said I murdered your first husband.

JOCASTA
Wait. Wait. Come here. *(pulls him to the side, private)* She said that?

OEDIPUS
Yes.

JOCASTA
That is ridiculous.

OEDIPUS
Yes, but...

JOCASTA
You could never kill anyone.

OEDIPUS
That is not true.

JOCASTA
You would have to have good reason then.

OEDIPUS
So you would think.

JOCASTA
Prophets and their powers. I do not have any faith in their methods. They might get the answers right a third of the time.

OEDIPUS
Creon encouraged me to call on her and to listen to her tales...

JOCASTA
That is why you and Creon are fighting?

OEDIPUS
(overlapping) Yes, he is...

JOCASTA
(overlapping) Over something so ridiculous.

OEDIPUS
Many people swear by...

JOCASTA
I know what the old country people say about these oracles and seers.

OEDIPUS
There have been stories of...

JOCASTA
Oh yes, the stories. I have been told so many of them. Let me tell you about a "prophecy" – Long ago, Laius was told by the Oracle – a "Prophecy", the priests told him– that he would die at the hands of his own son – our child. In reality, Laius was killed by thieves! Highwaymen, in broad daylight, killed him at a crossroads on his journey to Delphi! His son was nowhere near, because when the boy was but 3 days old, the King stripped the baby from my arms, both of us screaming as if we were being torn open and sent him to be abandoned in the mountains, to die from exposure to the elements. And with all that, we were supposed to feel safe and secure knowing that his fate had changed, all of our fates had. But the joke was on us – the prophecy was false, you see! Nothing but a fiction! A cruel game played at my expense. *(silence as she holds him)* That was a lifetime ago.

OEDIPUS
That really happened?

JOCASTA
Yes.

OEDIPUS
Why did you not ever tell me this?

JOCASTA
Would you have thought differently of me?

OEDIPUS
Because if this is true. If this is really true.

JOCASTA
It is. Painfully so.

OEDIPUS
How could you keep this from me? How could you...

JOCASTA
You have no reason to be angry with me. I suffered a great loss.

OEDIPUS
Laius was killed at a crossroads? Not in Delphi?

JOCASTA
I told you this long ago..

OEDIPUS
Tell me again.

JOCASTA
The crossroads in the foothills, where the paths to Delphi, Dahlia and Thebes all meet.

OEDIPUS
How long ago?

JOCASTA
You did not murder him. I know you did not. You would remember if you killed someone, would you not?

OEDIPUS
Yes. I would. I do. *(pause)* When exactly was he killed?

(Pause)

JOCASTA
It was just before you came to Thebes, I guess. Nearly 20 years now. Just before you won this kingdom.

OEDIPUS
Tell me what he looked like.

JOCASTA
Love, he was much older than me. White hair and beard. Blue eyes...

OEDIPUS
She was right.

JOCASTA
Tiresias?

OEDIPUS
I think I...

JOCASTA
Do not say it.

OEDIPUS
Do you remember how many people were with him? How many people went...

JOCASTA
I do not remember. I cannot remember.

OEDIPUS
Think quickly.

JOCASTA
There were... five I think. Laius's chief of staff, his guards. And Alec, a servant. And then Laius. They took one carriage.

OEDIPUS
You are sure?

JOCASTA
Yes. That is what Alec told us. He would know more than...

OEDIPUS
Alec?

JOCASTA
The only person who survived. He was Laius's assistant.

OEDIPUS
Creon told me he is still alive.

JOCASTA
Yes – he has moved away from here, but...

OEDIPUS
Where is he now? We need to find him.

JOCASTA
I can do that. I helped him leave town right after you became King, after we became engaged. In fact, I remember when we had the Spring festival. .. remember the parades. It was our first time together in public. Alec found me amongst the people and asked for a moment of my time. Oh, Oedipus, what a broken man. He said he was not sure

he could stay with a new King and did not want to ruin my happiness. I understood. His life had been working with Laius, so I helped him secure work as a farmer. It was the least I could do - Breaks my heart to think of him.

OEDIPUS
You need to get him back here. Now.

JOCASTA
But why? To interrogate the poor man? I have told you he is innocent. He has been through enough, I will not allow you to subject him to...

(OEDIPUS grabs JOCASTA's arms)

OEDIPUS
I am trying to save this city.

JOCASTA
(as OEDIPUS squeezes her arms harder)
You are hurting me.

OEDIPUS
Help me.

JOCASTA
I will always help you. You know that.

OEDIPUS
(letting go) Yes.

JOCASTA
It is alright.

OEDIPUS
No. No. It is not alright.

JOCASTA
You are jumping to conclusions. Love, look at me.

OEDIPUS
I cannot.

JOCASTA
There is nothing you can say that will harm me more than seeing you like this. Trust me. Talk to me. We can figure this out together. You are not alone.

OEDIPUS
You are too good to me.

JOCASTA
If that is true, then talk to me. I would never judge you

OEDIPUS
I know. You never have

JOCASTA
Then talk to me. Let me in.

OEDIPUS
You know I came from Corinth...

JOCASTA
Of course – you were Prince there - your parents are King Polybus and Queen Merope, but you have not spoken to them in years.

OEDIPUS
Jocasta, forgive me. I have told you half truth and lies. Not to deceive you, but rather hide myself from that world in Corinth.

JOCASTA
I have respected your privacy, Oedipus, never asked what drove such a wedge between you and your family, but what does this have to do with Laius?

OEDIPUS
I was living a very charmed life there. I was happy and full of good fortune. Until one night my parents held a state dinner. I was 17. It was a huge gala and there was an encounter with a drunk servant in the kitchen. And that was the beginning of my end.

(Lights change. Flashback to the party where OEDIPUS first had the encounter as a boy)

DRUNK SERVANT (Man #2)
You shouldn't be in here!

OEDIPUS
(startled to see a man) Oh, I am sorry.

DRUNK SERVANT
What?

OEDIPUS
I was just looking for…

DRUNK SERVANT
Not me, huh?

OEDIPUS
No. Not you. Can I help you?

DRUNK SERVANT
So you are the famous Oedipus?

OEDIPUS.
I am famous, huh?

DRUNK SERVANT
Have a drink with me.

OEDIPUS
I can't. I would get in trouble with my mother. And you should really be moving along. Take a walk and get some fresh air. You do not want my father to find you like this.

DRUNK SERVANT
A drunk and a bastard. We'd make a good team. Have a drink?

OEDIPUS
What did you call me?

DRUNK SERVANT
Come drink, Bastard. Drink.

OEDIPUS
I am not a bastard.

DRUNK SERVANT
The whispers in town say differently. Sit and have a glass. We can discuss it.

OEDIPUS
(in the man's face) You are drunk.

DRUNK SERVANT
I know what I've been told. Worst kept secret in the kingdom…

OEDIPUS
Have you forgotten who I am?

DRUNK SERVANT
I know exactly who you are.

(Lights change. Back to JOCASTA)

OEDIPUS
(to JOCASTA) That man, that conversation just… never left me. Put something in my head I just could not get away from.

JOCASTA
Did you ask your parents?

OEDIPUS
I did. I asked them point blank. At first they were so angry at that man, but then they explained that this is what happens in politics and government. I had to put it behind me.

JOCASTA
That is exactly what I would tell our daughters, love.

OEDIPUS
They did make me feel better. Months went by, but the seed was planted in my head.

JOCASTA
Of course.

OEDIPUS
So I went to see a fortune teller—one that my parents had mentioned and trusted. But they also feared him, I think, as I had never been allowed to even meet him before. I did not tell them where I was going, but I needed

to make sure. Needed further confirmation so I could sleep again.

JOCASTA
Yes. It makes sense.

OEDIPUS
Horrible doesn't begin to describe his words.

(Lights change. Flashback to OEDIPUS with the FORTUNE TELLER)

TELLER (Man #3)
You have to tell me whether you want to hear everything. Everything that the gods give me. Because I am unable to conceal the information.

OEDIPUS
That is why I have come.

TELLER
Very well.

(The TELLER flips the cards and something about the teller's face drops upon seeing the cards on the table)

TELLER
Oh. Gods.

OEDIPUS
What? What are they telling you?

TELLER
Oh. You should go home.

OEDIPUS
Am I not my father's son. Is that what it says?

TELLER
I did not get an answer to the question you asked.

OEDIPUS
Then what does it say?

TELLER
Sometimes in life, there are burdens in which—

OEDIPUS
I do not want your advice, I want the truth!

(Pause)

TELLER
The cards foretell a future where you will murder your father.

(Silence)

OEDIPUS
Murder?

TELLER
Yes.

OEDIPUS
My father?

TELLER
I cannot get a different answer.

OEDIPUS
No. No. I would never hurt him. I love him.

TELLER
Today you do. But tomorrow, next week, month, year, this is in the future.

OEDIPUS
I... I...

TELLER
And after you murder your father, you will have an unnatural relationship with your mother.

OEDIPUS
My - ?!

TELLER
I can only say what I see.

(Lights change. Back to JOCASTA)

OEDIPUS
I just ran.

JOCASTA
Oh my gods.

OEDIPUS
I ran from the fortune teller, from my parents, from Corinth. I never went back. Occasionally I sent word back home; just to tell them I was still alive, where I was, but I could never go back. They begged me to, tried to see me, but I refused them. It was the only thing I could think to do. I was barely eighteen.

JOCASTA
You were just a boy.

OEDIPUS
For years, if they knew where I was they sent messengers, gifts. I had money, of course, and for several years I just traveled, alone, aimlessly, never telling anyone why. It was during these travels I came to that crossroad you mentioned. Where Laius was believed to have been killed.

JOCASTA
Yes?

OEDIPUS
On that road, I had an encounter. *(pause)* More than an encounter.

JOCASTA
Yes.

OEDIPUS
I was walking... unsure even of where I was going, just headed to whatever was next. Lost in my thoughts, I heard and saw too late a carriage, coming at me quickly. I had to dive off the road to avoid being trampled to death! The driver had seen me, and hadn't even slowed! In anger, I leapt up and threw a stone, hitting one of the men riding on the top of the carriage. Then it stopped, and the man leapt down, charging back at me, fire in his eyes, and I... before the chariot had even turned around, I -

JOCASTA
You killed him?

OEDIPUS
I killed them all. I went into a rage. They charged out of the carriage one at a time, and I killed them. The last man... the last man out... he was the man you described to me.

JOCASTA
Oedipus. Oh Oedipus.

OEDIPUS
To say the words... I have uttered them to no one. Ever. *(silence)* You now look at me differently.

JOCASTA
No.

OEDIPUS
I am evil. Cursed.

JOCASTA
No you are not.

OEDIPUS
I have angered the gods and I bring death to every place I touch.

JOCASTA
Please. Please do not. Let us think about what...

OEDIPUS
I fled my home to protect it, and brought death to another.

JOCASTA
We do not know. We do not know any of this. This is not you. This is not my Oedipus. It is a mistake.

OEDIPUS
There have been no mistakes. I have ruined you, our children, our people.

Look around. Oh Gods, these hands! I have touched you with these hands – the hands that killed your husband!

JOCASTA
No! I will prove you wrong. You are wrong. They were attacked by robbers. Not just one man, but a gang of them. That is the story he told me. I remember so clearly. *(calls out)* Someone get me Alec now. He needs to be brought to us immediately. IMMEDIATELY. *(to OEDIPUS)* I have hope. Have hope.

OEDIPUS
I cannot have hope until I can hear him confirm it from his own lips.

JOCASTA
Yes. Yes. But the whole city can confirm what is well known. Everyone can. It was robbers. Robbers. *(gets up and goes to the town people in the courtyard)* Was it not said that King Laius was murdered by robbers?

MAN #3
Yes. Everyone knows that.

JOCASTA
It was not just one man. There were many of them.

MAN #3
Yes. Yes.

JOCASTA
See, love, but we will talk to Alec. We will confirm this.

OEDIPUS
(whispers) But if it was only one person, then it was me. We can only assume that…

JOCASTA
No. No we will not assume that. We will assume that these fortune tellers, these seers are liars. Laius was supposed to be murdered by his son. And our son is not living in this city because he perished at his own father's hand. And now they try to tell us that Laius' murderer lives in the city. Are you listening to this? It does not make sense. It does not add up. You have been tortured by what they are telling you. I have been tortured. We will expose this. Everything has been turned around. Do you not see?

OEDIPUS
I have caused you great pain and I'll never forgive myself. I changed your life…

JOCASTA
For the better. You saved me. You have loved and respected me. Given me beautiful children. Allowed me to govern with you. While I never wished Laius' harm, he was not good to… I was forced to marry, so young, and he – I - we were not good for each other. He was not the man you are. Not in any way. Do you hear me?

OEDIPUS
Jocasta, I love you.

(They kiss)

JOCASTA
You are my world.

OEDIPUS
And you are mine. You, our children, this city…

JOCASTA
We will solve this—together. I promise.

OEDIPUS
I just need to know. Look at these people.

JOCASTA
We are all suffering, but together, we will solve it. But you cannot stay out

here. Let us get you to sleep, eat, in clean clothes. The world will seem better I promise.

OEDIPUS
I should stay with them.

JOCASTA
They need you to be at your best. You are their leader.

OEDIPUS
Yes.

(They exit. CELLIST plays and speaks)

CELLIST
Time moved forward. Babies still cried, stomachs still churned, and dark clouds still hung over Thebes. A day passes.

(JOCASTA enters the courtyard with the citizens and approaches an altar to the gods. She passes with nods and salutations. She lays flowers on the altar and remains in prayer)

JOCASTA
(whispering to herself) Begging you to guide him and protect him. He believes that he is cursed by you, but how can that be true? I have never questioned you. Never asked for much. I have been at the hands of cruelty in the past, but you have allowed him to free me. If you could allow me to free him, to return his love and forgiveness, I would be so grateful.

(During this time a MESENGER appears on the stage asking very quietly if an OEDIPUS lives nearby)

MAN #2
That is his wife, Queen Jocasta.

MESSENGER (Man #3)
(approaches JOCASTA) Excuse me, ma'am.

JOCASTA
(startled) Yes.

MESSENGER
I am sorry. I did not mean to scare you.

JOCASTA
What is it?

MESSENGER
I am eager to learn if you are indeed King Oedipus' wife and if he...

JOCASTA
I am.

MESSENGER
Wonderful. Wonderful news. And can I inquire as to whether his highness is at home and available to meet with me?

JOCASTA
I am afraid my husband is in need of much peace as we are waiting for an answer, a visitor.

MESSENGER
Oh dear, is he ill?

JOCASTA
As you can see we are all ill in these parts.

MESSENGER
Yes. Word has spread. Nevertheless, I have a message for King Oedipus.

JOCASTA
I would be happy to deliver your message to him.

MESSENGER
I come with news from Corinth.

JOCASTA
Corinth?

MESSENGER
Yes.

JOCASTA
That is his hometown.

MESSENGER
Which is why I am here. To offer him his rightful place in our land.

JOCASTA
Rightful place?

MESSENGER
The people are demanding, begging for him to return and fulfill his family line.

JOCASTA
They want him as King?

MESSENGER
We have lost our monarch.

JOCASTA
Polybus.

MESSENGER
Yes.

JOCASTA
Polybus died?

MESSENGER
Yes.

JOCASTA
He is dead?!?

MESSENGER
I'm afraid so.

JOCASTA
(Jumps around and hugs him) What wonderful news. Bless you. Bless you. The weight... I can breathe... *(yells)* Someone get him. Someone get the King out immediately. *(yells)* Oedipus!!! Oedipus.

MESSENGER
Ma'am? Are you...?

JOCASTA
I owe you the world you kind fellow. The world. *(to the sky)* There is no curse. You silly gods. You silly silly gods.

MESSENGER
Curse?

(enters OEDIPUS)

OEDIPUS
Jocasta. What has happened?

JOCASTA
(hugging him) Only good things, my love.

OEDIPUS
What is it?

JOCASTA
This dear sweet man. This wonderful man now etched forever into my heart. He has come with the best of news.

MESSENGER
It is bittersweet, your highness.

JOCASTA
He is from Corinth. Corinth, darling.

MESSENGER
Yes. I am sorry to report that...

JOCASTA
Your father is dead. Dead and gone.

MESSENGER
Yes.

(Pause)

OEDIPUS
Polybus is dead?

JOCASTA
Yes.

MESSENGER
Yes.

OEDIPUS
(to the MESSENGER) When?

MESSENGER
Your father passed about two weeks ago. I have been sent for you to...

OEDIPUS
Was his death brought upon by sickness or someone's hand?

MESSENGER
It was an infection that...

OEDIPUS
(to Jocasta) It was natural.

JOCASTA
Thank you dear god.

OEDIPUS
Jocasta...

JOCASTA
You have been freed.

OEDIPUS
I feel it.

MESSENGER
Infection is never easy to fight at such an old age.

JOCASTA
(to the MESSENGER) You must find this all strange. We are of course very sad to hear about the King's demise, but it represents truth. A new truth that has been covered up with lies for so long.

MESSENGER
I assumed there must be something.

OEDIPUS
Not just something. A curse that was nothing more than a tall tale.

MESSENGER
Oh.

JOCASTA
I told you, darling. I told you!

(They hug)

JOCASTA
(whispers in his ear) There is no more reason to fear. It has all gone.

(Pause)

OEDIPUS
Should I be worried about my... my mother? About the second half of the prophecy?

JOCASTA
(to OEDIPUS) No. No. You either accept the prophecy or you do not. The first part was not true and therefore, the second half is also a lie. It is that simple.

MESSENGER
Sir, will you be following me back to your true home? I have orders to bring you back as soon as possible to take your place among your kinsman.

OEDIPUS
I cannot leave here. No. No. I have no interest in going back.

JOCASTA
Perhaps once things here in Thebes are set right?

OEDIPUS
(to JOCASTA) No. I cannot. When I left, I left for good. Call me superstitious, but I cannot overcome the fear of those damned words.

MESSENGER
You speak of a prophecy, but I have never heard of you attached to any cursed sentiments. Can you speak to what drives your fears, or is that something you would prefer to keep to yourself?

JOCASTA
Tell him, Oedipus. There is no shame in something you had no control over.

MESSENGER
I just want to help if I can. Perhaps shed any light.

OEDIPUS
It is shame that has held my tongue for all these years. I was told by a prophet that I would murder my own father and bed my mother. It is disgusting to hear those words drip from my lips, even now.

MESSENGER
Is this the reason you left Corinth so many years ago?

OEDIPUS
Did I need a better reason than that? I loved my father dearly! And for the rest of it, well...

MESSENGER
Yes. Of course. But sir, I have even better news for you. I can cure your fear.

OEDIPUS
Well.

JOCASTA
Speak now. Do not be shy.

OEDIPUS
Not if you can enlighten us.

MESSENGER
Polybus was not your father.

OEDIPUS
Excuse me?

MESSENGER
While he was indeed a father in name, in blood you are not related.

JOCASTA
Explain yourself.

OEDIPUS
My mother was unfaithful to my father?

MESSENGER
She was not your mother. They took you in as a small boy. So you understand that that silly curse meant...

JOCASTA
How are you so sure of this? How do we know that you are telling us the truth?

OEDIPUS
The drunkard said I was a bastard.

MESSENGER
(to JOCASTA) I know because I held him as a baby. I in fact put him... *(to OEDIPUS)* I put you in the arms of your mother and father, the King and Queen.

JOCASTA
They had no other children?

MESSENGER
They had been unable to conceive a child no matter how hard they prayed. And then you arrived for them.

OEDIPUS
From where?

MESSENGER
You were found or rather saved. In the mountains just North of...

OEDIPUS
So I was abandoned?

JOCASTA
Who found him?

MESSENGER
I took him. I was the rancher who was charged with his immediate supervision.

OEDIPUS
Did you not check where I was from? Perhaps I was kidnapped or...

MESSENGER
I was not worried about that. My main concern was getting you well. You were barely a week old and injured.

OEDIPUS
Injured?

MESSENGER
Your feet or rather your ankles had been sliced somehow.

(JOCASTA sinks backwards)

OEDIPUS
I still bear those scars today.

MESSENGER
Oedipus was the name we gave you while you healed in our home.

OEDIPUS
So you have no idea where I came from?

MESSENGER
I know how you came to me. A man. A friend of my cousins arrived with you.

OEDIPUS
What was his name? Where was he from?

MESSENGER
All I know is he worked in the palace and his name was Alec.

(JOCASTA has put the pieces together and is stunned still)

OEDIPUS
Alec? Jocasta, this is the same man. He could hold all the answers. He could set everything right.

JOCASTA
(grabbing OEDIPUS) Oedipus. Oedipus.

OEDIPUS
What? *(looks at her)* What is wrong?

JOCASTA
(whispers/whimpers) I need you to listen to me.

OEDIPUS
Alec holds the answers.

JOCASTA
I need you to listen to me.

OEDIPUS
Are you hearing me?

JOCASTA
I am.

OEDIPUS
We are so close.

JOCASTA
I am begging you to stop.

OEDIPUS
Why?

JOCASTA
This is a waste of time. A waste of time.

OEDIPUS
The truth is upon us.

JOCASTA
Do you love me?

OEDIPUS
Jocasta.

JOCASTA
Do you love me?

OEDIPUS
Yes. Yes.

JOCASTA
If you have ever truly loved me...

OEDIPUS
There's no time for...

JOCASTA
Please stop. This search. Now. Now before you find out

OEDIPUS
Do not fear the truth. Maybe I am from a slave or maybe I am the bastard of a whore, but this will not reflect poorly upon you. I promise.

JOCASTA
Let us go inside for just a moment.

Please. Let us take just a minute and allow me to persuade you of...

OEDIPUS
I love you, but...

JOCASTA
Then follow me. Follow me inside. *(gets up crying)*

OEDIPUS
You will not persuade me. This is about the truth, our city's truth.

JOCASTA
I have never led you astray. Never.

OEDIPUS
So do not start now.

JOCASTA
Please lend me your ear. Allow me to counsel you on these issues. You have always let me have my say.

OEDIPUS
When it pleased me, I let you have your say.

JOCASTA
(overlapping) I am just asking that you think.

OEDIPUS
(overlapping) And now. Now you are standing in my way. Acting as a fool, scared of what the truth holds.

JOCASTA
I fear what we are about to...

OEDIPUS
I do not fear the truth, I respect it. That is why I left Corinth.

JOCASTA
I beg a moment of your time?

OEDIPUS
You are merely wasting it.

JOCASTA
As your wife, as your Queen.

OEDIPUS
(loudly and puffing out his chest) Remember your place.

JOCASTA
(crying) The gods help you.

OEDIPUS
Exactly. They do!

JOCASTA
Unhappy Oedipus. That is all I can call you and will be all that I or anyone shall ever call you.

OEDIPUS
Go.

(JOCASTA exits)

OEDIPUS
(to the crowd) You need not concern yourself with her. Nor should any of you. The fights between a man and wife are exactly that . . . between man and wife. But she is fearful of what old Alec has to say about my birth right. I may be from common slaves or even worse. But citizens, I am fortunate; fortunate indeed. Whoever my parents are, I am about to learn the truth. And finding out the truth will lead us to salvation. For myself, for our country, for our world. I do not worry about whatever I find out; in fact I will not be whole until then.

(The HERDSMAN enters)

MESSENGER
Is that him?

OEDIPUS
(to the old man coming his way) I can only guess that you are Alec. Am I right? *(to the MESSENGER)* Am I?

MESSENGER
Yes. You can be sure this is him

OEDIPUS
(to HERDSMAN) Many blessings. Thank you for coming. I have two questions for you, and many lives hang in the balance of your answers.

HERDSMAN (Man #2)
Yes, sir.

OEDIPUS
You were the assistant to Laius, were you not?

HERDSMAN
I was. I started to work for him when I was just a boy.

OEDIPUS
So you are indeed the right man. What work did you do for the King?

HERDSMAN
Anything he needed done, was what I did sir.

OEDIPUS
And somewhere, you met this man here. (indicated to the MESSENGER)

HERDSMAN
(looks) No. I do not think so.

OEDIPUS
Look closely.

HERDSMAN
No, not that I can recall.

MESSENGER
You knew my cousins well. Creed and...

HERDSMAN
Yes. Yes I knew them. Indeed.

MESSENGER
And you one day appeared with a baby for me to bring up. Do you remember...

HERDSMAN
Why are you asking me these questions?

MESSENGER
This King is that baby.

HERDSMAN
Gods, no.

MESSENGER
Yes. Yes. The child you gave to me.

HERDSMAN
HOLD YOUR TONGUE!

OEDIPUS
Excuse me, old man. He asks on behalf of me. On my orders.

HERDSMAN
King Oedipus, I meant no disrespect but...

OEDIPUS
Then show respect by speaking of the child.

HERDSMAN
He is speaking of things... he is speaking about... He does not know what he talks about.

MESSENGER
That is not true.

OEDIPUS
You are in no trouble.

HERDSMAN
I am always troubled.

OEDIPUS
Just answer our questions.

HERDSMAN
My mind does not allow the words to form.

OEDIPUS
Tell your mind that the King commands it so.

HERDSMAN
I am unable to speak about...

OEDIPUS
I consider myself a reasonable man. A fair man. But I do not have the time to argue and somehow appease your sensibilities.

HERDSMAN
Then allow me to return to my home.

OEDIPUS
I cannot.

HERDSMAN
And I cannot help you.

OEDIPUS
It is for the city's good.

HERDSMAN
There is no such thing as good in my case.

OEDIPUS
Speak now, or I will make you speak.

HERDSMAN
You cannot.

(OEDIPUS *steps to him to beat him*)

HERDSMAN
God help me. No. No. Please.

OEDIPUS
Did you give him a child?

HERDSMAN
I did. And had the Gods been kind they would have struck me dead right after.

OEDIPUS
Dead is what you will be unless you tell me everything you know.

HERDSMAN
Dead is what I already am. Dead is what I have been. And once you know, I am sure I will perish into the ground.

OEDIPUS
So you will tell me no more? *(to the* CHORUS*)* Then take away this man that holds up the cure to our plague and do with him what you will.

HERDSMAN
No. No! I have answered your questions. Have I not?

OEDIPUS
Where did I come from? Are you my father or did I come to you by a different...

HERDSMAN
You are not mine. You were given me.

OEDIPUS
By whom?

HERDSMAN
I throw myself upon your mercy. I beg you to stop asking these questions of me. I beg you. I beg you.

OEDIPUS
Old man, you try my patience! I do not want to hurt you, but I will. So do not make me ask again.

HERDSMAN
(crying) Laius.

OEDIPUS
Who?

HERDSMAN
You are a child of Laius.

OEDIPUS
(whispers) Jocasta.

HERDSMAN
I should stop.

OEDIPUS
I wish I could ask you to.

HERDSMAN
Please.

OEDIPUS
But you must tell me everything.

HERDSMAN
You are indeed Laius' son, but your wife the Queen would best tell you how all this came to be.

OEDIPUS
You took the baby from her?

HERDSMAN
Laius would not touch him, so I had to upon his orders.

OEDIPUS
What were you to do with the child?

HERDSMAN
Make it go away forever.

OEDIPUS
And did the mother not protest, did the father not reconsider…

HERDSMAN
It was a fearful time. The Queen's protests did not matter, but she was not told the entire truth either. An oracle had given them a terrible proclamation.

OEDIPUS
Was it that…

HERDSMAN and OEDIPUS
The child would kill his father and lie with his mother.

HERDSMAN
Then you know.

OEDIPUS
Why did you not kill me?

HERDSMAN
It was an innocent baby. I pitied it and thought I could solve the problem by taking you far from here. But there is no fooling the Gods. I was so selfish. If you are indeed the baby, you were born to misery.

OEDIPUS
I must… you are telling me truth?

HERDSMAN
I could never make up such lies.

OEDIPUS
And the crossroads? You remember me from there as well?

HERDSMAN
I am sorry.

OEDIPUS
(to the crowd) We have solved the riddle. I am your… *(moaning)* I AM YOUR PLAGUE!

CELLIST
Oedipus the King bolted for the palace, crying the Queen's name.

(OEDIPUS yells JOCASTA's name and stays on stage reacting to it all. A big beat change. The cellist takes focus, as she narrates the next bit she sets her cello down, crosses to the stage, and orchestrates the chorus in setting up the drapes. As they narrate, they set banners and begin to get the linens ready to be raised during the shadow play)

MAN #3
A thunderous silence fell over the darkened courtyard.

MAN #2
The people of Thebes could not . . .

MAN #3
Believe.

MAN #2
Comprehend.

WOMAN
Breathe.

CELLIST
They had become a city of victims.

MAN #3
Victims of lies

WOMAN
Victims of truths.

CELLIST
More pain than relief. More questions than answers

MAN #2
How could the gods condemn anyone to such a fate?

WOMAN
What were they supposed to do next?

MAN #2
Were they to banish Oedipus?

MAN #3
Kill Oedipus?

CELLIST
As the story spread through Thebes, chaos went with it. And deep within the palace,

WOMAN
Queen Jocasta ran to her bedchambers, barring the door, screaming to the sky, "Laius",

MAN #3
(using the words of JOCASTA) "Laius you coward among men! You damned us all!"

CELLIST
(words of JOCASTA) "He has returned, Laius—the son you feared."

MAN #2
(words of JOCASTA) "—the son who was to have killed you and made children with his mother!"

MAN #3
(words of JOCASTA) "This bed!"

WOMAN
(words of JOCASTA) "This bed has witnessed all of our sins!"

CELLIST
And Oedipus burst into the palace, eyes wide with rage, sword in hand, howling...

OEDIPUS
JOCASTA! DEAR SWEET WIFE AND MOTHER! Let me take away your cursed womb from whence I sprang, me and our cursed children!

MAN #2
Hurling himself against their bedchamber doors, he shattered the hinges and collapsed into the room...

MAN #3
Finding Jocasta...

OEDIPUS
NO!

MAN #3
...dead by her own hands

(With this line, the shadow play linen curtains are slowly raised as OEDIPUS slowly sinks to his knees)

OEDIPUS
No! No! No!

WOMAN
Hanging from a noose she had fashioned from their own bed linens...

(This next section is done with OEDIPUS enclosed in the shadowplay curtains, silhouetted on all four sides)

OEDIPUS
What have you done to me, Jocasta? Don't leave me. I cannot face this without you. I cannot face our people. I cannot face our children. Jocasta! Oh Gods! Why did you not take me with you?

CELLIST
Tearing from her robes the clasps of gold, he held them to the heavens, crying—

OEDIPUS
These were my gift to you, love... at the birth of our daughter... my sister... Oh GODS! Grief! You have caused me nothing but grief. You have shown me nothing but pain. You have blinded me even in sight. And so blind I shall be.

CELLIST
And Oedipus drove the pins deep into his own eyes

(OEDIPUS uses the broach, stabbing out his eyes. His unbearable screams are heard for miles. The citizens moan at the screams)

OEDIPUS
(stabs away again) My memories are all that I will see now. Memories that were so full of good fortune and beauty will now be tainted with the dark clouds of truth. You wretched eyes, get out. GET OUT! *(collapses, weeping)*

CELLIST
His servants went to him then, bandaging his wounds, and offering comfort – but Oedipus wanted none.

OEDIPUS
Take me to the people of Thebes who have waited so long for their answer. Please. They deserve to see who I truly am. Laius' killer. I will free them.

CELLIST
And so he came –was led—to his people.

(The shadow play curtains are dropped, revealing OEDIPUS on his knees at center, bandaged. Gasps and some prayers from the chorus, maybe a few cries)

OEDIPUS
Dear friends—friends is what you've all been to me. If I could, I would weep for the unnecessary kindness you have shown to me.

WOMAN
You were not yourself, causing yourself such harm.

MAN #2
None of us can argue against your sins.

MAN #3
But we know the Gods were behind them. That whispered for you to...

OEDIPUS
While I am not a friend to the gods and they none to me... I can say that no spirit called me to harm myself. These injuries came from me. And why not? Why should the world be mine to see? Why should I enjoy the beauty of life when I have been responsible for so much death? Do I not deserve worse than death? *(down on his knees)* I beg of just one of you to take me from here. Please. Please.

WOMAN
Please get up. Get up.

MAN #3
Creon is upon us.

(CREON enters)

CREON
(kneels down to OEDIPUS) Oedipus. *(to the people)* Help me.

(CREON and the chorus move any banners or cloth in there way)

CREON
(to OEDIPUS) What have you done?

OEDIPUS
Your people need you

(OEDIPUS hands CREON the crown and

CREON is slow to put it on)

WOMAN
Our new King.

OEDIPUS
I am ready for what you have for me.

CREON
I do not come to mock or taunt you.

OEDIPUS
Oh Creon.

CREON
I do not forgive you, but we are still kin.

OEDIPUS
You are treating me so nobly even though I have been most cruel and vicious—

CREON
No one should have to see you like this. *(tries to lead him from the crowd)*

OEDIPUS
Then take me away from Thebes. Quickly. Get me away from all these tortured people.

CREON
I wish it were that easy. But I can not. Not until I hear directly from the gods what I am to do with you.

OEDIPUS
The murderer must leave or die.

CREON
I know that was said, but everything has changed. Circumstances have changed and the gods can change their minds. I must consult with them...

OEDIPUS
Thank you...

CREON
(helping OEDIPUS up) Do not thank me. Penance will be paid, Oedipus.

OEDIPUS
Creon - Jocasta... she lies in the house. Promise me you will give her a proper burial, one befitting of the Queen she was. Let her not be shamed by...

CREON
She is my sister always. She will be properly remembered.

OEDIPUS
Dear Creon. Uncle? King? Brother? Creon, my brother - Please do not punish my children. My sons are grown men now, they can rely upon themselves. But... but dear sweet Antigone and Ismene... my beautiful girls. Take pity on them, please. They are so young and innocent. Please look upon them with kindness.

(CELLIST voices the daughters)

ANTIGONE and ISMENE
Daddy?

OEDIPUS
Antigone? Ismene? Creon is that . .

CREON
Girls! Get back inside!

OEDIPUS
(to his girls) Oh girls. My beautiful daughters.

CREON
I will bring him to you!

OEDIPUS
I am sorry. I am so sorry.

CREON
Go. Now.

OEDIPUS
I love you girls!

CREON
You have frightened the children.

OEDIPUS
They are children no more. Oh Gods - I will become a folktale told to children at bedtime.

CREON
Let us go into the palace. You will rest in privacy, hidden, until your fate can be determined.

OEDIPUS
Just promise me - the girls...

CREON
Oedipus, you are no longer in control of their affairs. You are no longer in charge of anyone's well being in this land including your own. Your knowledge has not led you to the greater good. Now come as I commanded and ask for nothing more.

(CREON and OEDIPUS exit. CHORUS is now on stage. The lights change so that it appears as if a sun is slowing rising)

CELLIST
This was a story about darkness.

MAN #3
A city in darkness.

WOMAN
Cursed.

MAN #1
A city begging to be saved.

MAN #2
Saved by the same hero who had saved them before.

WOMAN
Oedipus

MAN #1
So this was really the story of a King.

MAN #2
No. This was the story of a man.

MAN #3
And his fall.

WOMAN
This was a story about the dangers of being human.

MAN #1
Of being flawed.

MAN #2
Of having the best of intentions.

CHORUS
This was a story about truth.

CELLIST
This was the story.

(Lights fade. Blackout)

END OF PLAY

Northern Aggression

ORIGINALLY ENTITLED
And The Creek Don't Rise

A PLAY BY
Joseph Zettelmaier

CAST OF CHARACTERS

ROB GRAFF - an unemployed automotive engineer, 45
MADDIE GRAFF - his wife, a veterinarian, 30
DR. BENJAMIN "DOC" BOGGS - a retired physician, 70s

TIME
The Present

PLACE
Various locations in Carson, Georgia

NORTHERN AGGRESSION (originally entitled AND THE CREEK DON'T RISE) received its world premiere on July 7, 2011 at Williamston Theatre (Williamston, MI). It was directed by Joseph Albright. Set Design by Daniel C. Walker, Lighting Design by Reid G. Johnson, Costume Design by Holly Iler, Sound Design by Will Myers. Stage managed by Nan Luchini.

The cast was as follows:

ROB GRAFF: John Lepard
MADDIE GRAFF: Kate Peckham
DOC BOGGS: Thomas D. Mahard

For information about production rights, visit www.jzettelmaier.com.

Northern Aggression

ACT I
SCENE 1

(The kitchen of ROB & MADDIE's new house. It is set up-tables, chairs, etc. MADDIE is checking everything out. ROB can be heard offstage shouting)

MADDIE
Honey?! What is...

(ROB rushes onstage, holding a large suitcase)

ROB
Oh my god. I just...oh god...it was...

MADDIE
What was it?

ROB
Like a rat...except huge...possibly prehistoric...

MADDIE
Just slow down.

ROB
You should've seen this thing! It was... like... *(He spreads out his hands, showing her how large the animal was)* And it hissed!

MADDIE
Hissed? Like a snake?

ROB
No! Like some sort of demon-rat! Get me a gun and a bible.

MADDIE
Rob. Rob.

ROB
Yeah?

MADDIE
Was it a possum?

ROB
No! It was...I don't know.

MADDIE
Grey. Hairless tail. Close-together eyes?

ROB
Yes! Prehistoric demon rat!

MADDIE
Honey, that was a possum.

ROB
That's a possum?

MADDIE
Don't worry. They're harmless. It just hissed because you scared it.

ROB
No, no, no. It hissed to scare me. I'm very confident about that.

MADDIE
Stay here. I'll take care of it. *(She heads off)*

ROB
No! Trust me! That thing is looking for a fight!

MADDIE
I've got this. *(She can be heard offstage)* Go on! Go! Get out of here! *(After a moment, she returns)* The possum says you scream like a girl.

(He laughs)

ROB
Please just tell me it's not living here.

MADDIE
It ran into a burrow across the street. I think it was just investigating. You've really never seen one before?

ROB
Yeah. On the Discovery Channel, I think. *(Beat)* So let's just load everything back into the car and get out of here.

MADDIE
Rob...

ROB
No, no. The possum has clearly marked his territory. I say we just give him the house and cut our losses.

MADDIE
You're hilarious. *(She goes to him, hugs him)*

ROB
New rule - you have to deal with the wildlife.

MADDIE
That's fair.

ROB
I'll handle the home-repair, you handle the giant rodents.

MADDIE
It's a marsupial, actually.

ROB
Show off. *(Beat. ROB looks around the room)* Wait. This place looks different.

MADDIE
Is it because we've got everything moved in?

(He stares at her, shocked & thrilled)

ROB
We're moved in?

MADDIE
We're moved in.

(She runs at him, jumping up. He catches her)

ROB
Careful. I stink.

MADDIE
I don't care. I do not care. We're unpacked.

ROB
Yes we are. *(He kisses her, then sets her down)*

MADDIE
How's your back, old man?

ROB
It's fine.

(He sits down tenderly in a chair. She stares at him)

ROB
It's fine.

MADDIE
Uh-huh.

ROB
This is not my back. This is an old baseball injury.

MADDIE
Located in your back.

ROB
It's an amazing coincidence.

MADDIE
Pansy.

(She rubs his shoulders. He winces in pain)

MADDIE
Too hard?

ROB
Yeah.

MADDIE
Want some ice?

ROB
No, just... *(He rises, then lies down on the table)* Oh yeah. There we go.

MADDIE
I threw your back out.

ROB
No, no, no. No. It's from moving.

MADDIE
Am I getting heavy?

ROB
Oh dear lord...

MADDIE
'Cause you can tell me if I am.

(Beat)

ROB
You're getting heavy.

(She hits him. He laughs)

ROB
See?! You told me I could tell you, but you lied.

MADDIE
It's the damn food here! You don't know! I was here for a month before you got here. You don't know what it was like. Set up the office, go to the Chic-Fillet. Meet with the staff, go to Krystals. It's all fat, Rob. It looks like meat, like vegetables, but it's all fat. And the next thing I know, I...

ROB
(taking her hand) Honey, I was joking. You're like 110 pounds. No one anywhere, ever, would call that heavy.

MADDIE
Oh! New rule-If you make fun of my weight, I can make fun of your age.

ROB
Sure. Why not? *(He rises and heads offstage)*

MADDIE
Where are you going?

ROB
Tylenol.

(They continue talking, though he remains offstage)

MADDIE
Know what you need?

ROB
Tylenol?

MADDIE
You need to get out. Check out the town.

ROB
This isn't a town. It's where culture goes to die.

MADDIE
Come on.

ROB
...churches and antique stores as far as the eye can see...

MADDIE
Could you try, for like a second, to pretend you're happy here?

ROB
(Returning, waving his arms and using a silly voice) Woooo! Look at me! I'm Happy Rob, the world's greatest house husband!

MADDIE
Stop it.

ROB
I hope the girls at the book club like my new sundress!

MADDIE
Rob. Stop.

(Beat)

ROB
You used to like it when I did my stupid voice.

MADDIE
This isn't a joke.

ROB
OK. Sorry.

MADDIE
I just...aren't you at all excited about this? We have a house. We have a new life.

ROB
See, that's the...you say that like there was something wrong with our old life.

MADDIE
You want me to make a list?

ROB
Ah, Jesus....

MADDIE
One...

ROB
Maddie, don't...

MADDIE
One – We were living in a condo half this size for twice as much.

ROB
I know. I....

MADDIE
Two – Said condo got broken into twice TWICE last year alone.

ROB
That could happen anywhere!

MADDIE
Three – You were unemployed, and I...

ROB
OK! I'm still unemployed!

MADDIE
But I'm not! No one in Michigan was making me the kind of offer I have now.

ROB
I know.

MADDIE
We made a sacrifice. I get that. But... God, isn't it worth it?

ROB
I don't know.

(Beat)

MADDIE
What exactly does that mean?

ROB
It means I've been here for a day. You've been here for a month. You can't expect me to be completely

adjusted.

MADDIE
Ok. That's fair.

ROB
Ok.

MADDIE
Ok.

(ROB sits down. She joins him, laying her head on his shoulder)

MADDIE
Think of this like a vacation. Relax. Have some fun.

ROB
(Kisses her) I'm gonna be OK. Really. I'm just a little disconnected.

MADDIE
You need friends.

ROB
I have you.

MADDIE
You need guy friends.

ROB
You could wear a moustache and pretend to be a guy friend.

(She just stares at him)

ROB
Nope. Bad idea.

MADDIE
There's a social this weekend. We should go.

ROB
A social?

MADDIE
You know. Like a…a social.

ROB
You have no idea what that is.

MADDIE
I know that there will be people there. People from town. They'll want to meet us.

ROB
I'm sure.

MADDIE
Really. The last month…I've been stopped like three times at the supermarket. Total strangers coming up, asking me if I'm the veterinarian.

ROB
How did they know that?

MADDIE
Small towns. People talk.

ROB
Wonderful.

MADDIE
This is our home now. It's time to make friends.

ROB
I get the distinct impression these people do not want to be our friends.

MADDIE
Not true.

ROB
What about that good ol' boy at the gas station? He just kept staring at our license plate, then at his gun rack.

MADDIE
He did not.

ROB
I swear to God! There was this moment where I was like "Do these people think the Civil War's still going on?"

MADDIE
You're reading too much into it.

(The doorbell rings. MADDIE goes to get

it. DOC is standing there in full Southern General uniform. He has a small box in his hand)

DOC
I hope I'm not interrupting anything.

(They just stare at him)

MADDIE
I'm sorry. Are you lost?

DOC
Oh, not at all. I'm y'all's neighbor.

MADDIE
We have neighbors?

DOC
Ha! Isn't that something. Yes, I just live right 'round that bend.

ROB
I didn't see any houses out there for like a mile.

DOC
1.8 miles. That would be me. Benjamin Wilford Boggs. Most folks 'round here call me Doc.

ROB
You're a doctor?

DOC
No, I'm a place you tie your boat. Ha! 'Course I am, son. 'Course I am.

ROB
Well, I'm...

DOC
Retired 4 years now. Had my own private practice for 30 before that. Lord, I do miss it sometimes but... *(Pause. He offers ROB his hand)* Well, listen to me go on. Doc Boggs. Who might you be?

ROB
Rob Graff. This is my wife, Maddie.

MADDIE
Pleased to meet you.

(They shake hands. DOC smiles, taking in their accents)

DOC
Where y'all from, exactly?

MADDIE
Detroit.

DOC
(Laughing loudly) Bless my soul, I've got me some genuine Yankees for neighbors. Isn't that something. Wilson's gonna love this.

ROB
Wilson?

DOC
Hasn't he showed up yet? Well, give him a day or two. He's got the rheumatism, you know? Up in his joints. Not so fast as he used to be. Why, I remember back in...oh, it would have to be '68...Wilson used to be the fastest runner old Carson High'd ever seen. Man could jump anything...and I do mean anything. Hurtles, fences... one time, I saw him jump clear over a 1960 Rambler Rebel. Damndest thing. Oh, back then, we weren't driving around SUVs or whathaveyou. I suppose jumpin' over one of those monsters would really be something to see.

MADDIE
Excuse me. I'm really sorry. Who's Wilson?

DOC
Lord, where's my head today? Wilson Hadley. President of the Carson Welcoming Committee.

ROB
There's a Welcoming Committee?

DOC
Oh, yes, yes. He's probably just a little behind today, trying to get everything set for the battle.

(Beat)

ROB
There's a battle?

(DOC just stares at him, uncertain what he means. Then he suddenly laughs loudly)

DOC
For the Recreationists! The Civil War Recreationists!

MADDIE
Of course.

DOC
Oh lord, I don't want to even guess what you were thinking.

ROB
No, you probably don't.

DOC
Probably thought Old Doc Boggs had plum fallen off his rocker.

ROB
And there it is.

DOC
Lemme guess, lemme guess. You think I got the entire Light Infantry camped out in your back yard.

ROB
Not the entire Light Infantry, no.

DOC
Ha! Boy, you're a funny one, and don't let anybody tell you otherwise.

(He hands them the package)

MADDIE
Oh. Thank you! What's this?

DOC
Just a little somethin' to say "Welcome to Carson, Georgia-Prettiest little town you're ever likely to meet."

(She opens it. It's full of jarred preserves)

ROB
What's in there, hon?

DOC
That'd be Doc Boggs's famous Peach Preserves. What you want to do is toast up an English muffin, then spread 'em on top. You'll think you died and gone to heaven.

MADDIE
That is so sweet!

DOC
I'd hope so. They're made with my own peaches.

MADDIE
No, I meant…

DOC
I know what you meant, darlin'. I was just funnin' with you.

(There is a beat, as no one is entirely certain how to keep the conversation moving)

MADDIE
Your costume is amazing.

DOC
Thank you, Madeline. That's right kind. But it's not a costume. It's a uniform.

MADDIE
Oh. I'm sorry.

DOC
Not at all.

(They notice he's been pulling on a tear in his coat jacket)

ROB
Hey, not sure if you know it, but you've got a tear there.

DOC
Beg pardon?

ROB
On your...costu...um...grey jacket.

DOC
Oh yes, of course. Wouldn't you know it. I was trying it on for tomorrow, and damn if I didn't catch my arm on a loose nail. *(He holds up his coat. The arm is torn on the seam)* Actually, I must confess to a bit of duplicity on my part. My visit wasn't entirely motivated by neighborly kindness.

ROB
OK

DOC
Miss Madeline, might you know your way around a thread and needle?

MADDIE
Oh.

DOC
If it's not an inconvenience. After all, General Braxton Bragg shouldn't show up to the battle threadbare.

MADDIE
Oh. Of course. Right. It's just...I don't really sew.

DOC
You don't?

MADDIE
I don't.

DOC
Not even a little?

MADDIE
Not really. I mean, sutures. But that's about it.

DOC
Well I'll be.

ROB
Weird, right? A woman who can't sew. And still I married her.

MADDIE
Rob can sew.

DOC
What?

ROB
Hold on.

MADDIE
He can! He even taught a Home Economics class through the Rec & Ed.

(ROB stares at her. Clearly he doesn't feel this should be public knowledge)

ROB
I...I have three sisters.

DOC
Oh. I see. *(Beat)* Well, I don't...that is...would you perhaps...

ROB
Lemme take a look at it.

(DOC hands him the coat. ROB examines it)

ROB
Oh, this is nothing.

DOC
Then it's repairable?

ROB
Yeah. Gimme a few minutes.

DOC
Sir, you are a gentleman and a seamstr...oh. I'm...not entirely certain what one calls a male seamstress.

ROB
A tailor.

DOC
Oh. Yes, of course. That certainly... yes.

(ROB *heads off*)

MADDIE
Would you like something to drink?

DOC
Well now, I'll tell you, I'd be very grateful for a glass of sweet tea.

MADDIE
Oh. I think all we have is water and Pepsi.

DOC
Water would be lovely.

MADDIE
We're just moving in and... Actually, I've been living here for a month. Rob was in Michigan finishing up the sale. Of our old house.

DOC
Well, you've found yourself a fine new home and that's God's honest truth. The Abeline's...they lived here before y'all, you know...they took real good care of this house. I helped them move in. Did you know that?

MADDIE
No.

DOC
Oh yes, this would've been...let me see...oh, 1970 or thereabouts. Mr. Abeline, he came up from Savannah to be the new superintendant. Filmore, that was his name. Filmore Abeline. Don't that beat all?

(MADDIE *laughs*)

DOC
Well, he and his wife Katy lived here 'til 2005, I believe it was. She passed away, you see. Bad ticker. He moved back to Savannah after that. Not really certain what he's up to there. Filmore and I weren't overly close, you see.

MADDIE
Really?

DOC
Oh, I'm afraid so. We had something of a disagreement as to where his property line ended and mine began. But I can already tell I'm gonna get along with you Michiganders just fine. Yes, sir. And let me just say, I apologize for not visiting sooner. I kept meaning to stop by, but the days just slipped away from me, I reckon.

MADDIE
My mom calls it Southern Time.

DOC
How's that?

MADDIE
She's from Virginia. She says "however long you think something should take, double it. That's how Southern Time works."

DOC
Southern Time! I like that, Madeline! I surely do! She's from Virginia, you say?

MADDIE
Yeah. Danville.

DOC
Why, that must be why I took such a shine to you. You've got rebel blood in your veins.

MADDIE
I guess so.

DOC
Wonderful history up in Virginia. I myself am partial to the First Battle

of Bull Run.

(She doesn't respond, as she isn't overly familiar with the topic)

DOC
I suppose y'all might call it The Battle of Manassas. *(DOC reads her expression and smiles)* There I go again. I beg your pardon, Madeline. The War of Northern Aggression is a passion of mine. Just ask Barksdale.

MADDIE
Who's Barksdale?

DOC
He is the last in a line of proud, purebred British Bulldogs that have been in my family since the 60s. He's 13 years old now, but a better friend I couldn't ask for. And named after the famous Confederate General William Barksdale.

MADDIE
Oh! I love bulldogs!

DOC
Do you now?

MADDIE
I'm a veterinarian, actually.

DOC
You're the one who replaced old George Hathaway, am I correct?

MADDIE
You are correct.

DOC
Well, if you don't mind my saying, you're a far sight prettier than George.

MADDIE
I don't mind at all.

(Beat)

DOC
Now where was I again?

MADDIE
Bulldogs? Or the Re-enactments?

DOC
Oh! Yes! The Re-enactments, they're very popular 'round these parts. We Georgians take that sort of thing very seriously. It's half historical recreation, half social club. Y'all should come to one of our battles.

MADDIE
I didn't realize people could just…go to those.

DOC
Oh yes, it's quite the to-do. What you want to do is pack yourself a nice picnic lunch and drag your husband to the battlefield. After the smoke clears, I'll introduce y'all around.

MADDIE
Oh my God. You would do that?

DOC
It would be my pleasure.

MADDIE
It's just…we don't know anyone here, really. Rob's having a hard time adjusting. He's been trying to find a job and…

DOC
He's unemployed, you say?

MADDIE
Yeah. He's getting discouraged, I think. Don't tell him I said that, but…

DOC
Your secret is safe with me, darlin'.

MADDIE
We need to spend more time in town, you know? It'll help us…

DOC
Don't you say another word. Old Doc Boggs is working out a plan as we speak.

(ROB returns with the jacket)

ROB
Here you go.

DOC
(Inspecting it) Well, bless my soul! Would you look at that! My mother couldn't have done a better job herself. Robert, you have my thanks.

ROB
No problem. And you can call me…

DOC
Robert, I am having a thought.

ROB
Oh. Um…good?

DOC
My thought is this. Have you ever handled a rifle before?

(Beat)

ROB
I was an engineer.

DOC
Is that a no?

ROB
I mean, my dad took me hunting a couple of…

DOC
Wonderful! It just so happens that our James Longstreet got himself the gout. His big toe is the size of a bowling ball. How would you like to join the South in glorious battle?

(Beat)

ROB
I mostly watch hockey.

MADDIE
Honey, I think Doc is asking you to join the recreationists.

ROB
Oh. Yeah. It's ok. I mean, thank you, but…

DOC
It just so happens that most of Carson's City Fathers are re-enactors, just like yours truly. You're just about Carl Rossom's size…Carl was our Longstreet, don't you know. Yes, yes. This is providence at work.

ROB
I've never really done anything like that before.

DOC
Don't you worry about a thing. I'll be there the whole time, walking you 'round the curves.

ROB
It's just that we just moved in and…

MADDIE
He'll do it.

(ROB stares at her. She stares back)

ROB
I think I just got drafted.

DOC
Wonderful! I tell you what I'll do. I'll drop by tomorrow and give you Carl's uniform. Then y'all come to Peachtree Park round about noon, and I'll give you the benefit of my knowledge.

MADDIE
Sounds like a plan.

DOC
Trust me, Robert. You will not regret this.

ROB
I'm choosing to believe that.

DOC
Well, I'll leave you to your settlin' in. Until tomorrow, then. Madeline. Robert. *(Turns to go)* Ha! Those Yankees won't know what hit 'em! *(Exits)*

(ROB just stares at MADDIE)

ROB
What the hell just happened?

(Lights change)

SCENE 2

(DOC & ROB, outdoors, are in full Confederate outfits. ROB's doesn't fit as well as it could. DOC is quizzing ROB on his information)

DOC
So you understand?

ROB
I understand.

DOC
This is a key moment in the Battle of Chickamauga. Rosencrans has ordered the general retreat, and we're gonna take the field. The victory is due to the actions of...

ROB
Of the left wing.

DOC
Exactly. Denied reinforcements from the failed right wing, we will lead the left wing to Snodgrass Hill and...

ROB
I know!

DOC
I know, SIR.

ROB
What?

DOC
I am your commanding officer. You shall address me as "sir."

(Beat. ROB mumbles something under his breath)

DOC
I'm gonna assume there was a "sir" in there.

ROB
That's a fantastic assumption.

DOC
Something got you riled, boy?

ROB
Sorry, I'm surrounded by men with guns. It makes me edgy.

DOC
I told you. They're firing blanks. They're harmless.

ROB
Yes, sir.

DOC
Unless you get shot in the face. Or at very close range.

(ROB stares at him)

DOC
Don't worry. I'm a doctor. You won't die under my command.

ROB
I'm going home.

DOC
And let those damned Yankees take Snodgrass Hill! Never!

ROB
I'm a damn...!

(ROB realizes others are looking at him.

He speaks quietly to DOC)

ROB
I'm a damn Yankee.

DOC
Not today, you're not. Today you are...

ROB
General James Longstreet, commander of the Left Wing.

DOC
Lieutenant General James Longstreet.

ROB
Right.

DOC
Son, if you want to make inroads with the city fathers, trust me. This is the side you want to be on.

ROB
I feel like these guys want to slide a bayonet into my spleen.

DOC
Now, to be fair, if you're gonna bayonet someone, you want to hit a lung. It'll drop them faster.

(ROB stares at DOC)

DOC
I'm sure you'll be fine.

(The sound of a gunshot. ROB jumps)

ROB
What the hell was that?!

DOC
Oh, one of Polk's boys got jumpy. *(Calls off)* Henry! Keep your pants on or I'll staple them to your ass! *(To ROB)* That's Henry Buckner. He runs Buckner Chevrolet. Good man, good man. He's playing Lt. General Leonidas Polk, who...

ROB
That sounded like a real gun!

DOC
Well, it's supposed to. Why are you gettin' so agitated? You're from Detroit aren't you?

ROB
What the hell is that supposed to mean?

DOC
Now then. We've only got a few minutes before the battle starts. This is fairly basic re-enacting. Your men know that you're just a ringer, so they're gonna go through their maneuvers on their own. You just stay by me and wave that saber when I tell you to.

ROB
Fine.

DOC
There's gonna be a lot of gunfire and shouting. And some horseback work. And some simulated cannonfire. Don't let it spook you.

ROB
I don't spook that easy.

DOC
Son, you nearly defecated from the sound of a blank-firing pistol.

ROB
I wasn't ready for it. That's all.

DOC
Then hush up and listen. When I sound the charge, the men are gonna run up there and take on three Yankee regiments. The 21st Ohio, the 89th Ohio, and the 22nd Michigan.

ROB
Wait. We're fighting a Michigan regiment?

DOC
Did I not mention that?

ROB
No, you did not mention that.

DOC
Well, it's not overly important. This is a decisive Confederate victory. Our men are gonna charge the hill, on your order. We'll catch the Union with their pants down and give them the spanking of a lifetime. They're just gonna roll over and take it, like they're supposed to.

(ROB *is clearly taking offense to this, and is fighting to keep his mouth shut*)

DOC
All you gotta do is wave your sword, give the order, and watch us send those Union bastards straight to black, burning Hell. Got it?

ROB
Oh, I'm getting it.

DOC
Good. (*Sees someone motioning to him in the distance. He nods in response*) All right. It's time. Now - What is Doc Bogg's #1 rule of Re-Enactment?

ROB
Don't get shot in the face?

DOC
There's no time for your addle-pated jibes, boy! WHAT IS THE #1 RULE!?

ROB
Above all else, do not alter the outcome of the battle!

DOC
Yes! Yes! That's the spirit! Now, let's go slaughter those Michiganders!

(*The sounds of the troops getting ready, drums & fifes.* DOC *addresses his troops*)

DOC
Proud sons of Georgia, the day is ours! Due to the inept leadership of our opponents, a hole has opened in their ranks; A hole that we shall press through, and deliver final and lasting defeat to the great oppressors!

ROB
(*quietly, to himself*) Oh come on.

DOC
Remember this day, you brave soldiers all! For on this day, you shall raise your eyes to the Lord Our Creator and say "We are Georgia! We shall stand tall against unjust law and suffer no invader to sully our land!" Let them look into our eyes, and know their own defeat! Let the mighty Chickamauga flow red with the blood of the enemy! And let us praise God who lifted us...TO VICTORY! FOR GEORGIA!

(*The troops cheer in response.* DOC *nudges* ROB *to sound the attack.* ROB *half-heartedly swings his saber*)

ROB
Go get 'em.

(*Trumpets sound. The sound of the Army charging forward, and battle starting.* ROB *starts getting jumpy*)

DOC
Settle down, son. You're more nervous than a long-tailed cat on a porch full of rockin' chairs.

(*A cannon goes off*)

ROB
Jesus Christ!

DOC
My God, but don't it get your blood

flowin'! *(Calls off)* Shore up the line, boys! Here they come!

ROB
Here they...?! They're coming here!?

DOC
This here's what you call a counter-attack.

(More battle sounds as the Union forces press forward. DOC takes out his saber. ROB jumps again)

ROB
What do we do? What do I do?!

DOC
You show some gumption, boy! And leave the orders to me! *(Calls off again)* Polk, attack the right flank! Go, man!

ROB
Those people are dying!

DOC
They're just play-acting, son!

ROB
I think that guy's bleeding!

DOC
Calm down! Henderson always brings ketchup packets!

(More gunshots, much closer. ROB lets out a girlish cry. DOC shouts orders)

DOC
When you're out of shot, fix bayonets and draw sabers!

ROB
Oh my God! They're coming right at us!

DOC
This is war, boy!

ROB
It's supposed to be pretend-war!

DOC
(To the unseen combatants) Die, you Yankee bastards!

(The battle surrounds them. ROB starts to really panic. He swings his saber like a man who has never done so before)

DOC
(to his opponents) This invasion of our sovereign land shall not be allowed! We shall fight you in the forests, we shall fight you in the hills! We shall fight you in the swamps, we shall...!

(ROB, swinging wildly, accidently fake-stabs DOC. The battle grows quieter as the unseen fighters all stop and stare at what has just happened. Their voices can be heard)

VOICE 1
He just stabbed General Bragg!

VOICE 2
What the hell're you doin'?!

VOICE 3
That Yankee idjit just killed General Bragg!

VOICE 1
Stop the fight! Stop the damn fight!

VOICE 2
We can't stop! We're about to drive them back!

VOICE 3
Well, what the hell're we supposed to do?!

(DOC has been glaring at the shocked & confused ROB. Finally DOC, still holding ROB's saber, lowers himself to the ground & "dies." ROB looks out at the unseen fighters)

ROB
I...I'm so sorry.

(ROB turns out to look at the men)

ROB
My bad.

(The sound of the men charging. ROB gets his arms up to defend himself. Blackout)

SCENE 3

(Lights up. Later that night. ROB's porch. DOC sits alone at first, clearly displeased. ROB soon re-enters, holding an icepack to his head. He sits down. They share a long uncomfortable silence. Finally—)

DOC
Thirty-five years.

ROB
I said I was sorry.

DOC
Thirty-five years.

ROB
You want me to say it again?

DOC
I've been a re-enactor for thirty-five years, never once in all that time did I witness such an atrocity.

ROB
Fine. OK. But I…

DOC
Even when Clayton O'Toole showed up to the Battle of Peachtree Hill completely inebriated, he still managed to carry himself with some semblance of dignity!

ROB
I feel like, at this point, I should point out that I was the one who got beat up.

DOC
Oh, you may have taken the odd lump, but make no mistake. I am the one bearing the scars of this battle.

ROB
Can you even hear yourself?

DOC
Can you?!

(ROB is silent)

DOC
Those people are my friends, my colleagues. And I looked all of them square in the eye and vouched for you. My god, I must've been out of my mind.

ROB
I never asked you to do this.

DOC
Of course you did. You moved in next to me.

ROB
That wasn't an invitation for you to drag me into this…whatever the hell this is.

DOC
It's called being neighborly, Robert. But I reckon that's a foreign concept to you.

(Beat)

ROB
And just how is that a foreign concept to me?

DOC
I'm going home. Thank you for driving us to the field. Please give my regards to Madeline…

ROB
You want to say something to me, Doc? Here I am.

DOC
A gentleman doesn't disparage his

host.

ROB
It's just you and me.

DOC
Yes, and fortunately one of us is a gentleman.

ROB
How is that not disparaging me?!

DOC
I never said which one of us I was referring to.

ROB
You think I can't see through this? I'm not an idiot, you know.

DOC
I say good evening.

ROB
You can stand there and smile and laugh and just...ooze this Southern charm, but I'm not an idiot, and I'm not deaf.

DOC
I'm sure I have no idea what you're talking about.

ROB
I can hear all the little digs you throw at me.

DOC
Well, I never!

ROB
Come on! The stabs at Detroit, and sewing, and Madeline...

DOC
That's quite enough! I've never said a thing about your darling wife.

ROB
When you introduced us to...what's his name...Buddy something...

DOC
Buddy Maddocks.

ROB
He asked if Maddie was my daughter!

DOC
And I corrected him!

ROB
Right, after you laughed for like two minutes.

DOC
My God. Are all Michiganians as dour and humorless as you?

ROB
It's "Michiganders" and you know it!

DOC
I have shown you nothing but hospitality, and you repaid me with humiliation.

ROB
It was an accident!

DOC
Was it? Or was it another Yankee trying to stick it to the South?

ROB
Come on!

DOC
Oh, I've seen your type before. You think we're all ignorant rednecks. We couldn't possibly be as smart and cultured as our enlightened Northern brethren.

ROB
You're going to want to back off.

DOC
Does it feel good, Robert, looking down your nose at us Southerners?

ROB
I don't have a problem with

Southerners, Doc.

DOC
Oh? Indeed?

ROB
I have a problem with you.

(Beat. DOC silently rages)

ROB
You can call it "hospitality" all you want, but from where I'm standing, it looks like you're trying to humiliate me. And I'll tell you this right now, I am not a man to mess with. You get me?

DOC
Sir, I pray that is your concussion talking. Because you do not want to make an enemy of Benjamin W. Boggs.

ROB
Yeah, what are you gonna do? Smother me in your rancid preserves?

DOC
You leave my preserves out...! *(Collects himself, still furious)* I gave my word to your dear wife that I will endeavor to help you. And that I shall do. But know this, Robert. There is a line between we two, and you were the one who crossed it. Good evening to you.

(DOC starts to walk off. ROB calls to him)

ROB
Hey! Don't do me no favors!

(ROB storms in, slamming the door. DOC smiles)

DOC
Oh, I've got a favor for you all right. Thirty-five years.

(He exits. Lights fade)

SCENE 4

(The next morning. ROB is downstairs, eating cereal and still angry. MADDIE enters, dressed for work)

MADDIE
Hey, there you are. I ...Honey?

(She sees him eating)

ROB
Yeah?

MADDIE
Why are you eating breakfast outside? Are you watching Doc's house?

ROB
When the attack comes, it'll come from there.

MADDIE
Oh, boy,

ROB
It's quiet out here, Maddie. Too quiet.

MADDIE
It was just a misunderstanding.

ROB
(Noticing he's out of Cookie Crisp) Dammit.

MADDIE
I bet Doc isn't even thinking about it anymore.

ROB
Oh, he's thinking about it. Sitting there drinking a mint julep and twirling his big Georgia moustache and...

MADDIE
He called.

ROB
Who called?

MADDIE
Doc.

ROB
Did he want you to get out of the house before he opens fire?

MADDIE
He found you a job.

ROB
What?

MADDIE
It's with the guy we met yesterday... Buddy something.

ROB
Wait, wait, wait. What kind of job are we talking about here?

MADDIE
He said it was in automotives.

ROB
You gotta be kidding me.

(She hands him a piece of paper)

MADDIE
He said you had to come in today, to meet with the boss. It's on the corner of Main and Church St.

ROB
What am I doing?

MADDIE
He didn't say. He just said to come in at nine.

ROB
Nine?! Hon, it's 8:30! Why didn't you tell me?!

MADDIE
You were in the shower!

ROB
I need pants! *(He jumps up, pantsless. He grabs MADDIE, hugging her. She smiles at him)*

MADDIE
So, which one of us was right about Doc? Was it me? 'Cause it feels like it was me.

ROB
Could you pick up some more Cookie Crisp on the way home? *(Runs offstage)*

MADDIE
Go kick butt today, baby! Baby?! *(He's gone)* That's my man.

(Lights change)

SCENE 5

(In the darkness, the sounds of phones ringing. As lights rise, ROB can be seen answering them)

ROB
Maddocks Toyota, Rob speaking. How can I help you? Please hold. *(ROB stares at the phone, unsure how to work it)* OK. OK. You can do this. It's just a phone. *(He hits a button and talks into the receiver)* Buddy, you've got a call on... *(He quickly realizes he's not on the intercom. He tries to make sure he hasn't hung up on the caller)* Hello? Are you still... hello? *(He hung up on them. He's also hit the intercom without realizing it)* Stupid piece of crap phone... *(His voice booms over the dealership. He madly scrambles to turn off the intercom)* Oh god. Sorry.... everyone...sorry... *(He manages to turn off the intercom. He seethes in quiet rage and tries to calm himself)* ...calm blue ocean, calm blue ocean... *(The phone rings again. He answers)* Maddocks Toyota. Rob Speaking, how can I... Yeah, sorry about that. It's my first day and...Mm-hmm...Mm-hmm...Ah, from Michigan, actually. Mm-hmm... Please hold. *(ROB puts the customer on hold, then stares at the phone, again unable to figure out how to work the inter-*

com) Ah, the hell with it. *(He shouts across the room)* Hey, Buddy! You've got a call on line one! *(He sits back down at his desk, defeated. He rests his head on the desk, then slowly grabs some scissors, making as though he might stab the phone)*

(MADDIE enters. She is singing something to the tune of 9 to 5 by Dollar Parton. She has lunch with her)

MADDIE
WORKIN' 9 TO 5, 'CAUSE MY HUSBAND IS SO AWESOME...
WORKIN' 9 TO 5, SOMETHING ELSE THAT RHYMES WITH AWESOME...

(ROB rises and hugs her)

MADDIE
How's it goin', working man?

ROB
It's goin'.

MADDIE
This is great! Look at you, back in the mix!

ROB
Honey, I'm a secretary.

MADDIE
Oh. You're not covering for someone 'til...?

ROB
Oh no. No no no. *(He taps the sign on the desk that reads ROB GRAFF)* This desk is aaaallll mine. And the beauty... THE BEAUTY of it is, they figured that, with my experience, I only needed one hour of training.

MADDIE
Honey...

ROB
This phone...the space shuttle doesn't have this many buttons!

MADDIE
You're getting loud.

(He quiets down, trying to reign himself in)

ROB
He said "automotive", right? That's what he said?

MADDIE
What?

ROB
That's what Doc Boggs said to you, yeah?

MADDIE
Oh. Yeah.

ROB
(to himself) ...very nice, you crafty son of a...

MADDIE
It's just your first day.

ROB
This is his opening salvo. And it's brilliant.

MADDIE
You're losing me.

ROB
He knows I need this job. He knows I'll just sit here and take the humiliation because...

MADDIE
Rob.

(He stops, looks at her)

MADDIE
Honey, I love you. But calling your new job "humiliating" on the sales floor is maybe not a great idea.

(He clearly wants to say more, but keeps

his mouth shut)

MADDIE
I...brought you lunch? *(She opens the bag)*

ROB
Oh my god, that smells amazing.

MADDIE
It's from this little barbeque place next to my office.

ROB
Thank you.

MADDIE
And...look! *(She takes a slice of pie out of the bag)*

ROB
Oh my god. Please tell me that's pecan pie.

MADDIE
Just for you, babycakes.

ROB
Best wife ever.

MADDIE
Is it ok if we eat together? Or should I...?

ROB
(Calling over her head) Buddy, am I cool to take my lunch now? *(Buddy agrees)* Yeah, we're good. There's a picnic table outside and...

(Just as they start to head out, DOC enters. He is very pleased with himself)

DOC
Well now! Look at the happy couple. *(He kisses her hand)* Madeline. *(He offers his hand to ROB. Smiles)* Robert.

(ROB grudgingly shakes it)

DOC
I was in the neighborhood and thought I might check in on you.

ROB
Awesome.

DOC
Do you find this situation to your liking, Robert? I know it's not the assembly line, but...

ROB
I didn't work the assembly line. I was an engineer.

DOC
Oh. My mistake. I'm afraid the distinction is lost on an old sawbones like me.

MADDIE
He's settling in nicely. Aren't you, Rob?

ROB
Yuh-huh.

DOC
Excellent! And Robert, there's no need to thank me.

ROB
OK.

DOC
After all. I was only being neighborly. Ooh, what have we here? *(Notices their lunch)*

MADDIE
I brought Rob lunch.

DOC
Do my nostrils detect the enticing aroma of Miss Cody's Homestyle Barbecue?

MADDIE
Oh. Actually, yeah.

DOC
An excellent choice, Madeline. There are few things I savor more than her

pulled pork in my mouth.

(Beat. ROB is trying hard not to laugh)

DOC
Did I say something funny, Robert?

ROB
Nope.

DOC
Well, I won't keep you from your well-earned repast. Y'all have a lovely... (He gets the slightest bit dizzy, stabling himself on ROB's desk)

MADDIE
Are you alright?

DOC
Oh, nothing to concern yourself over. I'm just a bit winded is all. Walking down to the dealership must've taken more out of me than I'd guessed.

MADDIE
You should sit down.

DOC
No, no. It's all right. (He chuckles a little)

ROB
What is it?

DOC
Well, in my haste to get started this morning, I must've skipped my breakfast. My blood sugar must be low is all.

(MADDIE checks his pulse)

MADDIE
Your heart's racing. Just sit down.

(He does so. MADDIE opens the lunch bag and pulls out the slice of pie)

ROB
Whoa. What're you doing?

MADDIE
He needs something sweet, to get his blood sugar up.

ROB
OK. Fine. There's a gumball machine right over...

DOC
I don't want to be a bother.

MADDIE
A gumball isn't gonna do it, Rob.

ROB
But...it's my pie.

DOC
Perhaps if I just rest my eyes...

MADDIE
I can get you more on my way home.

ROB
Right. I know. I just...it's been a rough day and...

MADDIE
Honey.

(She looks at him. ROB stares at her, then to DOC. DOC smiles sweetly. ROB hands the piece of pie to DOC)

ROB
Here you go.

DOC
Well, I do appreciate it.

MADDIE
It's nothing.

DOC
No, no. It's an act of kindness, one I'll not soon forget.

ROB
So I guess we're even.

DOC
Well, if you think that a piece of pie

is of equal value to finding you a job, then...

ROB
Just...enjoy it.

DOC
Don't mind if I do. *(DOC takes out a napkin, tucks it into his shirt, gets a fork, and takes a bite. He savors it, smiling)* Now. That is good pie. *(He continues to eat, smiling. Lights fade)*

SCENE 6

(Later that night. MADDIE is still cleaning/unpacking. ROB enters with an armful of library books)

MADDIE
Hey, baby.

ROB
Hey.

(They kiss. ROB sets the books on the table and starts to go through them)

MADDIE
Those are books.

ROB
Yuh-huh.

MADDIE
I thought you were getting mosquito netting.

(While reading, he sets a small paper bag on the table)

MADDIE
Honey?

ROB
Yeah?

MADDIE
Why do you have... *(She picks up one of the books)* Chattanooga: A Death Grip on the Confederacy?

ROB
He thinks I'm gonna roll over and surrender. That's his first mistake.

MADDIE
Who?

ROB
Doc Boggs. He's a crafty old bird, I'll give him that. But...

MADDIE
Rob, what are you doing?

ROB
Don't you see? It's all part of a plan! Making me a secretary was only step one. He's got this weird revenge-kick going on.

(Beat)

MADDIE
I'm guessing you can't hear how crazy you sound right now.

ROB
I'm sitting there today, answering these phones, and it hits me. If I'm going to strike back at him, I've got to be smart about it. So why not do the last thing he'd expect me to do?

MADDIE
Act like a sane person?

ROB
No! Study up on Civil War battles, but from the Northern side. That's his blindspot, honey! See what I'm saying?

MADDIE
Not...entirely.

ROB
He's got zero respect for the Union. So when my counter-attack comes, he won't...

MADDIE
Honey. Stop.

(He stares at her)

MADDIE
You're turning this into something it isn't.

ROB
But...but...counter-attack...

MADDIE
Doc hasn't done anything to you, except help you get a job. I know you've got this...intense competitive streak, but...

ROB
I do not!

MADDIE
Red Wings at the playoffs.

(Beat)

ROB
Go on.

MADDIE
I've seen you take things personally when they aren't. This is one of those times. I'm saying this 'cause I love you, and I really, really don't want you to burn down Doc's house.

ROB
I wasn't going to burn down his house!

(She holds up another book)

MADDIE
You checked out Sherman's March. That doesn't inspire confidence.

ROB
I just...you weren't there, OK. He threatened me.

MADDIE
Then why did he get you a job?!

ROB
To put me under his thumb! I'm telling you, this is just the beginning! I don't know what's coming next, but it's gonna be worse, more humiliating than...

MADDIE
Stop! He's our neighbor, ok? He's our one friend here. Just let it go. You guys got off on the wrong foot. I'll give you that. But he's a nice old man who's just trying to help us get settled. I promise you.

(ROB stares at her. Finally—)

ROB
Jeez, I was really heading for the deep end, wasn't I?

MADDIE
Without water wings.

ROB
Sorry about that. I just...it was a rough day.

(She sits with him, holds him)

MADDIE
I know, honey. But we just moved in. Give it a little time.

ROB
I know. Yeah. Just need to focus on the positive.

MADDIE
Now, see? That's sensible-Rob. I like sensible-Rob. I like to kiss sensible-Rob.

ROB
Sensible-Rob likes that too.

(They kiss. She rises)

MADDIE
I'm gonna hit the shower. Wanna join me?

ROB
Let me finish working on the porch. I'll be up in a bit.

MADDIE
OK. Love you.

ROB
I love you too.

(She heads upstairs. ROB watches her go. When he's confident that she's gone, he cracks open the books again)

ROB
Let's do this.

(Lights fade)

SCENE 7
VENGEANCE MONTAGE

(Lights change. What follows is a quick montage of scenarios, over the course of several weeks, detailing ROB & DOC's continued battle. When Johnny Comes Marching Home plays underneath. Between each scenario is the sound of a single shot fired. ROB comes home, wearing goggles. He speaks to himself)

ROB
Know what, Doc? That peach tree is close to my property line. Too close.

(Bang. Lights up on DOC)

DOC
Well Rodney, I think 9pm is a little late to be running a chain saw. Perhaps you could drive by in your squad car and ask him to keep it down. Thank you, Rodney.

(Bang. MADDIE & ROB at home)

MADDIE
What you got there?

ROB
Fox pee. Scares away raccoons and possums…*(MADDIE exits)* and smells mighty good on your neighbor's Camry.

(Bang. MADDIE and DOC at the supermarket)

MADDIE
Weird, animals don't usually mark their territory on cars.

DOC
I can think of one animal that might.

MADDIE
Huh, they're all out of Cookie Crisp, that's Rob's favorite.

DOC
Yes, I believe you mentioned that. *(MADDIE exits)* And now they're my favorite too.

(Bang. ROB is at the dealership, he speaks with Buddy)

ROB
Hey, Buddy! Is this the work order for Doc Boggs Camry? Yeah, I'll put it right through, no problem. *(crumples up the paper)* Call the cops on me will ya?

(Bang. DOC & MADDIE speak on the phone)

DOC
Oh, well… you see, I dropped my van off at the dealership nearly a week ago, and it turns out they're still waiting on a part. And sadly I don't have another vehicle so…

MADDIE
So…wait. How are you getting around?

DOC
Well, frankly, I'm not.

MADDIE
Why didn't you say so? Would you like to borrow Rob's car?

DOC
Oh, I couldn't do that.

MADDIE
It's not a big deal. I can drive him in to the dealership on my way to work.

DOC
Well, if you're sure it wouldn't be a problem.

MADDIE
Doc, I insist.

(There's a beep. MADDIE looks at her phone)

MADDIE
Speak of the devil. Rob's on the other line.

DOC
Well, you tell him I said thank you for the loaner. I'll take good care of his vehicle.

MADDIE
You bet.

DOC
And thank you again for tending to Barksdale.

MADDIE
No problem. Goodnight, Doc.

DOC
And to you.

(Bang. Lights down on Doc. Rise on Robert)

MADDIE
Hey, baby.

ROB
Hey, I'm thinking of picking up a pizza on the way home. You in?

MADDIE
I am so very, very in. But go ahead and start without me. I'm heading over to Doc's.

ROB
Uhm…why?

MADDIE
Nothing serious. His bulldog's arthritis is acting up. I'm just gonna drop off some Rimadyl.

(Beat. ROB smiles at this)

ROB
Doc has a dog?

(Bang. The next day. ROB is at home, still working on the porch)

DOC
Graff!

(DOC enters, furious. ROB sits up)

ROB
What's up, Doc?

DOC
Explain yourself.

(Beat)

ROB
Really? You've never seen Bugs Bunny?

DOC
Don't you barb with me, boy! You know damn well what I'm talking about!

ROB
I do?

DOC
Explain to me why, when I returned home from my Historical Society meeting, I was greeted by my beloved Barksdale…WEARING THIS! *(He slams a small dog costume on the table.*

ROB *examines it. It's a New York Yankees costume)*

ROB
Maybe Barksdale likes their chances this year.

DOC
That dog would never root for anyone but his beloved Braves! This costume is an outrage!

ROB
Sounds to me like you should be talking to him.

DOC
Do you think me a fool, sir?

ROB
Nope.

DOC
I know exactly where this...outfit came from. You crept into my home, and took advantage of my sweet canine's gentle and trusting nature.

ROB
(Straightening up and walking right up to DOC, nose to nose) Prove it.

(DOC doesn't flinch, but smiles a sinister smile)

DOC
Boy, you're too young a kitten to fool an old cat like me.

(ROB backs off a little)

DOC
These little skirmishes between us, they've provided a nice distraction. I'll give you that. But what I say now, I say for your own benefit. Desist. You are perilously close to awakening a sleeping bear. And this bear has claws you have not yet seen.

(Beat)

ROB
So...wait. Are you a cat or a bear?

DOC
(Storming out, he stops at the door) This isn't over, boy. Oh no. Not by a country mile.

(DOC leaves, slamming the door. ROB grabs a beer from the fridge, opens and drinks)

ROB
You got that right.

(Bang. Lights fade)

SCENE 8

(A few days later. The park, just before another re-enactment battle. DOC is there, putting on the last of his outfit. They are re-enacting The Battle of Perryville. As DOC prepares himself mentally for the battle, he waves to the occasional, unseen participant)

DOC
(muttering to himself) ...good god, it's a hot one...

(ROB enters, wearing a full Union soldier's uniform)

ROB
Good thing the battle hasn't started yet. I'd love to tell my commanding officer that I captured General Braxton Bragg.

DOC
Graff.

ROB
Boggs.

DOC
What the hell do you think you're doing?

ROB
Really? You can't tell?

DOC
Am I to assume you've joined the Union's cause?

ROB
I'd like to think I traded up.

DOC
Traded up?! This is the Battle of Perryville, boy! A resounding Confederate victory!

ROB
Well, yes and no.

DOC
Yes and...?! My god, the sheer hubris! We stopped Buell's advance! AND captured over 4,000 Union troops. We...

ROB
Retreated.

(DOC stops, flustered and stammering)

ROB
Oh yeah. That's right. This dumb Yankee knows how to read. Bragg had real victory in his hand, and what did he do, Doc?

DOC
It...it was a strategic withdrawal! He...I...

ROB
He got word that the other Confederate armies around him had gotten SPANKED by the Union. He knew that, even if he kept Perryville, he'd be surrounded by the enemy. So against the advice of two of his own generals, he turned tail and ran.

(DOC just glares at him)

ROB
One of his own soldiers said...hold on...*(Riffles through his pockets, finding his notes)* Here we go..."Bragg showed a perplexity and vacillation that had become simply appalling."

DOC
That may be factually accurate, but...

ROB
But nothing! See, I've decided to play the long war here, Doc. I'm willing to lose the occasional battle, 'cause I got my eye on the prize.

(The sound of gunfire. The battle is starting)

DOC
The battle's on, you idiot! Get out of...

ROB
It stings, doesn't it? Knowing that you're wearing the name of a Loser! Oh, he enjoyed a win here and there, but Bragg went down in flames!

DOC
(calling to his troops) McPherson! Shore your line up to the East! They're gonna...

ROB
You started this war, pal, but don't forget who's gonna win in the end!

DOC
Get out of here, Yankee Jim!

(ROB starts to sing badly, at the top of his lungs)

ROB
So we sang the chorus from Atlanta to the sea
While we were marching through Georgia

(In a fit of anger, DOC stabs ROB. ROB just stands there)

DOC
You want to stay where you don't belong, don't be surprised if you get skewered.

(ROB glares at DOC)

DOC
You took a saber to the lung, son. Now be a good Yankee, lie down and die.

(ROB lies down, but refuses to remain silent. DOC is jubilant, but seems shaky and a bit unfocused)

DOC
We've done it! Beat those bastards back, men!

ROB
You can't stab the truth, Doc.

DOC
Sound the charge!

ROB
Your army is just a bunch of rednecks in matching pajamas.

DOC
Polk! Move those damn cannons!

ROB
The North won…

DOC
No!

ROB
…because they were smarter, better equipped and just better fighters.

DOC
Be silent, corpse!

ROB
Don't hate me 'cause I'm right, grandpa.

DOC
You're not right! You're a rude, thoughtless punk working a woman's job!

ROB
Hey!

DOC
My god…you're a secretary and a seamstress! It would almost be funny if it weren't so damn sad.

ROB
(Rising) You are so lucky I don't hit senior citizens.

DOC
Back on the ground, Lazarus!

(ROB lies back down. As they argue, DOC starts to get noticeably weaker)

DOC
Your one and only achievement was somehow convincing a woman half your age to be your wife. And even she's more a man than you!

ROB
She's not half my age!

DOC
You're the poster child for midlife crisis, and you can't even see it.

ROB
At least I'm not a walking, talking stereotype!

DOC
How dare you!

ROB
I mean, do you wake up in the morning and ask yourself "How can I be more like Foghorn Leghorn?"

DOC
I am descended from philosophers and generals! I was raised in a time when

breeding counted for something! When a man worked hard, provided for his family and treated every man... be he a stranger or relation..like they were his...neighbor...

(DOC has gone to one knee, clutching his chest. ROB hasn't noticed at first)

ROB
Like hell!

DOC
Oh Christ...my heart...

ROB
You've been riding my ass ever since...

DOC
Medic...call a medic...

ROB
Oh! Sorry! Corpses don't talk back, do they?

(DOC grabs ROB. ROB now realizes that something's wrong)

DOC
...Ambulance...damn you...

ROB
Holy...Doc? What's...?

DOC
It's...my damn...heart, you imbecile...

(DOC collapses to the ground, still conscious, but in rough shape. He grabs ROB's arm, but doesn't look at him)

DOC
I shall...rise again. *(He lets go of ROB and lies there)*

ROB
(Scared, unsure what to do) Medic... Medic!

(Lights fade)

END OF ACT ONE

ACT II
SCENE 1

(The hospital. MADDIE & ROB are waiting. MADDIE has a bouquet of flowers. She's looking around)

MADDIE
God, are we the only ones here?

(She notices ROB's anxiety)

MADDIE
Honey, it's not your fault.

ROB
I know it's not my fault.

(Beat)

MADDIE
It's maybe a tiny, little bit your fault.

ROB
No it isn't.

MADDIE
You were antagonizing him. In 103 degree weather.

ROB
You don't know that.

MADDIE
I was in the stands.

ROB
There were...you know, things always look bad when you take them out of context, but...

MADDIE
I just...don't you even feel a little bad?

ROB
No. 'Cause he's faking it.

(Beat)

MADDIE
I don't think he's faking it.

ROB
Sweet, innocent Maddie.

MADDIE
I mean, if it was nothing, they would've released him already.

ROB
The guy's 102 years old. I'm not saying nothing's wrong with him. I'm just saying he didn't have a heart attack.

MADDIE
Rob...

ROB
It's Fort Macon all over again.

MADDIE
I get this feeling like you can't hear yourself talking.

ROB
It was this old fort that General Sherman turned into a prison. The conditions there were terrible. Eventually, the imprisoned solders started faking illness so they...

MADDIE
Rob!

(He stops talking)

MADDIE
Our neighbor had a heart attack. It happened.

ROB
I just...

MADDIE
It happened. And I need to know that, when we go in there, you're not going to...provoke him. OK?

ROB
What if he starts into me?

MADDIE
I don't care if he punches you in the face. You are NOT going to push his buttons, y'hear?

ROB
I'll be good.

MADDIE
OK. Let's go.

(Lights rise on the rest of the stage. DOC is lying in a hospital bed, comfortable & reading a book. He smiles when he sees them)

DOC
Well now. My day just got a little brighter.

MADDIE
Hello, Doc.

DOC
And a fine hello to you.

(She hugs him. ROB comes to him, unsure how to react)

ROB
Hiya.

DOC
Robert. Good to see you. *(Shakes ROB's hand, seemingly without any rancor)*

MADDIE
I hope we're not bothering you.

DOC
Not at all. It's a balm to my soul to finally have some visitors.

MADDIE
Are we the first people to visit?

(Beat)

DOC
And what do you have there? Lilies?

ROB
Oh. Yeah. Lemme just... *(Sets them on*

a table)

MADDIE
They're from our garden.

DOC
I thought they might be.

ROB
You're not allergic or anything, are you?

DOC
To neighborly kindness? No, sir. I'd say it's just what the doctor ordered.

MADDIE
(Sitting with him) How are you doing?

DOC
Well, I'll tell you. They brought me in here all agitated, and it turned out to be nothin' but a little Atrial Flutter.

ROB
So not a heart attack?

DOC
Not exactly, no. Turns out my heartbeat just had a hitch in its step.

ROB
OK then.

MADDIE
So the prognosis is good?

DOC
I wouldn't go that far.

(Beat)

DOC
Looks like I'm gonna have to pass on the biscuits and gravy from this day forward. And for a lifelong gourmand like myself, that's a serious prognosis indeed. Beware the Southern cuisine. It's put many a man in the ground.

(Beat. No one is entirely certain how to keep the conversation going)

DOC
Madeline, would you be so kind as to give me a moment with your husband?

ROB
What?

MADDIE
Of course.

ROB
What?

(She pats ROB on the arm as she leaves)

ROB
So…how about that…hospital food…?

DOC
Are you nervous, Robert?

ROB
(Laughing unconvincingly) What? No.

DOC
I'm just an old, bedridden man. You can cease your perspirations.

ROB
I'm fine, OK? *(Has seated himself on the other side of the room)*

DOC
Come closer.

ROB
I can hear you fine from here.

DOC
Come. Closer.

(ROB moves closer to DOC's bed)

DOC
Robert, Robert, Robert….we've made quite a mess.

(Beat)

ROB
Do…do you want me to get the nurse?

DOC
That's not what I meant, you...! *(Reigns himself in)* I'm a proud man. And I don't take kindly to folks rubbin' my rhubarb. That's not to say I'm without a sense of humor. But you have tested my patience, time and again.

(ROB wants to argue, but fights the urge)

DOC
However, geography has bound the two of us together. And as such, I must swallow my pride, and ask you to do me a favor. *(Grabs ROB's arm)* My dog, Robert. Take care of my dog.

ROB
Are you serious?

DOC
Barksdale...he's a good boy. But he's old, and he needs someone to take care of him.

ROB
You want us to take him?

DOC
Not unless you're overly fond of dog urine. He gets nervous in new places.

ROB
So...you want me to go to your house?

DOC
I don't have another choice! Please, you must do this for me.

ROB
I really think you'd be more comfortable with Buddy. Or that guy with the goiter.

DOC
They're not my neighbors, son! You're my neighbor. There is a sacred bond between us, and I'm asking you to honor that.

(ROB says nothing, hesitant)

DOC
I'm not asking so much. Just to feed him, to walk him...to keep him company. Of course, I would do it myself, but the events of yesterday have left me temporarily bedridden. Yes, yes. Yesterday took quite its toll. It surely did. I...

ROB
I'll do it.

DOC
And here's my key. *(Hands ROB his key)*

DOC
He takes a bowl of kibble at 7 in the morning, and another at 5 in the evening. And he needs to be walked at least twice a day. At least. And no outfits. Y'hear me?

ROB
Yes.

(DOC offers his hand. ROB shakes it. DOC grabs his arm)

DOC
You can insult a man all you'd like. But not his dog, Robert. Never his dog.

(Lights fade)

SCENE 2

(DOC's house. ROB is sitting in a chair, holding a photo. A knock on the door. An old dog can be heard sort-of barking offstage)

MADDIE
Rob?

ROB
Barksdale, no. Barksdale...just...

(Calls offstage) It's unlocked! *(Back to Barksdale)* It's not Doc, buddy. Just hang on...

(ROB goes off, opening the door. MADDIE enters)

MADDIE
Hey, honey.

ROB
Hey.

MADDIE
I got your voicemail. What's the problem?

ROB
He's not going outside! And he won't make a mess inside either! I'm worried his colon's gonna explode.

MADDIE
(Chuckling a little) Really? You don't get what's wrong here?

ROB
No!

MADDIE
Baby, you've got to go outside first.

(Beat)

ROB
For real?

MADDIE
For real.

ROB
But...but...the door's open.

MADDIE
Hon, this isn't unusual, not with a bulldog. They get really attached to people. He wants to be able to see you when he's outside. It makes him feel safe.

ROB
He's been going out there for years.

MADDIE
Yeah, probably with Doc standing out there with him the whole time.

ROB
So...I've got to watch him poop?

MADDIE
No, you just need to be within his line of sight.

(He stands there unconvinced. MADDIE takes the door from him)

MADDIE
Go on, get. Scoot.

ROB
Fine. *(Exits. He can be heard from outside)* Barksdale. Get your wrinkled butt out here. *(The sound of a dog dashing outside)* Holy crap! It worked!

MADDIE
Told you.

ROB
Oh man...you just saved this dog's life. I think he's been holding it in all day.

MADDIE
Rob! Why didn't you call me before?

ROB
I kinda got...Can I come inside?

MADDIE
Not unless you wanna give Barksdale a panic attack. Just wait.

ROB
Seriously, this is gonna take a while.

MADDIE
Then just wait. *(Looks around the house. She eventually finds the photo that ROB had. ROB can be heard offstage still)*

ROB
You can't still be going! *(The dog barks)*

Ok, ok!

MADDIE
Dogs can sense when you're judging them.

ROB
Awesome. *(Barksdale can be heard running inside)* How the hell does a dog that small hold so much poop?

MADDIE
They're big eaters.

ROB
Honestly. I think I'm kind of impressed.

(ROB enters)

MADDIE
Is he ok?

ROB
Yeah. Went right to his dog bed. *(He sits with her)* Why do they do that thing?

MADDIE
What thing?

ROB
That thing where they spin around before they lie down.

MADDIE
It's just something they do.

ROB
It's kind of…

MADDIE
Cute?

ROB
I…yeah.

MADDIE
I told you he's a good dog.

ROB
There's something about that wrinkly, snaggletooth face. I admit it. You should've seen him in the Yankees outfit.

MADDIE
In the what?

ROB
What'cha got there?

(She holds up the picture)

ROB
Yeah, that's what I was trying to tell you. I didn't call before because…

MADDIE
Because you were snooping through Doc's house.

(Beat)

ROB
No. Because it's not snooping when you're invited.

MADDIE
Is this Doc?

ROB
Yeah, probably twenty years ago.

MADDIE
Then who is she?

ROB
His daughter?

MADDIE
He has a kid?

ROB
I don't know. I was hoping maybe he told you.

MADDIE
Not a word.

ROB
It gets weirder.

MADDIE
Yeah?

ROB
That's the only picture I found of her. There isn't another one, even in the attic.

MADDIE
Oh my god! You went into the attic?

ROB
I'm a very thorough dogsitter.

MADDIE
Rob...

ROB
I just wanna know, ok? I feel like there's a clue here.

MADDIE
A clue to what?

ROB
To why he hates me!

MADDIE
He doesn't hate you!

ROB
Come on. We've been after each other for two months. You know this. He's only nice to me when you're around, so that you don't figure out what's going on.

MADDIE
Fine. What's going on?

ROB
War. This is war.

MADDIE
Then I'm ending it.

(He stares at her, ready to argue)

MADDIE
Whatever's going on between you two, it's got to end.

ROB
Look. I didn't start this.

MADDIE
I don't care. I do. Not. Care. When someone ends up in the hospital, then it's time to stop.

ROB
He said he was fine.

MADDIE
Yeah, this time. But he's an old man, he's retired, and he has no friends.

(Beat)

ROB
What?

MADDIE
I just...Rob, people hate Doc.

ROB
Like hell. He's got all his buddies in the Civil War re-enactors, and...

MADDIE
When he brought Barksdale in, the guys in the office starting talking. They couldn't believe we were neighbors. Hon, Doc didn't want to retire. He had to. No one would go to him anymore.

ROB
Come on.

MADDIE
It's true. People would drive twenty minutes out of their way to go to another doctor. They say he's been this way for years.

ROB
And what way is that?

MADDIE
Come on. You know.

ROB
You're right. I do know. And I want to hear you say it.

MADDIE
I think...maybe you're not totally wrong about him, OK?

ROB
I want you to know that I could totally gloat right now, but I'm taking the high road. What I want to know is why you couldn't admit it 'til now.

MADDIE
Because he's all alone, and I wanted to be his friend. I think he's trying to change, Rob. I mean...he gave us peach preserves.

ROB
Oh my god. I get it now. It all makes sense.

MADDIE
What?

ROB
Why he's been making my life hell. It's a classic reversal. He knows no one likes him. And all of a sudden, this Yankee moves in. He knows that, if he jumps on the Yankee-Hate-Wagon first, he'll get on everyone's good side. That clever bastard...

MADDIE
That sounds kind of nuts.

ROB
I know! He's totally mental.

MADDIE
No, I mean...

ROB
Oh my god, I gotta ask Buddy about this.

MADDIE
I thought Buddy hated you.

ROB
He hated me before 'cause we had nothing in common. But now...if he hates Doc like everyone else does...

MADDIE
No. No. Stop it.

ROB
Honey! This is my chance to fit in here! You gotta give me this.

MADDIE
Not a chance.

ROB
I've been waiting for months! Listening to every snide comment, watching people laugh at my license plate. But now...now there's common ground.

MADDIE
Rob. Listen to yourself. You're talking about ganging up on a sick old man to make yourself feel better. That is wrong on so many levels.

ROB
I...no, that's an oversimplification...

MADDIE
Go home.

ROB
What?

MADDIE
You need to go home. I'll take care of Barksdale.

ROB
Doc asked me to.

MADDIE
Because he's trying to rebuild the bridge. Clearly, that isn't what you want, so go home.

(Beat)

ROB
Fine.

(He storms out. MADDIE sits on the couch. Barksdale begins to whimper offstage. MADDIE rises, heading offstage to him)

MADDIE
It's OK, little guy. He'll be back soon.

(Lights fade)

SCENE 3

(Back at the hospital. It's night time. DOC is lying in the bed, watching TV with little interest. He has a cup of Jello. ROB enters)

DOC
What happened to my dog?

ROB
He's fine. Maddie's there right now.

DOC
Did something happen?

ROB
No. She's just…being neighborly. *(Sits next to DOC)* So you get to go home tomorrow, yeah?

DOC
That's what they tell me.

ROB
Too bad. Bet you're gonna miss flirting with the nurses. Am I right?

(DOC just stares at him)

ROB
I just…it was a joke.

(DOC eats his Jello)

ROB
Doc, what's your problem with me?

DOC
At the moment, you're interrupting my program.

ROB
All night, I've been going over this… thing between us. And it doesn't make sense. I mean, so I killed you on the battlefield. It was an accident.

DOC
Which incident are you referring to? When you stabbed me with your saber, or when you harangued me into a coronary episode?

ROB
Fine. You want me to say I'm a bad neighbor? I'm a bad neighbor. Are you happy now?

(Instead of fighting back, the question genuinely makes DOC think)

DOC
Happiness is a funny thing, Robert. *(Shakes off his reverie)* Why are you here?

ROB
I…don't really know. I wanted to come over, I guess.

DOC
Why? Were you going to put me in a Detroit Tigers jersey while I slept?

ROB
No, I just…thought you'd want some company.

DOC
Well, you made the trip for nothing. I'll have you know that I was resting from a day full of visitors and well-wishers. In fact…

ROB
No you weren't.

DOC
Don't interrupt me, boy. I was just saying…

ROB
Doc, it's fine. You don't have to…it's fine.

(DOC just stares at him, then goes back to his Jello. ROB turns on the TV)

ROB
Bass Masters?

DOC
You know it?

ROB
I'm from the Great Lake State. I know from fishing.

DOC
Hmmm.

(They watch for a while)

ROB
Holy crap! Look at the size of that thing!

DOC
That's a fifteen-pounder if I ever saw one.

ROB
The way he was fighting it, I thought he had a pike or something.

DOC
No, no. A pike would jump more.

ROB
I don't know. I heard sometimes they go deep, to try and tangle the line.

DOC
What? Who told you that?

ROB
My dad.

DOC
Oh. Well.

(They watch in silence a little bit more. ROB gets up to leave)

ROB
You know, I'm just…I'm gonna head out. Take care of yourself Doc.

DOC
I always do.

(ROB exits as lights fade)

SCENE 4

(ROB and MADDIE's house, a few days later. MADDIE is sitting at the table, lost in her own thoughts. ROB enters)

ROB
Hey, honey.

MADDIE
Hey.

ROB
I quit my job.

MADDIE
What?

ROB
This has been an extremely weird day.

MADDIE
What happened?

ROB
It starts out pretty normal. I'm answering phones, shooting the shit with Mark from maintenance. And Buddy comes over. He wants to ask me all about Doc. Someone told him I was dogsitting and…hon, you were right. He doesn't like Doc. Most of them don't. He wanted to know if he was out of the Re-enactors. Turns out Buddy's been gunning for the General Bragg spot for years. And I'm like "Hey, I thought you guys were all on the same team or something." Yeah, turns out the only reason they let Doc stay is because he

started the entire Carson Community Re-Enactors in 1980. He's the only founding member left. No one's had the balls to kick him out, but now that he's sick, they figure...anyway, so he's sitting there, just dishing all this crap about Doc and...I don't know. I got mad. I don't know why, but...there were these people in the showroom, asking about one of the hybrids. And I just walk right over to them, tell them about Toyota issuing a recall on a bunch of their hybrids 'cause of the anti-lock brake software. And when I say I "told them", I mean top of my lungs. Like, people two blocks over could hear me. Then I go on a tear about the unintended acceleration recalls, the floor mat recalls...and yeah. That was that.

MADDIE
Wait. Did you quit, or did you get fired?

ROB
Um...kind of a grey area.

MADDIE
Oh my God.

ROB
Hon, I know it's sudden. I swear to you, I did not go in today intending to quit. It just happened. But I'll find something else. I promise. Mark asked me to be his assistant coach at Little League this year. I mean, that'll be fun, right? Next week, he's taking the kids to Turner Field, and I get to come! Honest to god, free trip to Turner Field! We're gonna...

(Beat. ROB realizes that MADDIE is just staring at him)

ROB
You're mad.

MADDIE
No.

ROB
I'm really sorry. I am. I just...I couldn't work there anymore. Buddy's a total dick, and it just...I want to do something else, you know? That thing you were saying before, about being able to do something else with my life. I think you're right. Maybe this is my chance to start over. Maybe I just need to...

MADDIE
Rob. I'm not mad. Really.

(He sits down next to her, takes her hands)

ROB
Baby? What is it?

(Lights fade)

SCENE 5

(DOC's house. ROB is sitting alone on the couch. He is alone w/ his thoughts for a while. After a moment, DOC enters and hands him a beer. DOC has a bottled water)

ROB
Thanks.

DOC
Well, I'm switching to red wine with dinner now, so why waste them?

ROB
Fair enough.

(They drink in silence for a bit)

DOC
So what brings you here, Robert? Surely you don't miss Barksdale that much.

ROB
Maddie's pregnant.

(Beat)

DOC
I see. Am I to assume this wasn't planned?

ROB
Yeah.

DOC
I see.

ROB
I mean...we wanted to have a kid, at some point. And...Christ, I'm 45 years old. Some point is now, isn't it?

DOC
That's one way to look at it.

ROB
It's just...now? Right now? Maddie's freaked out 'cause she just started this job that she loves, and she's already got to ask for maternity leave. She's worried that...

DOC
Don't worry about it.

ROB
Well, it's maybe a legit concern.

DOC
I'll make some calls. People 'round here owe me some favors. Perhaps I could...

ROB
Doc, I know.

DOC
Know what?

ROB
That you're...

DOC
What? I'm what?

ROB
Not the most popular guy in town.

(Beat)

DOC
Doesn't mean that I'm not owed some favors.

ROB
That's not what I came here for.

DOC
I know that. I'm simply offering to help.

ROB
You're not really offering though. You're just going to go ahead and do it.

DOC
I'm not a thumb-twiddler, Robert. And I make no apologies for that.

ROB
(Laughs a little) Man, we just can't stop pushing each other's buttons, can we?

(DOC thinks on that, & laughs a bit himself)

DOC
You might be right about that.

(They drink in silence for a bit)

DOC
So what did you come here for?

ROB
Hmm?

DOC
You said you didn't come here for my favors. So why then?

ROB
Because, as screwed up as it sounds, you're the closest thing I've got to a friend in this town.

DOC
I'm fairly certain you didn't mean that to sound as insulting as it did.

ROB
No, I didn't. Sorry.

DOC
It's all right, son. You've had a long day.

ROB
Yes I have, Doc. Yes I have.

(Beat. ROB finally gets to the heart of the problem)

ROB
My child is going to be born in Georgia.

(DOC stares at him)

ROB
Maddie's right about me. I've made pretty much no effort to make this place my home. And now...it's going to be my kid's home.

DOC
Is that such a bad thing?

ROB
No. Not in theory. It's just...There's a part of me that's always had one foot out the door, you know? Like...Maddie would get a job offer somewhere else, we'd sell the house...we'd go back to Michigan or...I don't know. But...

DOC
Reality's setting in. This is your home now.

ROB
Oh God.

DOC
This is a nice town, Robert. In a nice state. You'll come to see that. God willing and the creek don't rise.

(ROB just stares at him)

ROB
I gotta be honest. I only understand maybe fifty percent of your Southern... thingies.

DOC
It means "let's hope everything works out."

ROB
Oh. OK.

(Beat)

DOC
I'm going to tell you a story, Robert.

ROB
No, it's OK. You...

DOC
I knew a gentleman in medical school...Jim Bodine...he was a Hoosier. He asked me one time about Civil War Re-Enactments. Asked me if the Confederates ever change the outcome of the battles, to allow ourselves to win. It was one of the single dumbest questions I've ever been asked. Y'see, we're not trying to rewrite history. We're trying to honor it. Jim...he had it in his head that we're all bigoted rednecks or somesuch. It's the reason we often get so... defensive around Yankees. *(Gets them both another drink)* The South lost the war because we were in the wrong. Because we forgot we were all brothers, Blue and Grey and Black and White. Nowadays, we focus so much on the few things that divide us, that we constantly forget the multitude of things which unite us. It's like watching two grown men scream at each other, because one says donkey and the other says mule. In the end,

they're still jackasses. If you'll pardon the colloquialism.

(Beat)

ROB
Good beer.

DOC
I'm glad you enjoy it.

(They sit in silence again. ROB rises)

ROB
I should probably head back.

DOC
Oh.

ROB
I know you've only been home for a little bit. Probably want to get settled.

DOC
Of course.

ROB
But thanks again, for the beer. And for…yeah, thanks.

DOC
You're welcome.

(ROB goes to the door, but doesn't go. DOC notices him staring)

DOC
You want to ask me about Evelyn, don't you?

ROB
I…don't know who that is.

DOC
Yes you do. The young woman, in the picture you took from my bedroom.

(ROB has no response. DOC smiles a bit)

DOC
You put her back on the wrong side of the chifarobe, Robert.

ROB
Dammit. I thought so, but I wasn't sure.

DOC
It's all right.

ROB
I'm sorry if I…

DOC
She was my wife.

ROB
Oh. I didn't…really?

DOC
Yes.

ROB
But she's so…

DOC
Young?

ROB
Yeah.

DOC
You of all people should be sympathetic of that.

ROB
That's…fair.

DOC
She passed away. Almost twenty years ago.

ROB
Oh. I…I'm not sure what to say.

DOC
"Sorry" seems a paltry word, doesn't it?

ROB
Yeah.

DOC
I appreciate your sentiment, Robert.

Yes, she was all of 32 when she passed. Heart aneurism. We'd only been together for five years. If you were wondering why I'm something of a…pariah in this town, that's why. I couldn't see past the injustice of it. It made me a difficult sort to be around. *(Gets his water)* I doubt anyone intends to reach the end of their days alone. But it does happen. It shouldn't, but it does. *(DOC notices ROB staring at him, & smiles a little)* Do you expect me to go on, Robert? To bear my soul?

ROB
I…maybe?

DOC
I'm grateful for your attending to Barksdale. And for this visit. But let's face each other honestly. We are not the closest of friends, are we?

ROB
You got me a job as a secretary. For Toyota.

DOC
You broke into my house and played dress-up with my dog.

(Beat. They laugh)

ROB
Truce?

DOC
Truce.

(They shake hands. ROB starts to go)

DOC
Robert, I…could I request a favor of you?

ROB
Knock yourself out.

(DOC stares at him, not familiar with the expression)

ROB
Go ahead.

DOC
It's about the re-enactors.

ROB
Yeah, I should tell you right off, I think I'm done with that. It's a little too intense for me.

DOC
I understand. My physician has ordered me to resign my commission as well.

ROB
Oh. I'm sorry. I know that was kinda your thing.

DOC
Well, I'll still go, but only to watch. My battlefield days are over.

(Beat)

DOC
I hate Buddy Maddocks.

ROB
Yeah, so do I.

DOC
The arrogant upstart has been circling me like a vulture for years.

ROB
Yeah…he was after your part.

DOC
I'm well aware. He's left me two messages, trying to worm his way into my good graces.

ROB
Why?

DOC
It's a by-law I wrote into this county's Rules of Re-Enactment. Commanding officers can name their successors.

ROB
So he's trying to sweet-talk you into making him the new Braxton Bragg?

DOC
So it would appear.

ROB
That's insane! He doesn't have the discipline! Bragg was a by-the-book soldier. Buddy doesn't know Jefferson Davis from Jefferson Starship! *(Notices DOC staring at him)* I've been studying. This stuff is kind of addictive.

(DOC puts his hand on ROB's shoulder)

DOC
Yes it is, Robert. Yes it is.

(Lights fade)

SCENE 6

(The battlefield. The sound of a crowd gathering, and "soldiers" getting ready. ROB enters, donning his new costume as Gen. Braxton Bragg. MADDIE is with him)

MADDIE
You look amazing.

ROB
I wish I'd had more time to take in the waist…

MADDIE
Stop fidgeting. It's un-Generally.

ROB
The hat doesn't look too big? *(She kisses him)*

MADDIE
It looks great. You look great.

ROB
I don't want to make a bad impression. This is a big deal.

MADDIE
Look at those people. They're not seeing Rob Graff anymore. They're seeing one of their own.

ROB
For today.

MADDIE
It's a start, honey.

ROB
I know.

(Beat)

ROB
Are you feeling ok? Do you wanna sit down?

MADDIE
And it begins.

ROB
I'm just saying.

MADDIE
Rob, I'm pregnant. I'm not an invalid.

ROB
Are you sure? I asked Doc to bring a wheelchair for you. And a hot compress for those swollen ankles.

MADDIE
You're so lucky you're in public right now.

ROB
Honey, don't get upset. The baby can sense that.

MADDIE
I owe you such an ass-kicking.

ROB
(Calling off to unseen "soldiers") Gentlemen, please remove this civilian from the battlefield. *(He sees that they're coming over)*

ROB
Guys, wait. Just kidding. Really.

(DOC has joined them)

DOC
Ms. Madeline, you look radiant.

MADDIE
Hi, Doc. (She hugs him)

DOC
Careful, now. I'm fragile.

MADDIE
Like hell.

ROB
(Offering his hand) Doc.

DOC
Robert.

(They shake hands, warmly)

DOC
The Confederate Stripes suit you well.

ROB
Thanks. The hat doesn't look too big?

MADDIE
Oh my lord.

DOC
You look every inch a commanding officer. How do you feel?

ROB
Well, the men and I went through the maneuvers one more time, just like you showed me. You should've seen Buddy's face when I told him he has to die in the first wave. I read up on the battle last night, and…

DOC
Robert. How do you feel?

ROB
Oh. (Thinks on that) Good. I feel good.

DOC
All right then.

(A trumpet sounds)

DOC
Looks like they're gearing up. I don't want to keep you from your troops.

ROB
OK.

MADDIE
I brought us some sandwiches and Coke.

DOC
What kind of Coke?

MADDIE
Diet Sprite.

DOC
Aren't you a dear?

MADDIE
I surely am.

DOC
Now, Robert. I always found that a pep-talk before the battle really enhanced the enjoyment of the day. Something stirring, but not too long.

ROB
All right.

DOC
And don't forget. This is the Battle of Chattanooga. The Army of the Cumberland will come charging up that hill, guns a-blazing.

ROB
Yep.

DOC
And most importantly, you must call the retreat. Can you do that, Robert? Can you lose the battle?

ROB
Doc. I got this.

DOC
(DOC claps ROB on the shoulder) I know you do, son.

MADDIE
Come here. *(She kisses him)*

ROB
Honey, not in front of the Army.

(She smacks his bottom, hard)

MADDIE
Go get 'em, General.

(DOC & MADDIE walk off a little bit. ROB faces the audience, his "soldiers")

ROB
Ok, guys. Circle up. *(The crowd gathers)* Ok. Yeah…so…here goes… Today, we are fighting for our…um…brothers and sisters…who have fought bravely…well, not our sisters…Not that they couldn't, just that historically they… *(He stops, collects himself)* I know you're probably as shocked to see me standing here as I am to be standing here. But it's important, I think. That we're all here, honoring the events as they happened. Not how they could have happened, but how they did happen. We're gonna lose today, fellas. But we're going to go down fighting. Together. We are fighting together. When they carry us from the field, they won't be carrying soldiers; they'll be carrying brothers. So…don't fear defeat. Just be proud, knowing that you have good men, brave men at your side. 'Cause that's how I'm gonna feel, out there with all of you. *(ROB raises his saber)* CHARGE!!!!

(The crowd cheers, lights fade)

SCENE 7

(ROB & MADDIE's porch. The evening of July 4th. MADDIE is sitting on the porch by herself. She's on the phone with her mother)

MADDIE
No, he's still looking. Actually, nothing in automotives. I don't…mom. Mom. He just wants to try something else with his… 45 is not to… It's not. It's not. I'm just… OK. I'm just saying, everything's new for us here. So why not? We're going to be fine. I promise.

ROB
(Can be heard calling from inside) Maddie! There's a freaking bat in the kitchen! Holy crap! He's got a knife! You gotta do something!

MADDIE
Mom, I gotta go. Yeah, there are bats in Georgia too. Big ones. With attitudes. Love you. Bye. Bye. Bye. *(Hangs up)*

ROB
(Entering with a tray, three glasses, & a pitcher) Did it work?

MADDIE
Like a charm. She hates bats.

ROB
Everyone hates bats.

MADDIE
I don't hate bats.

(He just stares at her)

MADDIE
What? They've got those cute little scrunched up faces, and those big ears. They're like terriers with wings.

ROB
(Holds her) I love you 'cause you're

weird.

MADDIE
You love me 'cause I'm awesome. And weird.

(They kiss)

ROB
Shiloh.

MADDIE
No.

ROB
Ulysses? Like Ulysses S...?

MADDIE
No.

ROB
What about Tyrus?

MADDIE
All signs point to "no".

ROB
But...no, hear me out. That was Ty Cobb's real name. And he was born in Georgia, but played for the Detroit Tigers, so we kinda have this "best of both worlds" thing.

MADDIE
I would maybe consider "Tyler". Also, it might not be a boy.

ROB
Totally fine. I have the perfect name if it's a girl.

MADDIE
I'm going to hate this, aren't I?

ROB
Robertina.

(Beat)

MADDIE
Honey, I'm going to need you to give me the baby name book. So I can burn it.

(A knock at the door. ROB goes for it)

ROB
Settle down, wifey. You're wisecracking for two now. *(He exits)*

MADDIE
How many ass-kickings do I owe you?

ROB
(offstage) Seven. *(Re-enters with DOC)*

DOC
Good evening, Madeline.

MADDIE
Hi, Doc. *(They hug)*

DOC
Oh my. Look at you. You've got the glow.

MADDIE
I do?

DOC
You most certainly do. It's very becoming.

ROB
Are you flirting with my wife?

DOC
If I were, you wouldn't stand a chance. *(Looks out at the view)* My goodness. I forgot how lovely the view is out here.

ROB
Is it that different than yours?

DOC
You've got a better view of the city, down there. Close enough to see it, but not so close that you can hear it.

ROB
You want some sweet tea?

DOC
You have sweet tea?

MADDIE
Yeah. Miss Cody gave me her recipe.

DOC
Well, I couldn't imagine a better teacher.

ROB
(Gives DOC a glass and grabs him a chair) Make yourself comfortable already.

DOC
Don't mind if I do. *(DOC sits. ROB & MADDIE sit together)*

DOC
Quite a night, isn't it?

ROB
Yeah.

DOC
A little brisk, but lovely.

ROB
It's 82 degrees.

DOC
That's why I brought an overshirt. *(Beat)* While I appreciate the invitation, I'm not entirely certain why it was offered.

ROB
Just checking in. Saying howdy.

DOC
That's very kind of you.

ROB
(Shrugging) Besides, I didn't want you to miss the show.

DOC
What show?

(ROB waits, looking out over the horizon. Finally—)

ROB
Dammit. I was hoping it would start right then. The timing would've been incredible.

DOC
Madeline, am I missing something?

MADDIE
Give it a second. You'll...

(Suddenly, the stage fills with light as some fireworks go off)

ROB
There we go.

DOC
Oh. Oh my. I...I forgot what day it was.

MADDIE
You were right. It's a hell of a view.

DOC
Would you look at that. *(More fireworks go off. DOC just stares)* It's been a while since...thank you.

ROB
No problem.

DOC
It's lovely, isn't it? Just so...lovely.

ROB
You got that right.

(ROB & MADDIE smile, as they see DOC lost in the spectacle)

MADDIE
Happy 4th, Benjamin. *(She clinks his glass with her own)*

DOC
Oh. Yes, I...to you, as well, darling. And Robert. *(They watch the fireworks. After a while)* Did you know I proposed to my wife on the 4th of July?

(They look at each other then back at the fireworks. Lights fade)

END OF PLAY

Available Plays by Joseph Zettelmaier

All Childish Things

Dead Man's Shoes

Ebeneezer - a Christmas Play

The Gravedigger - a Frankenstein Play
adapted from the novel by Mary Shelly

It Came From Mars

Northern Aggression
(formerly And The Creek Don't Rise)

The Scullery Maid

For information about production rights, visit:
www.jzettelmaier.com

More Plays From Sordelet Ink

Once A Ponzi Time
by Joe Foust

A Tale of Two Cities
by Christoper M Walsh
adapted from the novel by Charles Dickens

The Count of Monte Cristo
by Christoper M Walsh
adapted from the novel by Alexandre Dumas

The Moonstone
by Robert Kauzlaric
adapted from the novel by Wilkie Collins

The Woman in White
by Robert Kauzlaric
adapted from the novel by Wilkie Collins

Season on the Line
by Shawn Pfautsch
adapted from Herman Melville's Moby-Dick

Hatfield & McCoy
by Shawn Pfautsch

The League of Awesome
by Corrbette Pasko and Sarah Sevigny

Eve of Ides
by David Blixt

Visit www.sordeletink.com for more!

NOVELS FROM
SORDELET INK

The Star-Cross'd Series

THE MASTER OF VERONA
VOICE OF THE FALCONER
FORTUNE'S FOOL
THE PRINCE'S DOOM
VARNISH'D FACES - STAR-CROSS'D SHORT STORIES

The Colossus Series

COLOSSUS: STONE & STEEL
COLOSSUS: THE FOUR EMPERORS

and coming 2016
COLOSSUS: WAIL OF THE FALLEN

HER MAJESTY'S WILL
a novel of Wit & Kit

All by bestselling author David Blixt!

And on sale now:
THE DRAGONTAIL BUTTONHOLE
by Peter Curtis

VISIT WWW.SORDELETINK.COM FOR MORE!

www.ingramcontent.com/pod-product-compliance
Lightning Source LLC
Chambersburg PA
CBHW080723300426
44114CB00019B/2477